CARTHAGE PAPERS

JOURNAL OF ROMAN ARCHAEOLOGY

SUPPLEMENTARY SERIES NUMBER 28

GENERAL EDITOR: J. H. HUMPHREY
ASSISTANT EDITOR: D. STONE

AN INTERNATIONAL JOURNAL

CARTHAGE PAPERS

THE EARLY COLONY'S ECONOMY, WATER SUPPLY, A PUBLIC BATH, AND THE MOBILIZATION OF STATE OLIVE OIL

by
J. T. Peña,
J. J. Rossiter,
A. I. Wilson,
C. Wells, M. Carroll, J. Freed & D. Godden

PORTSMOUTH, RI
1998

ISBN 1-887829-28-8
ISSN 1063-4304 (for the supplementary series)

Printed by Cushing-Malloy, Ann Arbor, Michigan.

This and other supplements to the *Journal of Roman Archaeology* may be ordered from:
JRA, 95 Peleg Road, Portsmouth, RI 02871, U.S.A.
or by telephone (USA) 401 683 1955, telefax (USA) 401 683 1975 (fax only), or e-mail jra@wsii.com

CONTENTS

1. The construction of *decumanus* VI N and the economy of the early colony of Carthage 7
Colin Wells, Maureen Carroll, Joann Freed and David Godden

2. Water supply in ancient Carthage 65
Andrew Wilson

3. A Roman bath-house at Bir el Jebbana: preliminary report on the excavations (1994-1997) 103
J. J. Rossiter

4. The mobilization of state olive oil in Roman Africa: the evidence of late 4th-c. *ostraca* from Carthage 117
J. T. Peña

The construction of *decumanus* VI N and the economy of the early colony of Carthage

Colin Wells, Maureen Carroll, Joann Freed, and David Godden

The aims and importance of the excavation

This is a report on a small but crucial excavation, lasting only two weeks in June 1996, on the summit of the Odeon hill at Carthage (fig. 1).[1] We cut a longitudinal section through *decumanus* VI N, at a point just east of the central axis of the Odeon and just west of the intersection with *cardo* VI E (fig. 2). Here *decumanus* VI is bounded on the south side by the N wall of the courtyard that preceded the N façade of the Roman Odeon. The aim of the excavation was to obtain a section through the successive street levels down to the natural subsoil, with a view to obtaining pottery as dating evidence for the construction and the phases of repair of the street. It was hoped in this way to throw light on the question of when this sector of the Roman city was first occupied and on the relationship between the street grid and the Odeon itself.

The excavation produced the most narrowly datable sequence of Augustan and Julio-Claudian contexts yet found at Carthage. It showed that the first *decumanus* VI was laid out before the end of the 1st c. B.C., suggesting that from the very start of the new Roman colony there was official concern for the building and maintenance of the street grid, even in what was then an outlying area of the city. It also revealed Punic material *in situ* beneath the Roman levels and in an occupation context with no sign of burials, despite the fact that the Odeon hill is known to have been a cemetery in the Punic period. In the Roman contexts, where the material comes solely from street layers, it is clear that the pottery was deliberately re-deposited, but there is no evidence, such as fragments of human bone or plaster from destroyed tombs, to suggest disturbance of graves.

Summary of earlier excavations in the area

In 1976, as part of the UNESCO Save Carthage campaign, a Canadian team under the direction of C. M. Wells (then of the University of Ottawa) and E. M. Wightman (McMaster University) began excavations on the top of the Odeon hill at Carthage. These excavations extended over 8 seasons, ending in 1986.[2] The main excavations (trench 2CC1/2), directed by Wells, lay astride *decumanus* VI N between *cardines* II and III E. They revealed that the so-called Theodosian Wall of *c.*A.D. 425 had been built over the line of *cardo* II, coming up from the

---

1 C. M. Wells (Trinity University, San Antonio) bears overall responsibility for the excavations in and around the Odeon. He and his colleagues wish to express their deepest thanks to A. Ennabli, Director of the Musée de Carthage, for his confidence and unfailing support. Field directors for 1996 were M. Carroll and D. Godden (Römisch-Germanisches Museum, Köln). The pottery specialist was J. Freed (Wilfrid Laurier University). Among our Tunisian workmen for the 1996 season special thanks are due to Noureddine Yacoubi for his skill and devotion. Expenses for the field season were defrayed by generous contributions from friends in San Antonio, especially William Scanlan, Jr., Olive Brewster, and members of the Southwest Texas Archaeological Society and the History Club. For subsequent study of the pottery the authors gratefully acknowledge financial support from a grant partly funded by Wilfrid Laurier University and partly by the SSHRC General Research Grant of Canada awarded to Wilfrid Laurier University.

2 The results are summarised by C. M. Wells, "Le mur de Théodose et le secteur nord-est de la ville romaine," and by L. Neuru, "Le secteur nord-est de la ville," in A. Ennabli (ed.), *Pour sauver Carthage* (Paris–Tunis 1992) 114-23 and 135-42 respectively, with bibliographies of earlier reports.

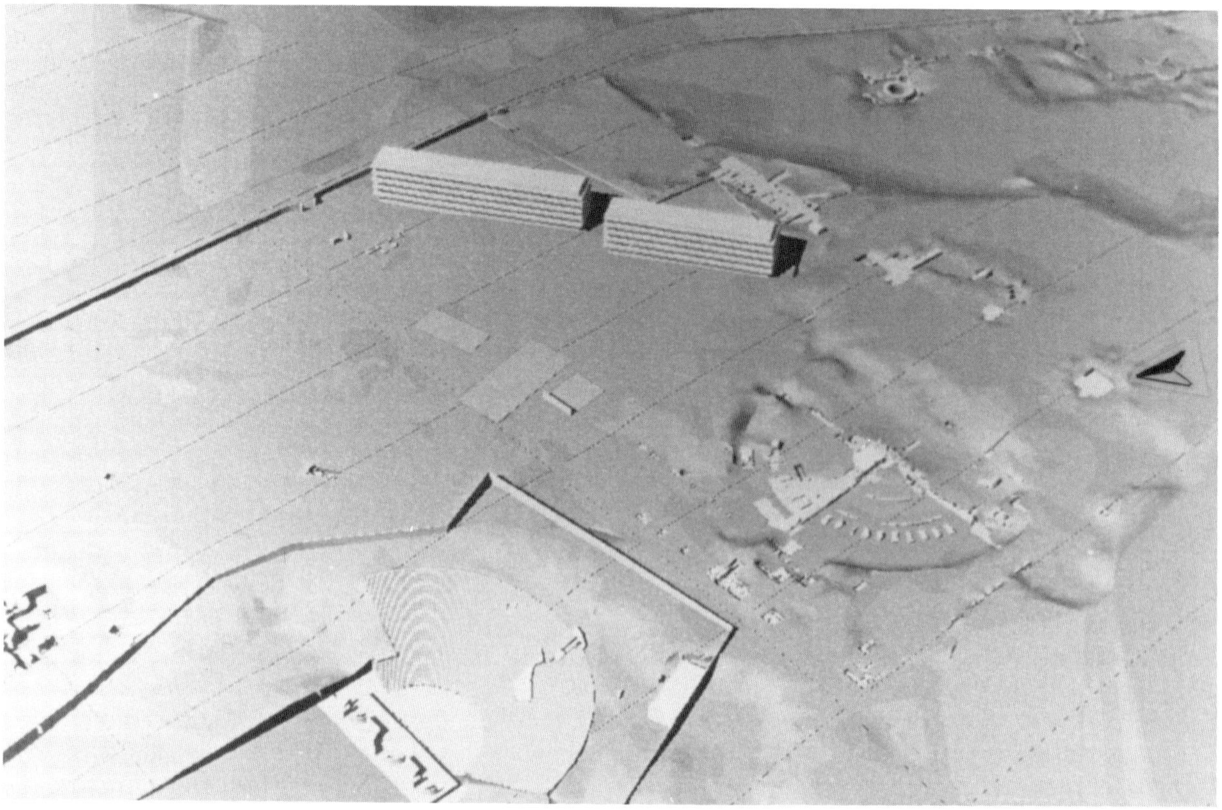

Fig. 1. Computer model of Odeon hill with Odeon near lower right hand corner. The Roman street grid is also indicated. The 1996 excavation lies in the center of the right-hand side of the image (arrow).

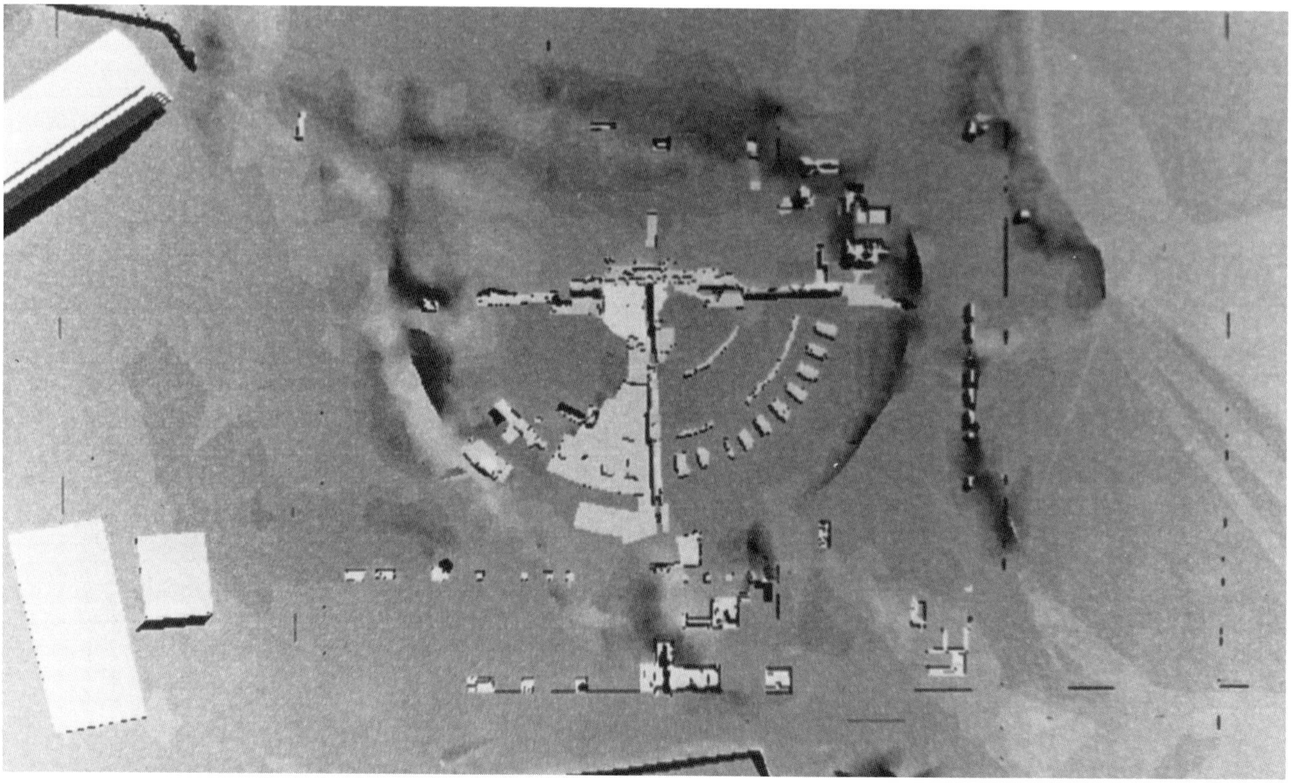

Fig. 2. Computer model of Odeon, viewed from above. North is to the top of the photograph.

S, and that the Wall then turned E along *decumanus* VI at its junction with *cardo* II, thereby obliterating *decumanus* VI to a point about 7.70 m short of its junction with *cardo* III, at which point the Wall turned off to the NE, following the rural cadastration.

A number of trial trenches were opened by E. Wightman further E along both *decumanus* VI and the Theodosian Wall beyond the point where they diverged. Three trenches along *decumanus* VI aimed at finding the intersections of *decumanus* VI and *cardines* IV, V, and VI. Wightman's tragic and untimely death in 1983 prevented her from publishing the final report. Her work at the presumed intersection with *cardo* IV (trench 2CC6) was, however, taken up again in 1990, as described in the next paragraph, and the excavations of 1996 also made use of her trench at the presumed intersection of *decumanus* VI and *cardo* VI (trench 2CC8), which facilitated access to the section of the *decumanus* which we removed.[3]

In 2CC6, Wightman had found the remains of a hypocaust in the SW corner of the presumed intersection, with an apse projecting into the line of the *decumanus*. Further excavation (1990-92) undertaken under the direction of C. M. Wells and M. B. Garrison showed the hypocaust to be part of a small Roman bath complex, probably inserted into the shell of an earlier house.[4] What appears to be the original corner-stone of this house is still *in situ*, and a similar corner-stone belonging to a building north of *decumanus* VI in the NE corner of 2CC6 (square 6C)[5] was associated with occupation levels dating from *c.*A.D. 200.[6] The bath complex was abandoned by the first quarter of the 6th c. A.D. at the latest: there was no sign of a *cardo* IV during the period when the baths were in use, although it could possibly have existed earlier. After the bath complex was abandoned, there appeared to be road surfaces extending on the south side of *decumanus* VI into the line of *cardo* IV,[7] but their significance is unclear.

In 1994, Wells, in partnership with E. Haldenby (University of Waterloo), began to work in the Odeon itself, which had been discovered and partly excavated in 1900-1 by P. Gauckler, then Director of Antiquities for Tunisia.[8] The massive concrete foundation of the auditorium and orchestra and certain other structures, including the base of the wall forming the front of the stage itself, are still visible. The Odeon lies between *decumani* VI and V and occupies the width of 3 city blocks, bounded on the west by *cardo* IV and on the east by *cardo* VII, so that *cardines* V and VI S between *decumani* VI and V must either never have existed or have been removed and destroyed when the Odeon was built. The stage is on the north side of the building and the semicircle of the *cavea* extends to the south, mirroring that of the theater which

---

3 M. Carroll as a graduate student in 1979-80 had been one of Wightman's site supervisors in 2CC8; in the absence of Wightman's original records her own notes and memory were invaluable. The dates in the present article, based on excavations in the 1990s, differ considerably from those in Neuru (supra n.2), based on Wightman's excavations in 1978-80. For the dating of *decumanus* VI, however, the pottery evidence published in full by Freed below is conclusive.

4 M. B. Garrison, P. Foss, and C. M. Wells, "A newly discovered cryptoporticus and bath at Carthage," *JRA* 6 (1993) 251-60. Nothing that we observed in these excavations supports the view (Neuru, supra n.2, 136) that any building in 2CC6 antedates the laying out of *decumanus* VI.

5 In the absence of a plan, there is a vertical photograph of Wightman's 2CC6 trench in C. M. Wells and E. M. Wightman, "Canadian excavations at Carthage, 1976 and 1978: the Theodosian Wall, northern sector," *JFA* 7 (1980) 58 fig. 14.

6 Two superimposed floor levels (C94, C95) that had been left exposed by Wightman's excavations were identified and carefully removed by C. Wells when the entire trench was being cleaned up in 1990. They proved to contain a small amount of pottery, dated to the late 2nd or early 3rd c. A.D. by ARS coarse ware forms 197, 23, and 26.

7 Garrison *et al.* (supra n.4) 260.

8 The most comprehensive account of his excavations appears as part of a longer article: P. Gauckler. "Les fouilles de Tunisie," *RA* 3e sér., 41 (juillet-déc. 1902) 369-408. C. M. Wells, "Paul Gauckler et la colline de l'Odéon à Carthage" in *Hommage à Edmond Frézouls* II (Strasbourg, forthcoming), provides a detailed analysis of Gauckler's work.

extends to the north on the other side of *decumanus* V. Gauckler claimed that the façade of the building north of the stage faced onto a porticoed courtyard enclosed by a perimeter wall ("mur d'enceinte"), of which he had established the precise dimensions by trial trenches ("au moyen de tranchées et sondages"), although he gives no indication where these trenches were.[9] The plan by Sadoux which accompanies Gauckler's report shows the courtyard extending roughly to the line of *decumanus* VI on the north, *cardo* IV on the west, and *cardo* VII on the east,[10] though it should be noted that at the time when Gauckler was excavating in the Odeon, he had not yet located the regular Roman street grid and did not know where the adjacent streets were.[11]

Gauckler's report also spoke of Roman tombs lying in ruins beneath the perimeter wall, tombs which he describes in language reminiscent of that which he used for the tombs in the cemetery of the *officiales*, apparently of Flavian date, on the west side of the city.[12] He dated these tombs on the Odeon hill to the 1st c. B.C., however, and concluded that the area where they were found was therefore at this date outside the *pomerium*. He assumed that the early Roman city was limited to the coastal strip where the original Punic settlement also lay.[13] We have found no trace of such tombs in the area, and there are other reasons for scepticism. One wonders if the débris that Gauckler saw might have been brought to the site as fill. This is not perhaps a very happy solution, but a problem certainly exists if in fact the layout of the Roman colony does go back to the Augustan period and *decumanus* VI represents the *decumanus ultimus*, as was first argued — correctly, it would seem — by Saumagne.[14]

Now Gauckler assumed and Saumagne seems to imply that the site of the Odeon was left vacant until the Odeon was built around A.D. 200 (fig. 2). Against this militate several indications of earlier structures. Gauckler himself in a wholly different context spoke of mosaics belonging to houses of the 1st and 2nd c. A.D. that were demolished when the Odeon was built, although there is no mention of such in his specific writings on the Odeon.[15] The drain **D27** of *decumanus* VI, which cannot be later than the second half of the 2nd c. A.D., has a branch (**D29**) running into it from *cardo* VI, of which only the junction with the *decumanus* drain and 1 m or so of the *cardo* drain survive (fig. 3). The two drains are contemporary and their walls of one build. The rough appearance of the existing ends of the walls of this truncated section appears more consistent with the hypothesis that the *cardo* drain was built and later demolished than with its never having been built. This would suggest that *cardo* VI itself was built and presumably lined with houses, and the dating would be consistent with its having been obliterated when the Odeon was built.

Further evidence for buildings south of *decumanus* VI predating the Odeon was found in 1997, when excavation further west along the line of *decumanus* VI near the theoretical junction with *cardo* V revealed two earlier cisterns south of the street, which had been demolished to allow the perimeter wall of the Odeon courtyard to pass over them. Whether *cardo* V or *cardo* IV ex-

---

9 Gauckler (supra n.7) 394.

10 Plan in Gauckler (supra n.7) 392, fig. 2.

11 On Gauckler's discovery of the principle of the Roman street grid, see P. Gauckler, *Compte-rendu de la Marche du Service en 1903* (Tunis 1904) 11-13.

12 Gauckler (supra n.7) 398: "Le mur d'enceinte ... est établi sur de nombreux débris de tombes maçonnées en blocage et revêtues de stucs, autels ou caissons, entassés pêle-mêle avec des fragments de lampes romaines de la première époque et de coupes ou de patères signées, en fine terre rouge d'Arezzo"; parallels in P. Gauckler, "Fouilles dans le premier cimetière des *officiales* à Carthage," *MémSocAntFr* 56 (1897) 83-124.

13 Gauckler (supra n.7) 398. Cf. R. Lantier, "Notes de topographie carthaginoise. Cimetières romains et chrétiens de Carthage," *CRAI* 1922, 22-28.

14 C. Saumagne, "Colonia Iulia Karthago," *BAC* 1924, 131-39; E. M. Wightman, "The plan of Roman Carthage," in J. G. Pedley (ed.), *New light on ancient Carthage* (Ann Arbor 1980) 29-46.

15 P. Gauckler, *Inventaire des mosaïques de la Gaule et de l'Afrique* 2: *Afrique proconsulaire (Tunisie)* (Paris 1910) 208-9, nos. 619, 620, where the reference to the *Marche du Service* is transparently wrong.

Fig. 3. Junction of sewers of *decumanus* VI N with *cardo* VI E (on right).

isted at this early period is impossible to tell without further excavation. If the site of the Odeon was previously occupied, the earlier properties must have been bought up or expropriated, but this would have been no problem if the emperor approved:

> "Erection of public buildings frequently led to the destruction of existing private ones and therefore to charges on the Imperial purse. ... It is emphasized over and over again that building is not to be embarked on even in the provinces without the emperor's knowledge", but if that were forthcoming, "where land was needed for the construction or improvement" of public buildings, "the owners had little choice in the matter."[16]

In this case, moreover, it may even have been the emperor himself who commissioned this building of unparalleled size, great magnificence, and in an unrivalled position, where it will have been visible for miles around and dominated the approach to Carthage by sea, particularly if the building was connected with the celebration of the Pythian Games in the presence of the emperor Septimius Severus himself.[17] Now that the 1996 excavations have proven that *decumanus* VI was already in existence by the end of the 1st c. B.C., it becomes even less likely that 3 full city blocks just south of it in a prime location were left vacant for over two centuries.

Stratigraphic report

(a) Punic period (figs. 6-8)

The stratigraphically earliest feature was a compact layer (**31**) of hard red clayey sand and chunks of chalk (fig. 4). As it was only partially excavated, its thickness could not be estimated. It contained no finds and appeared to be the undisturbed subsoil, subsequently identified by

---

16 See J. W. Jones, "Expropriation in Roman law," *Law Quarterly Review* 153 (1929) 512-27, esp. 524, 522, for the passages quoted here.

17 T. D. Barnes, *Tertullian: a historical and literary study* (Oxford, rev. ed. 1985) 34-35, 188-89, despite L. Robert, "Une vision de Perpétue martyre à Carthage en 203," *CRAI* 1982, 228-76, esp. 232-33, who argues that the grant to Carthage of the *Pythicus agon* belongs to the start of the reign of Septimius Severus and has nothing to do with the emperor's visit to the city.

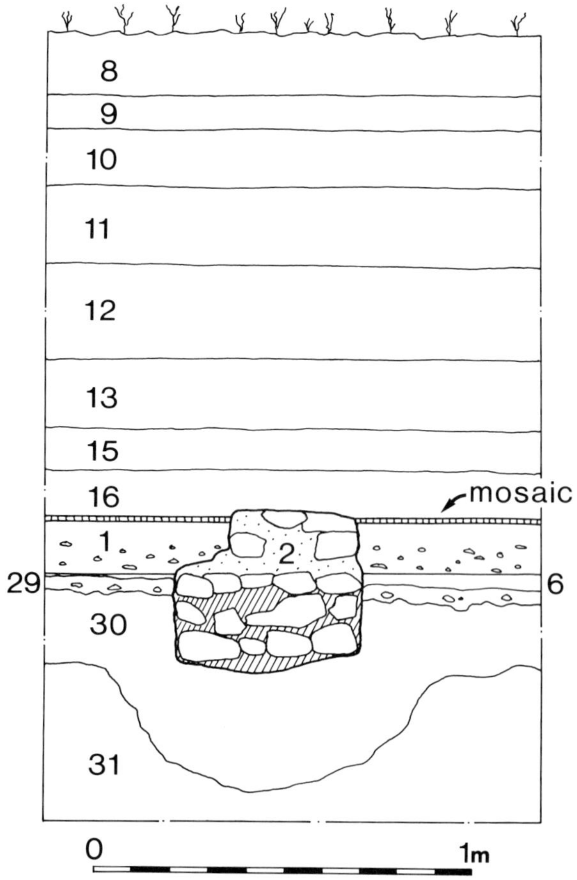

Fig. 4. Composite section of remains of Punic building and overlying road levels of *decumanus* VI.

a geologist as "a palaeosol, probably of the B horizon, a sandy soil of marine origin with significant Aeolian additions of silt and carbonate dust, reddish in color due to the presence of iron, with nodules of calcium carbonate".[18] The layer was observed not only in the 1996 excavations, but also *in situ* to the north of the house wall (Wall 4) in the E part of the trench where it had been exposed by Wightman's excavations of 1979-80.

Immediately above this undisturbed subsoil lay a thick (20 cm) layer (**30**) of sandy soil containing chalk, pebbles, and pottery clearly dating from *c.*300 B.C. Into this layer a pit (**32**) was cut in the SW part of the trench, filled with loose, sandy soil (**33**) mixed with pottery, roughly half of which was of similar date to the pottery in **30**, but with other material clearly of the first quarter of the 2nd c. B.C., including Campana A. This fill also contained creamy white wall-plaster with traces of red paint, as well as fragments of buff-colored *opus signinum* floor and white mosaic. Some of the chunks of *opus signinum* showed signs of burning. Adhering to the underside of one of the mosaic fragments, in what must have been the original make-up layer on which it lay, were 3 sherds dating to

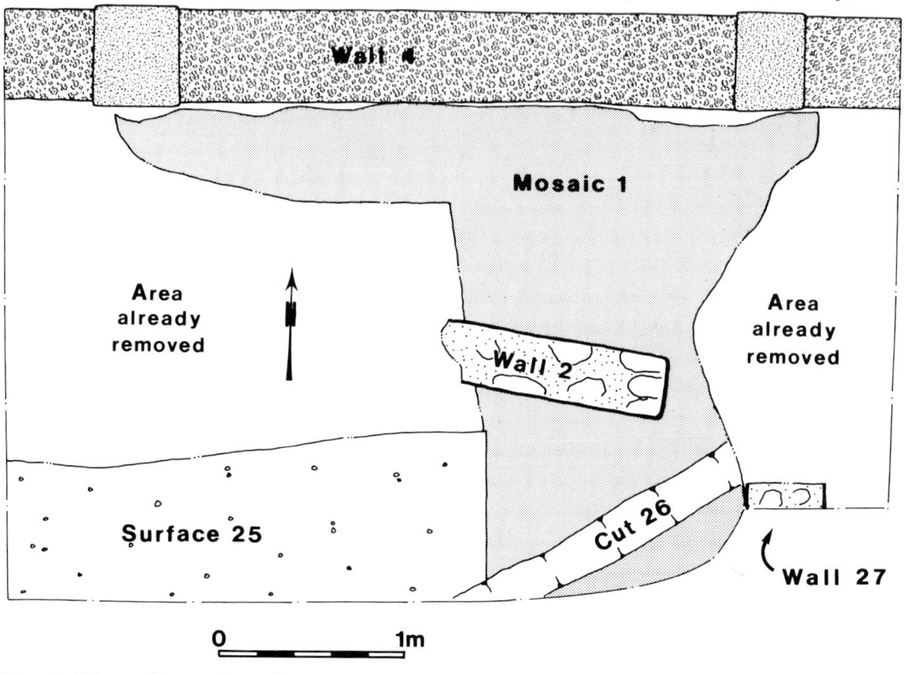

Fig. 5. Plan of remains of Punic building with *opus figlinum* mosaic and late Roman wall **4**.

18 Our thanks are due to T. W. Gardner (Trinity University) for identifying samples of this layer.

Fig. 6. Excavation in progress in line of *decumanus* VI (compare fig. 7, SW corner of trench).

c.300 B.C. This cut **32**, however, may not have been a true pit, but part of a robber trench that removed an earlier building. Not enough was dug to say which was the case.

A beaten earth surface **25**, 5 cm thick (fig. 5), covered **32** and its fill **33**. It contained almost 50 sherds of which none is obviously later than *c*.300 B.C., despite the fact that it post-dates the pit fill **33**, which, as we have just seen, cannot be earlier than the first quarter of the 2nd c. B.C. The surface **25** may have been contemporary with the building discussed below, as it abutted its floor construction. The lowest layer that appeared to be part of this later building was one of clayey sand **29** containing some large pebbles and chalk which may represent a leveling surface from which the construction took place. It contained pottery generally datable to the first half of the 2nd c. B.C. Into this surface went the construction cut **3** for wall **2** running roughly E-W (figs. 4-5). Wall **2** had a rubble foundation *c*.50 cm in width with red clayey bonding material, while the upright masonry of the wall above the *opus figlinum* floor that rests on the bedding **6** and **1** (see below) was set in chalky mortar and was about 35-40 cm thick. From the wall came a fragment of a small table amphora of *c*.300 B.C. Wall **2** was cut at the W end, so that its original length is unknown. To the east, however, the wall properly terminated at the level of the *opus figlinum*, although its foundations continued underneath that floor. Another wall (**27**), partially preserved and disappearing into the S section of the trench, probably represented another wall of the building, though disturbance had obliterated any connection between walls **2** and **27** at foundation level.

This building had a mortar floor layer (**6**), 2 cm thick, overlying **29** and containing a small amount of pottery of the late Punic period, which cannot be more precisely dated. Above **6** was a three-part make-up layer (**1**), devoid of finds, that formed the bedding for a tile mosaic floor of the *opus figlinum* type commonly found in Punic houses (fig. 8).[19] The lowest part of this

---

19 On floors of this type, see K. M. D. Dunbabin, "The pavement fragments and their typology," in J. H. Humphrey (ed.), *Excavations at Carthage 1976 conducted by the University of Michigan* IV (Ann Arbor 1978) 169-80, esp. 176-78 with pl. 4, E-F; and F. Rakob, "Pavimenta punica und Ausstattungselemente der punischen und römischen Häuser", in F. Rakob (ed.), *Karthago* I: *Die deutschen Ausgrabungen in Karthago* (Mainz 1991) 220-25 with pl. 50, g-k. Even if it is true that this type of floor was still being

Fig. 7. Street layers of *decumanus* VI (left) and wall **2** (center) after the removal of *opus figlinum* floor.

Fig. 8. *Opus figlinum* floor cut by late wall (**4**) of building on north side of street.

---

laid in the Roman period (Neuru [supra n.2] 136), the evidence of the pottery in our case leaves no doubt that the floor is Punic.

make-up consisted of coarse, orangey-brown mortar with pebbles (5 cm thick); the next layer (3 cm thick) was of greyish-white mortar with some charcoal flecks; the top layer (1 cm thick) was fine white mortar. The tightly packed but randomly arranged tile tesserae, primarily red and orange in color, were on average 2 x 2 cm square, and the whole surface was "polished" to give a very fine, flat appearance. It appears that **29**, **6**, **1**, and the *opus figlinum* floor itself all represent a single construction phase for which a date in the first quarter of the 2nd c. B.C. best accords with the totality of the ceramic evidence. There is no evidence for the occupation of the building, since any evidence that there might have been was cleared away to floor level before the first Roman street was laid (see below).

At some stage a small irregular channel, **26**, 9 cm in depth, was cut into the mosaic floor (fig. 5). Neither the date nor the purpose of the cut can be determined, but the pottery in the fill of this channel was of Roman date and is discussed below.

(b) Roman and later periods:

After the building was demolished, a new street was laid down immediately on top of the old mosaic floor (fig. 4). This street, which is Roman *decumanus* VI, is on a different alignment from the earlier building, indicating new development on a different plan. The fact that we found no humic build-up or collapsed building material lying on top of the Punic *opus figlinum* floor and beneath the lowest street level is surprising. It must mean that all débris was cleared off the floor at the time when the new street was constructed, so that the mosaic itself at this point formed the actual surface on which the street was laid down. It is not likely that the building remained standing into the Roman period, unless it were still occupied and maintained after 146 B.C., for which there is no evidence. Nor does it seem likely that the building was destroyed in 146 and the débris carted off immediately. Firstly, who is likely to have done it? Secondly, one would then expect there to have been a humic build-up which would have been at least as difficult for the road-builders to clean off as the débris would have been. Therefore we prefer the following as the most plausible hypothesis. First, the building was destroyed in 146 and left as a heap of ruins. Over a century later, the Roman surveyors came along to lay out the street grid of the new *colonia*. They surveyed in the line of the planned *decumanus* VI and ordered it to be leveled, whether by filling in depressions or by smoothing out obstacles, to reach the elevation at which they intended to lay the foundations of the new road. The road gang removed the pile of old building débris and by chance hit upon the mosaic beneath at approximately the right level. They were just starting to pick through the mosaic — hence the irregular channel with the fill **26** — when a supervisor stopped them, pointing out that the mosaic itself, if cleaned off, would serve perfectly well as a foundation for the lowest street layer, as indeed it did. This lively reconstruction at least accounts for all the evidence.

The earliest street layers **16**, **15**, **23**, **13**, **12** and **11**, in ascending order, which have a combined depth of about 1 m, are compact and clearly defined. They are composed of light brown clayey sand. Layers **16** and **15** contain pottery of the last decade of the 1st c. B.C., and we feel justified in concluding that the first street was actually laid out at this period. Layers **23**, **13**, and **12** contain pottery of *c.* A.D. 15, and layer **11** pottery of *c.*A.D. 50. Layer **10**, however, lying immediately above **11**, contained pottery from the mid 2nd c. A.D., so that there was a gap of at least a century between **11** and **10**. In 1979-80, a large vaulted street drain **D27**, 1 m wide and 1.30 m high to the start of the vault, was found to originate a few meters to the east of our subsequent (1996) operations and to run east towards the sea. Although we did not excavate in the area of the drain in 1996, and although it was never built to extend as far west as the area of the 1996 trench, it could be seen that our layer **10** extended east into the area of the drain and was the first layer to pass over the top of the drain, which must therefore have been constructed in the second half of the 2nd c. A.D. at the latest. The drain cuts down through all earlier Roman street layers and the floor of the drain is at a level below that of the *opus figlinum* floor. As already stated, a drain serving *cardo* VI (**D29**) enters the drain **D27** of the *decumanus* just east of the point where it begins, but had been demolished, presumably when the Odeon was built and the *cardo* therefore obliterated.[20]

If layer **10** was originally covered with paving stones, as seems likely by analogy with the paving covering the similar drain that runs west beneath *decumanus* VI in the old Canadian trench 2CC1/2, these stones and any accumulation above them were removed before the first of the preserved later street layers **9** and **8** was laid down. These two street layers displayed well-defined hard trampled surfaces and both date to the first half of the 6th c., leaving a gap of over 300 years between layers **10** and **9**. They also contain fragments of grey mortar characteristic of the Theodosian Wall and later periods. The south wall **4** of a building fronting onto *decumanus* VI cut through these upper street surfaces, making it the latest feature in the area (figs. 5, 8). The building was approached by a shallow flight of steps leading down from the street. No pottery was recovered from wall **4** itself or from the construction cut **5**. This wall was of substantial build, being 50 cm thick and consisting of rubble masonry bonded between piers of blocks set 2-3 m apart in *opus africanum* technique. The stratigraphically latest feature was layer **7** which was a loose layer lying on the street and against wall **4**. It contained a few sherds of late Roman pottery and appeared to be surface build-up as the area went out of use. It is not shown in the section drawing.

FREQUENTLY CITED ABBREVIATIONS USED IN FOLLOWING POTTERY REPORT

Bailey, *BM* 1980	D. M. Bailey, *A catalogue of the lamps in the British Museum* II, *Roman lamps made in Italy* (London)
Bailey, *BM* 1988	D. M. Bailey, *A catalogue of the lamps in the British Museum* III, *Roman provincial Lamps* (London)
Beltrán, *Guia* 1990	M. Beltrán, "Cerámica pintada," in *Guia de la cerámica romana* (Zaragoza) 161-69
Byrsa I 1979	S. Lancel and J.-P. Thuillier, "Niveaux puniques," *Byrsa* I: *Mission archéologique française à Carthage* (Rome)
Byrsa II 1982	*Byrsa* II: *Rapports préliminaires sur les fouilles 1977/1978 (niveaux et vestiges puniques) sous la direction de S. Lancel* (Rome)
Carandini *et al.* 1981	L. Anselmino and A. Carandini (edd.), *Enciclopedia dell'Arte Antica Classica e Orientale, Atlante delle forme ceramiche* I: *Ceramica fine romana nel bacino mediterraneo (media e tardo impero)* (Rome)
Cintas 1950	P. Cintas, *Céramique punique* (Paris)
CMich I 1976	J. W. Hayes, "Pottery: stratified groups and typology," 47-107, and J. Riley, "The amphoras," 108-23, in J. H. Humphrey (ed.), *Excavations at Carthage 1975 conducted by the University of Michigan* I (Tunis)
CMich IV 1978	J. W. Hayes, "Pottery report — 1976," in J. H. Humphrey (ed.), *Excavations at Carthage 1976 conducted by the University of Michigan* IV (Ann Arbor) 23-98
Conspectus	E. Ettlinger *et al.*, *Conspectus formarum terrae sigillatae italico modo confectae* (Bonn 1990)

20 The building of the Odeon and the courtyard to the north involved massive earth-moving operations, so that today it is impossible to recover the profile of the Odeon hill before the Odeon was built. If a drain from *cardo* VI flowed into that of *decumanus* VI, the hill at this point must have sloped down, no matter how gently, towards the north, which is no longer the case. There are similar indications of changed contours elsewhere, but this is not the place to attempt to marshal all the evidence.

Freed 1996 — J. Freed, "Early Roman amphoras in the collection of the Museum of Carthage," *EMC/Classical Views* 15, 119-55

Harbour 1994 — M. G. Fulford and D. P. S. Peacock, *Excavations at Carthage, The British Mission* II, 2. *The Circular Harbour, North Side: The pottery* (Oxford)

Harden 1937 — D. B. Harden, "The pottery from the precinct of Tanit at Salammbo, Carthage," *Iraq* 4, 59-89

Hayes, *LRP* — J. W. Hayes, *Late Roman pottery* (London 1972)

Hayes 1985 — J. W. Hayes, "Sigillate orientali," 1-96 and pls. 1-23, in I. Baldassare *et al.*, (coord.), *Atlante delle forme ceramiche* II

Hesnard 1980 — A. Hesnard, "Un dépôt augustéen d'amphores à La Longarina, Ostie," in J. H. D'Arms and E. C. Kopff (edd.), *The seaborne commerce of ancient Rome* (MAAR 36) 141-56 and plates

Karthago 1991 — F. Rakob, *et al.*, *Die deutschen Ausgrabungen in Karthago* I (Mainz-am-Rhein)

Kenrick, *Benghazi* 1985 — P. M. Kenrick, *Excavations at Sidi Khrebish Benghazi* III.1, *The fine pottery* (Tripoli)

Leptiminus 1992 — N. Ben Lazreg and D. J. Mattingly (ed.), *Leptiminus (Lamta), a Roman port city in Tunisia, Report no. 1* (JRA Suppl. 4)

Martin-Kilcher, *Augst* 1987 — S. Martin-Kilcher, *Die römischen Amphoren aus Augst und Kaiseraugst* 1. *Die Südspanischen Ölamphoren (Gruppe 1)* (Augst)

Mayet 1975 — F. Mayet, *Les céramiques à parois fines dans la péninsule ibérique* (Paris 1975)

Morel 1981 — J.-P. Morel, *Céramique campanienne: les formes* I, II (Rome)

Ostia III 1973 — C. Panella, "Le anfore," *Le Terme del Nuotatore* III = *StMisc* 21, 460-633

Oxé–Comfort 1968 — A. Oxé and H. Comfort, *Corpus vasorum arretinorum. A catalogue of the signatures, shapes and chronology of Italian sigillata* (Bonn)

Panella and Fano 1977 — C. Panella and M. Fano, "Le anfore con anse bifide conservate a Pompei: contributo ad una loro classificazione," *Méthodes classiques et méthodes formelles dans les études des amphores* (Rome) 133-77

Peacock, 'Petrology' 1984 — M. Fulford and D. P. S. Peacock, *Excavations at Carthage, The British Mission* I,2. *The Habib Bourguiba Site: The pottery* (Sheffield) 6-28

Peacock & Williams 1986 — D. P. S. Peacock and D. F. Williams, *Amphorae and the Roman economy: an introductory guide* (London)

Ricci 1985 — A. Ricci, 'Ceramica a pareti sottili," in I. Baldassare *et al.* (ed.), *Atlante delle forme ceramiche* II: *Ceramica fine romana nel bacino Mediterraneo (tardo ellenismo e primo impero)* (EAA Supp., Rome) 231-358, pls. 78-104, maps 150-59

Riley, *Benghazi* 1979 — J. A. Riley, "The coarse pottery from Benghazi," in J. A. Lloyd (ed.), *Excavations at Berenice Benghazi* II (Tripoli)

Sabratha 1994 — M. Fulford and R. Tomber (edd.), *Excavations at Sabratha, 1948-1951* II, *The finds*, pt. 2, *The fine-wares and lamps* (London)

Sanmartí 1984 — E. Sanmartí (ed.), *El fòrum romà d'Empúries* (Barcelona)

Tomber 1986 — R. Tomber, "Pottery from the south side of the Circular Harbour," *CEDAC Carthage* 7, 34-58

Toscanos 1964 — H. G. Niemeyer and H. Schubart, *Toscanos 1964. Die altpunische Faktorei an der Mündung des Río de Vélez, Grabungskampagne 1964* (Berlin 1969)

van der Werff 1977-78 — J. H. van der Werff, "Amphores de tradition punique à Uzita," *BABesch* 52-53, 171-200

van der Werff 1986 — Id. in J. Boersma *et al.*, "Excavations in the House of the Porch (V.ii.4-5) at Ostia," *BABesch* 61, 77-137

Vegas, 'Karthago' 1994 — M. Vegas, "Ein frühkaiserzeitlicher Fundkomplex aus Karthago," *RömMitt* 101, 339-64.

Pottery report

Joann Freed

General survey of ceramic finds

Discrete and well articulated stratigraphic sequences combine with high counts of diagnostic pottery for both the Punic and early Roman contexts. The ceramic material is abundant and in excellent condition and includes a wide variety of wares and forms which are distinctive and identifiable almost without exception. The excavation has provided an ideal opportunity to utilize recent scholarship that has greatly refined the dating of black-glazed[21] and Italian terra sigillata[22] fine wares and early Roman lamps.[23] In addition, publication of stratified pottery horizons for the Punic and early Roman periods have been accruing steadily since J. W. Hayes' *Late Roman pottery* first illuminated the pottery production of Roman Tunisia.[24] In 1972, the class of fine wares which Hayes dubbed 'African Red Slip' were only just conceded to be a production of North Africa; today we can clearly distinguish at least between productions of Carthage/Nabeul and Byzacena in fine wares, cooking wares and perhaps even in amphoras. With the accumulation of evidence from relevant contexts at Carthage and elsewhere in North Africa, the range of fabrics and forms presented here can now be considered diagnostic for the date of the contexts in which they appear.

For the Punic contexts, the publications of the French[25] and German[26] teams have provided comparative material. The pottery from the levels of *decumanus* VI reveals a more articulated picture of the first half of the 1st c. A.D. than earlier treatments of material of comparable date from Carthage. Nevertheless, important comparative material was available in the publication by J. W. Hayes and J. A. Riley of 1st c. A.D. deposits from the Michigan excavations of 1975-76;[27] in the recent publication by M. Fulford and D. P. S. Peacock of contexts of the 1st c. B.C./A.D. from the British excavations in the harbour,[28] and by M. Vegas of several 1st c. A.D. deposits[29] and another deposit of the third quarter of the 1st c. A.D. from the German excavations.[30] Our level of the mid 2nd c. A.D. was scantier and less closely dated; nevertheless, comparative material published by R. Tomber[31] was useful. By contrast with the earlier levels, the two topmost street levels **9**, **8**, and level **7**, all of which date to the first half of the 6th c., contained very little pottery, and this material offered no new information. As the importance of the site lies in the Punic and, especially, in the early Roman material, the later material is only briefly summarized.

The early Roman contexts provide new dating evidence for Kenrick's 'Tripolitanian' (Campanian) sigillata, Sanmartí's 'Ampuritan grey ware', Hayes' local 'early African Red Slip A', Byzacena blacktop cooking ware (Hayes' 'Early Roman Cooking Ware 2'), Carthage/Nabeul blacktop cooking ware (the forms in African blacktop coarse ware typed by Hayes in 1972, and his 'Early Roman Cooking Ware 1'), local neo-Punic early Roman amphoras, coastal

---

21 Morel 1981.

22 E. Ettlinger *et al.*, *Conspectus formarum terrae sigillatae italico modo confectae* (Bonn 1990).

23 D. M. Bailey, "Part IV. Lamps," in *Sabratha* 1994; also Bailey, *BM* 1980 and Bailey, *BM* 1988.

24 Hayes, *LRP*, included the earliest forms in the blacktop cooking ware, forms 181-200 (pp. 200-11), and the earliest exported forms in the local Carthage/Nabeul production of African Red Slip 'A' fine ware, which dated from the late 1st c. A.D.

25 *Byrsa* I 1979; *Byrsa* II 1982.

26 *Karthago* 1991.

27 *CMich* I 1976; also *CMich* IV.

28 *Harbour* 1994.

29 M. Vegas, passim in *Karthago* 1991.

30 Vegas, 'Karthago' 1994.

31 Tomber 1986.

Tarraconensian Dressel 2 and the small ovoid North African and Italian(?) amphoras of Panella's class *Ostia* III, 44-46 (see discussion of these types below).

Especially in the early Roman street levels, the percentage and absolute numbers of diagnostic rims were high: the Augustan and Julio-Claudian levels of *decumanus* VI had a total of 211 diagnostic rims. Fine ware counts were relatively high in all contexts and highest (11-14%) in the levels of c.A.D. 15. Both the Punic and the Roman layers also showed a high concentration of amphoras. In the Punic contexts as a whole, the percentage of amphoras averaged about 52% by weight, varying from 40 to 76% in the different layers. In the Roman street layers, the overall average was 61% of amphoras by weight, but there was a much greater variation by layer (from 23 to 100%).

Despite the limited size of the excavation, the material returned was more than adequate for dating, by both count and weight (1,233 sherds, 27.087 kg). Ceramic material from the Punic levels totalled 6.957 kg; from the earliest Roman street levels **26**, **16**, **15** it totalled 5.995 kg (10-1 B.C.); from the next later group of strata **23**, **13**, **12**, 7.730 kg (c.A.D. 15). A particularly high count and percentage of diagnostic and publishable pottery was recovered from layer **12**. Relatively less material, 1.555 kg, came from the last Julio-Claudian layer **11** of c.A.D. 50 (see Tables 1-4 for a detailed analysis of the Augustan and Julio-Claudian levels). From the level of the mid 2nd c. A.D. **10**, 3.130 kg was recovered. By contrast, the two early 6th-c. street layers **8** and **9** had little pottery (1.546 kg combined).

Pottery methodology

In the excavation, the pottery was not sieved and no extreme measures were taken to extract every sherd; on the other hand, the broad range of pottery in fabric, type and size indicates that the pottery recovered was representative. Proceeding layer by layer, every sherd returned from the site was assigned to a fabric class (for example, 'ARS A'); rims, bases, handles and wall sherds in each fabric class were counted, identifiable forms were noted, and the fabric class as a whole was weighed. Fabrics and types are also classified by one of 4 functional categories: fine wares, service and cooking wares, and amphoras. Across all periods, there were a minimum of 20 distinguishable fine wares; 11 service and cooking wares and 11 amphora fabrics. Fifteen distinctive Punic fabrics and 27 early Roman fabrics (see Tables 1-4) were identified. Nearly all the catalogued early Roman pottery occurs in wares which have been previously documented to the point of identification of their general provenance. A reference to a general fabric description is given when the fabric is first discussed; the description in the catalogue is therefore minimal.

The date of each context was determined by the fine wares, confirmed by lamps in the early Roman layers. C. Wells consulted with P. Kenrick on the stamped fragments of Italian terra sigillata[32] and J. Freed consulted with J. W. Hayes on a broad range of pieces. A number of calculations were made for every layer and context: sample size, average sherd size, the ratio of imports to local production, and the percentages of residual and intrusive pottery. These calculations are listed with the summary of each layer in the catalogue below. I consider average sherd size to be important evidence; according to my experience with excavation pottery, average sherd weights in urban deposits of 25-75 g for amphora and 10-12 g for other pottery are normal but not necessarily indicative of primary deposition. When the average size of pottery sherds is large (more than 100 g for amphora and more than 25 g for other pottery), primary and undisturbed deposition is likely. On the other hand, where sherds are particularly small (less than 20 g for amphora and less than 8 g for other pottery), the pottery has been crushed, possibly deliberately, and is certainly re-deposited and possibly disturbed as well. On this site, most layers are clearly re-deposited, but the pottery in the two largest Punic layers and in the early Roman street levels has not been crushed. Among the 1,233 sherds analysed, 2 sherds are certainly intrusive.[33] They are absolutely outweighed by the consistency of the other 1,231 sherds returned from the site, which form a clearly articulated sequence.

Most of the catalogued sherds were drawn in pencil by Freed; a number of pieces, including the stamped Italian terra sigillata and the lamps were drawn by A. Leung, who also inked all the drawings.

---

32 P. M. Kenrick published the fine wares at Benghazi (*Benghazi* 1985) and is one of the authors of the *Conspectus*. He is preparing a new edition of the catalogue of Italian terra sigillata and stamps, originally Oxé–Comfort 1968.

33 These are a small wall sherd of local blacktop cooking ware Hayes Form 197 in **29** and a bit of burnt Hayes Type 1 lamp in **13**. As I note below, large lid knobs in Hayes' 'Early Roman Cooking Ware 2' are not necessarily intrusive in Punic and early Roman layers.

Characterization and dating of the Punic layers

The area was occupied by *c*.300 B.C. (layer **30**) and the Punic building, the floor of which underlies the Roman street levels, was probably built *c*.175 B.C., which is the latest likely date for the pit fill **33** and other layers **25**, **29**, **6** at and below the floor. The lowest Punic layer **30** and the fill from the pit **33** both had a relatively high pottery count and a high percentage of diagnostic sherds. Particularly in **30**, the sherds other than amphoras are large, an indicator of possible primary deposition.

Somewhat unexpectedly, there were no lamps in any of the Punic layers. One sherd of burnished red slipped fine ware may be as early as the 7th/6th c. B.C.[34] A wide range of black-glazed fabrics of the 3rd/2nd c. B.C. includes Attic, local, various Italian productions including possible Campana B, and definite Campana A; most is not very fine quality. Identification and dating of the black-glazed types follow Morel, quoting his wording as appropriate.[35] Local buff coarse ware appears, often with painted bands, a type of decoration typical at Carthage from the 7th to the 3rd c. B.C.[36] Transport amphora fabrics are mainly local Tunisian; Greco-Italic amphora also appears. The great majority of the Punic sherds are entirely appropriate to the contexts in which they are found; the few problematic sherds are specifically noted in the layer descriptions.

Layers **30** and pit fill **33** are differentiated in date by the appearance in **33** of Campana A, by a great increase in the quantity of Byzacena blacktop red cooking ware,[37] and by Greco-Italic amphora (no. 25). The remaining Punic layers **25**, **29**, **2**, **6** have little pottery; none has a sherd count large enough to ensure an entirely reliable date. The sherds are also much smaller; they were perhaps disturbed in construction of the Punic building, and the sherd size reflects this.

The first layer **30** above natural soil is dated to *c*.300 B.C. by fine wares, which include a local black-glazed version of small hemispherical bowl Lamboglia 22/28 (no. 1) and an elegant sherd, probably from Teanum Sidicinum, with characteristic red gloss on the underside of the base (no. 2); banded service wares (nos. 4 and 5) support the general date. A single burnished handmade sherd in this context may be residual, perhaps of the 7th or 6th c. B.C.[38] A type of slipped and banded jug or table amphora appears (no. 4) that is typical of Punic burials at Carthage from the earliest to latest contexts.[39] The fill in the pit **33** dug into layer **30** is a much later context; two fine ware bowls in layer **33** (nos. 8 and 9) shared the earlier context date of the material in **30**, but half the fine wares in **33** date to the first quarter of the 2nd c. B.C. Three forms, including Lamboglia 36B, occur in black-glazed Campana A from Naples/Ischia (cf. nos. 11-13); the fabric began to be widely exported only around 220 B.C.[40] Vegas dates a comparable deposit, with a local version of Lamboglia 22/28 (as no. 8), Punic blacktop red cooking ware casserole as Hayes 194 (as no. 24) and thin-walled lids (as nos. 22-23), a Punic basin with beveled rim (as no. 20) and a Greco-Italic amphora with dropped triangular rim, to the first quarter of the 2nd c. B.C.; this date agrees well with the Campana A in **33**.[41]

An Attic black-glazed *guttus* (no. 26), which dates to the second half of the 4th c. B.C., is significantly earlier than its context in **25**, a probable beaten earth floor surface over pit fill **33**. Otherwise, the two larger Punic contexts indicate that some black-glazed ware was imported

34 For Punic fine wares of this period, cf. *Toscanos 1964*.

35 Morel 1981

36 Cf. Cintas 1950.

37 There were 5 sherds (30 g) in layer **30** compared to 32 sherds (385 g) in layer **33**.

38 *Toscanos 1964*, 105-16.

39 It can date as early as the 8th c. B.C.: Cintas 1950, 153. According to Harden, it is far more usual in 7th and 6th c. contexts than in 5th and 4th c. contexts, but a debased version is found even in the 3rd and 2nd c. B.C.: Harden 1937, 74, 87.

40 Morel 1981, 47.

41 Vegas, *Karthago* 1991, fig. 36.1-30 and 179-81.

from both Campania (Teanum Sidicinum) and Sicily around 300 B.C. (but only 2% of layer **30** by weight), and that in the first quarter of the 2nd c. B.C. Campana A from Naples/Ischia and Greco-Italic amphora were imported (at least 14% of layer **33** by weight).

There were few surprises among the Punic material. However, a wall sherd of Tunisian cylindrical amphora with a maximum body diameter of only 15.0 cm in layer **30** was noteworthy, as I do not know of other evidence for fractional median sizes of Punic cylindrical amphoras[42] before the neo-Punic types (see below).

Byzacena blacktop red cooking ware

This excavation clarified the definition and date of a wheelmade cooking ware which is important in Punic contexts at Carthage. The ware which Hayes dubbed 'Early Roman Cooking Ware 2' in a first analysis of early Roman contexts at Carthage[43] is the only cooking ware in our Punic contexts, occurring first, but rarely, in **33**, which is dated to the first quarter of the 2nd c. B.C. It is proportionally very uncommon in the early Roman layers, occurring only in layers **15** (5 sherds, 100 g, of which one is a large string-cut lid knob) and **11** (2 sherds, 30 g).

Hayes' 'Early Roman Cooking Ware 2' is a North African fabric, slightly abrasive and usually dark red; the ware can have a 'blacktop' treatment (reduced surfaces) similar to that found on local blacktop orange cooking ware, which Hayes labelled 'Early Roman Cooking Ware 1' in the first Michigan volume.[44] From long experience of excavated pottery at Carthage, and from observations of pottery in Tunisian museums, I associate very thin-walled miniature casseroles and lids in the abrasive red blacktop fabric with the Hellenistic period. Forms of Hellenistic/Punic date also often have characteristic lateral rolled handles. The miniature forms in which the ware appears in the Hellenistic period are in fact imitations of normal-sized Greek cooking ware forms,[45] and a regular range of cooking ware was manufactured alongside the miniatures, which must have had a special function, perhaps as toys or funerary gifts.

Before studying the evidence from this excavation, I had associated a more 'normal' range of sizes and wall thickness in this fabric with the early Roman period and Hayes' 'Early Roman Cooking Ware 2'. Hayes noted three forms in the ware, forms quite similar to his early Roman Forms 191 cooking pot, 194 casserole, and 196 lid in local (Carthage/Nabeul) blacktop orange cooking ware.[46] Of these, the latter two forms appear in Punic layers in this excavation. All three of the forms which Hayes noted occur in normal sizes in contexts of the first half of the

---

42 A mini version of Cintas 315, the cigar-shaped amphora with hole mouth and ridged shoulder, is on display in the introductory gallery of the Musée National de Carthage; it should be dated to the 4th c. B.C.; cf. Cintas 1950.

43 Hayes, *CMich* I 1976 93-95. The cooking ware forms which were analysed in Hayes, *LRP* were those of the local Carthage/Nabeul blacktop orange cooking ware fabric, which the evidence of this excavation suggests begins only with the founding of the Roman colony. I suggest that this ware, which is now inadequately labelled 'African blacktop coarse ware', should be re-named Carthage/Nabeul blacktop cooking ware.

44 While the 'Byzacena blacktop red cooking ware' is easily distinguished visually by colour and surface treatment, and also by its 'sandpaper' texture, from local blacktop cooking ware ware, the two fabrics are not petrologically distinguishable; Fulford, *Harbour* 1994, fig. 75, coarse ware lid forms 3 and 4, p. 197, evidently classes it as Peacock's Fabric 2.3, 'quartz-limestone fabrics of Africa', 'black surface ware', D. P. S. Peacock, "Petrology and origins," 17, in Peacock, 'Petrology' 1984.

45 H. A. Thompson, "Two centuries of Hellenistic pottery," *Hesperia* 3 (1934) fig. 121, and 466-68. These forms were widely distributed around the Mediterranean where Greek influence was strong, probably ordinarily copied in local fabrics.

46 These forms were first defined in blacktop cooking ware in Hayes, *LRP*; the form designations have been applied to forms in both the local Carthage/Nabeul and the Byzacena blacktop fabrics.

2nd c. B.C. in the French excavations on the Byrsa.[47] At Leptiminus, Dore identified a few examples similar to the Form 194 casserole, as identical in both form and fabric to Sabratha Form 35, which appeared in the 4th c. B.C. and became common from the end of the 3rd c. B.C.; that is slightly earlier than the date of layer **33**, the context in which it appears on *decumanus* VI. Interestingly — given that it does not appear in our excavation — Dore dates the first appearance of a casserole Hayes Form 191 in this ware to slightly later, from the 2nd c. B.C. and lasting into the 1st c. A.D.[48]

Since this blacktop red cooking ware, in the range of forms which Hayes described, is common in the Punic pit fill **33** of the first quarter of the 2nd c. B.C. and hardly occurs in the overlying early Roman street levels, it may be incorrectly described as 'Early Roman', at least at Carthage (but see below).[49] For the purpose of this report, I will designate the ware 'Byzacena blacktop red cooking ware'. Designation by area of manufacture is most helpful, where it is known; and since the same general class appears at Carthage, Leptiminus, Uzita,[50] and Sabratha, it is most likely a product of central Tunisia (Byzacena).

Large thick-walled forms in a very similar fabric are common at Carthage in the late Roman period. Hayes labelled the late range, in new forms and with thicker walls, 'Late Roman Cooking Ware I',[51] but the fabric is essentially the same in red colour, grey surfaces and abrasive surface. A large string-cut lid knob (no. 21), which appears in layer **33** and again in Roman layer **15**, is not distinguishable from a Late Roman/Vandal lid knob in 'Late Roman Cooking Ware I'. It is possible that this piece is intrusive in the Punic context, but I am less certain than I would once have been.[52]

Characterization and dating of the Augustan and Julio-Claudian street levels

Like the Punic, the Julio-Claudian material seems to be domestic; however, lamps are very common. The Roman street layers other than the lowest (**16**) and the highest (**8**), where the sherds are notably small, have normal average sherd sizes. In the Augustan and Julio-Claudian street layers, for wares other than amphoras, which can nearly all be individually dated, residual sherds make up 3% by sherd count and less than 2% by weight, which is very low. It is more difficult to calculate the percentage of residual amphoras. All the non-Tunisian amphora types in layer **12** are imported types contemporary with their contexts; the average weight is 115 g, which is very large. The Tunisian cylindrical amphora sherds, in contrast, averaged only 30 g. While wall sherds of Punic Tunisian cylindrical amphoras were not distinguished from early Roman ones at the point of processing, the early Roman neo-Punic amphora described by van der Werff as Type 2 is both smaller and thinner-walled than the Punic Cintas 312/313. Although the neo-Punic type represented in the early Roman contexts of *decumanus* VI is not equivalent to van der Werff Type 2, it is contemporary, and may also be relatively small and thin-walled. There is 1 clearly residual Punic (Cintas 315) *versus* 10 neo-Punic rims, suggesting a sherd count ratio of 8% of Punic residual amphoras among the Tunisian amphoras; this is

---

47 *Byrsa* I 1979, 204, layer A147, fig. 28, no. 9 = as Hayes Form 191, rim diam. 34.0; no. 10 = as Form 194, rim diam. 23.0; no. 11 = as Form 196, rim diam. 22.0.

48 J. N. Dore, "First report on the pottery," in *Leptiminus* 1992, 136, cooking ware forms nos. 2 and 3 (as Hayes 194 and 191), illustrated p. 139.

49 Fulford notes that the overall evidence for forms in this fabric suggests residuality, but a version as Form 194 with beveled interior angles is extremely common in Augustan contexts: *Harbour* 1994, fig. 1.1-3, pp. 56-59. It therefore seems possible that the ware was used at Carthage in the early Augustan period, although the local blacktop orange cooking ware replaced the earlier ware by the mid Augustan period.

50 Hayes, *CMich* I 1976, 95, citing van der Werff, pers. comm.

51 Hayes, *CMich* I 1976, 95-96; the similarity to 'Early Roman Cooking Ware 2' is not noted.

52 Fulford, *Harbour* 1994, 67 notes that coarse ware lids cannot be trusted as chronological markers. See also the discussion below of coarse wares in the early Roman street levels.

quite possibly anomalous, but it does seem that the rate of residual Tunisian amphoras was relatively, but not absolutely, high.

A high proportion of imports appeared in the Augustan and Julio-Claudian layers, particularly those dated 10-1 B.C. and those dated *c*.A.D. 15. Again the percentages are based on relatively small numbers of sherds and should be treated with caution, but they are very suggestive. The overall count of imports in the Punic contexts was 12% by sherd count and 13% by weight. By contrast, imports were 42% by weight in the Augustan street levels **16** and **15** dated 10-1 B.C., and increased to 48% by weight in levels **23**, **13**, **12** dated *c*.A.D. 15. They then dropped back to 29% by *c*.A.D. 50 (layer **11**) and to 18% in the mid 2nd c. A.D. (**10**). The two periods with very high imports, 10-1 B.C. and *c*.A.D. 15, also showed a very great variety in both imported household wares and amphoras.[53] The evidence that imports were both high and varied at these two points, still relatively close in date to the foundation of the Roman colony, and that they dropped back as the local economy became established is intuitively obvious, but detailed analysis shows how well the new city was supported, either by the wealth of its new citizens or by outside subventions.

Layers **16** and **15**, which are stratigraphically discrete street levels, cannot be distinguished in date and a rim sherd from the same neo-Punic amphora occurred in both **16** and **15**.[54] There was then a chronological gap between **15** and **23**, shown by the introduction of Italian terra sigillata hemispherical cups with areas of rouletting and the flat-based amphora class *Ostia* III.44-46.[55] Layers **13** and **12**, which cannot be differentiated in date by Italian terra sigillata forms and stamps, showed a possible gap, as **12** introduced metallic-glazed thin-walled ware and an Italian Tyrrhenian cooking ware, possibly from Latium. A distinct chronological gap was evident between **12** and **11**, with the introduction of Italian terra sigillata in *Conspectus* Form 3.3 and simple plates/platters which take appliqué decoration, and Carthage/Nabeul blacktop cooking ware Hayes Form 183 casserole and Form 26 bread-baking dish.

Overview of fabrics in the Augustan and Julio-Claudian street levels

There were 7 general classes of fine wares in the Augustan and Julio-Claudian levels. Residual mostly Italian black-glazed wares formed about 8% of the fine wares by weight. Of the 6 contemporary classes, Italian fine wares were predominant (63%). The Italian fine wares included Italian terra sigillata (48% of contemporary fine wares) from a number of production centers, of which only the Campanian ('Tripolitanian') sigillata could be differentiated visually by form and wall thickness, although this distinction was not made in the original registration. Italian thin-walled wares occurred in 4 types: an unglazed red orange dark-surfaced 'Republican' fabric; an Etrurian production of dark-surfaced mugs with fine vertical combing; a matte-slipped barbotine fabric, perhaps made near Cosa, and, finally, a sandcast metallic-glazed fabric. No probable Spanish thin-walled types occurred in these contexts. Ampuritan grey ware was relatively important by weight; North Syrian Eastern Sigillata A was not always differentiated from other unusual red fine wares in the original registration, but it was certainly relatively uncommon. The appearance of the local production of proto-African Red Slip A in levels of *c*.A.D. 15 and *c*.A.D. 50, although negligible numerically, is historically important; the ware appears in both thin-walled beaker or mug forms and in small hemispher-

53 Delattre's 'First Amphora Wall', a context closed by 10 B.C., and 'Second Amphora Wall', dated to the second quarter of the 1st c. A.D., are both almost entirely made up of a wide range of imported early Roman amphoras, although the actual types recovered in the two contexts are different; cf. Freed 1996.

54 Most likely an accident of excavation.

55 C. Panella, *Ostia* III 1973, summarizes the known typology of the class in her discussion of amphoras of small dimensions by illustrating 3 complete profiles (nos. 44-46, p. 632) of forms which appear only as fragments in the Ostia excavations. The illustrated example of Form *Ostia* III.44 occurred at Pompeii, therefore before A.D. 79, and Panella believed Form *Ostia* III.45 to occur by the 1st c. A.D. as well.

ical bowls. The rarest category by far was Spanish painted ware,[56] a sherd of which occurred in level **12** (see quantification, Table 1).

Table 1: Fine wares in the Augustan and Julio-Claudian levels of *decumanus* VI
Number of sherds/*grams* [number of catalogued examples]. Present: √; absent: -.

	(16) 10-1 B.C.	**(15)** 10-1 B.C.	**(23)** *c.*A.D. 15	**(13)** *c.*A.D. 15	**(12)** *c.*A.D. 15	**(11)** *c.*A.D. 50	Totals
undiff. BG	4/10	1/1	-	7/30	6/70 [1]	-	18/111
Amp. grey	-	2/110	-	2/60	3/25 [1]	1/15 [1]	8/210
undiff. ITS	5/14 [1]	9/65 [2]	6/35 [2]	8/180 [7]	25/285 [8]	10/60 [3]	63/639
Camp. ITS	-	-	-	√ [1]	√ [3]	-	
ESA	√	√ [1]	-	4/40 [3]	?	-	4/40
undiff. red fw (not ITS)	-	10/100	-	4/30	2/35	-	16/165
undiff. TW	√	√	√	√	15/60	√	48/195
'Republican'	3/5	12/40	2/10 [1]	13/50	√	-	
combed	-	√ [1]	-	-	√	2/20 [1]	
barbotine	-	-	-	-	√ [1]	-	
metallic glaze	-	-	-	-	√ [1]	1/10	
proto-ARS A	-	-	√	√	√	√	12/60
TW forms	-	-	5/30	-	1/5	1/5 [1]	
hemi bowl	-	-	1/10 [1]	4/10	√	-	
Spanish painted	-	-	-	-	1/10 [1]	-	1/10
Totals	12/29	34/316	14/85	42/400	53/490	15/110	170/1430

Without exception, the service wares are in quartz and limestone local fabrics, about equally divided between a buff coarse or plain ware (Peacock's Fabric 2.5, 'cream sandy ware' and a local orange coarse ware, not distinguished by Peacock). There is more variety in levels dating *c.*A.D. 15 and later, but the variety is still within the range of essentially local fabrics described by Peacock in the first report of the British excavations[57] (see quantification, Table 2).

Table 2: Service wares in the Augustan and Julio-Claudian levels of *decumanus* VI
Number of sherds/*grams* [number of catalogued examples]. Present: √; absent: -.

	(16) 10-1 B.C.	**(15)** 10-1 B.C.	**(23)** *c.*A.D. 15	**(13)** *c.*A.D. 15	**(12)** *c.*A.D. 15	**(11)** *c.*A.D. 50	Totals
local buff/ local orange	16/410	32/470 [2]	10/160 [2]	32/490 [1]	28/445	16/380 [3]	134/2355
misc. local	-	-	-	8/100	5/50	1/15	14/165
Totals	16/410	32/470	10/160	40/590	33/495	17/395	148/2520

Six cooking ware fabrics appear in the Julio-Claudian street levels. Two are North African; the local production of blacktop orange coarse ware quickly becomes predominant, while a sherd or two appears of a regional fabric exactly as the 'Byzacena blacktop red cooking ware' described above, which may or may not be residual.[58] Four distinctive Italian Tyrrhenian early Roman wares occur, although none is statistically common: Pompeian red ware appears in small

56 The early Roman version of the ware is discussed by Beltrán 1990.

57 Peacock, 'Petrology' 1984 "Quartz-limestone fabrics of Africa", Fabric 2.2, "White surface ware", pp.15-16 and particularly Fabric 2.5, "Cream sandy ware", 17.

58 Fulford does not reliably distinguish between the Byzacena blacktop cooking ware, which is Fabric 2.6, 'Central Tunisian ware' and includes specks of (angular) lime, as opposed to the Carthage/Nabeul blacktop cooking ware, which is Fabric 2.3, 'Black surface ware', the inclusions of which are largely quartz sand; Peacock, 'Petrology' 1984, 14-18.

and decreasing quantities (no. 56);[59] an orange-brown coarse ware which to the naked eye resembles the local blacktop orange cooking ware is rare but evidently most common in the mid 1st c. A.D. (no. 101); a possibly Latian ware ('Porta Pia coarse ware') appears rarely (nos. 102 and 136);[60] and, finally, a soft brown coarse ware, possibly sometimes originally slipped on the inside, is also rare (nos. 57 and 125) (see quantification, Table 3).[61]

Table 3: Cooking wares in the Augustan and Julio-Claudian levels of *decumanus* VI
Number of sherds/*grams* [number of catalogued examples]. Present: √; absent: -.

	(16) *c.*10-1 B.C.	**(15)** *c.*10-1 B.C.	**(23)** *c.*A.D. 15	**(13)** *c.*A.D. 15	**(12)** *c.*A.D. 15	**(11)** *c.*A.D. 50	Totals
ARS bt cw	3/*25*	16/*125* [2]	10/*150* [2]	45/*530*	29/*400* [1]	39/*480* [4]	142/*1710*
Ital. bt cw	-	-	-	-	√[1]	√ [1]	
'ERCW2'	-	5/*100*	-	-	-	2/*30*	7/*130*
Pompeian red ware	-	6/*70*	2/*30* [1]	6/*100*	3/*45*	-	17/*245*
Ital. soft brown cw	-	-	√ [1]	-	2/*35* [1]	√ [1]	2/*35*
'Porta Pia'	-	-	-	-	6/*65*		6/*65*
Totals	3/*25*	27/*295*	12/*180*	51/*630*	40/*545*	41/*510*	174/*2185*

There are 9 identifiable amphora classes in the Augustan and Julio-Claudian layers, which represent 9 identifiable contemporary types: Tunisian, probably local, neo-Punic; Campanian Dressel 4; Tyrrhenian Dressel 3; Adriatic Dressel 6A (chronologically more likely than Lamboglia 2); Baetican coastal Haltern 70; Baetican Guadalquivir valley Dressel 20; Tarraconensian coastal Dressel 2; regional North African and Italian(?) small flat-based *Ostia* III.44-46, and the Koan amphora. All but the regional small ovoid wine amphora and the rare Koan amphora appear here in the contexts of 10-1 B.C., **16** and **15**, and this is the period which shows the greatest variety. All the Italian amphoras are wine amphoras, as are Haltern 70, Tarraconensian Dressel 2 and Koan amphoras, underlining the importance of wine imports to the new Roman colony.[62] The local neo-Punic amphora may have contained *garum* or olive oil (see below).

Absolute dating by Italian Terra Sigillata

The absolute dating of the Augustan and Julio-Claudian levels of *decumanus* VI was determined by the forms of Italian terra sigillata. There were 33 diagnostic rims of Italian terra sigillata in the early Roman street levels.

J. W. Hayes and P. M. Kenrick identified a variety of fabrics, including possible examples of Padane, Pisan and Puteolan workshops (no physical analysis was done on the sherds). Kenrick has seen and commented on the 5 stamped pieces. I am very grateful to both for their observations. For the identification and dating of the Italian terra sigillata forms, I follow the numbering of the *Conspectus*,[63] using its actual phrasing to describe

59 The fabric is the most common, Fabric 1, the Campanian 'black sand' fabric, in Peacock's analysis of Pompeian red: D. P. S. Peacock, *Pottery and early commerce. Characterization and trade in Roman and later ceramics* (London 1977) 149-53. Pompeian red ware occurs as 6 sherds, 100 g in layer **13**; 3 sherds, 45 g in **12** and 3 sherds, 10 g in **10**.

60 J. Bird *et al.*, "Porta Pia. Excavations and survey in an area of suburban Rome," *PBSR* 61 (1993) 51-113; the ware is described on p. 83. 'Porta Pia coarse ware' appears as 6 sherds, 65 g in layer **12**, no. 126 cooking pot, and 5 sherds, 75 g in **10**, no. 137 jar.

61 S. Dyson, *Cosa. The utilitarian pottery* (MAAR 33, 1976), soft brown fabric of Class 11, p. 91.

62 The early Roman imported cylindrical amphoras occurring in two amphora walls at Carthage, *c.*15 B.C. and *c.*A.D. 25-50, have recently been discussed in detail, with sources on the fabric of each type; see Freed 1996.

63 *Conspectus* 1990 (see n.22 above).

the forms and dates wherever appropriate. Hayes, who commented on a selection of pottery from the early Roman levels of *decumanus* VI, identified the presence of 'Tripolitanian' sigillata, originally so named by Kenrick because of its common occurrence at Benghazi; it is now identified as a Campanian fabric.[64] Hayes had in fact noted the relative importance of this fabric at Carthage earlier.[65] Finds reported by M. Fulford and J. Timby from the harbour of Carthage also show its numerical importance; they also observe that the typology of this fabric is conservative in relation to the whole range of forms in Italian terra sigillata.[66]

From the Italian terra sigillata, layers **16** and **15** may be dated as early as 10 B.C., since exterior rouletting, which appears then, does not occur. There is evidently a gap of at least 10 years between **15** and the next group of layers, **23**, **13**, **12**, all of which show the use of rouletting as all-over decoration (nos. 51 and 67); this type of decoration is concentrated between A.D. 1 and 40.[67] Italian terra sigillata in layer **23** suggests a general date in the first quarter of the 1st c. A.D.; however, as **13** and **12**, which lie above and cannot be distinguished in date, have pieces dating to *c*.A.D. 15 and must end by *c*.A.D. 15, judging by the presence of exclusively rectangular stamps (nos. 67-68, 84-86), the end date for **23** must be put back to A.D. 15 as well. A gap of 15-25 years intervenes between layers **12** and **11**. Layer **11** is characterized by two examples of *Conspectus* plate Form 20.4, which ordinarily bears varied appliqué motifs (no. 114). This type of decoration began in *c*.A.D. 30, while Form 20.4 is particularly characteristic of the mid 1st c. A.D. Finally, a single poor-quality wall sherd of Italian terra sigillata in **10** suggests a date in the later 1st c. A.D. Local African Red Slip A in this layer includes a possible Form 9B, which should belong to the later 2nd c. A.D.; however, while Carthage/Nabeul blacktop orange cooking ware is plentiful, the Form 197 casserole, which is a characteristic export form of the late 2nd/early 3rd c., is completely missing, suggesting an end date even before the mid 2nd c. A.D.

The earliest Italian terra sigillata form to appear in the early Roman road surfaces (in **16**) is a bell-shaped cup, *Conspectus* Form 14, 15 or 17 (no. 33); a larger-scale version of this form occurs in 'Tripolitanian' sigillata in layer **12** (no. 89), but the form does not otherwise occur again in the excavation. The most common Italian terra sigillata form in these contexts is *Conspectus* Form 18, the 'plate with concave vertical rim'. The 6 examples, which were typed without reference to their context, show the appropriate developmental sequence: 18.1.2 in **15** (no. 38); 18.2 in **23** (no. 50); three examples of 18.2.1 in **13** (no. 71), and 18.3 in **12** (no. 92). The 3 examples of *Conspectus* Form 33, 'hemispherical cup with flange', in **23** and **13** make a strong impression because the example in **13** (no. 67) is more than two-thirds complete. Hemispherical cups other than Form 33 occur in **23** (no. 51), **13** (no. 72) and **12** (2 bases); cylindrical cups (*Conspectus* Forms 26 or 28) occur in **15**, **13** (no. 73) and **11** (no. 112). Relief-moulded decoration from chalices occurs only in layers **13** and **12** (nos. 70 and 82-83), that is, *c*.A.D. 15, with two examples in each layer. The two examples of Form 20.4 in layer **11** (no. 114) confirm its discrete and later date. Layer **11** also includes a late version of *Conspectus* dish Form 3 (3.3.1) (no. 113), which is one of the two latest-surviving forms in Italian terra sigillata. Overall, the correlation of the dated Italian terra sigillata with the layer sequence is perfect and clearly articulated.

There are 5 stamped bases among the diagnostic sherds. Stamps appear only in **13** and **12**, the layers which also produced the greatest number of examples of Italian terra sigillata and which are very closely dated by their forms to *c*.A.D. 15. The stamps are all rectangular rather than *in planta pedis*, which supports an end date by A.D. 15. The makers (following Kenrick's observations on provenance of these pieces) are Priamus (Pisan or possibly Arretine) (no. 67);

---

64 E. Ettlinger, "Tripolitanische Sigillata," *Conspectus* 1990, 12-13.

65 Hayes discussed the fabric as 'Imitation Terra Sigillata', noting 125 sherds as against 573 for other Italian terra sigillata; in other words, it is quite an important fine ware numerically at Carthage. He was aware of its presence at Benghazi, at Tharros in Sardinia, and at Tipasa; Hayes, *CMich* I 1976, 75-76, fig. 13, A25-40 and p. 82.

66 'Tripolitanian' makes up 28.7% of imported sigillata on the harbour site: Fulford and Timby, *Harbour* 1994, I, 5-7 and fig. 1.3, 42-60.

67 Kenrick, *Conspectus* 1990, 149.

Atticus (possibly Puteolan) (no. 68); Umbricius (possibly Arretine by distribution) (no. 84); Ateius (probably Pisan) (no. 85), and Crestus (not Arretine) (no. 86).[68] The evident variety of Italian workshops reflects a similar variety in the other Italian terra sigillata sherds. In Kenrick's opinion, all 5 stamped pieces are similar in date to finds from Haltern (7 B.C.-A.D. 9); the forms in layers **13, 12** generally agree, but a few pieces suggest a slightly later date.

Three or four sherds belong to the Campanian fabric which Kenrick originally designated 'Tripolitanian'. The forms are characteristically on a somewhat large scale, with little articulation. The examples are close to *Conspectus* Form 12, 'platter with narrow hanging lip' in **13** and **12** (nos. 74 and 88); Form 14, 'bell-shaped cup with narrow hanging lip' in **12** (no. 89), and Form 19, 'plate with concave vertical rim and quarter round moulding' in **12** (no. 90). All examples of this fabric occurred in layers **13** and **12**, which date *c.*A.D. 15.

The lamps in the early Roman street levels

All the lamps recovered from early Roman street levels are of Italian manufacture.[69] Although the typology of these lamps has been worked out in immense detail by Bailey, it can be difficult to apply precise designation of type to small fragments. Fortunately, Bailey's recent publication of the lamps from Sabratha provided good comparanda for all but one lamp in the street levels of *decumanus* VI. The suggested dates of the lamps in the early Roman contexts fit perfectly with the context dates supplied by the Italian terra sigillata. All the lamps in the contexts of 10-1 B.C. and *c.*A.D. 15, elegantly slipped thin-walled examples with sharply angled shoulders, belong either to Loeschcke Type I or to Broneer Type XXI with two nozzles. The occurrence of a tiny fragment of a lamp in lead-glazed fabric in a context of 10-1 B.C. (no. 36) is important because of the infrequency of publication of early Roman lead-glazed fabrics as well as the dearth of closely-dated contexts for them.[70] Loeschcke Type IA, of Augustan/Tiberian date, is predominant, with two certain examples, one with flared nozzle (no. 32) and one with nozzle channel (no. 76), and 6 others are very likely. The most complete discus figure, a standing gladiator (no. 48), agrees with other evidence that lamps with gladiators were extremely popular in the Augustan/Tiberian era at Carthage.[71] In these contexts there is only one probable example of late Augustan to early Flavian Loeschcke Type 1B (Deneauve Type IVA) (no. 63 in **13**).

The lamps in the context of c. A.D. 50 are similar, with an undifferentiated Loeschcke Type I and another Loeschcke Type IB (Deneauve Type IVA) (nos. 109 and 110). The lamps in Vegas' context of the third quarter of the 1st c. A.D. are clearly slightly later in date than those in the *decumanus* VI context of c. A.D. 50, since Vegas' context includes a significant group of examples of Loeschcke Types IV and VIII.[72] Loeschcke Type VIII with rounded shoulder, of which Italian versions date to the 'last two decades of the 1st c. and most of the 2nd c. A.D.',[73] first appears only in the mid 2nd c. A.D. level of *decumanus* VI (no. 128). The other identifiable lamp in

---

68 P. M. Kenrick to C. M. Wells, July 1996.

69 Bailey, *BM* 1988, 170, has pointed out that North Africa relied on Italian lamps until late Flavian times. The first lamp type to appear in a North African fabric copies Loeschcke Type VIII, with North African examples appearing from *c.*A.D. 100 (Bailey, *Sabratha* 1994, 175), but the fabric of no. 128 in layer **10** does not seem to be local.

70 Cf. A. Hochuli-Gysel, "Ein bleiglasierter kleinasiatischer Skyphos oder Kantharos aus Karthago," *RömMitt* 101 (1994) 365-67.

71 K. Knowles, *Harbour* 1994, has published a group of Loeschcke Types IA and IB from the British excavations at Carthage, figs. 2.1-8.21, p. 27 and 2.2.22-27, p. 30, among which nos. 7, 10 and 11 show gladiators; also, J. Deneauve, *Lampes de Carthage* (Aix-en-Provence 1969) pls. 37-38 and 313-23, none like ours.

72 Vegas, 'Karthago' 1994, for the lamps, fig. 8 and 362-63, 346-47, and table 1 on 349.

73 Bailey, *Sabratha* 1994, 175.

that level is a North Italian factory lamp of Loeschcke Type X (no. 129), dated to the Flavian period or a little later, a type which does not occur in Vegas' context.

Other fine wares and glass from the early Roman street levels

Thin-walled wares made up about 13.5% by weight of fine wares in the Augustan and Julio-Claudian layers. There were 48 sherds, weighing a total of 195 g, of which only 4 pieces could be drawn and catalogued meaningfully. One clearly recognizable fabric occurred in layers **16**, **15**, **23** and **13**; this is a very thin-walled (less than 2 mm) unglazed coarse orange fabric of which the exterior surfaces, where exposed by stacking in the kiln, are reduced to a matte grey (no. 53). Such a fabric is described by Ricci as central Italian, beginning in the mid 2nd c. B.C. and continuing no later than the Augustan period.[74] A matte slipped *poculum* with barbotine decoration in a central Italian fabric appears in **12** (no. 94); this has close parallels at Cosa and should be of Augustan rather than Tiberian date because the wall of the cup is curved.[75] Both matte-slipped (no. 95) and metallic-glazed *pocula* in sandcast fabric appear in layers **12** and **11**; the fabric is uniformly coarse, with shiny angular volcanic inclusions, suggesting manufacture in a volcanic area of Tyrrhenian Italy. The metallic-glazed type is the most common thin-walled fabric and form, with a wide distribution in the western Mediterranean, occurring in Tiberian-Claudian to Flavian contexts.[76] An Etrurian production of vertically combed thin-walled mugs, Mayet's Form XXIV, of Augustan and later date, certainly occurs in **12** and **11** (no. 116).[77] Mayet's distribution map shows that the form is very common in the Mediterranean in the first half of the 1st c. A.D., with North African finds well attested, and suggests production in Tyrrhenian N Italy.[78] The thin-walled wares generally confirm the dating based on the Italian terra sigillata, but also distinguish the horizon of level **12**, where barbotine decoration and metallic-glazed first appear, from **13**, both otherwise dated *c.*A.D. 15.

A few, but interestingly varied, pieces of N Syrian Eastern Sigillata A ware occur in contexts of 10-1 B.C. and *c.*A.D. 15. This ware, which has a long history, has rarely been recognized at Carthage. Its lack of recognition may possibly be because the period of its import was particularly early and short, belonging to the era (documented on our site) when imports and variety among imports was extremely high (see Table 1 above). Eastern Sigillata A is strongly represented in an early Augustan context at the harbour of Carthage, and Fulford and Timby suggest that its import may have preceded that of Italian terra sigillata in the Augustan period.[79] J. Hayes' summary of the forms, fabrics and decoration in this ware has been followed here.[80]

A 'Hellenistic grey ware' occurs in Punic contexts on the Byrsa, sometimes in bowls, but often in biconical jars which are characteristically decorated with horizontal rounded ridges.[81] There are no examples of such a ware in the Punic levels under *decumanus* VI, but there are a few examples of grey ware bowls and platters with thin matte black slip in the early Roman levels of *decumanus* VI, present in ever smaller quantities in contexts dated from *c.*10-1 B.C.to

74 Ricci 1985, 231-358, pls. 78-104 and maps 150-59. Ricci's map 151 shows the wide distribution (including Carthage) of her 'Central Italian' thin-walled fabric, which is described, p.248, associated with her Form 1/30 olla, and earlier Form 1/1-4 beaker.

75 M. T. Marabini Moevs, *The Roman thin-walled pottery from Cosa (1948-1954)* (MAAR 32, 1973) pls. 21 and 67, nos. 209-10 and Form 36 Group B, especially nos. 222-26, pl. 22-24, pp. 133-34.

76 Mayet 1975, 5 and 73-74.

77 Mayet 1975, Form XXIV, nos. 201-7, pl. XXVII and pp. 58-59.

78 Mayet 1975, map 134.

79 Fulford and Timby, *Harbour* 1994, 1.

80 Hayes 1985.

81 *Byrsa* I 1979, particularly in layer A148, p. 205, fig. 30.14 and 14bis (hemispherical bowl with bead rim) and no. 43 (as Lamboglia 27). The context dates to the first half of the 2nd c. B.C. (p. 206). Iberian forms in this ware also occur at Ostia and at Ventimiglia, where they may date to the first decades of the 1st c. A.D. (*Ostia* II, pl. 19 and pp. 87-89) and cf. Riley, *Benghazi* 1979, fig. 244.6-8 and p. 197.

A.D. 50 (see Table 1). The ware occurs in at least two 1st c. A.D. contexts published by M. Vegas, who identified the ware as Ampuritan (coastal Tarraconensis).[82] In his analysis of early Roman contexts at Carthage, Hayes had noted such a ware and assigned it a provisional Augustan date.[83] The ware has a long history; 'grey monochrome ware' made in Iberian biconical jars in the earlier Hellenistic period[84] also appeared in Italian black-glazed bowl and platter forms and with a poor quality thin matte black slip by the 2nd c. B.C., and this production was evidently local to Ampurias.[85] The bowl in **12** (no. 81) is an example of the most characteristic Augustan and early imperial form in this ware, although the form can appear as early as the 2nd c. B.C.[86] A small bowl with a similar rim was published by Vegas in a context probably of Tiberian date.[87] A hemispherical bowl with a bifid rim occurs in **11** (no. 111). Vegas does not note this ware in a fairly large context at Carthage of the third quarter of the 1st c. A.D. which she has published in detail;[88] when combined with the evidence from other sites, the evidence from *decumanus* VI suggests that the import of Ampuritan grey ware decreased to essentially nil at Carthage by the third quarter of the 1st c. A.D. On the other hand, the ware can be seen, with Iberian thin-walled metallic-glazed cups and the Tarraconensian coastal production of Dressel 2 amphoras, to mark a period in the first half of the 1st c. A.D. in which imports from Spain achieved their greatest presence in early Roman Carthage.

A fabric which is evidently the earliest version of local (Carthage/Nabeul) African Red Slip A is here designated 'proto-African Red Slip A'. This is a somewhat coarse orange fabric with a single layer of matte orange slip, usually on either the interior or the exterior. It occurs in a thin-walled beaker with slightly flared rim and also in a hemispherical bowl (no. 52) in a context dated *c.*A.D. 15 (**23**). A mug with horizontal rim also occurs in **11** (no. 116). In the first publication from Michigan's Carthage excavations, Hayes identified a fabric he called 'Early ARS', with a thin dullish slip, as appearing by the mid 1st c. A.D., and "immediately prior to the introduction of the classic African Red Slip Ware"; the forms he identified included a hemispherical bowl.[89] Vegas has recently shown that a number of bowl forms in this ware are firmly established by the third quarter of the 1st c. A.D.[90] Although the ware has been documented at other sites at Carthage in the 1st c. A.D., including the same bowls and thin-walled forms which appear in our *decumanus* VI street levels,[91] our contexts of A.D. 15 are the earliest in which the ware is known.

---

82 Vegas, *Karthago* 1991, between figs. 16 and 22 and fig. 39.14, p. 195, in a context correctly dated Augustan/early Tiberian (amphora fig. 39.22 appears in the first amphora wall at Carthage, by *c.*15 B.C.). Fulford, *Harbour* 1994 notes only a ridged jar in this fabric, fig. 1.6.101.

83 Hayes, *CMich* I 1976, 74 and 59, deposit IX, no. 3 (not illustrated) = Lamboglia 5/7; reproduced as F2277a1 in Morel 1981, 160, dated 1st c. B.C.

84 The identification is made by Vegas, *Karthago* 1991, bowl, fig. 39.14, p. 195. The Iberian forms of Hellenistic date have been studied by C. Aranegui Gasco, "Las jarritas bicónicas grises de tipo ampuritano," in *Ceràmiques gregues i hel·lenístiques a la península iberica, Taula rodona amb motiu del 75e aniversari de les excavacions d'Empúries, 18-20 març 1983* (Barcelona 1985).

85 J. Barbera Farrás reviews the chronology of the fabric in "Las cerámicas grises de La Penya del More do Sant Just Desvern (Barcelonès)," in *Ceràmiques gregues* (ibid.) 115-31, esp. 117.

86 E. Sanmartí, "Ceramica empuritana," 'Form 14', fig. 130.12 and 394-95 in Sanmartí 1984.

87 Vegas, *Karthago* 1991, fig. 39.14, rim diam. 13.0; she considers the context later than Augustan/Tiberian only by the amphora illustrated in fig. 39.22 and by a thin-walled cup of Mayet Form XXIV, as our no. 116, p. 195; however, the amphora type occurs in the first amphora wall, for which the *terminus post quem* is 15 B.C., and the thin-walled type can certainly be Tiberian.

88 See Vegas, 'Karthago' 1994.

89 Hayes, 1976, *CMich* I, 77 and 82, A53.

90 Vegas, 'Karthago' 1994, fig. 3.42-48 and pp.354-55.

91 See no. 53 below. Fulford, *Harbour* 1994, fig.1.7.3, 'proto-ARS', among which he documents '14/16', slipped on either the inside or the outside, but not both. The form is among the earliest stratified forms in

Two pieces of glass were recovered from the early Roman layers. One is a thick wall sherd from a small cobalt blue lathe-turned bottle in **16.** The second piece, no. 61 in **13**, is a small moulded bowl with double convex wall of which only the upper curve survives. In opaque milky green thin-walled glass, it is a characteristic type of the first half of the 1st c. A.D. The fact that the form occurs first in Italian and then in Gaulish sigillata suggests that the glass was of Italian rather than eastern manufacture.[92] The elegance and Italian provenance of this small bowl confirm the general character of the levels of *decumanus* VI dated to A.D. 15.

Carthage/Nabeul cooking wares in the early Roman street levels

The common forms of the blacktop cooking ware produced in the Carthage/Nabeul area were described by Hayes in 1972,[93] although its specific provenance was not recognized until 1978.[94] This fabric, which in its widely exported versions of the late 2nd and early 3rd c. A.D. had a characteristic orange colour, is closely related to African Red Slip fine ware 'A', which is early Roman, and 'D', which is late Roman;[95] all three wares are more or less local to Carthage.[96] The cooking ware is 'Fabric 2.3' in Peacock's designation.[97] An early Roman version of Carthage/Nabeul cooking ware (not necessarily 'blacktop') was dubbed 'Early Roman Cooking Ware 1' in Hayes' first analysis of early Roman contexts at Carthage; the yellowish or brownish fabric colour which Hayes described as typical[98] is not obvious in the early examples from *decumanus* VI.

In 1978, Hayes noted that the early Carthage blacktop cooking ware was widely exported from the early 1st c. A.D., and was certainly familiar in Italian markets long before the fine wares.[99] The evidence from our closely dated excavation indicates that the locally produced blacktop cooking ware completely dominated the local market for cooking ware by A.D. 15. The ware is already more than negligible in levels **16** and **15** in 10-1 B.C., but by A.D. 15 it is remarkably prominent both by sherd count and weight.[100] The 4 forms which appear in street levels of *decumanus* VI of 10-1 B.C. — Hayes Forms 196 lid, 194 casserole, bread-baking pan with bifid rim (Hayes' 'Type G') and 198 jar — were identified by Hayes among 5 forms which appear in the early version of the ware; Form 191, originally identified by Hayes as beginning in the late 2nd and 1st c. B.C.,[101] does not appear in the early Roman street levels of *decumanus* VI.

---

proto-ARS, but Fulford (pp.16-17) conservatively dated its earliest appearance to the late 1st/early 2nd c. A.D.

92 The type belongs to D. Grose's Family III, 'monochrome opaque colored fine wares', occurring in small carinated and hemispherical bowls, dated to the first half of the 1st c. A.D., although usually found in Claudian/Neronian contexts: D. F. Grose, *The Toledo Museum of Art: early ancient glass* (New York 1989) 254-56, nos. 419-22, drawn on p. 421, catalogued on 306-7, colour photograph.

93 Hayes, *LRP*, Forms 181-200, pp. 200-11; Hayes' dates for forms in blacktop orange cooking ware were admittedly tentative because he had seen few dated examples, but he did note that the Form 191 casserole could be traced back to the Hellenistic period (p.205). I suggest that the form but not the ware can be traced to the Hellenistic period.

94 Hayes, *CMich* IV 1978, 75.

95 Hayes' term 'African Red Slip' covers a variety of fabrics with different production areas and dates; the letters which distinguish a number of productions were adopted and further subdivided by the Italian team of A. Carandini; the fabrics distinguished are described in Carandini *et al.* 1981.

96 Hayes, *CMich* I 1976, 84.

97 Peacock, 'Petrology' 1984 for 'Fabric 2' and its sub-types, 14-19.

98 Hayes, *CMich* I 1976, 93-95; cf. also J. W. Hayes, *A supplement to Late Roman Pottery* (London 1980) 518/lii.

99 Hayes, *CMich* IV 1978 75.

100 Local blacktop orange cooking ware makes up 20% by weight of level **13**; 10% of level **12**, and 25% of level **11** (see Table 3).

101 Hayes, *LRP* 205; the form also appears in Augustan contexts at the Athenian Agora and is known at Pompeii.

The Form 196 lid appears by 10-1 B.C.; at this early date it is thin-walled and the rim of the form does not show thickening. It is ubiquitous in the early Roman street layers, and is the most commonly occurring form from the site. Form 194 appears by 10-1 B.C., but is not common, appearing only in layers **15** and later in **11**. Hayes' 'Type G', a bread-baking pan with a bifid rim, occurs sometimes in the local fabric and sometimes in an Italian fabric[102] from *c.*10-1 B.C., and it is still found in all the contexts of A.D. 15 (**15**, **13**, **12**), but it was evidently replaced by Forms 26 and 23, also bread-baking pans, in later contexts. Form 198, originally provisionally dated by Hayes to the 1st c. A.D.,[103] appears by 10-1 B.C. and continues to appear in the whole range of early Roman contexts, including the 2nd c. No examples of Form 183 casserole or Form 26 bread-baking pan appear before A.D. 50 (layer **11**). The mid 2nd-c. context **10** saw the introduction of Forms 23A, 23B (no. 137) and 195. Form 197 casserole, a predominant form at Carthage and certainly on the export market from the late 2nd c. A.D., does not appear at all in the early Roman layers, not even in the context of the 2nd c. A.D.[104]

These are the earliest attested dates I know for any of the 9 Carthage/Nabeul blacktop cooking ware forms which occur in the street levels of *decumanus* VI.[105] It is well known that the wide export of forms in this cooking ware (particularly casserole 197 and lid 196 with thickened rim) from the later 2nd and into the early 3rd c. is strongly linked with the rise of Carthage as a great port. Our early dates for the establishment of the ware suggest that it began to be manufactured very soon after the founding of the Roman colony. The earliest forms, 194 and 191 casseroles and 196 lids, imitate existing forms in the 'Byzacena blacktop red cooking ware', which in turn were copied from Greek cooking ware.

Both the bifid rim bread-baking 'Type G' pan and Form 198 jar appear both in Carthage/Nabeul blacktop cooking ware and in the second Italian cooking ware noted above; bifid rim pans which superficially look like local blacktop cooking ware but are in fact in this Tyrrhenian orange coarseware fabric occur in layers **12** (no. 101) and **11** (no. 121). I have also seen a lid/dish superfically like Hayes Form 196 in a similar Italian ware in late Republican contexts (unpublished) on the Via Gabina near Rome; an Italian example occurs in Punic layer **25** (no. 27, with Punic banding in the floor) in our excavation. It is therefore clear that the makers of the local blacktop cooking ware copied forms which were Italian as well as the Greek forms produced in the regional Punic blacktop red cooking ware of Byzacena. Clear Italian influence on some of the forms also suggests that the beginning of production of Carthage/Nabeul blacktop cooking ware must be linked with the foundation of the Roman colony.

Two strap handles and a large string-cut lid knob in 'Byzacena blacktop red cooking ware' (see above) appear in layer **15**. This North African ware, perhaps manufactured in central Tunisia, had dominated the market at Carthage in Punic times and would regain a significant market share by no later than the 4th c. A.D., as Hayes' 'Late Roman Cooking Ware I'. Byzacena blacktop red cooking ware continued to be made in the early Roman period, despite its relative rarity at Carthage. A trefoil rim jug in this fabric occurs on the Byrsa in a Punic context of the first half of the 2nd c. B.C.,[106] and a number of similar trefoil rim jugs appear in a large

---

102 Hayes points out that the pan with bifid rim was originally an Italian form and is evidently copied in the proto-ARS coarse ware; he dubs the form 'Type G': Hayes, *CMich* 1 1976, 93-94, 98-99.

103 Hayes, *LRP* 210.

104 Evidence from the harbour confirms that Form 197 does not appear before the late 2nd c. A.D.: Fulford, *Harbour* 1994, 60, fig. 4.6, casserole Form 26. Tomber 1986, 38 suggested a Hadrianic date for a 2nd-c. context in which Hayes Form 197 does not occur, although Hayes had earlier suggested a Hadrianic date for deposits with elegant early variants of the form (Deposit XVI, *CMich* I 1976 and Deposit XIX, *CMich* IV 1978.

105 Vegas, 'Karthago' 1994, shows 6 forms: the bifid rim pan = Hayes 'Type G'; Form 194 casserole; a cooking pot and a jar which Hayes described as 'Type C' (*CMich* I 1976, 94); Form 196 lid and Form 198 jar, all in a context of the third quarter of the 1st c. A.D. (figs. 3-5, nos. 52-60).

106 *Byrsa* I 1979, layer A148, p. 208, fig. 16, no. 16.

unpublished context of the late 2nd/early 3rd c. A.D. from Canadian excavations on the Theodosian Wall site. A lid knob identical to that in layer **15** was noted above from Punic layer **33** on our site (no. 21), but a similar type is extremely common in late-Roman contexts at Carthage. The present evidence does not allow certainty as to whether the pieces in early Roman contexts from this excavation are contemporary examples of a very long-lived form or not. The fact that no similar jug or heavy lid form appears in the repertory of Carthage/Nabeul blacktop cooking ware ware may suggest that these pieces were contemporary imports, although the ware perhaps never had a significant share of the early Roman market.

Amphoras from the early Roman street levels

The amphoras in the Augustan and Julio-Claudian contexts are very varied, and echo the evidence first presented by J. Riley from 1st-c. contexts and more recently by M. Vegas from a context of the third quarter of the 1st c. A.D. The important types are, first, Punic-derived forms of Tunisian manufacture contemporary with the neo-Punic types described by van der Werff at Uzita;[107] the contents of these amphoras are uncertain. Then come imported wine amphoras: Campanian Dressel 4, Italian Tyrrhenian Dressel 3, Tarraconensian coastal Dressel 2 with fake double rolled handles, Adriatic Lamboglia 2/Dressel 6A, Baetican coastal Haltern 70, and Koan. Baetican river-valley Dressel 20 (oil) amphoras also appear.[108] Finally, there is the small ovoid flat-based wine amphora *Ostia* III.44-46; for the first time we have compelling evidence for this form appearing so early at Carthage.

In the early Roman contexts, no. 106 is a sub-type of Dressel Form 3, Panella and Fano Type 8;[109] some examples of this Tyrrhenian amphora type have been identified as of Falernian provenance.[110] Four fragments, weighing a total of 1.0 kg, an unusually large survival of one individual amphora, were excavated in **12**, a context dating to A.D. 15. The amphora has a vertical stamp, anomalously placed on the neck; neither the stamp nor this placement are previously attested. The general form (Panella and Fano 8/9) is well attested by *c*.15 B.C. in the 'First Amphora Wall' at Carthage, where, however, stamps do not appear.[111] Examples of the stamps typical of Type 8, placed vertically on the toe, appear in the collection of the Musée National de Carthage, but from unstratified contexts.[112] Although the stamp on no. 106 is new and its placement is anomalous, the context provides a date relevant to the appearance of stamped examples.

A handle of Tarraconensian Dressel 2, an amphora which is characterized by fake double rolled handles and a massive spike toe, is dated to *c*.10-1 B.C. by its appearance in layer **15**. I believe this is its earliest attested date; this form does not appear in the First Amphora Wall at Carthage, dated *c*.15 B.C., but a variant of the more carefully made and elegant Tarraconensian Dressel 3 does appear.[113] On the other hand, Tarraconensian Dressel 2 is by far the most common amphora in the Second Amphora Wall at Carthage, which was built of imported

---

107 van der Werff 1977-78, 194, fig. 10. Cf. Peacock and Williams 1986, Class 32A, B and C.

108 Early Roman imported amphoras from the German excavations at Carthage have recently been published by S. Martin-Kilcher, "Amphoren der späten Republik und der frühen Kaiserzeit in Karthago: Zu den Lebensmittelimporten der Colonia Iulia Concordia," *RömMitt* 100 (1993) 269-320. Martin-Kilcher p.275 usefully presents the relative percentages of the types and their contents; among 416 fragments, she found only one related to van der Werff Type 2 (Vindonissa 592, fig. 1, 273), fig. 27.95, and does not note examples of *Ostia* III, 44-46.

109 Panella and Fano 1977, Type 8, 154-55, figs. 39-48; Fabric B, 147.

110 A. Hesnard and C. Lemoine, "Les amphores du Cécube et du Falerne, prospections, typologie, analyses," *MEFRA* 93 (1981) esp. 257-64.

111 Freed 1996, 148.

112 I have catalogued 3 examples of the known stamps in the collection of the Musée National de Carthage: 92.149, PRAT; 94.48, CERD; 95.359, MAR.OF.

113 Freed 1996, 148-49.

cylindrical amphoras at some time in the second quarter of the 1st c. A.D., and it is common in other contexts at Carthage in the 1st c. A.D. While Dressel 3 appears in the deposit at La Longarina (Ostia), dated A.D. 1-12,[114] Dressel 2 does not. I would therefore date the first appearance of this form to the turn of the millennium, as much as a quarter-century earlier than previous evidence suggested.

The amphora class *Ostia* III.44-46 (provenance unidentified, but fabric indicates that at least some of the production is North African, with the rest quite likely to be Italian, as Panella suggested), and Baetican Dressel 20[115] certainly appear in the contexts dated A.D. 15. This is the earliest attested date I know for the class *Ostia* III.44-46 (see below), and the earliest date at Carthage for Dressel 20. Earlier examples of Dressel 20, from the first decade of the 1st c. A.D., are known at La Longarina at Ostia.[116] While no complete examples of Dressel 20 survive in the Carthage Museum, Delattre indicated that the type appeared in the Second Amphora Wall (second quarter of 1st c. A.D.).[117]

While no great weight can be placed on observations based on quantification of such small contexts, in the earliest context (10-1 B.C.) imported types overall weigh equally with the local Tunisian amphora fabric; but by A.D. 15 the imports are more than double the local fabric (2.910 vs 1.205 kg), and Campanian and Tyrrhenian wine amphoras each approximately equal the weight of local Tunisian amphoras (for which the contents are unknown). The evidence here suggests that A.D. 15 marked a high point in the dominance of Italian amphora imports, since local fabric and imports were approximately equal again in the contexts of A.D. 50 and of the mid 2nd c. A.D. The context of *c.*A.D. 50 also confirms other evidence that Italian wine amphoras were almost totally replaced in trade to Carthage by the Tarraconensian coastal Dressel 2 amphora, perhaps by the second quarter of the 1st c. A.D.[118]

The Carthage/Nabeul neo-Punic amphora

In the period since van der Werff described three classes of neo-Punic amphoras from contexts of the 1st c. A.D. on the site of Uzita in Byzacena,[119] the existence of neo-Punic amphoras extending into the 1st c. A.D. has been accepted, and the general outline of three classes of production — Form 1 centered on N Tunisia (Carthage/Nabeul), Form 2 on central Tunisia (Byzacena), and Form 3 on Tripolitania — has gained acceptance.[120] The issue has been complicated by van der Werff's subsequent statement that his N Tunisian Form 1 is identical with Carthage-produced Punic Cintas 312/313 with trumpet-flared rim, the production of which ended by the first quarter of the 1st c. B.C.; Form 1 at Uzita is therefore residual.[121]

Although Cintas 312/313 is probably the correct identification of the exiguous number of examples of van der Werff Form 1 found at Uzita, van der Werff collected examples of neo-Punic amphoras as comparanda to his Form 1 from other sites, and many examples are more likely to be relevant to the 1st c. A.D. than to the Punic period.[122] In 1978, Hayes used the designation 'Dressel 18' to refer to neo-Punic amphoras at Carthage;[123] van der Werff had considered

---

114 Hesnard 1980, pl. 3, fig. 2 and 145-46; the deposit dates to the first decade of the 1st c. A.D. by comparison with stamps at Haltern (p.145).
115 Martin-Kilcher, *Augst* 1987.
116 Hesnard 1980, 148 and pl. 6, figs. 1 and 2.
117 Freed 1996, 143.
118 Freed 1996.
119 van der Werff 1977-78.
120 Peacock and Williams 1986, Class 32, 151-56, although fabric analysis suggests that Form 3 was also produced in Byzacena: van der Werff 1977-78, 174-75.
121 van der Werff 1986, 109.
122 van der Werff 1977-78, 176-77, n.33.
123 Hayes, *CMich* IV 1978, 83.

Dressel 18, an amphora from excavations of the *Castra Praetoria* which bore the dipinto *hal(lec)*, as not accurately fitting his type series.[124] Examples of neo-Punic amphoras which are clearly not either van der Werff's Form 2 or 3, both of which are fairly clearly defined, have continued to accrue. In fact, in an amphora wall dated *c*.30 B.C. at the House of the Porch at Ostia, van der Werff found that the general class of neo-Punic amphoras, among which 6 amphoras are closest to his Form 1, was the second most numerous after Dressel 1B.[125] As van der Werff has pointed out, the Uzita type series does not cover all neo-Punic amphora types.

There is therefore a pressing need to re-evalute the locally-produced neo-Punic amphoras at Carthage. The finds from the Augustan and Julio-Claudian levels of *decumanus* VI, when combined with the evidence of similar amphoras from other sites at Carthage, show that an amphora class which evolved from Cintas 312/313 was still consistently in production to at least the third quarter of the 1st c. A.D. The neo-Punic amphoras from Carthage are difficult to define adequately, because only rims and the characteristic long hollow toe[126] have been identified. A consistent group of rims appears in *decumanus* VI; in contexts published by Hayes and Riley from the Michigan excavations;[127] by Vegas in a context of the third quarter of the 1st c. A.D. at the German excavations,[128] and by Peacock from the British excavations.[129]

Our small excavation, with much more narrowly dated contexts than the others noted, recovered 5 rims in contexts of 10-1 B.C., 3 rims in contexts of A.D. 15, and 2 in the context of A.D. 50. Ten rims of one amphora type is a high number from such a small excavation. These rims vary from 18.0-20.0 cm[130] and their body diameters are probably not much wider than the rim. The small size of the average Tunisian amphora sherd from the contexts of *decumanus* VI in which rims of these amphoras appear also suggests that, like van der Werff Form 2 from Byzacena, the neo-Punic amphoras from Carthage are relatively thin-walled and reduced in size compared to the Punic amphora type.[131] Unlike van der Werff's Form 2, the rim variations attested are all strongly flared, and the curve of the neck is continuous, whereas van der Werff's Form 2 is characterized by a change of angle where the neck joins a convex shoulder.

Vegas has observed that the early Roman neo-Punic amphora at Carthage is equivalent to Riley's 'Early Amphora IIa' and occurs in small numbers relative only to the very common residual Punic amphoras.[132] In fact, Riley's Types IIa and IIb, with the smaller rim diameter, are both neo-Punic while the more numerous Type IIc is equivalent to Cintas 312/313.[133] Riley certainly imagined that his Type II had its handles on the upper body, and neo-Punic

---

124 van der Werff 1977-78, 176, n.31; he later stated (1986, 110) that the 'precise typological attribution of this amphora has proved almost impossible to establish'. However, Dressel's drawing is accurate enough to say that Dressel 18 is closer to van der Werff's general Northern Tunisian Form 1, as opposed to Byzacena Form 2 or Tripolitanian Form 3.

125 van der Werff 1986, 109-12 and fig. III.7.37-42.

126 For the toe, Vegas, "Karthago" 1994, fig. 7.89-90 and p.360. The bottom of a similar toe was recovered from *decumanus* VI layer **13.**

127 Hayes, *CMich* I, Deposit IX, fig. 5.13 (top); Deposit X, fig. 5.32, 33, 36 (bottom); Riley, *CMich* 1, Early Roman Amphora Type series, fig. 19.2-3 = Type IIa.

128 Vegas, "Karthago" 1994, 345-46, fig. 7.87-90.

129 Peacock, *Harbour* 1994, neo-Punic amphoras, 42-43, fig. 3.2.18-20 and 25; no. 18 with late Augustan material, no. 19 from a 1st-2nd c. context, no. 20 from a 2nd-1st c. B.C. context. See also Tomber 1986, 47, fig. 7.208, from a context of the 1st to mid 2nd c.

130 The dimensions are more suited to a slightly larger variant of Form 2 which van der Werff reports; an illustrated rim of this variant is very much like our no. 34: van der Werff 1977-78, fig. 7.034-205.

131 Cintas 312/313 was over 1 m tall and had a consistent body and rim diameter of *c*.24.0 cm, according to the dimensions of examples I have catalogued in the Musée de Carthage.

132 Vegas, "Karthago" 1994, 346. In fact, Riley did not attempt to date the Punic and Punic-derived amphoras he defined, but his Types IIa and IIb have rim diameters of *c*.20.0 cm (*CMich* I 1976, 108-10).

133 For the definition of the local amphoras, Riley, *CMich* 1 (1976) 108-10 and fig. 19.

amphoras with this handle placement, such as Dressel 18, do exist.[134] However, matters are complicated by the fact that Vegas describes a neo-Punic profile recovered in the German excavations of 1993 with handles running from neck to shoulder.[135] In that case, an amphora published by Riley, from a context of the later 1st c. A.D., with a similar rim and the upper handle attached at mid neck must be related.[136] More evidence is necessary, but this suggests that there are two versions of an otherwise similar amphora that have different handle placements, one 'neo-Punic' and one 'Roman' — a situation of cultural confusion which has already been demonstrated for the Tripolitanian amphoras at Pompeii in the 1st c. A.D.[137]

A clear definition of the Carthage/Nabeul neo-Punic amphora type will allow the evidence of export, especially to Italy, of all 3 neo-Punic amphora types to be evaluated analytically. Finally, the presence of local neo-Punic amphoras in the Augustan and Julio-Claudian levels of *decumanus* VI, which have an extremely high percentage of imports, suggests that the contents were important to the diet of the colonists. Oil and *garum* are the two most likely contents, and both of these foodstuffs have a place in the Roman diet by *c.*10 B.C.[138] It is relevant that there is almost no evidence for import of either oil or *garum* to Carthage before the 'Second Amphora Wall' in the second quarter of the 1st c. A.D., when the numbers of imported oil and *garum* amphoras were still extremely small.[139] The dipinto on the example of Dressel 18 at the *Castra Praetoria* demonstrates that *garum* is possible; the reduced size of the amphora also suggests a parallel with the later 'Africano piccolo', which evidently held oil, to judge from its presence on Monte Testaccio.[140]

Small flat-based early Roman wine amphora (Panella's Forms *Ostia* III.44-46)

A small ovoid flat-based amphora class (Forms *Ostia* III.44-46 by Panella's typology) appears in levels of *decumanus* VI of A.D. 15, where it is a new class among what is otherwise the same range of amphoras as found in the contexts of *c.*10-1 B.C. Of 4 examples in the Augustan and Julio-Claudian contexts, three are in North African fabrics. This is the earliest closely dated context known for the class. Context **11** of A.D. 50 has a rim of Form *Ostia* III.44. In the later 2nd c. context **10** the general class *Ostia* III.44-46, despite its small size and relatively thin walls, makes up one-third of the amphora weight. Although this degree of predominance may be anomalous, the general class is usually well represented at Carthage in contexts of the 2nd to 4th c.[141] Amphoras from this thin-walled class break up easily; rims, handles (which often show wide lengthwise rills), profiled bases and even wall sherds can be identified as belonging to the class, but only a rim allows identification of a specific sub-type. Panella was clear on the existence of at least three forms, of which both *Ostia* III.44 and 45 certainly appeared during the 1st c. A.D. (*Ostia* III.44 appearing at Pompeii). Riley illustrated his Mid-Roman Amphora

134 Cf. A. Rodero Riaza, in M. Almagro-Gorbea (ed.), *El santuario de Juno en Gabii: excavaciones 1956-1969* (Rome 1982) esp. p. 528 and fig. 3.

135 Vegas, "Karthago" 1994, 345-46.

136 Riley, *CMich* I 1976, 110 and fig. 19, E11. In addition, note Hayes, *CMich* IV 1978, 84-85 and fig. 27.E44, residual in Deposit XX.

137 C. Panella, "Anfora tripolitane a Pompei," *L'instrumentum domesticum di Ercolano e di Pompei nella prima età imperiale* (Rome 1977) 135-49.

138 van der Werff 1986, 117-19, summarized a study by Panella of dated contexts demonstrating this.

139 Freed 1996, 143.

140 J. M. Blázquez Martínez *et al.*, *Excavaciones arqueológicas en el Monte Testaccio (Roma). Memoria campaña 1989* (Madrid 1994) 137 and figs. 63.2-3, 5-7 and 66.1.

141 Hayes and Riley did not note it in the deposits published in *CMich* I 1976, according to Riley, *Benghazi* 1979, 179, but in my own experience it is almost always present in mid- and late-Roman contexts, if only in small quantities. For example, Tomber 1986, 57, no. 213, shows a rim of *Ostia* III.45 in a North African fabric, dating from "at least mid-2nd c. A.D.". No. 132, p. 44 (not illustrated) is the same form in an imported micaceous fabric.

1 at Benghazi, which belongs to the class, with a figure resembling *Ostia* III.46; however, he described two variants in mid-Roman contexts, of which one is similar to Panella's *Ostia* III.44, suggesting that, even though the type began early, it continued at least into the mid-Roman period. Riley's distribution map shows that the class is common in Tunisia and Tripolitania.[142]

Certainty on production areas, fabric, and dating of individual types is lacking, since no kiln sites are known, although Panella's suggestion that the production was partly from Byzacena and partly Italian still seems most likely. The fabric colour ranges from pale red to pale brown, and vertical runnels of a light-coloured or, alternatively, reduced grey wash over the exterior are typical. The fabric is often highly levigated, and so not petrologically distinct to the eye; it does occasionally show mica or hematite, which makes a North African provenance for at least part of the production unlikely. Peacock and Williams present the petrology for a fabric with limestone, angular quartz (not desert sand), and mica but do not suggest a production area.[143]

Published analysis of this amphora class is still inadequate, while the evidence from excavation is both extensive and confusing. Some of the difficulty lies in the fact that the full participation of small flat-based amphoras in the world of trade and transport has been recognized only recently. Since distinctive flat-based wine amphoras (which were particularly suited to river traffic and rafts) are now recognized as occurring in the first half of the 1st c. A.D. or even earlier in Spain (Dressel 28), Central Italy (Dressel 29), and Gaul (Dressel 30), it is very likely that *Ostia* III.44-46 too carried wine.

The appearance of the class in a context of *c.*A.D. 15 is not devoid of support elsewhere. Panella has cited an example of *Ostia* III.44 in a context dated as early as Augustan/Tiberian from Lepcis Magna;[144] it is noteworthy that the class was more common at Ostia in the second half of the 1st c. A.D. than in later contexts,[145] which supports an early start. At Carthage, Vegas has recently demonstrated its presence by the third quarter of the 1st c. A.D,[146] noting that Form *Ostia* III.44 is also attested at Pompeii.[147]

Conclusions

This small excavation illustrates the economy of the early Roman colony of Carthage at three nodal points in the first half of the 1st c. A.D. Taken with material and contexts of the late 1st c. B.C. and 1st c. A.D. which have been previously published, especially a context of the third quarter of the 1st c. A.D. published by Vegas, it offers a new and clearly focused view of the early development of economic autonomy in a city that would become by the 2nd c. A.D. a great exporter of its local production of fine and cooking wares and a trader in local and regional cylindrical amphoras and their contents of oil and *garum*.

The change in sources of supply for all ceramic categories is documented minutely by these contexts, which illustrate over the first half of the 1st c. A.D. the early preponderance of imports, and Tyrrhenian Italian imports in particular, including lamps, Italian terra sigillata, a variety of Italian cooking wares, and Campanian and other Tyrrhenian Dressel 2-4 wine

---

142 Riley, *Benghazi* 1979, Mid Roman Amphora 1, 177-80 and figs.; unidentified flat-based body with runnels of light coloured paint over buff fabric with occasional white grits, fig. 80.207 and 176, Deposit 58; distribution map for Mid Roman Amphora 1, fig. 27, p. 178.

143 Peacock and Williams 1986, Class 40, 175-76.

144 Panella, *Ostia* III, 1973, 467.

145 Riley, *Benghazi* 1979, fig. 26, p. 178.

146 Vegas, 'Karthago' 1994, fig. 7, no. 93 and p.360; the example is in a 5YR 6/6 orange fabric with a light-coloured slip.

147 Vegas, 'Karthago' 1994, 346, referring to Riley, *Benghazi* 1979, 177; on p.178 Riley also shows that the class appears at both Ostia and Benghazi by the late 1st c. A.D. (fig. 26). A flat-based body published by Riley in early Roman Deposit 58 at Benghazi (supra n.142) is an earlier example of the class.

amphoras. The appearance of Ampuritan grey ware and N Syrian Eastern Sigillata A illustrates the participation of the whole Mediterranean in the supply of the new colony. These small contexts also suggest the change by the mid 1st c. A.D. away from imports of Italian wine amphoras to the Dressel 2 amphoras of coastal Tarraconensian Spain (see quantification, Table 4), a fact which has been previously demonstrated by analysis of the amphoras in the two early Roman amphora walls at Carthage.

Table 4: Amphora fabrics in the Augustan and Julio-Claudian levels of *decumanus* VI
Number of sherds/*grams* [number of catalogued examples]. Present: √; absent: -.

	(16) 10-1 B.C.	**(15)** 10-1 B.C.	**(23)** *c.*A.D. 15	**(13)** *c.*A.D. 15	**(12)** *c.*A.D. 15	**(11)** *c.*A.D. 50	Totals
Tunisian	39/*810* [1]	41/*1260*	-	13/*705*	15/*500* [3]	7/*200*	115/*3475*
Campanian	3/*175*	5/*700* [1]	1/*25*	2/*100*	5/*920* [1]	-	16/*1920*
Other Tyrrh.	-	1/*30* [1]	-	-	4/*1000* [1]	-	5/*1030*
Adriatic	-	2/*440*	-	-	-	-	2/*440*
Baetican coast	1/*150* [1]	1/*50* [1]	-	-	-	-	2/*200*
Baetican river valley	3/*200*	-	-	2/*400*	-	-	5/*600*
Tarrac. coast	1/*25*	2/*140*	-	-	-	1/*230* [1]	4/*395*
NAfrican+ Ostia III, 44-46	-	-	2/*100* [1]	-	8/*330*	1/*30* [1]	11/*460*
Koan	-	-	-	-	1/*60*	-	1/*60*
undiff. non-local	-	-	-	-	-	1/*80*	1/*80*
Totals	47/*1360*	52/*2620*	3/*125*	17/*1205*	33/*2810*	10/*540*	162/*8660*

The beginning of the Carthage/Nabeul production of 'blacktop cooking ware' can now be seen to be nearly contemporary with the Augustan founding of the colony. Although from the first publication of this class Hayes showed that the different forms appear in a series beginning in the 1st c. B.C., it has been a common error to read the presence of the ware as indicating a date not earlier than the 2nd c. A.D. and to confuse the local production with similar forms in 'Byzacena blacktop red cooking ware', which began much earlier. Understanding the order of appearance of forms in the local series (see above) allows much more accurate dating of contexts from the first two centuries of the colony. Probably because it had a model in the earlier regional production, the production of local cooking wares was confident from its first appearance and was commercially successful by A.D. 15 (see quantification, Table 3).

The excavation clarifies the dating of the earliest forms in Carthage/Nabeul African Red Slip A fine ware. Quite recently the first appearance of African Red Slip A has been dated to the Flavian era, but as this is the earliest period of wide export[148] it is not likely that it is also the date of its first appearance. In fact, the first era of local production had its own characteristic forms, a series of simple bowls and of thin-walled mugs and beakers, which can now be seen to appear as early as *c.*A.D. 15 (see Table 1). The first production of local fine ware was clearly not as technically confident as that of local blacktop cooking ware, and even these simple forms were only well established by the third quarter of the 1st c. A.D., confirming that the earliest range of exported forms did not appear before the fourth quarter of the 1st c.

---

148 Carandini *et al.* 1981, 13.

Perhaps the most surprising aspect of the local economy in the first half of the 1st c. A.D. is the predominance of a 'Punic-derived', probably local, cylindrical amphora class, in a variant slightly smaller and thinner-walled than the Punic production. The fact that such an amphora type, which may have contained *garum* or oil, maintained predominance in the local market until the Flavian era has not previously been well demonstrated. The small flat-based regional wine amphora was another mostly North African production which was in use at Carthage by the Tiberian period. In contrast, no trace of a certainly Greco-Roman derived Tunisian cylindrical amphora (such as Dressel 26) appears in these early Roman contexts.[149] This suggests that Carthage itself was not a leader in production of the new amphora types which would characterize the long period, from the early 2nd to the 7th c., in which the city achieved great economic power as a major exporter of ceramics and of the agricultural produce of its hinterland.

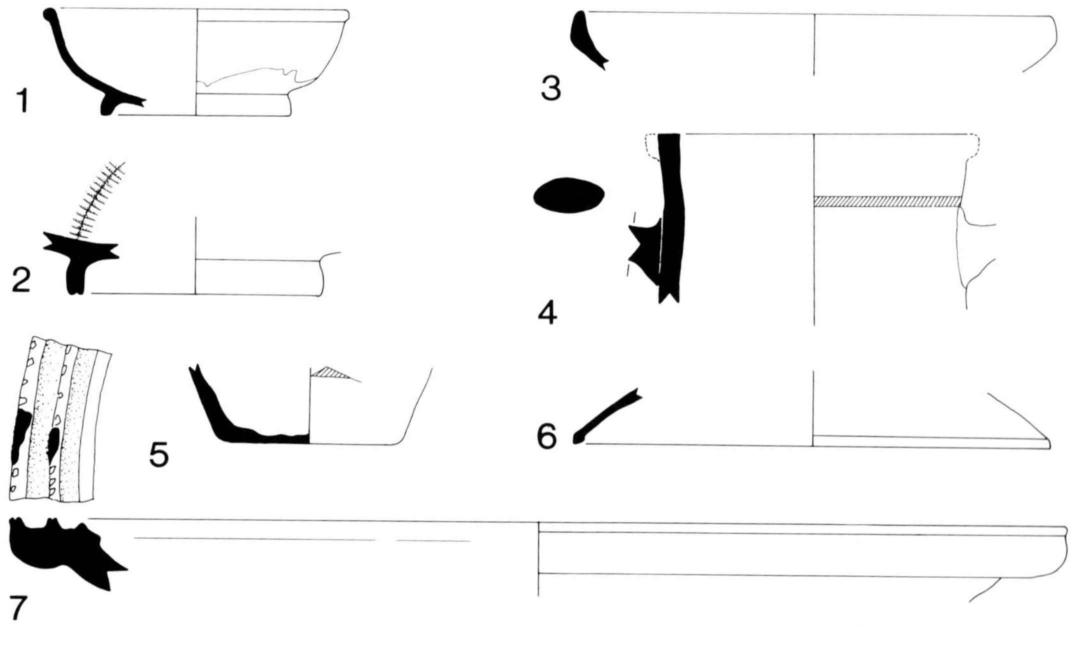

Fig. 1. Punic layer **30** (*c.*300 B.C.) 1-7. Scale 1:3

149 This is surprising in view of the discovery of an example of Tunisian Dressel 26 in a 1st c. A.D. context at Rome: E. Lissi Caronna, *NSc* 22-23 (1968-69) *Suppl.* 10-15.

CATALOGUE OF POTTERY
PUNIC CONTEXTS

30, sandy soil, first layer above natural (*c.*300 B.C.)

100 sherds (10 rims), 2.510 kg. Fine wares 13 sherds, 100 g (4% by weight); amphoras 39 sherds, 1.290 kg (51% by weight). Average sherd size for amphora 31g, for other pottery 21g.

Local, Campanian (Teanum Sidicinum) and possible 'Sicilian' black glaze; local, light surface service wares, regional thin-walled Punic blacktop red cooking ware, local hand-formed brazier. Amphora is almost entirely Tunisian.

Residual: Red fine ware, burnished on both sides, is earlier Punic, 2% by weight.

Imported: 2% by weight, fine wares of S Italy.

Fine wares

Black-glazed

1) Local Lamboglia 22/28 small carinated bowl. Fine fabric, minute quartz and rare white lime; 10YR 7/3 very pale brown (pale yellow buff) in break, matte black slip, worn on interior, upper exterior wall mottled matte 7.5YR 6/8 reddish yellow (dull orange) to black, slip ends in irregular demarcation. Mediocre quality.
Morel 1981, 204, dates 2672e1, the original Lamboglia 22/28, 'around 310-275'.

2) Campanian production of Teanum Sidicinum, bowl with foot-ring base, groove under foot. Extremely fine fabric, slightly micaceous, 5YR 6/6 light reddish brown (dull red orange) in break, glossy black slip on exterior, reserved at join of base to exterior wall and under bifid foot; 2.5YR 5/6 red gloss on entire underside of base, darker 2.5YR 6/8 red gloss circle (largely worn away) in floor, to line over diameter of base beyond which gloss is black. Circle of large-scale rouletting in floor over colour demarcation line. Excellent quality.
Morel 1981, pl. 223, Ba 14 and 446-47, dates this type of high foot-ring base with groove in base of foot to 'around the beginning of the 3rd c.'; the fabric of Teano is dated from the end of the 4th to the first third of the 3rd c. B.C., (Morel 50 and n.130).

3) Sicilian(?) bowl with plain incurved rim, wall thickens slightly below rim. Extremely fine hard fabric, 5YR 6/6 reddish yellow (dull pink) in break, slightly metallic black gloss on interior and exterior, worn over horizontal knife smoothing on upper exterior rim.
Most like 2725b1, in Sicilian black glaze, dated to the end of the 4th c. B.C. (Morel 1981, 211).

Service and cooking wares

Local buff coarse ware

4) Slipped and banded small jug/table amphora with tall neck, rim broken away, rising handle, small ovoid in cross-section, runs from mid-neck to shoulder. Crowded minute round reddish brown and white quartz inclusions, 2.5YR 6/4 light reddish brown in break, 10YR 8/2 white (cream) exterior slip continues over interior but thins downward, banded with 5YR 4/3 reddish brown (dark brown) paint on flat top of rim and in line just above attachment of handle.
Cf. Vegas, *Karthago* 1991, fig. 30, no. 107, pp. 148-49. Such a form is often identified as jug form Cintas Forms 90-94; a generally similar amphora (Cintas Forms 325h, 329-31) is equally likely.

5) Slipped small flat-bottomed jug, lower wall and base only. Round fairly crowded small light brown quartz inclusions, 5YR 6/6 reddish yellow in fresh break, 7.5YR 7/4 pink (dull orange) overall exterior slip, band of reddish yellow paint below mid-body at break. Nicely made.

Byzacena blacktop red cooking ware

6) Very thin walled large lid, rim not thickened but slightly beveled. Fine fabric, minute white lime (some shell?) and occasional red grog, colour 2.5YR 5/6 red mottled wet-smoothed exterior surface, underside and inner core 2.5YR 5/2 weak red (grey).

Local hand-formed coarse ware

7) Large shallow brazier, 4 high ridges on wide horizontal rim, outer 2 ridges decorated with fine irregular dents. Dark discolouration in floor. Large quartz and lime inclusions, some shell; fabric colour sandwich, wet-smoothed 2.5YR 6/6 light red (orange) surfaces, same colour outer edge of break around irregularly mottled core varying from 10YR 6/3 pale brown (yellowish grey) to 7.5YR N5/ grey.

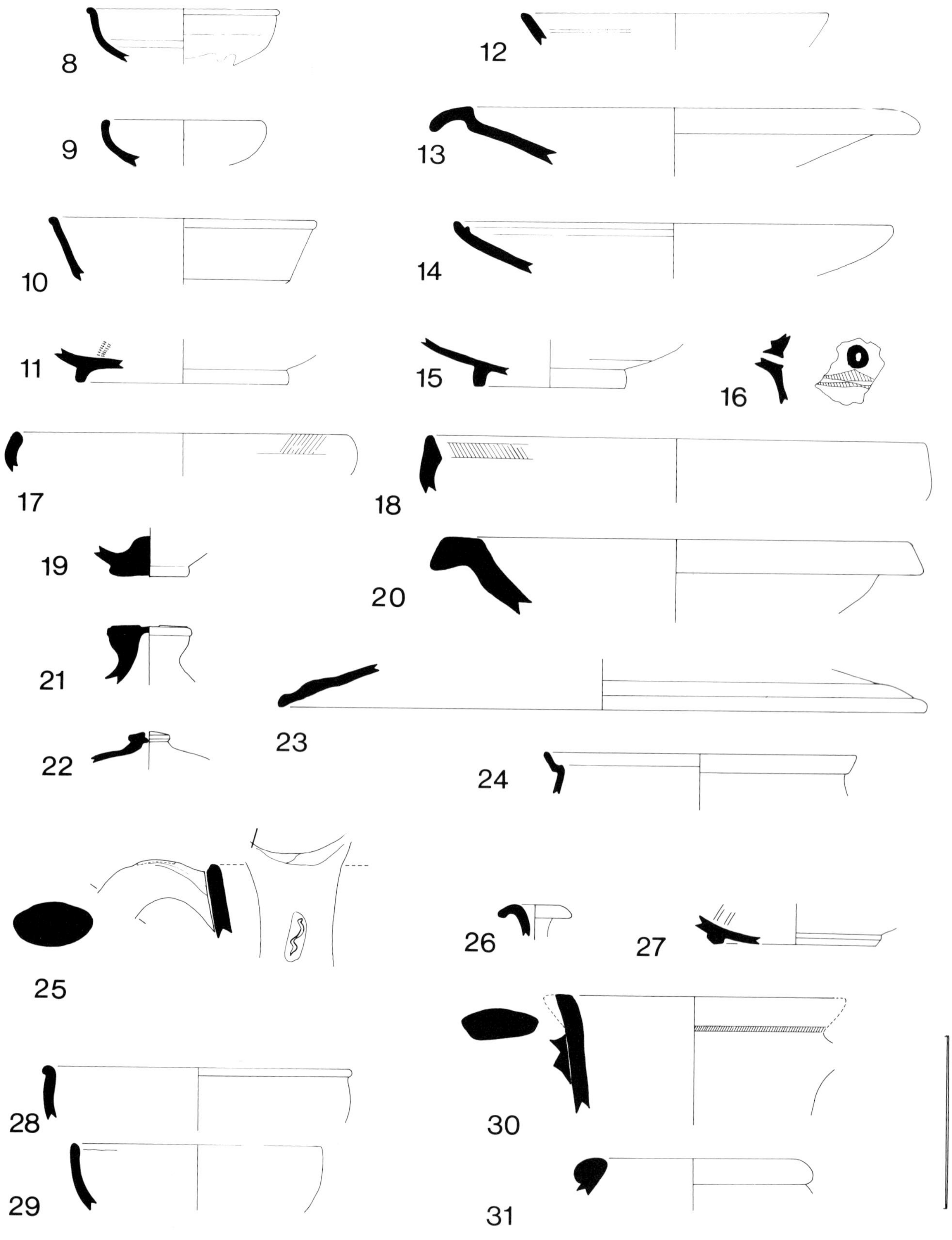

Fig. 2. Punic layer **33** (*c.*first quarter 2nd c. B.C.) 8-25. Scale 1:3.
Punic layers (all *c.*first quarter 2nd c. B.C.): (**25**) 26-27; (**29**) 28-29; (**2**) 30; (**6**) 31. Scale 1:3

Vegas, *Karthago* 1991 fig. 13, no. 127, basin with ridged rim, rd 32.0, red fabric, of first half 3rd c. B.C. *Byrsa* II, fig. 43, no. 35, rim diam. 33.0-34, with greenish fabric and pinkish white surfaces, context of first half 2nd c. B.C.; another example, fig. 175, no. 70, rd 32-33, very coarse beige fabric, beige surface, 'probably used for cooking', in destruction context.

33, Punic fill (first quarter 2nd c. B.C.) in a pit dug into layer 30

140 sherds (28 rims), 2.920 kg. Fine wares 24 sherds, 270 g (11% by weight); amphora 43 sherds, 1.360 kg (47% by weight). Average sherd size for amphora 32 g, for other pottery 16 g.

Campana A, local and Etrurian black-glazed. Banded and plain Punic coarse ware, probably local. Byzacena blacktop red cooking ware. Tunisian and Tyrrhenian Greco-Italic amphora. A small undecorated fragment of ostrich egg shell (a favourite Punic grave gift) was recovered from this layer.

Residual: As much as half the material in this context is residual; the earlier material is of the same date as that in layer **30**.

Imported: 14% by weight, fine wares and amphora of Tyrrhenian Italy (Campania and Etruria).

3 additional sherds, not catalogued here, were found adhering to the make-up on the underside of a fragment of white mosaic floor in this context. They were local black glaze Forms Lamboglia 21/25 (as no. 9) and 22/28 (as nos. 1 and 8), and Byzacena blacktop red cooking ware miniature Form 194 casserole.

Fine wares

Black-glazed

8) Local small gently carinated bowl with corniced rim, Lamboglia 22/28. Fine fabric, minute quartz, 10YR 7/3 very pale brown (pale buff) in break, matte black slip on interior, matte slip over upper two-thirds of exterior wall, 7.5YR 5/6 strong brown (yellowish brown) on upper half, brown black on lower half, colour change from stacking, irregular demarcation line where slip ends. Very well made.
Morel 1981, 204 dates 2672e1, the original Lamboglia 22/28, 'around 310-275 B.C.'

9) Local small bowl with incurved rim, Lamboglia 21/25. Fine fabric, minute white lime and some holes, colour 10YR 7/3 very pale brown (dull buff) in break, worn poor quality mottled dark brown to black matte slip, 10YR 6/4 dark yellowish brown above stacking line on upper exterior wall.
Lamboglia 21/25 = Morel 2765a1, end of 4th and 3rd c. B.C., common *c.*300 B.C.

10) Local carinated dish with slightly flared wall and small bead rim. Fine fabric, minute angular brown and grey quartz, some minute white lime; 10R 5/6 red in break, surface mottled matte 5YR 5/6 yellowish red (yellowish brown) slip on exterior of upper wall, 10R 5/8 red slip on interior and lower exterior wall. The colour change on the upper exterior wall, from stacking, is echoed by dark orange at edge of break.
Most like Morel 2642e1; the general form is common in a number of fabrics and associated with both the 3rd and 2nd c. B.C.

11) Campana A low foot-ring base of open bowl, unarticulated curve under base, 3 rounds of super-fine rouletting in floor. Extremely fine fabric, minute red grog, slightly micaceous, 2.5YR 5/6 red in break, elegant shiny black gloss, perfectly smooth on exterior, slightly pimply, with flaw over grog on the interior.
No exact comparanda in Morel 1981.

12) Campana A bowl with slightly flared wall, plain rim, thin line of white paint wash below rim on interior wall. Extremely fine fabric, 2.5YR 6/6 light red in break, silvery metallic black gloss, worn over rim.
Morel 2154, one of the earliest classes of Campana A to be widely exported, from 220 B.C. to the mid 2nd c. (Morel 1981, 348 and n.132, at the Athenian Agora).

13) Campana A shallow flared dish, wide dropped rim, Lamboglia 36B. Extremely fine fabric, 5YR 6/4 light reddish brown in fresh break, 5YR 7/4 pink where glaze is abraded over rim top and edge, surfaces silvery metallic black, poorly preserved in floor, badly scratched on outer side. Elegant example despite poor condition.
Morel 1312b1, the form appears almost exclusively in Campana A, and dates to the 2nd c. B.C., especially the first half (Morel 1981, 103).

14) Etrurian(?) shallow bowl with double ridge inside rim. Fine fabric, minute holes, some minute quartz and lime, including shell, one large lime inclusion, two small flaws in floor over exploded lime, slightly micaceous; 5YR 7/4 pink in break, 5YR 5/2 reddish grey (dark brown) matte slip over interior, worn over rim round, exterior slipped 2.5Y 7/3 light grey/pale yellow with traces of very worn trailed black slip. Not well made.
Morel 1646g1, dated "beginning of 2nd c.", a local or regional fabric from South or Central Etruria.

Service and cooking wares

Local buff common ware

15) Partial black slip on foot-ring base of open bowl. Fine fabric, minute quartz, black grits and holes; 10YR 7/3 very pale brown (dull buff) at break and unslipped surfaces, thin very slightly metallic black glaze in floor and over upper two-thirds of exterior wall, neat demarcation line, all very worn.
Rim of similar bowl in Italian fabric in the same layer, profile incurved near rim as Morel 2812a1, dated *c.*250-190 B.C.

16) Small 'feeding bottle' with applied nozzle directed slightly upward, hole drilled through wall from outside in. Fine fabric, minute black inclusions and holes, colour 10YR 7/2 light grey (pale dull buff) at break and surfaces, 2 irregular 10R 4/2 dark greyish brown horizontal lines of thin matte paint on wall below nozzle.
Cintas Forms 371-79; a common find of Delattre in the excavation of the Sainte-Monique necropolis, dating to the 4th and 3rd c. B.C. (Cintas 1950, 163). Very similar example at Nabeul Museum, dated to 4th c. B.C.

17) Slipped bowl with incurved plain rim. Fine orange fabric, minute subangular dark brown and red quartz inclusions, interior surface wet-smoothed 2.5YR 6/6 red, exterior slipped 10YR 7/3 very pale brown (greenish cream), banded at upper wall and at break on interior of floor in 2.5YR 5/4 reddish brown thin paint, very sharply defined.
Harden 1937, 83, fig. 7.K, and 84, 87, shows 'lids' of Greek cultural derivation, including a small carinated bowl with banding above carination lines, red fabric with reddish slip, red band of paint at outer rim, 3 concentric circles of purplish black paint in floor. This bowl occurred with an amphora which could date before 500 B.C. but is more likely later (that is, second half of 'Tanit II', *c.*500-350/300 B.C).

18) Slipped bowl with incurved rim, rim beveled on interior of wall. Very fine fabric, vari-coloured minute rounded quartz and grog; 2.5YR 6/6 light red in break, all-over slip varies from 10YR 8/3 very pale brown to 7.5YR 8/4 pink (pale orange), band of thin 2.5YR 4/4 reddish brown paint over upper inner angle of rim.
Byrsa II 1982, fig. 44, no. 48 and fig. 66, no. 29, context before 200 B.C. (p.59).

19) Slipped small deep bowl with profiled flat base and large *umbilicus* in center of floor. Fine fabric, 5YR 6/6 reddish yellow in core to pink at edges of break, all-over slip varies from 7.5YR 7/6 reddish yellow to 8/4 pink.
No comparanda.

20) Shallow basin, flat-topped beveled rim. Slightly coarse, well-sorted rounded quartz grains; colour 7.5YR 7/4 pink in core, very slightly redder towards edges, salt-fired 2.5Y 8/2 white (yellowish cream) surfaces. Well made.
Perhaps the most common service form in late Punic contexts; cf. Vegas in *Karthago* 1991 fig. 36.23 and p. 181, in context of first quarter 2nd c. B.C.; *Byrsa* II, fig. 43.31 and fig. 129.22, in context of destruction of 146 B.C., A172 (p. 106).

Byzacena blacktop red cooking ware

21) Steep-walled lid with large string-cut knob. Rare large subangular quartz and round white lime. Exterior 10R 5/6 red, interior 10R 5/2 weak red, break the same, mottled to dark grey.
Similar lid knobs occur in Hayes' 'Late Roman Cooking Ware 1' in about the 5th c.

22) Lid, rim very slightly thickened, beveled edge. Fine fabric, minute quartz and lime, occasional small dark grog, small holes and lamination lines; colour 2.5YR 5/6 red in break, matte 2.5YR 5/4 reddish brown wet-smoothed surfaces, mottled to grey in characteristic horizontal streaks on exterior, darkened to 5YR 5/2 reddish grey at edge of rim and about 1 cm up interior wall.

23) Thin-walled lid, sharply knife-cut beveled and perforated lid knob. Fine fabric, minute black and white inclusions, colour 2.5YR 6/6 light red in break, interior and exterior surfaces mottled 5YR 5/4 red brown to grey.
Same lid type as no. 6 in (30). Fulford in *Harbour* 1994, coarse ware lid Form 8, fig. 4.8.8, of probable Punic date.

24) Thin-walled casserole, form as Hayes 'Form 194'. Fine fabric, 2.5YR 5/4 reddish brown in core, 5YR 4/1 dark grey matte surface on exterior and over upper rim on interior, lower wall 5YR 5/2 reddish grey.
Byrsa II 1982, fig. 128, 8-10 in context of destruction of 146 B.C., A172 (p. 106).

Amphora

Sicilian/Campanian Greco-Italic amphora

25) Amphora, rim lost, small neck off-round, curved handle is wide ovoid in cross-section. Fine fabric, minute fairly common 'black sand' inclusions, minute silver mica; colour 7.5YR 7/4 pink in break, 10YR 8/3 very pale brown slip on all surfaces. Stamp on top of handle has rounded irregular ends, wiggly line in stamp may be anepigraphic.
Greco-Italic amphora of 3rd c. B.C. or earlier, should have projecting triangular rim.

25, Thin beaten earth surface over pit fill 33, floor abutting the *opus figlinum* floor (first quarter of 2nd c. B.C.)

48 sherds (4 rims), 0.515 kg. Fine ware 12 joining + 2 sherds, 15 g (3% by weight); amphora 10 sherds, 0.210 kg (40% by weight). Average of amphora 21 g; average of other 8 g.

Attic *guttus*, local plain ware *unguentarium*, Italian banded orange coarse, Byzacena blacktop red cooking ware, Tunisian amphora.

Residual: Attic *guttus*, 3% by weight.

Imported: 5% by weight, Tyrrhenian Italy, Athens.

Fine ware

Black-glazed

26) Attic '*guttus*' or slumped *askos* with vertical neck, wide curving dropped rim. Extremely fine, 5YR 6/6 reddish yellow (dull orange) fabric, shiny black gloss, worn in 'measle spots' on upper side of rim.
At the Kerameikos museum, Athens, such pieces are dated *c*.370-60 and 350-25 B.C. by context. Morel 5451c1, Attic fabric, dated '315 ± 30' (Morel 1981, 364-65).

Service ware

Italian Tyrrhenian banded orange coarse ware

27) Dish/lid with beveled low foot-ring. Minute lime, angular dark grey (volcanic?) and red quartz inclusions, some minute lime, one bit of gold mica, lamination lines; fabric colour 5YR 6/6 reddish yellow. Two poorly defined bands of dark grey wash at base diameter in floor.
Although the form and fabric suggest early Roman Carthage/Nabeul blacktop orange cooking ware Form Hayes 196, the fabric is actually Italian and the banding in the floor is a typical Hellenistic or Punic surface treatment.

29, Leveling surface for construction of *opus figlinum* floor of Punic structure (first quarter of 2nd c. B.C.)

52 sherds (4 rims), 0.815 kg. Fine wares 9 sherds, est. 30 g (less than 4% by weight); amphora 23 sherds, 0.620 kg (76% by weight). Average of amphora 27g; average of other 7g.

Black-glazed, Byzacena blacktop red cooking ware.

Residual: 5%, black-glazed and basin of same fabric as no. 7 in layer **30**.

Imported: 27%, Tyrrhenian Italy (one-third of amphora is Italian); Athens.

Intrusive: Carthage/Nabeul blacktop orange coarse ware (5 g), horizontally ridged interior, Hayes Form 197 or related, late 2nd/early 3rd c. A.D.

Fine wares

Black-glazed

28) Local deep bowl with curved wall, bead rim, sturdy manufacture. Fine fabric, minute quartz and lime, one large piece dull red grog, 7.5YR 7/4 pink (buff) in break, thin almost matte 5YR 5/3 reddish brown slip over exterior, 5YR 4/2 dark reddish grey (dark brown) on interior. Very well made.
Most like Morel's 2686 series; dates vary widely, 210 ± 30 B.C. is typical.

29) Local small bowl with plain rim, gently curved wall. Fine fabric, rare minute quartz and lime, 2.5YR 6/6 light red in break, with thin line of dull orange towards exterior. Upper exterior wall 5YR 5/6 yellowish red (red brown), with line of demarcation at stacking level, the rest of the exterior and the interior is 10R 5/8 red, except for a narrow line of brown black at top of inner wall. Very well-made.
Most like Morel's 2985 series; dates vary from 150 to 50 B.C.; the form is not very distinctive and these dates seem late for our context.

2, wall (first quarter 2nd c. B.C.) cleared off to just above upper surface of *opus figlinum* floor

5 sherds (1 rim), 0.90 g. No fine ware; amphora, 1 sherd, 60 g; average of other 8 g.
Local buff coarse ware, Tyrrhenian Greco-Italic amphora.
Imported: 67% by weight, Tyrrhenian Italy.

Amphora

Sicilian/Tyrrhenian Greco-Italic amphora

30) Slipped small table amphora, flat-topped triangular rim broken away; handle, applied just under rim, is wide ovoid in cross-section. Small rounded white and pale buff quartz grains, several small hematite balls; colour 2.5YR 6/8 light red in fresh break, 10YR 8/2 white (cream) slip, now mostly lost, still visible at inner side of rim, applied over 5YR 5/1 grey reduced surface. A band of cream slip survives at hollow under rim.
Cf. Cintas 1950 Forms 349 and 350, pls. 29 and 97, with foot-ring base, associated with cemeteries of 4th and especially 3rd c. B.C. (p.155).

6, Mortar floor layer (first quarter of 2nd c. B.C.) beneath 1, makeup of *opus figlinum* floor

10 sherds (2 rims), 0.107 kg. Fine wares 2 sherds, 5 g (less than 5% by weight); amphoras 2 sherds, 50 g (47% by weight). Average of amphora 25 g; average of other 7 g.
Black-glazed, thin-walled Campana B(?), orange coarse ware. Tunisian amphora.
Imported: Less than 5%, Tyrrhenian Italy(?).

Service ware/amphora

31) Non-local orange coarse ware jar/amphora, constricted at neck, with rolled bead rim. Small rounded pale buff and red quartz grains, some black hematite, occasional minute white lime, lamination lines, horizontal wet-smoothing.

1, Three-part make-up layer forming the bedding for the *opus figlinum* floor

No finds.

EARLY ROMAN CONTEXTS

26, fill (10-1 B.C.) in small channel cut into Punic *opus figlinum* floor

12 sherds (no rims), 0.470 kg. 100% amphora. Average of amphora sherd 39 g.
Campanian amphora, including a short spike toe with rounded end, and local Tunisian amphora sherds. The Campanian spike could belong to either Dressel 1A (produced during the period from *c.*140 to 80 B.C.) or Dressel 2-4 (30 B.C. to A.D. 79; a small spike toe is likely to be Augustan Dressel 4, Panella and Fano 1977, Type 1, fig. 1, p. 165). Without other evidence to support the Republican/Punic date — which is unlikely at Carthage — Dressel 4 is most likely the correct identification.
Imported: 64% by weight, Tyrrhenian Italy.

16, *Decumanus* VI: first street level (10-1 B.C.), laid directly on floor of Punic building

78 sherds (9 rims), 1.824 kg. Fine wares 12 sherds, 29 g (less than 2% by weight); amphora 47 sherds, 1.360 kg (75% by weight). Average of amphora 34 g; average of other 7 g (small sherds).
Italian terra sigillata or contemporary; Italian Tyrrhenian and local coarse ware; Campanian, Baetican coastal and river-valley amphora and Tarraconensian coastal amphora; Tunisian neo-Punic amphora. Wall of small cobalt blue lathe-turned glass bottle.
Residual: Punic local black-glazed Lamboglia 22/28 and Cintas Form 32 *unguentarium*, less than 2% by weight.
Imported: 31% by weight, Tyrrhenian Italy, coastal Tarraconensian, coastal and river-valley Baetican.

Italian lamp

32) Chip of flared nozzle, superfine 10YR 8/2 white in break, excellent 2.5YR 4/4 reddish brown slightly glossy slip over both exterior and interior.
Italian Loeschcke Type IA, Bailey, *Sabratha*, fig. 36.90, Augustan/Tiberian.

Fine ware

Italian terra sigillata

33) Cup base with tiny offset at edge of interior floor.
Conspectus Base Form 3.9 type characteristic of small bell-shaped cups (Forms 14, 15, 17); 3.9 is from Haltern (7 B.C.-A.D. 9).

Amphoras

Neo-Punic Tunisian amphora

34) Wide flared rim with ridge under rim, coarse fabric with rare minute to small white lime and holes; 2.5YR 6/6 light red in break, 2.5Y 8/2 white (yellowish cream) slip over outer rim and neck, mottled to pink on interior of rim and neck. Well made. An exactly similar rim, not illustrated, occurs in **15**.
As van der Werff 1977-78, 'Form 2 variant', fig. 7, C34-206, p. 191. Peacock in *Harbour* 1994, fig. 3.2.18 and pp. 46-47, earliest example is from a late Augustan context.

Baetican coastal Haltern 70 amphora stopper

35) Complete purpose-made flat amphora stopper, 4 narrow irregular ridges radiate from center knob(?), now broken away. Fabric shows rare dark grey hematite, minute mica; 10YR 8/3 very pale brown.
A similar lid with 4 radiating ridges and central knob, diam. 9.2, non-local pale green fabric (5Y 7/3) with dark grey grits at Benghazi in context with mainly Hellenistic to Augustan material (Riley, *Benghazi* 1979 fig. 81, no. D213, p. 176, citing Spanish contexts).

15, *Decumanus* VI: second street level (10-1 B.C.) above Punic structure

145 sherds (31 rims), 3.701 kg. Fine wares 34 sherds, 316 g (8.5% by weight); amphora 52 sherds, 2.620 kg (71% by weight). Average of amphora 50 g, average of other 12 g.

Italian terra sigillata, Spanish Ampuritan grey ware and N Syrian Eastern Sigillata A. Tyrrhenian bifid rim baking pan and Carthage/Nabeul blacktop cooking ware Hayes Forms 194 casserole and 195 lid/bowl, Byzacena blacktop red cooking ware lid knob and large grooved handle of jug. Campanian 'Fabric A' amphora, Adriatic Lamboglia 2/Dressel 6A, Tarraconensian coastal Dressel 2 with fake double handles, Tunisian neo-Punic amphora 2. Four Loeschcke Type I lamp fragments. Two small (diam. 1.0) flat gaming pieces, one ceramic, the other probably bone.

Residual: Punic black-glazed Campana A, less than 1%.

Imported: 46% by weight, fine wares and amphoras of Tyrrhenian Italy, Baetican coast, Adriatic Italy, coastal Tarraconensis, N Syria.

Intrusive(?): Byzacena blacktop red cooking ware large string-cut lid knob and strap handle (may be residual, contemporary or intrusive).

Lamp

36) Not illustrated. Lamp, from Asia Minor: chip of outer point of triangular handle with trace of raised decoration, very soft friable fabric with superminute angular grey inclusions, 10YR 8/1 white in break, slight traces of vitrified yellow to yellowish-green lead-glaze.
Broneer Type XXI = Bailey, *BM* 1980, Type D, cf. Bailey in *Sabratha* 1994, fig. 39, 151-52 (for form only), type can be Augustan–Tiberian.

Fine wares

North Syrian Eastern Sigillata A

37) Platter with curved vertical wall, very worn.
Hayes 1985, ESA Form 33, pl. 5.3-4; Form 34, pl. 5.6 is related but larger; the form imitates Haltern 2 (*Conspectus* 20) and dates *c*.1-30/50 A.D., Hayes 1985, 29.

Italian terra sigillata

38) Plate with concave vertical rim.
Conspectus Form 18, closest to 18.1.2. Form dated mid Augustan by its appearance at Dangstetten and Oberaden (15 B.C.-10 B.C.).

39) Cylindrical cup.
Probably *Conspectus* Form 26, carinated cylindrical cup with vertical rim, closest to 26.1. Form dated 7 B.C.-A.D. 9 by its appearance at Haltern.

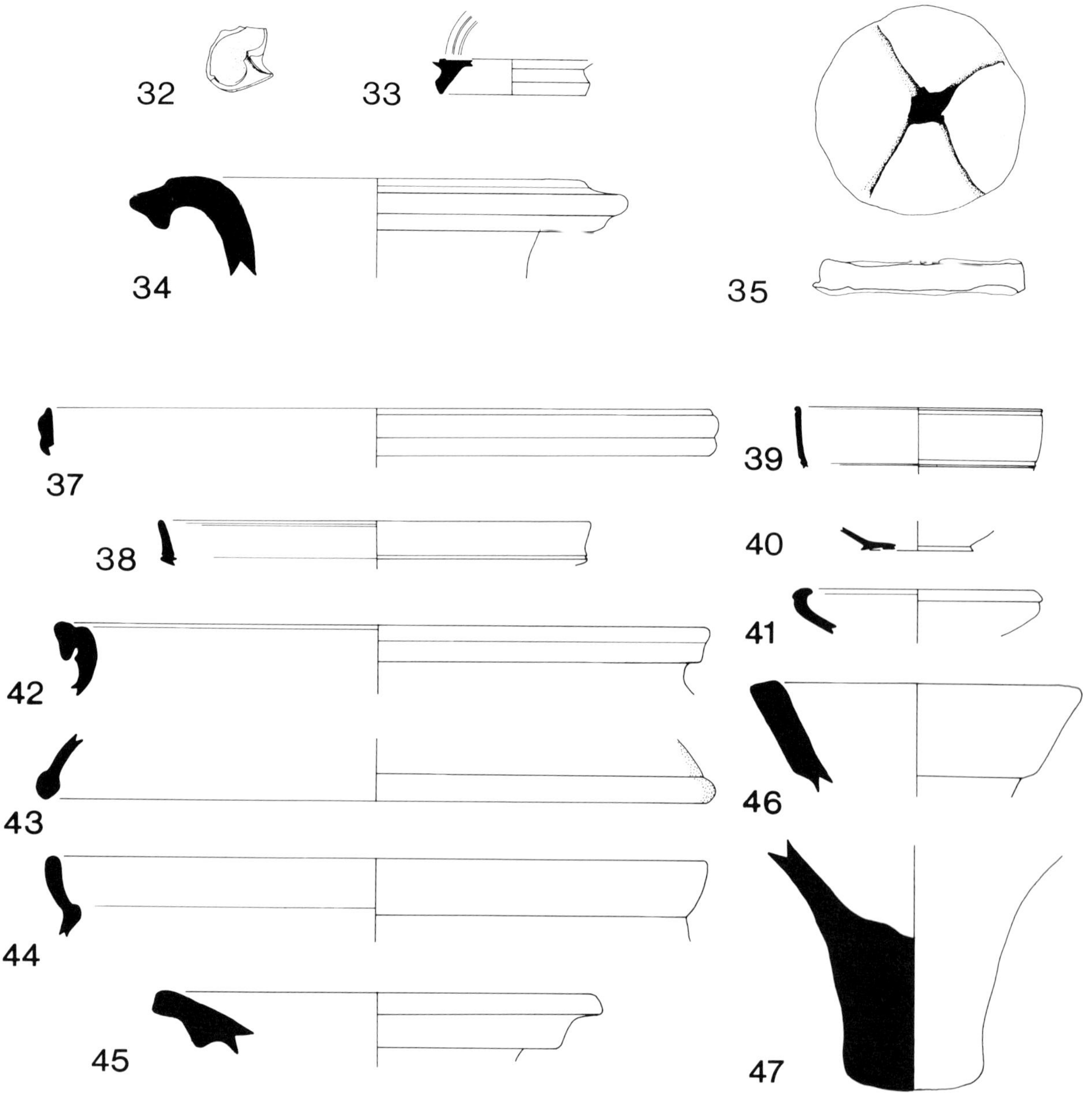

Fig. 3. Early Roman street layer 1 (**16**) (*c.*10-1 B.C.) 32-35. Scale 1:3.
Early Roman street layer 2 (**15**) (*c.*10-1 B.C.) 36-47. Scale 1:3

Central Tyrrhenian thin-walled

40) Profiled base, grey coarse ware, may be type with vertical combing, as no. 116 in layer **11**. Tiny curved handle with strongly marked groove down back may be from same *poculum*.
Cp. Fulford in *Harbour* 1994, fig. 1.5.81 and 82, pp. 13-14; both his examples in possibly local 'Fabric B'.

Service and cooking wares

Local buff coarse ware

41) Small bowl with early Roman bead rim.
Hayes in *CMich* I 1976, Type 1 early Roman bowl in local buff coarse ware (p.100). Fulford in *Harbour* 1994, fig.4.1.7.1-2 and 4.1.8.1-2, local Fabric 2.2 'white surface ware', possibly of 1st and 2nd c. (p.54).

42) Wide-mouthed basin with everted hollow T-rim, slight ridge under rim. Well-sorted sandy orange fabric, horizontally smoothed surfaces, fabric colour is 5YR 7/4 pink to 6/6 reddish yellow. The form clearly begins before the Augustan period and could still be in use in the mid 1st c. A.D. to judge by its appearance in layer **11**.

Form as nos. 55 in **23** and 125 in **11**; the form is also common in Italian fabric, no. 125.
Hayes in *CMich* I 1976, discusses 4 related early Roman forms as basin types 1-4, fig. 17.2-4; cf. Deposit XII, 1st c. A.D., fig. 6.4-5, p. 63; catalogue D8, variant of basin type 4, is closest to ours. The form is common in late Hellenistic and Augustan contexts elsewhere (pp.104-5). Fulford in *Harbour* 1994 fig. 4.2.19.1 and 5, pp. 56-57, coarse ware bowl Form 19, Fabric 2.2 'white surface ware', dated from late 1st c. B.C. Riley, *Benghazi* 1979, fig. 100.454 in early Roman cooking ware and fig. 120.803, 804, 806, 808 in early Roman plain ware, common in Augustan contexts. Dyson, *Cosa* 1976 (supra n.61), PD161, fig. 4, Class 11 in light-surfaced ware; Class 24 pots, PD54 and PD58, fig. 33 and p. 95, are related; the context ends by 30 B.C.

Byzacena blacktop cooking ware

43) Deep dish/lid, with small bead rim, thin-walled variant, burnished red slip on interior, grey exterior.
Hayes Form 185 variant; Form 185 has red slip and line burnishing on exterior, form 'perhaps early' (Hayes, *LRP* 204).
Fulford in *Harbour* 1994, Form 3 lid, fig. 4.8.4.3 lid; Fulford notes that such rims are present in the Augustan group at Sabratha, p.64.

Carthage/Nabeul blacktop cooking ware

44) Hayes Form 194 casserole, large-scale version.
As no. 123 in **11**. Hayes in *CMich* I 1976, Deposit XI, early 1st c. A.D., fig. 6.13, pp. 62-63. Vegas, 'Karthago' 1994, third quarter of 1st c. A.D., fig. 3.53-54, pp. 354-55.

Amphoras

Tunisian neo-Punic amphora

45) Very sharply defined flared rim with heavy ridge under flare. Slightly coarse fabric with some lime, red grog, minute holes; 5YR 7/4 pink in break, slip mottled 7.5YR 8/4 pink.
Hayes in *CMich* I 1976, Deposit X, early 1st c. A.D., Tiberian(?), fig. 5.33, pp. 60-61, catalogue E29; Deposit XI, early 1st c. A.D., fig. 6.20, pp. 62-63 is Riley Type IIb, catalogue E5. Peacock in *Harbour* 1994, cf. fig. 3.3.25 and pp. 46-48.

Baetican coastal Haltern 70 amphora

46) Slightly flared crown-shaped rim. Coarse dense fabric, with crowded minute brown, grey or clear quartz, occasional medium bits of flat gold and silver mica, pimply surfaces; 10YR 7/3 very pale brown, thin 10YR 8/3 very pale brown (cream buff) slip.
Haltern 70, which may have carried wine or must, appears in Delattre's 'First Amphora Wall (Freed 1996); Peacock in *Harbour* 1994, fig. 3.3.35, pp. 48-49; in context of early 1st c. A.D. (p. 43).

Campanian Dressel 2-4 amphora

47) Solid spike toe, break shows attachment of spike to cone-shaped original base. Hard coarse friable fabric, minute to small crowded subangular dark grey and exploded white lime inclusions, common minute gold mica; fabric colour 10R 5/6 red, exterior wet-smoothed, 7.5 YR 8/2 pinkish white (very pale grey) slip.
Panella and Fano 1977, Type 1, 149, fig. 1, or possibly Class 3, 150-51, figs. 4-5, 'Fabric A' (p.145).

23, *Decumanus* VI: lens (*c.*A.D. 15) between 2nd and 3rd street layers

39 sherds (18 rims), 0.550 kg. Fine wares 14 sherds, 85 g (15% by weight); amphora 3 sherds, 0.125 kg (23% by weight). Average of amphora 42 g, average of other 12 g.

Local proto-African Red Slip A hemispherical bowl, Italian terra sigillata, Carthage/Nabeul blacktop cooking ware Hayes Forms 198 jar, 196 dish/lid; North African *Ostia* III.44-46 flat-based amphora, Italian Loeschcke Type I and Broneer Type XXI lamps.

Imported: 18% by weight, Tyrrhenian Italy.

Italian lamps

48) Sharply angled shoulder with 3-4 narrow ridges, about one-fifth of discus, very fine fabric, 7.5YR 7/4 pink break and interior, 2.5YR 5/6 red very slightly glossy mottled slip, splotch of same slip on interior. The lamp was smoothed into the mould with a cloth, which has left characteristic markings (information from J. W. Hayes). On discus, torso and upper legs of single standing gladiator, large oval shield to left of gladiator with boss, gladiator wears loin cloth, folds of material diagonally across chest with left arm and left upper leg covered. A horizontal line just below his belt must be his sword or a dagger held across his body. Part of filling hole to right of figure.

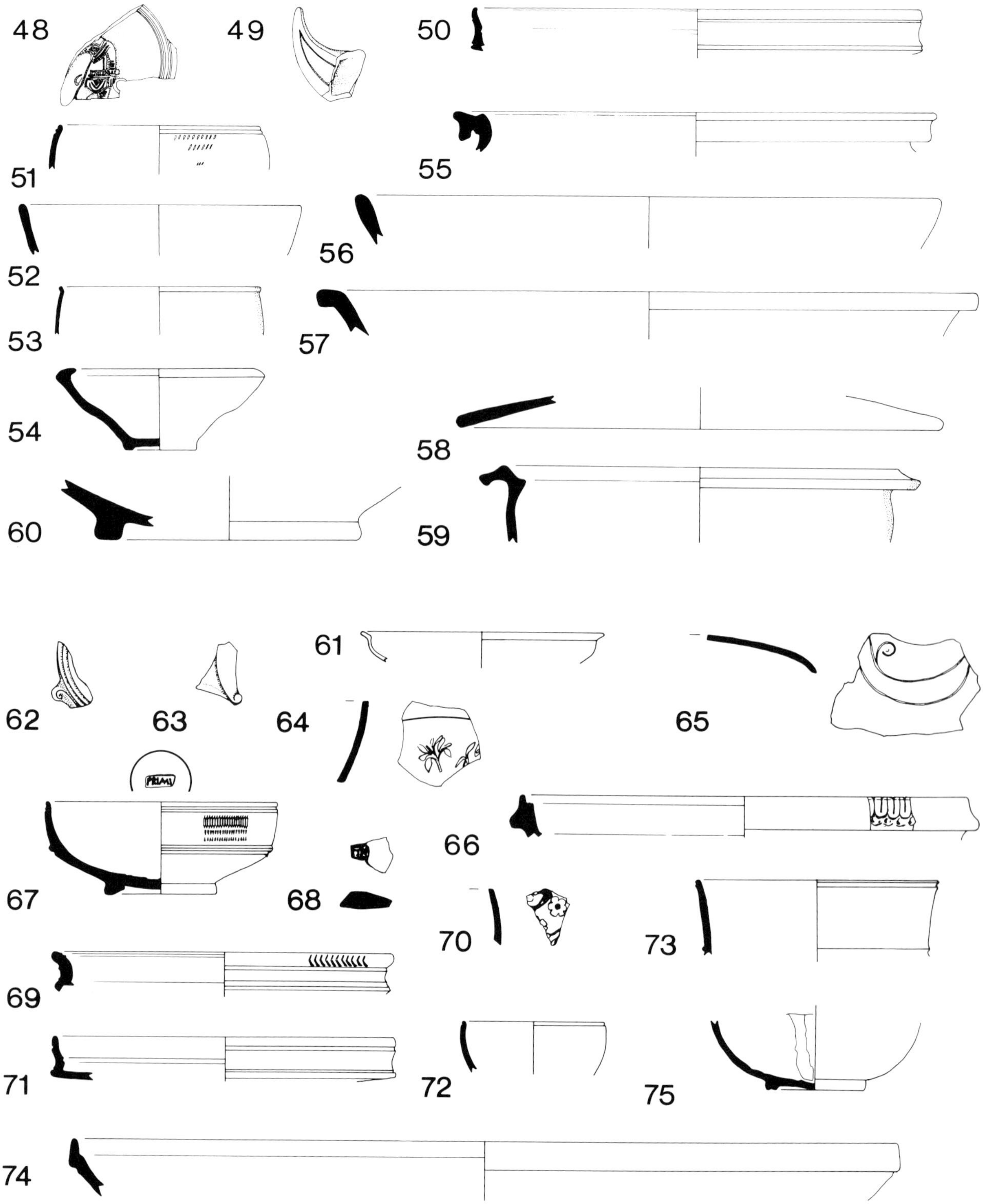

Fig. 4. Early Roman lens (**23**) (*c.*A.D. 15) between street levels 2 and 3, 48-60. Scale 1:3
Early Roman street level (**13**) (*c.*A.D. 15) 61-75. Scale 1:3

Italian Loeschcke Type I A, cf. Bailey, *Sabratha* 1994, fig. 36, 100 (form only), dated Augustan–Tiberian; a very different standing lone gladiator with filling hole at right hip, pl. 3.22, overall manufacture of lamp very similar to no. 48. Bailey, *BM* 1980, has no gladiator positioned or dressed like ours, although he designates other gladiators with oval shields as *myrmillones* (53-54). None of Deneauve's gladiators is good comparanda for this one (Deneauve [supra n.71] pl. 37, 313-14, 316; pl. 38, 317-23).

49) One horn of well-made crescent handle, very fine fabric, minute holes, 7.5YR 7/2 pinkish grey in break, mottled 2.5YR 5/8 slightly glossy good quality red slip, slightly worn over angles, some darkening from smoke.
Italian Broneer Type XXI, Bailey in *Sabratha* 1994, fig. 38.137-39; type dated late Augustan to well into 2nd c. A.D. (p.166). Deneauve shows examples with a double nozzle (Deneauve [supra n.71] pl. 56.544, 545, 551, 552 and 553; and pl. 59.569 with head of Diana at center of crescent handle).

Fine wares

Italian terra sigillata

50) Plate with concave vertical rim, very high gloss.
Conspectus Form 18, closest to 18.2.1, dated mid-Augustan to Tiberian. Same form as no. 71 in layer **13**. Hayes in *CMich* I 1976, Deposit XI, early 1st c. A.D., fig. 6.3, pp. 62-63.

51) Hemispherical thin-walled cup, with all-over rouletting on exterior.
Conspectus Form 38 hemispherical cup (the complete form should have ring-handles); the form is a N Italian production, dated Augustan to early Tiberian, but rouletted decoration pushes the date to the first two decades of the 1st c. A.D.

Proto-African Red Slip A

52) Hemispherical bowl.
Vegas, 'Karthago' 1994, fig. 3.42 and 44. In addition, a small flat-based bowl with flared wall and a shallow lid (42-48) (pp. 354-55), show that the ware is well established by the third quarter of the 1st c. A.D. Hayes in *CMich* I 1976, early ARS forms A47-59, especially A53 and A55, fig. 13, pp. 77 and 82, are the same form but with larger diameter; A55 occurs in Deposit IX.1, fig. 5, of the 1st c. A.D., p. 59. Hayes publishes corresponding bases, Deposit XIII, fig. 7.18, pp. 64-65, and esp. A58, fig. 13, pp. 82-83. Fulford in *Harbour* 1994, fig. 1.7.3, proto-ARS, among which '14/16', slipped on either the inside or the outside but not both, is among the earliest stratified forms.

Central Italian Republican thin-walled

53) Beaker, tiny flared rim, extremely thin walled (less than 2 mm).
Mayet 1975, earliest fabric group, with colour change from stacking (p.4). Hayes in *CMich* I 1976, fig. 5.9, Deposit X, early 1st c. A.D., Tiberian(?) (p.60).

Service and cooking wares

Local buff coarse ware

54) Small early Roman bowl.
Fulford in *Harbour* 1994, fig. 4.1.7.1-2, pp. 54-55, coarse ware bowl Form 7, in contexts of 1st and 2nd c. A.D.

55) Large Roman bowl or basin with everted hollow T-rim.
Form as nos. 42 in layer **15**, in local buff (orange) coarse ware and 125 in **11**, in Tyrrhenian coarse ware. For comparanda and date, see no. 42 above.

Pompeian red cooking ware

56) Baking dish with plain rim, normal Tyrrhenian ware (information from J. W. Hayes), much minute silver mica.
Hayes in *CMich* IV (1978) 34, fig. 4.27, rim diam. 34.0, Deposit XVIII.

Tyrrhenian soft brown cooking ware

57) Thick-walled brown coarse-ware baking dish, very even wet-smoothed surfaces, possibly originally red-slipped in floor. Not from Vesuvius area (information from J. W. Hayes).
Dyson, *Cosa* 1976, Class 11 large shallow pan with out-turned rim, granular brownish clay, 'probably imported to Cosa'; the type usually has interior glaze (p.91). Examples occurs at Cosa both in V-D (V-D14, to 60 B.C.), 67, and PD contexts (P-D20, P-D23, to 30 B.C.) (p.87).

Carthage/Nabeul blacktop cooking ware

58) Dish/lid with widely flared wall, no thickening at rim, completely reduced and overfired to maroon, change of gloss at rim indicates blacktop treatment.
Form as no. 122 in **11**. Hayes Form 196, *LRP* 1972. Hayes in *CMich* I 1976, in 'Early Roman cooking ware 1', Deposit XI, early 1st c. A.D., fig. 6.15 and pp. 62-63.

59) Wide-mouth cooking pot with dropped rim.
As form and fabric of nos. 100 in layer **12** and 124 in **11** with slightly modified rim. Hayes Form 198, *LRP* 1972; Hayes in *CMich* I 1976, Deposit XI, early 1st c. A.D., fig. 6.12 and pp. 62-63; Fulford in *Harbour* 1994, fig. 4.5.9.1-2, coarse ware Form 9, Fabric 2.3; the form does not appear in Punic contexts and therefore is early Roman (pp.60-61).

Amphora

North African small flat-based amphora as *Ostia* III.44-46(?)

60) Foot-ring base of closed form, slightly coarse fabric, vari-coloured (red, beige, dark grey) minute rounded fairly crowded quartz, some minute lime and holes; 5YR 7/6 reddish yellow at break and exterior, interior 7.5YR 8/4 peach (yellowish orange).
Note that Vegas, 'Karthago' 1994, context of third quarter of 1st c. A.D., shows a similar base with generic jugs, fig. 5.73, pp. 356 and 358.

13, *Decumanus* VI: third street level (*c.*A.D. 15)

150 sherds (59 rims), 2.825 kg. Fine wares 42 sherds, 400 g (14% by weight); amphora 17 sherds, 1.205 kg (43% by weight). Average of amphora 71 g, average of other 12 g.

Italian terra sigillata (3 pieces of stamped or moulded Italian Terra Sigillata from this layer seen by Kenrick are 'contemporary with Haltern'); proto-African Red Slip A hemispherical bowl; Carthage/Nabeul blacktop orange cooking ware Form 196 dish/lid, bifid rim pans; 12 fragments of Italian Loeschcke Type I or related lamps; shaft of bone pin.

Residual: Punic, less than 5% (miscellaneous black-glazed; rim of Tunisian Cintas 315 amphora).

Imported: 36% by weight, fine wares and amphora from Tyrrhenian Italy, Baetican Guadalquivir valley, N Syria.

Intrusive: tiny chip of grey (burnt) base of local Hayes Type I lamp, late 4th/early 5th.

Italian glass

61) Small thin-walled moulded bowl, everted rim, with double convex wall, preserved only to bottom of upper curve, opaque milky-green glass.
See discussion in text.

Italian lamps

62) Angular shoulder with two narrow ridges and projecting volute curl. Fabric has minute grey and white angular inclusions, some mica, 5YR 6/6 reddish yellow in break, worn matte 2.5YR 6/6 red matte slip, irregular thin splotch of slip on interior.
Loeschcke Type IA, Bailey in *Sabratha* 1994, fig. 37.98, Augustan/Tiberian; Vegas in *Karthago* 1991, fig. 39.23, in a horizon very similar to **13** (p.12).

63) Volute and bit of top of nozzle. Very fine fabric, some minute holes, 7.5YR 8/4 pink in break, 2.5YR 5/8 red mottled slip on exterior, a few spots on interior. Possibly Loeschcke Type I B, but more likely Broneer Type XXI; cf. Bailey in *Sabratha* 1994, fig. 38.141, from double-nozzle lamp, late Augustan to 2nd c. A.D.

Fine wares

North Syrian Eastern sigillata A

64) 'Megarian bowl' with vegetal spray in very light relief.
Hayes 1985, pl. IV.1-4, ESA Forms 24 and 25 (p.12). Moulded decoration in very light relief and 'impoverished' vegetal and figural motifs spaced at regular intervals appear on 'Megarian bowl' Forms 24 and 25 and occasionally on imitations of Arretine goblets; the type appears in the 1st c. B.C. and continued in the 1st and even into the 2nd c. A.D. (p.25).

65) Shoulder of jug with loosely hand-drawn *graffito*.
Hayes 1985, pl. IX.101 and 104, are jugs with wide shallow shoulders, dating from the 1st c. B.C. to 1st c. A.D.; although the only decoration which Hayes mentions (42-43) for this type is painted, he did not remark on this *graffito* decoration in 1996.

66) Bowl with very poor quality egg-and-dart moulded decoration at outer rim.
Hayes 1985, pl. 2.7, ESA Form 9, p. 18; egg and dart decoration is not common, dated to end of 1st c. B.C. (p.11). Hayes in *Sabratha* 1994, Form 9 plate in context of 10-1 B.C., fig. 25.14, p. 122.

Italian terra sigillata

67) Hemispherical cup with narrow corniced rim, rouletted band above narrow flange; two-thirds of the rim and the complete base survive.
Conspectus Form 33, closest to 33.1.1, dated late Augustan to Tiberian; possibly from Pisa or even Arezzo, since the distribution of this form is more common in the north than south of Italy (p.110).
Rectangular stamp in floor, PRIAMI, AM ligatured, no frame: Oxé-Comfort 1968, 1385, *CIL* 8.22645.294 a and b, no exact parallels for our stamp; examples of this potter are known from Sousse and Constantine as well as Nimes and Baden. New examples from the supplement (in progress) include North African sites Cherchel, Sale, Constantine and Sousse (information from P. Kenrick).

68) Base fragment, badly chipped, form unidentifiable.
Rectangular stamp,]TTICI, CI ligatured, 'Attici': Oxé-Comfort 1968, 207; *CIL* 8.22645.54a from Carthage but in *tabula ansata*. Provenance of new examples from the supplement include Volubilis, Sale, Banasa, Cherchel. and Lixus, Pozzuoli, Cordoba and Tarragona, Corinth, and Haltern; analysis of the Haltern example showed its fabric to be Pisan (information from P. Kenrick).

69) Chalice with moulded vertical rim of which the top round is finely rouletted, separated from relief decoration by a quarter-round.
Modiolus or chalice, cf. *Conspectus* Chalice Rim Form R6; the form suggests an Augustan to early Tiberian date. Similar to Puteolan fabric (information from J. Hayes).

70) Thin-walled sherd from relief-moulded cup or bowl, excellent gloss and workmanship, with all-over pattern of 6-lobed rosettes tied together by barbotine stems. One rosette is complete; its center is formed by a 6-lobed mini-rosette, almost invisible to the naked eye.
For form, cf. *Conspectus* relief-decorated rim R11.

71) Plate with concave vertical rim, elegantly articulated grooves. There are two additional uncatalogued examples of this form in the same layer.
Conspectus Form 18, closest to 18.2.1, mid-Augustan to end of Tiberian.

72) Simple hemispherical cup, tiny groove at top of rim on exterior, very pale dull pink fabric, good red gloss.
Conspectus Form 36 simple hemispherical cup, closest to 36.4.2, form possibly produced only in Padane workshops. Generally Tiberian, can be later.

73) Cylindrical cup (possibly but not certainly carinated) with plain vertical rim.
Conspectus Form 26 or 28, first half of 1st c. A.D.

Italian terra sigillata, Campanian fabric as Kenrick's 'Tripolitanian' sigillata

74) Platter with narrow hanging lip, horizontal knife-smoothing on interior of wall, red fabric, common minute mica, good gloss.
Conspectus Form 12, (the form is common in both Italian and provincial productions of terra sigillata), closest to Form 12.3.1, mid to late Augustan.
Cp. no. 88 in layer **12** (not illustrated), rim diam. 24.0. Hayes in *CMich* I 1976, fig. 13.A28 and A30, pp. 76 and 80; Kenrick, *Benghazi* 1985 fig. 53.403; Timby in *Sabratha* 1994, 82-84 and fig. 17.48; in all these cases, no. 74 has a much larger diameter; no. 88 is closer in size.

Service ware

Local buff coarse ware

75) Small closed jug, thin-walled, lower body and foot-ring only, elegant narrow foot-ring has groove cut neatly in bottom; 5YR 6/6 reddish yellow, interior surface 7.5YR 5/2 brown, exterior 2.5Y 8/2 white (cream yellow) slip, partly doubled, one vertical streak of slip on interior. Elegantly made, early Roman rather than Punic manufacture.
No comparanda.

12, *Decumanus* VI, fourth street level (*c*.A.D. 15)

159 sherds (55 rims) 4.340 kg. Fine wares 53 sherds, 490 g (11% by weight); amphora 33 sherds, 2.810 kg (65% by weight).

Average of amphora 85 g, average of other 12.5 g.

Fine wares in great variety: black-glazed Campana A, Italian terra sigillata (3 stamps, all rectangular), Spanish painted ware, N Syrian Eastern sigillata A, Ampuritan grey ware, local proto-African Red Slip A thin-walled beaker, central Italian thin-walled ware with extremely fine 4-line vertical combing, Pompeian red ware, Italian Tyrrhenian bifid rim pan, Carthage/Nabeul blacktop cooking ware Hayes Forms 196 dish/

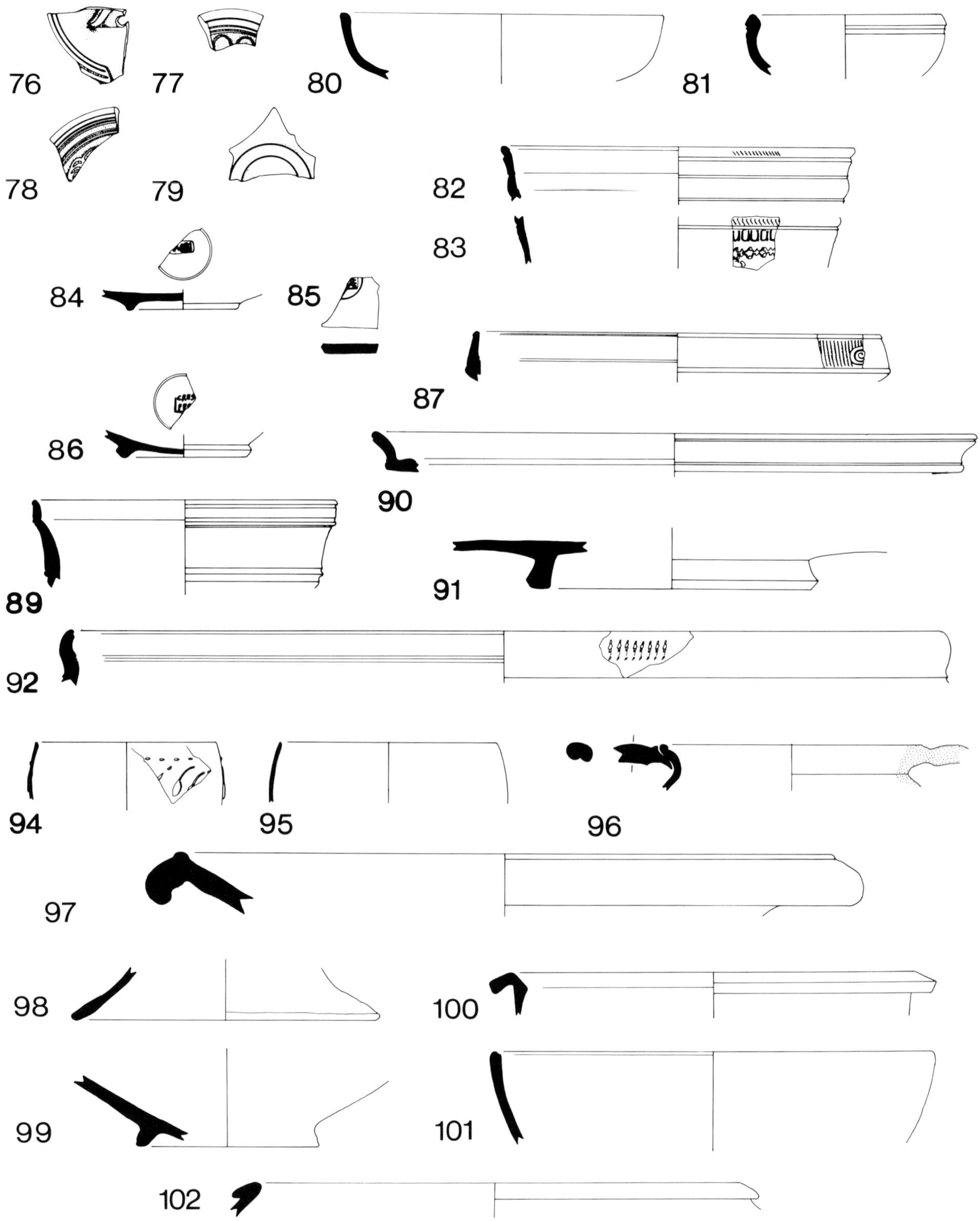

Fig. 5. Early Roman street level 4 (**12**) (*c*.A.D. 15) fine wares, service and cooking wares, 76-102. Scale 1:3

lid and 198 jar. Campanian Eumachius type amphora, Tunisian neo-Punic amphora, North African *Ostia* III.44-46. Three wall sherds of local thin-walled beaker with traces of pale blue pigment once stored in vessel.

Residual: 3% by weight, miscellaneous black-glazed.

Imported: 76% by weight, fine wares and amphora of Tyrrhenian Italy and Koan amphora.

Italian lamps

76) Narrow shoulder, 3-4 ridges, Loeschcke shoulder form I(?) or IIA, and one quarter of discus with half of channel nozzle, minute black grits, shell and holes, 7.5YR 7/4 pink in break, 7.5YR 4/2 brown matte slip survives only in grooves, front paws of animal standing on simple base-line in discus, filling-hole above ground line.
Loeschcke Type IA with channel nozzle, cf. Bailey in *Sabratha* 1994, fig. 37.90 and 103; channel nozzle indicates Augustan date (p.159).
For discus motif, cf. Bailey, *BM* 1980, Q821, fig. 86, p. 78, hound on ground-line with filling-hole under belly and above ground-line. While the mould is not the same as ours, Bailey notes many unpublished parallels from Benghazi and elsewhere in Loeschcke Type I.

77) Sharply angled wide shoulder with 2 wide outside and 2 narrow inside ridges, Loeschcke shoulder form IIa, with trace of rosette in discus. Fine fabric, minute grey and white inclusions, 10YR 8/3 very pale yellow in break, 10YR 6/3 pale brown (yellowish brown) worn thin matte slip.
Cp. Bailey, *BM* 1980, most like pl. 2, no. 367, for shape of shoulder and spacing of rosette petals, but without bisecting line down each petal of rosette. Italian proto-Loeschcke Type I, cf. Bailey in *Sabratha* 1994, fig. 36.81, Augustan date. Cp. Vegas in *Karthago* 1991, fig. 39.24, 196-197, in a horizon very similar to **13** and **12**, and Vegas, 'Karthago' 1994, fig. 8.105, 362-63.

78) Sharply angled wide shoulder with 6-7 narrow ridges, fine fabric, minute black grits, 10YR 7/3 very pale brown in break, mottled 5YR 5/8 yellowish red, nearly matte slip. Trace of low relief vegetal(?) decoration in discus.
Italian Loeschcke Type I A, Augustan/Tiberian. No good parallel in *Sabratha* 1994.

79) One-third of base with piece of steep wall, profiled base ring formed by two neatly-cut concentric grooves. Very fine, minute black grits and lamination lines, 10YR 7/3 very pale brown in break, 7.5YR 4/2 dark brown slightly mottled slip over exterior, matte thin splotch of slip on interior.
Italian Loeschcke Type I early variant, Augustan-Tiberian. Bailey, *Sabratha* 1994, 132.

Fine wares

Local(?) black-glazed

80) Low hemispherical bowl with slightly flared wall, flattened plain rim top, levigated fabric, all-over red-brown gloss, largely lost over upper exterior wall.
Cf. Vegas in *Karthago* 1991, pl. 36.52, same colour treatment on La22/28 in local black-glazed, dated 3rd/2nd c. B.C. The piece is probably residual.

Ampuritan grey ware

81) Small hemispherical bowl, plain thickened rim with clearly marked groove under rim, sturdily-made finely levigated fabric, occasional minute holes, reduced to grey.
Sanmartí 1984, fig. 130.12, Form 14, 394-95; although this bowl form first appears in the 2nd c. B.C., it is the most characteristic Augustan and early imperial form.

Italian terra sigillata

82) Articulated rim of large chalice with rouletting over top round, thin-walled fine fabric, high gloss.
Conspectus chalice Rim Form R7, most like 7.1.1, dated late Augustan and later.

83) Wall-sherd of relief-moulded chalice, thin-walled fine fabric, high gloss. Finely detailed small-scale egg-and-dart ovolo above continuous line of trefoil (ivy) leaves, above trace of freer vegetal motif. The fabric, fineness of detail, and wall thickness are exactly similar to the rim form above; they may belong to the same vessel.

84) Cup base, elegant gloss.
Conspectus cup Base Form B3, closest to B3.16, base diam. 5.5. This base is characteristic, among other forms, of Forms 33, 36 and 38 which are hemispherical cups (all occur in the Augustan/Tiberian layers of *decumanus* VI), but the interior floor of no. 84 does not curve before the break.
Rectangular stamp in floor, VMB(r)I(cius), VM ligatured, surrounded by single circular groove. The potter is Oxé-Comfort 2385. The fabric is possibly Arretine according to distribution of the stamp. Stamps of this potter are very widespread and very varied, with 144 new examples in the supplement. Previously found at Carthage, at Cherchel and Sabratha, in Italy, Spain, the south of France, Corinth, Haltern (therefore occurs by A.D. 9) and the Auerberg (information from P. Kenrick). Combination of hemispherical bowl form with rectangular stamp dates piece as late Augustan.

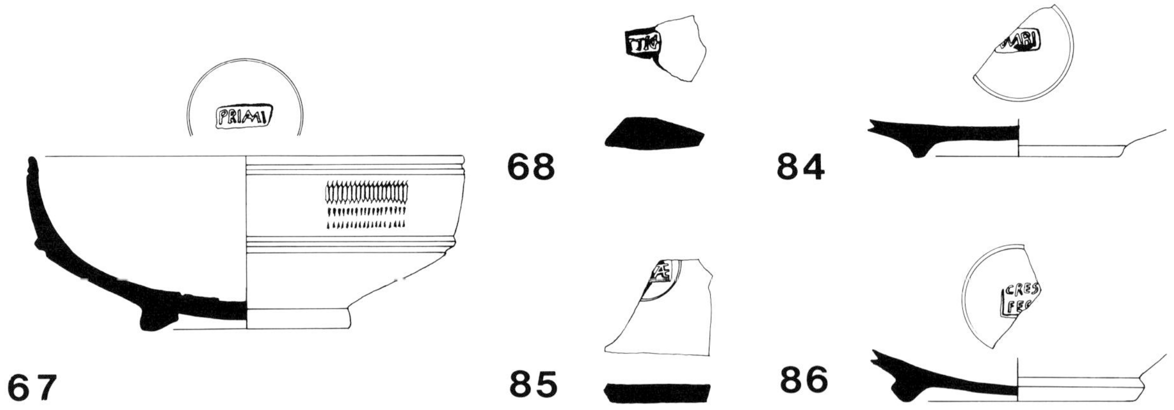

Fig.5b. Italian terra sigillata stamps from streets levels 3 (**13**) and 4 (**12**) (both *c*.A.D. 15), 67-68, 84-86. Scale 1:2.

85) Unidentifiable form, base sherd with rectangular stamp, perhaps the floor of a small plate, stamp]ATEI, 'Ateius', 4 letters form monogram (by far the most common potter's name in Italian terra sigillata, with far-flung production centers), stamp impressed just off-center inside small circular groove in center floor. "Probably Pisan" (information from P. Kenrick)

86) Low foot-ring base of unidentified cup form.
Conspectus Base Form B3, closest to B3.13, which is associated with a number of cup forms; of these, it is perhaps Form 36.4, hemispherical cup. The base illustrated as B3.13 occurs at Haltern; if Form 36.4, it is dated Tiberian and later. "Not Arretine" (information from P. Kenrick).
Two-line rectangular stamp, CRES· / FEC[; 'Crestus fecit'. This stamp is not in Oxé-Comfort 1968; there is one example in the supplement, from Ordona (information from P. Kenrick).

87) Plate with carinated vertical rim, fine vertical rouletting over upper zone, half of round of applied double spiral decoration.
Cp. *Conspectus* Forms 18-21, Form 21.2.1 for style. Estimated date late Augustan.

Italian terra sigillata, Campanian fabric as Kenrick's 'Tripolitanian' sigillata

88) (not drawn) Plate with narrow hanging lip, very soft fabric, with scratches and pitting.
As *Conspectus* Form 12, in Italian terra sigillata, closest to 12.2, form dated mid to late Augustan.
Same form as no.74 in **13**, above, but smaller; see comments under no. 74.

89) Bell-shaped cup with vertical overhanging lip, excellent red brown shiny gloss in interior, more matte on exterior.
A large-scale softened version of *Conspectus* Form 14 in Italian terra sigillata, closest to 14.2.3. Form dated mid to late Augustan.
Hayes in *CMich* 1 (1976) fig. 13.A39 and p.82.

90) Large simplified variant of plate with concave vertical rim and quarter-round moulding at angle of floor and inner wall, weak red gloss on exterior, good red-brown gloss on interior, knife-smoothing lines on outer wall.
As *Conspectus* Form 19 in Italian terra sigillata, closest to 19.2. Form dated late Augustan to Tiberian; it is rare at Haltern. A clearly related form without the quarter-round moulding is shown by Fulford in *Harbour* 1994, fig. 13.48; Kenrick, *Benghazi* 1985, fig. 53.409.1-2; cf. also Timby in *Sabratha* 1994, fig. 17.48, 'unclassified platter'.

Italian terra sigillata

91) Platter base on high angled foot, extremely fine hard fabric, fabric colour 10YR 6/6 light red, 10R 4/8 elegant thick gloss in floor, 10R 4/5 red on exterior, reserved at bottom and interior of base. Extremely narrow shallow double grooves in floor define an undecorated circular band *c*.2 cm wide over the foot. Stacking indicated by condition of floor over foot, which is slightly darker and pitted, with a few small rounded dark red stones (to 2 mm) still attached, which probably helped to separate stacked pieces.
Date probably Augustan.

92) Very large low platter with concave vertical rim, exterior top round has very fine rouletting, very well made.
Conspectus Form 18.3, form dated mid Augustan to mid Tiberian. "Possibly Pisan production" (information from J. Hayes).

Conspectus Form 18.3, form dated mid Augustan to mid Tiberian. "Possibly Pisan production" (information from J. Hayes).

Spanish painted ware

93) (not drawn). Small wall sherd of closed form jug, 2.5YR 6/4 reddish brown at break and interior, rounded small brown inclusions, very slightly micaceous fabric; on exterior, 2.5YR 4/4 shiny reddish brown paint in vertical runnels over a very smooth 5YR 7/3 pink slip.
Early Roman Spanish 'cerámica pintada', metallic red brown paint in vertical lines: Beltrán, *Guia* 1990, 161-69. Augustan to end of 1st c. A.D.

Italian thin-walled wares

94) Deep hemispherical drinking cup, very thin-walled (2 mm), plain rim, barbotine decoration, a row of applied dots above corresponding buds or leaves with stems curving up and to right. Central Italian thin-walled ware, coarse fabric, black grits and balls of hematite, matte dark brown slip starting to flake over exterior, red brown over rough surface on interior (not truly rough-cast).
Exactly as Moevs, *Cosa* 1973 (supra n.75), Form 42 (cup with two handles), pls. 21 and 67, nos. 209-10, and Form 36, Group B, especially nos. 222-26, pls. 22-24, pp. 133-34, with poor-quality brown glaze and floral decoration in barbotine. Augustan (p.180).
Vegas, 'Karthago' 1994, fig. 2.38-40, 352-53, with barbotine decoration; her fabric is evidently Baetican.

95) Wide hemispherical *poculum*, thin-walled, slightly profiled base. Italian Tyrrhenian thin-walled ware, very coarse fabric with small to medium angular volcanic black inclusions and rounded hematite, red brown matte slip over rough-cast finish inside and out.
A wall sherd of the same form and fabric, with all-over pinkish brown metallic glaze, also occurs in layer **12**; the base of a similar *poculum* with all-over pinkish grey metallic glaze occurs in **11.**
Ricci 1985, form 2/214 *poculum* with rough-cast finish and metallic glaze (Moevs 36/Mayet 35) pl. 37.297-305; immediately succeeded by the same with metallic glaze, Ricci Form 2/216 (Moevs 36/Mayet 37/Schindler-Kaudelka 115), Ricci 1985, 288-89.

Service and cooking wares

Carthage/Nabeul blacktop cooking ware

96) Most likely to be a wide mug, with one handle (rather than two as drawn); flared rim, semi-thin-walled, curved handle rises above rim. Note that a cooking ware is here used for a service form.
Vegas, 'Karthago' 1994, fig. 2.36, beaker with handle. Hayes in *CMich* I 1976, 65, fig. 7.17.

Local buff coarse ware

97) Wide shallow basin with rounded ridge marking inner edge of sharply dropped curved hooked rim, fairly coarse and dense, minute quartz and fairly common minute white lime, pimply wet-smoothed surfaces. Fabric colour is a sandwich of 10YR 7/3, very pale brown in core, surounded by narrow band of 2.5YR 6/6 light red, surface as core. Well made.
Hayes in *CMich* IV 1978 Deposit XVIII, mostly early 1st c. A.D., fig. 4.32, which has a large projecting handle on upper inner wall (p.33). Cf. Riley, *Benghazi* 1979, fig. 112.661, but with wide shallow ribbing on flange.

98) Deep lid with plain, very slightly thickened rim, fairly fine fabric.
Fulford in *Harbour* 1994, lid Form 6, esp. fig. 5.2.6.3, phase group 4.7 (p. 81).

Carthage/Nabeul blacktop orange cooking ware

99) Open dish/lid with applied base, 5YR 6/6 reddish yellow in break, exterior 7.5YR 7/4 pink, interior 5YR 6/4 light reddish brown, yellower than classic Carthage/Nabeul blacktop cooking ware, with common small angular white lime inclusions. Well made, surfaces neatly smoothed on wheel.
Hayes Form 196, see no 58 above.

100) Wide-mouth cooking pot with dropped rim, minute vari-coloured quartz, no lime, dull grey over exterior of rim, pale orange on interior.
As nos. 59 in layer **23**, and 124 in **11** with slightly modified rim. Hayes Form 198. For comparanda, see no. 59 above and no. 124 below.

Italian Tyrrhenian orange cooking ware

101) Fairly deep bread-baking pan with curved wall, plain rim with groove in rim top (bifid rim), coarse fabric with rare dark brown balls of hematite up to 2 mm across, wet-smoothed interior.

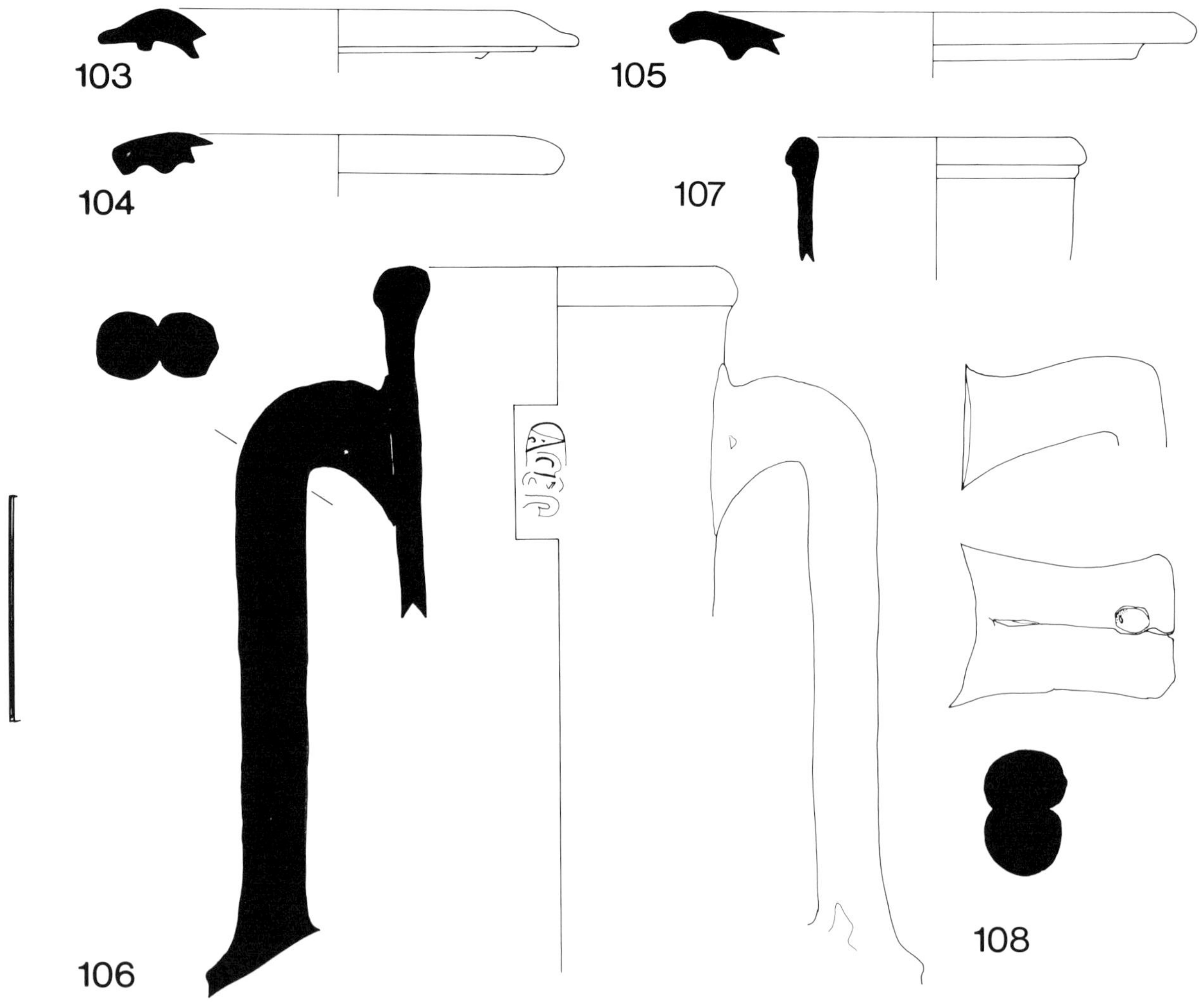

Fig. 6. Early Roman street level 4 (**12**) (*c.*A.D. 15) amphoras, 103-8. Scale 1:3

For a larger example of the same form in Carthage/Nabeul blacktop cooking ware, cf. no. 121 in layer **11**. The form was originally Italian, Dyson, *Cosa* 1976 (supra n.61), Class 1 flat-bottomed pans, 22-II-24/25 (p.119). It was widely exported. Hayes in *CMich* I 1976, Deposit X, early 1st c. A.D., Tiberian(?), fig. 5.12, and catalogue C18, fig. 15 and pp. 98-99; Riley, *Benghazi* 1979, fig. 100.446-50 and p. 248, in 'Campanian fabric' (no. 451 is in Tunisian fabric) in contexts of the early 1st c. B.C. to late 1st c. A.D.; at the Athenian Agora in a context of *c.*86 B.C., Thompson 1934, fig. 121.E145 (supra n.45).
Examples in Carthage/Nabeul blacktop cooking ware can be superficially identical: Hayes in *CMich* I 1976, 'Form G', 94, and Deposit XI, early 1st c. A.D., fig. 6.14, pp. 62-63. Fulford in *Harbour* 1994, fig. 4.7.1.1-6, dishes Form 1, examples 1.2 and 1.5 are in 'Campanian black sand fabric', the others in local Fabric 2.3 ('black surface ware'); examples in local fabric appear from mid 1st c. A.D., 60-63; Vegas, 'Karthago' 1994 fig. 3.52, in local fabric (pp.354-55).

Italian Tyrrhenian 'Porta Pia' coarse ware fabric

102) Jar with incurved bead rim.
Cp. no. 136 in layer **10** in same fabric. It is the most common coarse ware fabric in unpublished early Roman contexts at the Via Gabina Sites 11 and 10 on the via Praenestina. A few forms have been recently published and the ware, 'tempered with relatively large black volcanic grits and with lime fragments', is described and dated 1st to 3rd c. A.D. (Bird *et al.*, 1993 [supra n.60] 83).

Amphoras

Tunisian neo-Punic amphoras

103) Strongly flared and slightly dropped rim with sharply marked narrow ridge under rim, rim offset from neck. Coarse fabric, with fairly common minute exploded lime; 10R 5/6 red in core of break, salt-fired

2.5Y 8/2 white (cream yellow) outer surface affects colour well into break. Very nicely made.
Cp. Hayes in *CMich* I 1976 Deposit XIII, 1st c. A.D., Riley Type IIa, 109, catalogue E3, fig. 19 and p.112; also Deposit IX, mid 1st c. A.D.(?), fig. 5.13 and p.61; Vegas, 'Karthago' 1994, fig. 7.87 and p.360.

104) Strongly flared rim with wide rounded ridge under rim. Coarse sandy fabric, rare minute lime, dark inclusions and grog; 2.5YR 6/6 light red in break, variable mottled slip 10YR 8/2 white, thinning on inner side of rim top.
See comparanda for no. 105 below.

105) Strongly flared rim with sharply defined ridge on underside of rim. Coarse fabric, rounded quartz, minute dark inclusions and occasional red grog; 2.5YR 6/8 light red in core of fresh break, 2.5Y 8/2 white (cream yellow) salt-fired slip lightens colour into break, surface mottled to pink over rim top.
Hayes and Riley in *CMich* I 1976, Type IIa, catalogue E2, fig. 19 and p.112; Peacock in *Harbour* 1994, fig. 3.2.19 and 20 (19 dated 1st-2nd c. A.D.; 20 dated late 1st c. B.C./early 1st c. A.D.); Vegas, 'Karthago' 1994, fig. 7.87-88 and p.360; *Ostia* III 1973, no. 395, p.210, in a context dated 90 - 155/160 (most of the material is earlier).

Italian Tyrrhenian large Dressel 3 amphora, Panella and Fano Type 8

106) Four pieces, poorly defined large bead rim, neck, one set of true double-rolled handles, thick walled. Hard somewhat coarse fabric, minute white lime, some minute pale grey quartz, no mica, many minute holes; 2.5YR 6/6 light red, surfaces 5YR 7/4 pink.
Vertical stamp on neck, upper end rounded, lower end poorly impressed, 4.4 x 1.6 cm, ACEP, last 2 letters uncertain.
Panella and Fano 1977, Type 8, 154-55 and figs. 39-48; Fabric B, 147. This particular stamp (for which I can offer no obvious interpretation) and the placement of the vertical stamp on the neck have not been previously reported.

Campanian Dressel 4 amphora

107) Bead rim, thin-walled, smallish format. Break at rim shows it folded around hole. Coarse fabric with volcanic 'black sand', rare minute white lime and red grog, rare small to medium flat gold mica; 2.5YR 6/2 pale red in break, slip mottled 7.5YR 8/4-7/4 pink.
Panella and Fano 1977 Type 1, as Eumachius amphora, p.149, in Fabric A, fig. 1 and p. 145. Probable date 30 B.C. - *c*.A.D. 25+; common in First Amphora Wall (Freed 1996).

108) True double-rolled handles, flattened back of handles, large format, upper handle only. Hard coarse fabric with extremely crowded minute dark grey inclusions, minute white lime, small bits of iron oxide and minute mica; 2.5YR 5/4 reddish brown in break, surfaces 2.5Y 8/2 white slip.
Finger indentation on one roll of handle is typical of Eumachius-type amphoras in the collection of the Musée de Carthage. Type and date as no. 107 above.

11, *Decumanus* VI, fifth street level (*c*.A.D. 50)

83 sherds (39 rims), 1.555 kg. Fine wares 15 sherds, 110 g (7% by weight); amphora 10 sherds, 0.540 kg (35% by weight). Average of amphora 54 g; average of other 14 g (large sherds).

Italian terra sigillata, Ampuritan grey ware, metallic glaze sandcast thin-walled wide *poculum*. Proto-African Red Slip A thin-walled beaker, horizontal rim. Italian cooking pot, Carthage/Nabeul blacktop cooking ware Hayes Forms 196 thin-walled lid, Form 183 casserole, bifid rim pan, Form 194 casserole, Form 198 wide-mouthed cooking pot, Form 26 bread-baking pan, some Byzacena blacktop red cooking ware. Tarraconensian coastal Dressel 2, Tunisian neo-Punic amphoras. 4 early Roman lamps. Fragment of elegantly cut Chemtou revetment, 0.8 cm thick. Hard very smooth terracotta 'polishing tool', shaped like a Neolithic axe, 180 g.

Imported: 24% by weight, Tyrrhenian Italy, Tarraconensis.

Italian lamps

109) Angular shoulder with 2 fairly wide ridges around 4 narrow ridges, piece of outer discus with zone of fine radiating lines. Fine fabric, minute lamination lines and holes; 10YR 7/4 very pale brown in break, traces of matte 5YR 6/6 reddish yellow to 5YR 4/3 reddish brown slip.
Italian Loeschcke Type I, Bailey, *Sabratha* 1994, fig. 37.111, Augustan, or Broneer Type XXI, fig. 38.142, Claudian-Flavian. Cp. also Bailey 1980, Q926, Type B, group iii, pl. 17 and p. 175 (Loeschcke Type IV without handles), dated A.D. 40-90.

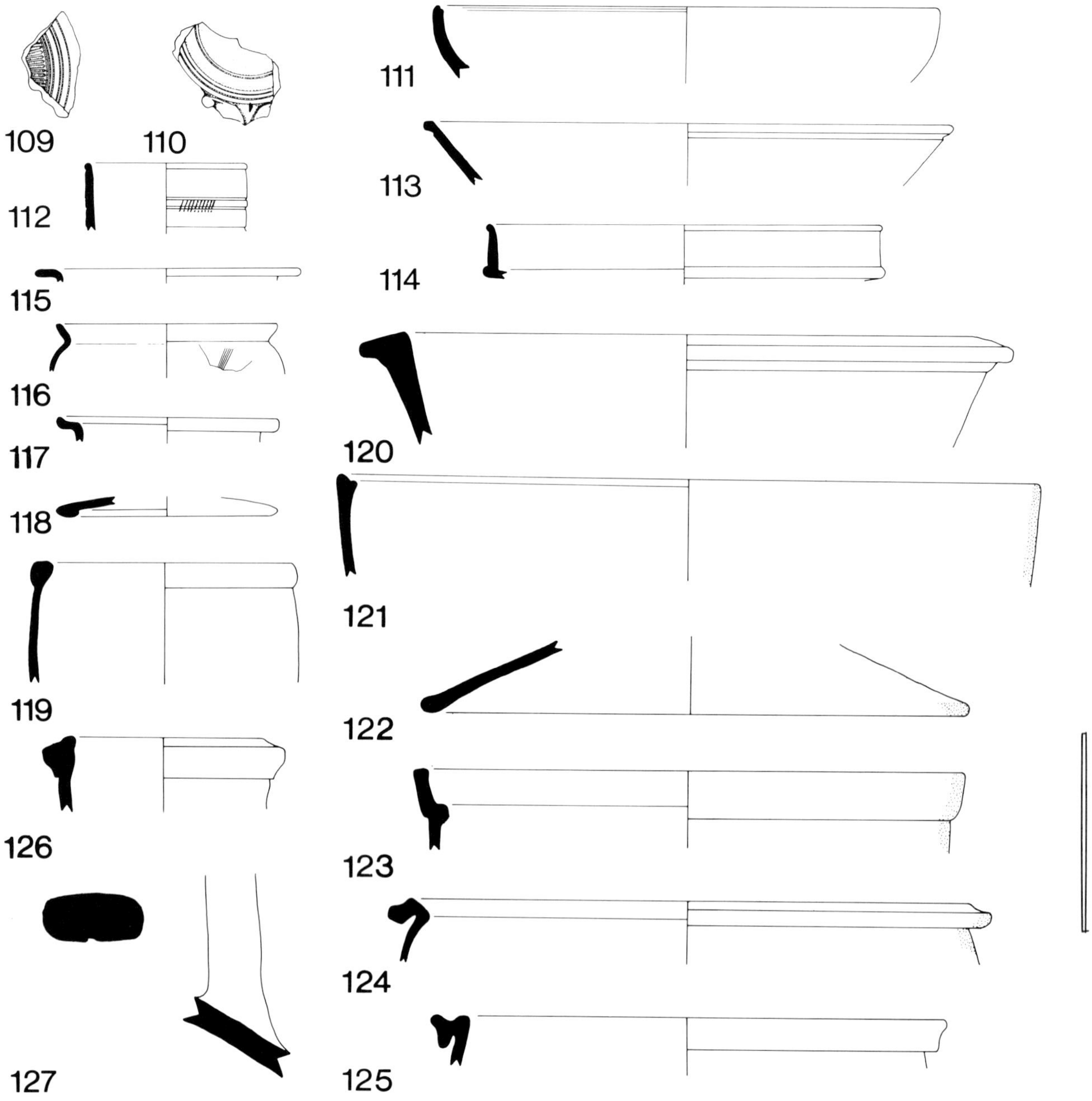

Fig. 7. Early Roman street level 5 (**11**) (*c.*A.D. 50) 109-27. Scale 1:3

110) Fairly wide shoulder with 3 fairly narrow ridges separated by wide hollow from 2 narrow ridges, partial volutes with small indentation which protrudes on interior marking center of join of nozzle to shoulder, bit of discus. Fine fabric, minute black and white grits; 10YR 8/3 very pale brown in break, 5YR 5/3 reddish brown doubled and darker in hollows and over discus, 5YR 6/6 yellowish red (warm brown) slightly glossy slip over interior.
Italian Loeschcke Type I B, shoulder IIIA, late Augustan to early Flavian, Bailey in *Sabratha* 1994. Deneauve 1969 (supra n.71) Type IV A, cf. 282-84 (pl. 35) and 291 (pl. 36).

Fine wares

Ampuritan grey ware

111) Hemispherical bowl, tiny groove in rim top. Highly levigated flour-like fabric, reduced to pale grey, matte slip slightly darker than fabric. Sturdily made but very worn.
No comparanda for form; fabric is 1st c. B.C./A.D. (cf. no. 81 above).

Italian terra sigillata

112) Carinated cylindrical cup with vertical rim, finely rouletted convex moulding at mid wall on exterior, plain interior wall, dull red brown levigated fabric, good red brown gloss.
Conspectus Form 26.2, form combined with decoration suggests *c.*A.D. 1-50.
Cp. pyxis base, Hayes in *CMich* I 1976, Deposit XI, early 1st c. A.D., fig. 6.4 (pp.62-63).

113) Dish with widely flared wall and flared bead rim, thin-walled. Careful knife-smoothing on interior, more roughly done on exterior.
Conspectus Form 3 (3.2/3.3) = Goudineau 43, appears before mid 1st c. A.D. but is most common in second half (*c.*A.D. 50-100).
Vegas, 'Karthago' 1994, fig. 1.1-4 and 6 (pp.350-51).

114) Plate with vertical rim, small offset at top and bottom of rim, probably had appliqué decoration. Dull red fabric, shiny all-over red brown gloss, some small chips on exterior.
An uncatalogued example of the same form in the same layer has a larger diameter (rim diam. 22.0) but lower vertical rim. *Conspectus* Form 20.4, the most common plate in the middle of the 1st c. A.D. Form dated A.D. 30-80+.
Vegas, 'Karthago' 1994, fig. 1.7 (pp. 350-51).

Local proto-African Red Slip A

115) Thin-walled beaker with horizontal rim, levigated fine fabric, glossy red orange slip.
Cp. Hayes mug Forms 131-140, especially Form 137 with horizontal rim, dated end 1st to mid 2nd c. and later, *LRP* 181. Vegas, 'Karthago' 1994, fig. 1.19, pp.350-51, similar form, thin-walled local product, but gloss is blackened on interior and over lower part of exterior.

Northern Tyrrhenian reduced thin-walled ware

116) Thin-walled mug with flared almond-shaped rim, very fine oblique 4-line vertical combing on wall, somewhat coarse very thin-walled (2 mm) fabric, minute white lime and black grits, fabric colour red brown, reduced grey brown surfaces.
Mayet Form XXIV for fabric, form and decoration, nos. 201-7, pl. XXVII and 58-59; it appears in Augustan contexts but is particularly common under Tiberius.
Vegas, 'Karthago' 1994, fig. 2.29-32, pp.352-53, identifies 3 or 4 examples as 'local'; Hayes in *CMich* I 1976, Deposit XIII, 1st c. A.D., fig. 7.16, pp.64-65, the same form with 3-line vertical combing; Fulford in *Harbour* 1994, fig. 1.4.4.

Service and cooking wares

Italian blacktop orange thin-walled ware

117) Thin-walled beaker or mug with hollow horizontal rim, Italian coarse ware superficially as Carthage/Nabeul blacktop cooking ware, red grog, dark grits, some holes, single layer matte dark exterior slip.
Cp. no. 96 in layer 12, in local ware. Vegas, 'Karthago' 1994, fig. 2.35, 352-53, the same thin-walled form but unslipped, with an ash grey surface. Hayes in *CMich* I 1976, Deposit XIII, 1st c. A.D., fig. 7.17, same fabric and form, with trace of handle at rim (pp.64-65). Fulford in *Harbour* 1994, small slipped thin-walled cup or beaker, fig. 1.7.4 and p. 18; also fig. 4.12, closed form 12, thin-walled, in Fabric 2.5 'cream sandy ware', with comparanda cited of second half 1st c. B.C./first half 1st c. A.D. at Sabratha.

Local buff coarse ware

118) Tiny lid with rim rounded under.
Hayes in *CMich* I 1976, Deposit XIII, 1st c. A.D., early Roman lid type 1, fig. 7.22, pp. 65-66 and 102; catalogue D9, fig. 17, pp. 104-5, with small hole in pinched vertical knob. Vegas, 'Karthago' 1994, fig. 6.83-85, pp.359-60, local buff coarse ware, rim diameters vary from 9.0 to 9.4 cm. Fulford in *Harbour* 1994, fig. 4.10.26.3 and p. 67, small lid Form 26, occurring in Fabrics 2.1, 'African red ware', and 2.5, 'cream sandy ware'; earliest context end 1st c. B.C./beginning 1st c. A.D.

119) Jar with vertical wall, folded rounded rim, pale buff fairly fine fabric, rare lime inclusions.
For the same form, probably in local fabric, but with much smaller rim diameter, cf. Vegas, 'Karthago' 1994, fig. 5.57 and 68 jugs (pp. 356-58); Fulford in *Harbour* 1994, fig. 4.12.31, pp.71-72, jug Form 31 in Fabric 2.5, 'cream sandy ware', evidently residual in 5th-c. context.

120) Deep basin with slightly depressed narrow squared rim, knife-cut and smoothed exterior, horizontal lines off straight. Fabric dense, with well-sorted sand, colour of inclusions unusually varied; 10YR 8/2 white (pale greenish grey) at break and surfaces, casual wet-smoothing.

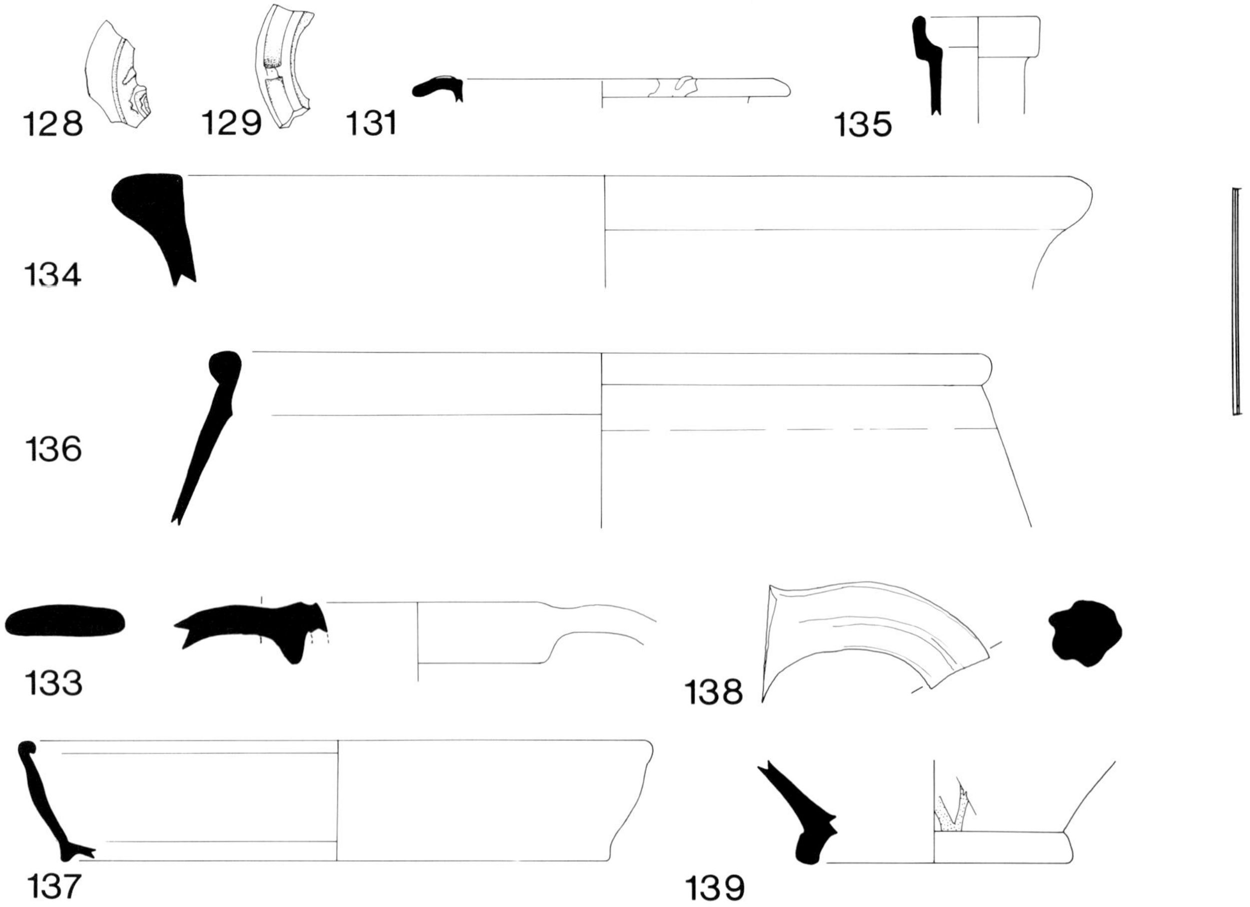

Fig. 8. Early-Roman street level 6 (**10**) (*c.*mid 2nd c. A.D.) 128-39. Scale 1:3

Vegas, 'Karthago' 1994, fig. 7.98, pp.360-61.

Carthage/Nabeul blacktop orange cooking ware

121) Deep bread-baking dish with bifid rim, inclusions of minute quartz, black grits, rare red grog, exterior uniformly grey.
For the same form, but smaller, in Italian Tyrrhenian fabric, and for comparanda for the form in both fabrics, see no. 101 in layer **12** above.

122) Dish/lid, inclusions of minute quartz and holes, grey over slightly thickened rim.
Hayes Form 196 as no. 58 in **12**. Vegas, 'Karthago' 1994, fig. 4.61-63, pp.356-67.

123) Casserole with vertical rim, lid ledge on interior wall, grey over exterior.
Hayes Form 194, as ware and form of no. 44 in layer **15** above.

124) Wide-mouthed cooking pot with soft rounded dropped rim, grey over round of rim and exterior wall, fabric has some black grits.
Hayes Form 198, cf. nos. 59 in layer **23** and 100 in layer **12**. Fulford in *Harbour* 1994, fig. 4.5.10.2, pp.60-61, coarse wares Form 10, Fabric 2.3, 'black surface ware', earliest context second half of 1st c. A.D.; Vegas, 'Karthago' 1994, fig. 5.58-60, pp.356 and 358.

Italian Tyrrhenian soft coarse ware

125) Wide-mouthed basin or cooking pot with everted T-rim, wide hollow in rim top and rim outer edge; fabric has black grits and lime, fabric colour soft red brown.
Form as nos. 42 in layer **15** and no. 55 in **23**, in local buff coarse ware; for comparanda for the form, see no. 42.

Amphoras

North African *Ostia* III.45 amphora

126) Beveled triangular rim, coarse fabric, sand-blown quartz and lime, weak red with reduced dark grey sur-

faces.
Vegas, 'Karthago' 1994, fig. 7.93, pp.360-61.

Coastal Tarraconensian Dressel 2 amphora

127) Shoulder and handle spring of fake double-rolled handles only. Crowded small white subangular quartz and small cream yellow inclusions, minute to small flat bronze mica; 2.5YR 6/8 light red at break and surfaces.
Tarraconensian Dressel 2 (Early Roman Amphora Type VI) is present in virtually all the 1st c. A.D. deposits published by Hayes and Riley in *CMich* I, 1976: cf. Deposit IX, fig. 5.15-16, p.61; Deposit XI, fig. 6.21, p.62, fig. 20.E12, etc.

Mid 2nd-c. street layer

10, *Decumanus* VI, sixth street level, first level above top of large drain D27 (*c.* mid 2nd c. A.D.)

104 sherds (29 rims) 3.130 kg. Fine wares 23 sherds, 150 g (5% by weight); amphora 35 sherds, 2.160 kg (69% by weight). Average of amphora 62 g, average of other 14 g.

Local African Red Slip A Forms 3B, 8A, 6, 9B, 2 closed forms; poor quality Italian terra sigillata, Carthage/Nabeul blacktop orange cooking ware elegant Form 23B bread-baking pan, Form 198 jar, Form 196 lid/bowl (6 examples), possible Form 23A pan, Form 195 lid/bowl. Campanian Pompeian Red ware and fragments of Italian Tyrrhenian jar in 'Porta Pia' coarse ware. Tunisian cylindrical amphora (1 kg), North African *Ostia* III.44-46 (700 g), Baetican Guadalquivir valley Dressel 20 (270 g), Campanian Dressel 2-4 (160 g). Two Italian lamps.

Residual: less than 1% overall: Punic Campana A and local black-glazed; early Roman Pompeian Red ware.

Imported: 18% by weight, Tyrrhenian Italy, Baetican Guadalquivir valley.

Italian lamps

128) Plain dropped shoulder and edge of discus with a little relief decoration. Fine fabric, minute angular grey and white inclusions, slightly micaceous; 5YR 7/3 pink in break, 5YR 6/6 reddish yellow to 3/2 reddish brown slightly shiny slip, worn off over shoulder.
Standard African and Italian Loeschcke Type VIII, Bailey in *Sabratha* 1994, figs. 41-42, pp.188-213. The form was first made in Central Italy by the last two decades of the 1st c. A.D. and then became the earliest form produced in Roman North Africa, continuing most of the 2nd c. A.D. (p.175).

129) Moulded flat beveled shoulder with small square raised lug. Slightly coarse fabric with minute black and white angular inclusions and holes; 10YR 7/3 very pale brown in break, matte 7.5YR 4/4 slightly worn dark brown slip.
North Italian *Firmalampen* ('factory lamps') of Loeschcke Type X, Bailey in *Sabratha* 1994, fig. 41, nos. 181-86, esp. 185, pp. 173-74, dated late Flavian and slightly later. Deneauve Type VIIC, nos. 878-98, pls. 80 and 81 (pp.188-91).

Fine wares

Italian terra sigillata

130) (not drawn). Wall sherd of large hemispherical cup, with very rough horizontal knife-smoothing over exterior wall, single deep groove in lower wall.
Later 1st into 2nd c. A.D.

Local African Red Slip A

131) Small shallow bowl with wide curved horizontal rim, bit of barbotine bud on rim top.
Hayes Form 3B, 2nd c. A.D.

Service and cooking wares

Local buff coarse ware

132) (not drawn) Jug with tall almond rim, strap handle projects from top of rim, piece not complete enough to draw, almond rim 2.7 cm tall, groove at top of rim.
Fulford in *Harbour* 1994, closed Form 3, esp. fig. 4.12.3.2 and 3.4, in Fabrics 2.2 and 2.5, earliest date attested second half of 1st c. A.D., common in contexts of early to mid 2nd c. A.D. (p.70). Tomber 1986, early Roman jug 2, 46 and 57, fig. 6.179, date 2nd c. A.D.

133) Jug rim and handle, unique form, plain rim with wide sharply-defined groove in rim top, deep vertical flange projects down around outside of neck, wide flat strap handle projects horizontally from top of rim/flange. Fabric shows well-sorted minute quartz grains; 2.5YR 8/2 white (yellowish cream) at break and surfaces, slight pink tinge in core.
No comparanda.

134) Wide deep basin, rounded bead rim, fairly thin wall. Very hard fine fabric, well-sorted minute buff sandy quartz inclusions; 10YR 8/2 pale brown in break, 2.5Y 8/2 white (pale buff) smoothed surfaces.
Hayes in *CMich* 1, Deposit XVI (from Rectangular harbor), fig. 11.13, 2nd-c. context with early Form 197 casserole (p.72).

135) Jug with wide vertical rim offset from neck.
Riley, *Benghazi* 1979, fig. 138.1133, with early- and mid-Roman jugs; he cites similar jugs in contexts of later 1st to 2nd c. A.D. at Ostia.
Vegas, 'Karthago' 1994, illustrates somewhat similar jugs with a more flared rim, fig. 5.65-66, pp.356 and 358.

Italian Tyrrhenian 'Porta Pia' coarse ware

136) Deep wide-mouthed coarse ware cooking pot with bead rim.
For the fabric, see no. 102 in layer **12**, above.

Italian Tyrrhenian? blacktop orange cooking ware

137) Bread-baking pan with small round at upper rim, slipped on interior and outer wall. While the finish is standard, the fabric seems to be Italian, with small black grits, angular quartz, superminute mica.
Hayes Form 23B; see discussion of form in the text; Italian Tyrrhenian manufacture of this particular form, which is characteristic of Carthage/Nabeul blacktop cooking ware, is entirely unexpected.

Amphoras

North African *Ostia* III.44-46 small flat-based amphora

138) Rolled handle with deep grooves, broken away from neck, fine fabric, minute subrounded white quartz and possible lime, occasional medium to large straw-holes; 5YR 5/6 yellowish red in break, thin 10YR 8/4 very pale brown slip over exterior.
See no. 139 below.

South Italian(?) *Ostia* III.44-46 small flat-based amphora

139) Ring base, flared wall, slightly micaceous fine fabric, rare minute black and white inclusions, rare hematite; 2.5YR 6/6 light red in break and inner surface, variably thick 10YR 8/4 very pale brown slip with two clear vertical streaks where slip has run doubled (characteristic of this form).
For nos. 138 and 139, see nos. 60 and 126 above, and discussion in text.

140) (not drawn). Baetican Guadalquivir valley Dressel 20 oil amphora, roll of handle from upper curve of handle only, round in cross-section, diameter of cross-section 5.0 cm. Fabric very hard and coarse, with white and pale grey minute rounded to subangular quartz inclusions, rare red-brown iron oxide. Fabric colour 7.5YR 8/6 reddish yellow (orange) in break, surface 8/4 pink.
Martin-Kilcher's diagram of cross-sections of handles suggests that ridges down the back of Dressel 20 handles are common in *c.*A.D. 50-150 (Martin-Kilcher, *Augst* 1987, fig. 32, p. 63), but handles which are round in cross-section are not unknown in this period. Ours is probably contemporary with the context, approx. second quarter of 2nd c. A.D.

Late Vandal/ Early Byzantine street levels

9, *Decumanus* VI, seventh street level (first half of 6th c. A.D.)

51 sherds (11 rims), 0.846 kg. Fine wares 9 sherds, 55 g (less than 7% by weight); amphora 22 sherds, 0.475 kg (56% by weight). Average of amphora 22 g, average of other 13 g.

Local African Red Slip D Hayes Forms 99A/B, 104A/B, British Carthage Closed Form 1, some residual African Red Slip A Forms 8A and 2. 'Late Roman Cooking Ware III', 'Late Roman Cooking Ware II', residual Carthage/Nabeul blacktop cooking ware 'classic' Hayes 196 and 197?, Pompeian Red ware. Tunisian Keay Type 26 *spatheion*, micaceous Aegean Anatolian Late Roman Amphora 3. No lamps. Grey mortar of type seen in Theodosian Wall.

Residual: Punic 8% by weight (local black-glazed, Greco-Italic amphora of *c.*300 B.C.); early Roman 15% by weight (African Red Slip A, classic Carthage/Nabeul blacktop cooking ware, Pompeian red ware, Adriatic amphora).

Imported: 23% by weight (mostly residual); contemporary imports from Italy(?) (hand-formed coarse ware) and Aegean Anatolia (Late Roman Amphora 3).

8, *Decumanus* VI, eighth and topmost street level (first half 6th c. A.D.)

50 sherds (11 rims), 0.700 kg. Fine wares 14 sherds, 80 g (11% by weight); amphora 17 sherds, 0.420 kg (60% by weight). Average of amphora 25 g, average of other 8 g.

Local African Red Slip D Hayes Forms 91 with grits in floor, 99B, 104A; African Red Slip A Hayes Form 9B. Carthage/Nabeul blacktop cooking ware 'classic', Hayes Forms 196, 197; 'Late Cooking Ware 1' lid knob. Amphora types are Tunisian cylindrical, North African *Ostia* III.44-46, and Tyrrhenian Dressel 2-4. Local lamp Hayes Type 2 (2 examples).

Residual: no Punic, 4% early Roman (Tyrrhenian Dressel 1-4).

Imported: 3% by weight, residual only.

7, Build-up over street layer 8 and lying against later wall 4 (after the first half 6th c. A.D.)

6 sherds (no rims), 0.175 kg (sherds and weight not counted in excavation totals). No fine wares; amphora 3 sherds, 0.120 kg (69% by weight). Average of amphora 40 g, average of other 18 g.

Local and non-local coarse wares, Southern Anatolian Late Roman Amphora 1, residual Campanian amphora with mortar.

Residual: Campanian amphora, 46% by weight.

Imported: residual as above, plus Late Roman Amphora 1, total 69% by weight.

Water supply in ancient Carthage

Andrew Wilson

The study of an ancient city's water supply presents a number of difficulties, and complete understanding is well-nigh impossible. There is often a lack of reliable topographical and chronological evidence that could establish connections between elements found in different parts of a city.[1] This is especially true of Carthage: the city's sheer size, coupled with the lack of precision and detail in early excavation reports, are two of the main problems; and although in recent years the UNESCO Save Carthage project has made great strides in understanding the city's history and topography (fig. 1), with it has come a realisation of the complexity of the stratigraphy and the fragility of earlier chronologies.[2] The picture is one of a highly complex process of urban development and change. It may therefore appear premature to attempt a survey of her water supply, but the effort seems necessary to correct some misconceptions which have in turn influenced wider views on aqueducts and the nature of Roman water supply. Study of the water supply of Carthage has been largely dominated by the monumental aqueduct from Zaghouan, and by the Antonine Baths, with the result that our view of this aqueduct's rôle within the total scheme of the city's water supply has been distorted. The rôle of the La Malga cisterns — the largest covered reservoirs in the Roman world — has been largely ignored, despite the evidence they provide for water storage on an unparalled scale before the construction of the Zaghouan aqueduct.

This article attempts to gather some of the more important data relating to Carthage's water supply — springs, wells, cisterns, aqueducts, and distribution network — in order to re-assess how it functioned. It does not pretend to be complete: reconstruction of infrastructure systems as complex as those of water supply is always hazardous where much of the ancient topography is unknown or lies under modern construction. Yet it is hoped that the study may provide a foundation for future research.

Punic Carthage

Punic Carthage had an important perennial spring (known as 'la fontaine aux mille amphores', from the large quantity of amphorae found inside it when it was excavated), situated on the shore by the hill of Bordj Djedid. It rises in a natural grotto, and was developed with a catchment chamber dug into the rock and walled with ashlar masonry, to which in Roman times was added a vaulted entry passage and monumental exterior façade.[3] Carton supposed that the spring would have attracted early settlement, and mentions evidence of early occupation on the shore in front of it — a layer of ash and cooking refuse, sealed by a layer containing Punic lamps.[4] Unfortunately no precise dating was given.

The German excavations on the seafront by the Avenue de la République showed that well-appointed residences of the 4th c. B.C. were originally supplied by wells, but that during the 3rd c. most if not all the houses underwent a radical change in their water supply. This involved the construction of underground cisterns with capacities of between 5.5 and 14.3 m^3, which

---

1 This paper has benefitted greatly from the comments of S. P. Ellis, F. Rakob, C. M. Wells and R. J. A. Wilson, to all of whom I am grateful for saving me from a number of mistakes. I am very grateful also to A. Ennabli, Conservateur en chef du site de Carthage, for his generous permission to study the cisterns and aqueduct at La Malga and to publish my interpretation of the site, as well as for all the assistance he gave me during my visit in October 1997. All opinions expressed in this article, and any remaining errors, are my own.

2 Humphrey 1980.

3 Carton 1919, 312-14; Carton 1920; Carton 1935, 76-80.

4 Carton 1920, 262, 264.

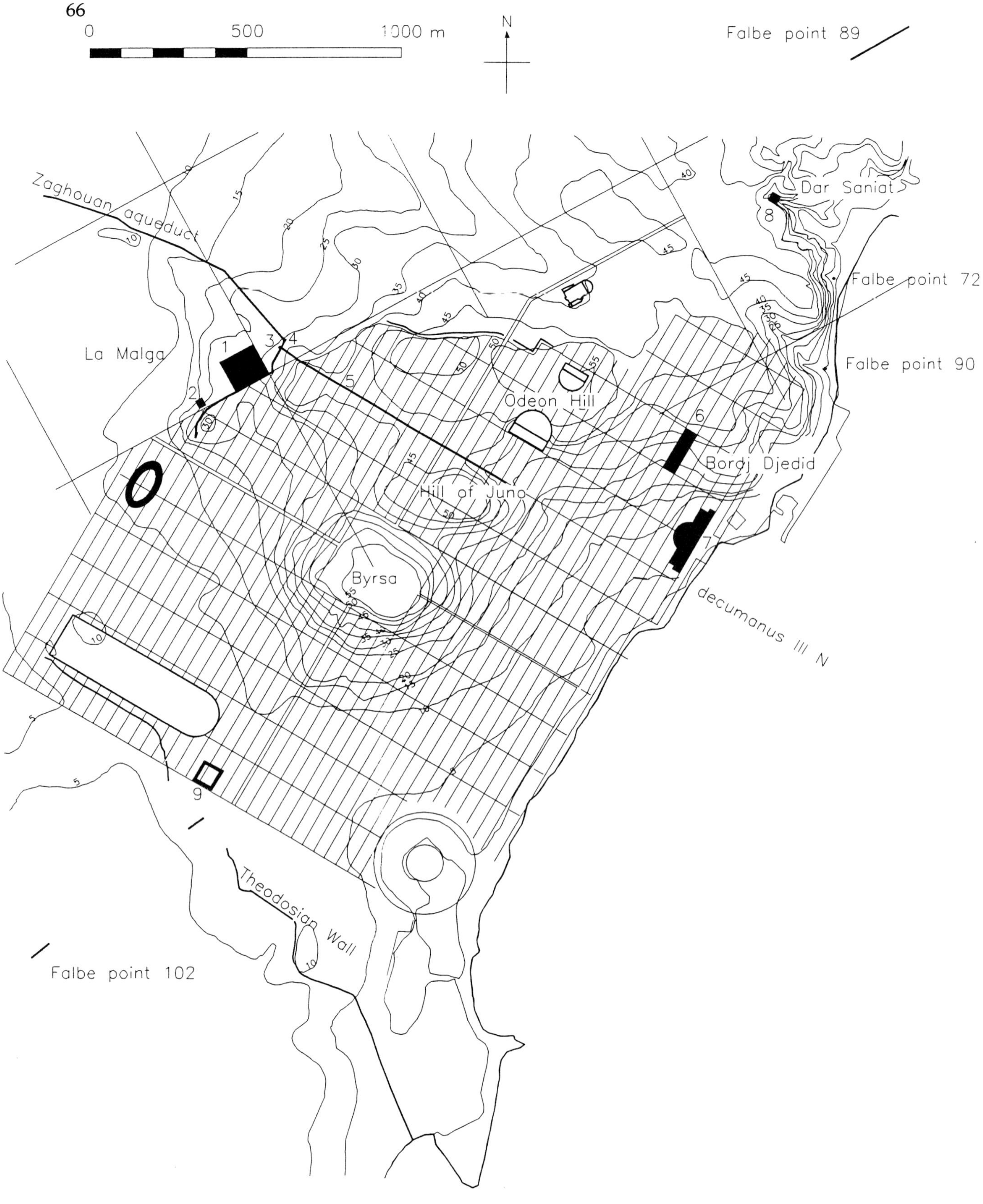

Fig. 1. Plan of Roman Carthage showing the main known elements of the water-supply infrastructure. 1. Large La Malga cisterns. 2. Small La Malga cisterns. 3. *Castellum* excavated by Vernaz. 4. *Castellum* excavated by Ellis. 5. Aqueduct branch traced by Vernaz under *decumanus* III N. 6. Bordj Djedid cisterns. 7. Antonine Baths. 8. Dar Saniat cisterns. 9. Turris Aquaria.

collected rain run-off from roofs and courtyards by means of terracotta downspouts.[5] The cisterns were of the classic Punic 'cigar-shaped' type, long and narrow with rounded ends.[6] Their narrowness results from the use of slabs for roofing, either laid flat or pitched in pairs against each other; the narrowness was compensated for by considerable depth. The insertion of such cisterns in the houses found in the German excavations must have caused considerable domestic upheaval and expense, necessitating the removal of floors, the excavation of many cubic metres of spoil, partial demolition of external walls to allow introduction of large cover slabs, and the subsequent raising of floor levels. The wells formerly in use were converted to soak drains to receive overflow from the cisterns.[7]

Ordinarily water from wells is preferable to water from cisterns, and at Carthage the water-table lies close to the surface and is of good quality, even close to the sea.[8] The change to cisterns is not, therefore, to be explained simply by the inhabitants taking advantage of new waterproofing technologies to reduce dependence on a poor water-table; rather, the disruption involved suggests that the change was a necessary response to changing conditions in water supply and population growth that rendered the wells insufficient. Possible explanations include a lowering of the water-table because of declining rainfall or through increasing abstraction by a growing population, or even because of contamination of the water-table by sewage and effluent, or a combination of several of these factors. On present evidence it is impossible to choose between these explanations, but as there is no firm evidence for increasing aridification in the climate of N Tunisia in the 3rd c. B.C. it would seem that the change from wells to cisterns occurred as a result of increasing human pressure on the hydrogeological environment.

Cigar-shaped cisterns are also found on the south slopes of the Byrsa, again supplied from roofs or courtyards by terracotta, or in some cases lead, pipes.[9] Here dimensions range from 2.90 to 5.20 m long by 0.90 to 1.25 m wide, with depths of 2.70-4.60 m.[10] But while they are similar to the cisterns by the seafront, they are dated several decades later, and are apparently contemporary with the first occupation phases on this site, settled as the city expanded in the first half of the 2nd c. B.C. As drainage in this area was led into soak pits, it is unsurprising that here too cisterns were preferred to groundwater utilisation,[11] although two Punic wells, of square cross-section, have also been found on the Byrsa (their date of construction is unknown).[12]

Besides the cigar-shaped cisterns, cisterns shaped like an upright carafe or bottle are occasionally found in Punic contexts. From Carthage two examples are known from the Byrsa and a third from a Punic house at Dar Saniat, all sealed by the destruction layer of 146 B.C.[13] Another carafe-shaped cistern (of unknown date) has been discovered by the Canadian excavations; the house above it (not necessarily contemporary with the cistern's construction) was destroyed in the 6th c. A.D.[14] These cisterns were made by digging a shaft down until reaching rock sufficiently firm to bear the weight of the ground above as the chamber is widened out to create a reasonable storage volume. Essentially the same technique is employed on a larger scale in the Punic quarries of El Haouaria on Cap Bon.[15] This relatively simple technique became common in

---

5 Rakob 1979a, 24; Stanzl 1991, 213.

6 On Punic cisterns generally, see Cintas, P. 1976, 134-35.

7 Rakob 1979a, 24.

8 F. Rakob, pers. comm.

9 Lancel 1995, 169-71; Thuillier 1982, 82-83.

10 Carrie and Sanviti 1979, 124 and n. 34.

11 Lancel and Morel 1992, 47.

12 Saumagne 1982, 300-1.

13 Lancel 1979, 77; Lancel 1982, 371 fig. 604; Renault, J. 1912a, 363. See also Vann 1981, 30-31.

14 The cistern is *c.*7 m deep, and lies on the S side of *decumanus* VI between *cardo* II and *cardo* III (C. M. Wells, pers. comm.).

15 I owe this point to R. J. A. Wilson.

the Greek world from the 4th c. B.C. (e.g., Athens,[16] Olynthos,[17] and Morgantina[18]) and its occurrence at Carthage probably reflects cultural contacts with Sicily and Magna Graecia (as also do the Hellenistic bathtubs and bathroom fittings at Punic Kerkouane[19]). Carafe-shaped cisterns were also used in the Roman world, but their distribution in North Africa (central and southern Tunisia along the coast and in the Tell, Tripolitania, and a few outlying examples in Syrtica and N Algeria[20]) correlates in large part with the zone of former Punic influence, suggesting a technological continuity between the Punic and Roman periods.

In addition to the evidence for cisterns and wells, there is tantalising evidence which may suggest a Punic aqueduct pipeline at Carthage. There are 8 terracotta pipes each bearing Punic graffiti interpreted as the word 'conduit' followed by a numeral. Unfortunately their findspot and context are not recorded.[21] A parallel is the Punic pipeline reported from Nora (Sardinia).[22] Although almost nothing is known about Punic aqueducts, contemporary Hellenistic cities had pipelines; given the other Hellenistic influences on Punic hydraulic technology, there would be nothing inherently improbable in a Punic aqueduct at Carthage. It could be further evidence that a growing urban population was requiring more water than local sources could provide. However, if such an aqueduct did exist, it did not serve any of the numerous private houses that have been excavated to date. Perhaps it served only public fountains, as in the Hellenistic world, though no examples of Punic fountains are known; alternatively the pipes may not have belonged to an aqueduct but have come from a localised rainwater catchment or drainage system.

Private and public cisterns in Roman Carthage

A prime concern of the builders of the Roman colony of Carthage appears to have been the discovery and re-use of Punic cisterns. In the area uncovered by the German excavators near the shore, walls and other traces of Punic constructions were systematically razed during the new building work of the Claudian period but the cisterns were put back into service wherever possible.[23] Similar re-use appears to have occurred at other sites within Carthage; the double cistern beneath the House with the mosaic of the Greek Charioteers is clearly two Punic cisterns joined together in the Punic period and re-used in the 1st c. A.D. with the addition of a vaulted roof.[24] Saumagne (1982, 301) refers to the re-use of a Punic cistern on the Byrsa.

New cisterns were also constructed, usually rectangular and barrel-vaulted, a technological advance enabling the creation of larger cisterns (one at Dermech [Michigan excavations] had a capacity of 75 m^3). The same techniques also facilitated the construction of large public cisterns. A great number of cisterns are visible among the houses on the Odeon hill and at Dermech, and it is clear that at Roman Carthage, as in many other North African cities, domestic cisterns formed a major part of the water-supply strategy;[25] as in the Punic period, rain run-off was preferred to groundwater.

16 H. A. Thompson *apud* Stillwell 1933, 126-29.

17 Robinson 1930, 56, 72, 100, 110; Robinson 1946, 118, 287-88 and pl. 101; Robinson and Graham 1938, 307-9 and pl. 76.1.

18 Stillwell and Sjöqvist 1957, 157.

19 For Punic bathrooms at Kerkouane see M. Fantar, *Kerkouane, cité punique de Cap Bon (Tunisie)* II (Tunis 1985) 305-58, 363-89.

20 Tunisia: Blanchet 1897; Maumené 1897; Carton 1903a; Carton 1903b, 141; Montalier 1903, 62-3; Gendre 1907; Ben Lazreg and Mattingly 1992; Slim 1990, 193-97. Syrtica: Reddé 1985, 178; Reddé 1988, 74. Algeria: Gsell 1911, f.12, 42 (near Cartennae); f.16, 357 (SW of Sitifis).

21 Berger 1911.

22 Patroni 1904, pl. VI point K; cf. Cintas, P. 1976, 136-37.

23 Rakob 1979a, 27; cf. Vann 1981, 37.

24 Vann 1981, 6-10.

25 Vann 1981.

In Carthage, as elsewhere, the large paved areas of public spaces and entertainment buildings were sometimes used as *impluvia* for cisterns. On the Byrsa hill, too high to be fed by either of the aqueducts discussed below, run-off from a portico, temple courtyard and perhaps also parts of the library was collected in a large channel lined with *opus signinum* (and therefore not a drain) and conveyed probably to a large cistern under the courtyard of the temple in the centre of the complex.[26] Comparable arrangements for the collection and storage of run-off from public spaces existed at Bararus (the forum), Thugga (Temple of Saturn and the public building known as Dar el-Acheb), and Sabratha (Temple portico and courtyard in the South Forum), as well as in the forum at Pompeii.[27] Such water could hardly have been used as drinking water, but it could have served other purposes. The use of different qualities of water for different purposes was commonplace in the ancient world.[28]

Although in some towns, such as Bararus and Thugga,[29] run-off from the orchestras and *caveae* of theatres supplied cisterns, there is no certain evidence for this at Carthage. The odeon had two cisterns (7 m deep) under its stage, but they probably collected water from the roof of the stage building rather than the orchestra.[30] The theatre possessed two small cisterns (each 2.5 x 3.1 m, but of unknown depth) under the stage but there is no information on how they were supplied.[31] It is unlikely that they were involved in flooding the orchestra for aquatic spectacles: they are too small and set too low, and, if Ros is right to argue that they were disused by the time the stage was paved in marble, they had fallen out of use before such aquatic events became popular. Nevertheless, Augustine, in a sermon preached in Carthage, does refer to such a show to be held on the following day: *cras illi habent, ut audivimus, mare in theatro; nos habeamus portum in Christo*. 'Tomorrow they will have, so we have heard, a sea in the theatre; let us have our haven in Christ.' (*Enarr. in Ps.* 80.23). Archaeological evidence for the provision of such spectacles in either the theatre or the odeon, however, is lacking.

Two large sets of cisterns existed on Bordj Djedid hill (distinct from the much larger Bordj Djedid cisterns feeding the Antonine Baths, discussed below).[32] One set was 13.40 m deep, the other 14.13 m deep; in both there were 12 chambers nearly 4 m square and communicating through narrow arches at the base (fig. 2). The proportions are unusual (leading Carton to the curious conclusion that they were Punic) but probably to be explained by the need for sufficient cross-bracing of the external walls to resist the pressure of the surrounding earth when water levels were low. Capacities would have been 2340 and 2160 m^3 for each group respectively, assuming water depths of 13 and 12 m. Their source of supply is unknown; Carton assumed that they were fed by local run-off, which could be the case — the hill was artificially terraced for either a temple or the barracks of the First Urban Cohort[33] and the terrace could have provided an *impluvium*. Carton notes that the surface of the hill lies at the 35-36 m contour;[34] even assuming a water level in the cisterns a few metres below that, there could hardly have

26 For the channel and monumental complex see Deneauve 1977, 62-64 and 61 fig. 7; for the cistern, Deneauve 1990, 152 fig. 10 no. 8 and p. 153. *Opus signinum*: personal observation.

27 Bararus: Hallier 1987; Thugga: Carton 1896, 561-63; Sabratha: personal observation. Pompeii: Eschebach 1979, 74.

28 Aristotle (*Pol.* 1330b): 'In sensible states, if the supply is not of equal quality and there is not an abundance of these kinds of running waters, it is necessary to separate the water for drinking from that for other uses.'

29 Lachaux 1979, 41; Carton 1896, 563. The theatre at Delos provides a non-African example: Homolle 1894, 166.

30 Gauckler 1902, 387-99; C. M. Wells, pers. comm.

31 Ros 1996, 471.

32 Carton 1912.

33 Gauckler 1904. For the suggestion of a temple, see Temple 1835, 107.

34 Carton 1912, 564.

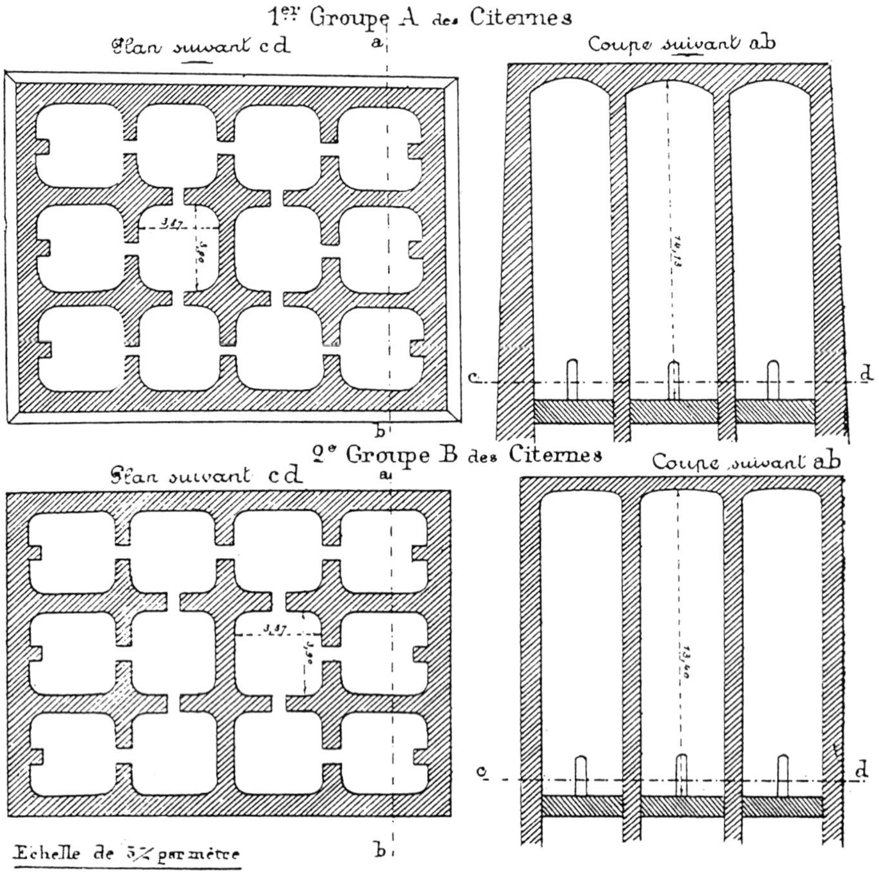

Fig. 2. Plan and sections of the smaller sets of cisterns at Bordj Djedid (Carton 1912, 562).

been sufficient gradient to supply them from the channel of the Zaghouan aqueduct near La Malga, where the aqueduct conduit is at *c*.27 m asl (fig. 1).

The cisterns of Dar Saniat

A curious set of large cisterns was excavated early this century at Dar Saniat in the northern suburbs (near the modern Hotel Amilcar), and published in an unusually full but strangely neglected series of articles by J. Renault (fig. 1 no. 8).[35] The cisterns were fed by an aqueduct whose course was traced for 30 m; further remains of an aqueduct were found upslope on the other side of a ravine. The cistern complex falls into two parts with different functions (fig. 3): a group of three settling tanks each 4.33 m deep, and two storage reservoirs each with two chambers. Total storage capacity (excluding the settling tanks) was 2780 m^3. Water from the aqueduct entered the first settling tank, oblong with rounded ends; the overflow went partly into the first of the two reservoirs and partly into the second (circular) settling tank (fig. 4). This communicates with the third settling tank through a lead pipe placed half-way up; an overflow at the top of the third tank fed the second two-chamber reservoir. Water entering the second reservoir had therefore gone through a second settling process and was of higher quality than water in the first reservoir. At the SE end of the complex there projected a circular chamber, roofed with vaulting tubes and accessible from the outside by a spiral stair of 16 steps. This was the tap control chamber, traversed by 3 lead pipes, long since robbed (fig. 5). One pipe left each of the two reservoirs at floor level; a third left the second reservoir about 1 m above the floor and carried a third grade of water, free of any sediment that had managed to enter the second reservoir. These three pipes were presumably provided with stopcocks in the tap room, from which they departed in a tunnel, two set into the floor, the third in a groove in the ceiling

35 Renault, J. 1912a; 1912b; 1912c; 1913b; cf. id. 1911; id. 1913a.

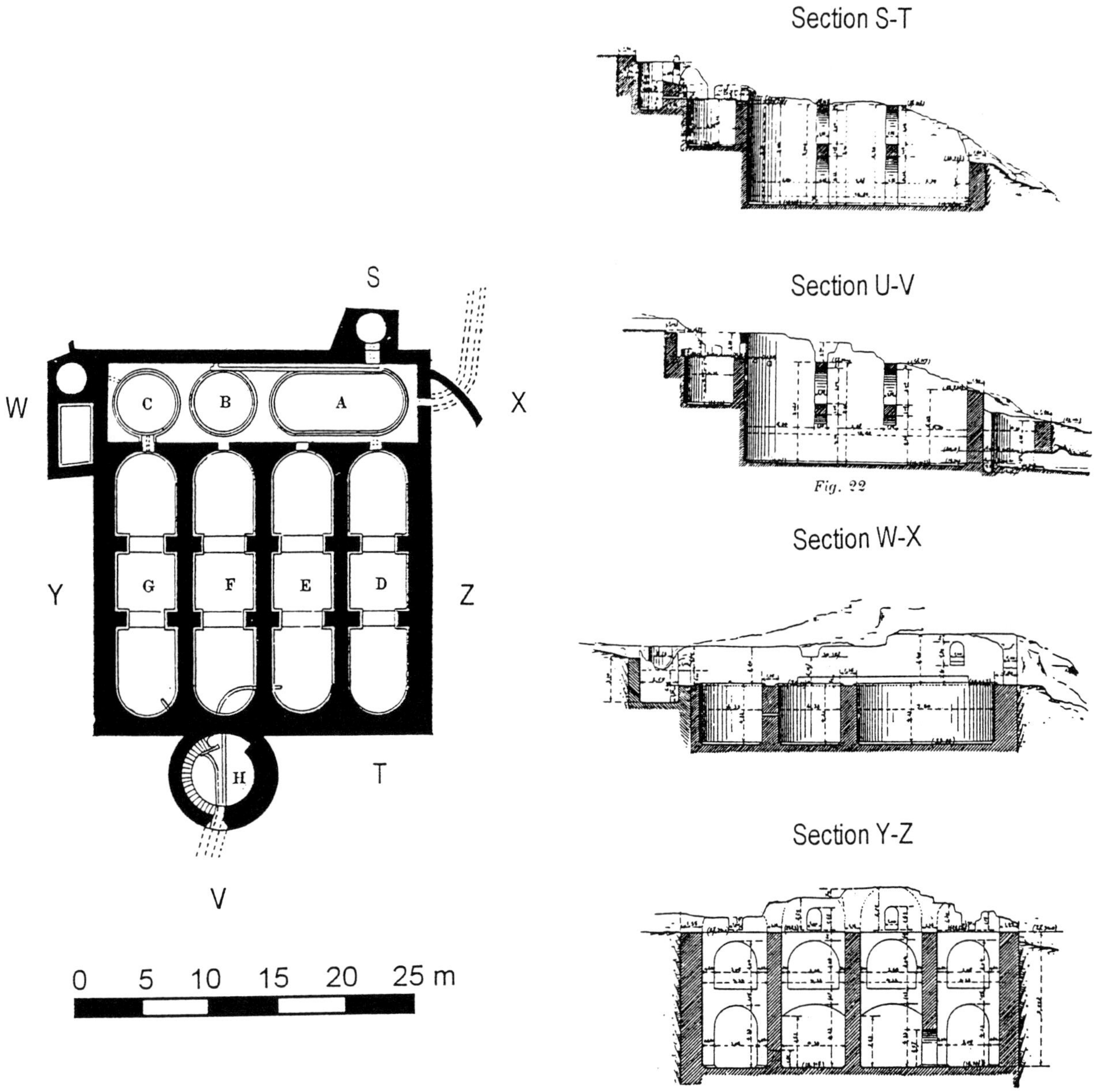

Fig. 3. Plan and sections of the cisterns at Dar Saniat (after Cagnat and Chapot 1916, vol. 1, 89 fig. 43 and Renault 1912b). A= primary settling tank; B and C = secondary settling tanks; D and E = reservoir of lower quality water; F and G = higher quality reservoir; H = tap chamber.

(fig. 6). The different pipes carrying the different grades of water must have supplied different structures, with a distinction probably between water for drinking, for washing and bathing, and for gardens, pools and fountains. The walls of the tap room were covered in graffiti, which Renault interpreted as the scribblings of prisoners incarcerated there (for which there is no direct evidence); they could equally have been the jottings of bored waterworks staff.[36]

The cisterns and settling tanks were vaulted over, and lit and aerated by holes in the vaults covered with stone lattice grilles to allow the entry of rainwater falling on the extrados of the vaults but not of foreign bodies.[37] Windows into the reservoirs from the area of the settling tanks allowed inspection of the water level. Surveillance galleries of a slightly different nat-

36 Renault, J. 1912b, 475-85.
37 Renault, J. 1912b, 488-89.

Fig. 4. The settling tanks of the Dar Saniat cisterns (*Excavations at Carthage .. University of Michigan* II pl. 18).

Fig. 5 (left). Engraving of the tap control room of the Dar Saniat cisterns, showing the 3 pipes coming from the reservoirs, and graffiti on the wall above them. The base of the spiral access stair is visible on the left (Renault 1912b, 484 fig. 29).
Fig. 6 (right). Dar Saniat cisterns: exit tunnel from the tap room, with grooves for two pipes in the floor and one in the roof (Renault 1912b, 482 fig. 26).

ure but serving the same function are known from cisterns at Hippo Regius, Cirta (Constantine), and Stora (all in Algeria) (where they are carried on the tops of dividing walls) and at Bordj Djedid (fig. 11 below), Uthina, and Thuburbo Maius (where they run around the perimeter of the reservoirs).[38] Tap control rooms are also found in the Bordj Djedid cisterns and at Hippo Regius, Rusicade, Stora and Sicca Veneria (El Kef).[39]

At some point it became necessary to supplement the aqueduct's supply (whether owing to falling levels of groundwater or increased demand is unclear) by constructing an impluvium surface uphill (west) of the cisterns, from which water was led by two circular shafts into the settling tanks. Later still, in the late 4th or early 5th c. (linked by Renault to the Vandal conquest, though this must remain supposition), collapse of the vaults rendered the cisterns unusable, and a dam was built across the disused supply aqueduct, behind which surface run-off was collected. Water was filtered through a bank (2 m high) of shells and sherds heaped against the dam, and collected by a channel discharging into another, pre-existing aqueduct.[40]

The original construction date of the cisterns is unknown. No construction phase intervenes between the destruction of a Punic house on the site and the building of the cisterns. Renault's date of the 1st c. A.D. is speculation;[41] architecturally the construction has similarities with the Bordj Djedid cisterns of the mid 2nd c., but that too is impressionistic. The source of the aqueduct feeding the cisterns is unknown. It appears too high to have been fed by the Zaghouan aqueduct (below); more probably it tapped a fairly local source of groundwater, whose abundance would explain the other aqueduct channels found in the vicinity — the channel aqueduct mentioned above, whose supply was later supplemented by the 4th- or 5th-c. dam, and Roman 'draining galleries' collecting fresh groundwater down by the shore.[42] Lastly, at Falbe's point

---

38 Gsell 1901 vol. I, 266, 268, 275; Babelon and Cagnat 1893, text to f. XXVIII; Ben Abed-Ben Khader 1987, plan 13.

39 Gsell 1901 vol. I, 264-66, 273; Renault, H. 1903, 90-98.

40 Renault, J. 1912a, 367.

41 Renault, J. 1912a, 366. His 1st-c. dating is based on a mosaic found in the vicinity (now in the Louvre) showing slaves carrying food and equipment for a banquet, but while the building from which it came may have been supplied by the cisterns, the two need not be contemporary. Dunbabin 1978, 124 n.52 dates the mosaic in question to the late 2nd or early 3rd c.

42 Renault, J. 1912a, 351-53.

89, a few hundred metres north of Dar Saniat, is an underground channel or drain aligned with the rural cadastration (cf. p. 80 below).[43]

The Dar Saniat cisterns provided a reserve of water that could be accumulated or drawn off as needed and distributed in different qualities according to function. They may have served a residential suburb, although the area below the cisterns, between them and the shore (now largely occupied by the hotel), is fairly restricted — a triangle some 250 m long and 200 m broad at the base, enclosed by two spurs.[44] Renault's suggestion that the proconsul's suburban palace was situated in this area, and that the cisterns served it, deserves serious consideration: firstly, the area downslope of the cisterns formerly contained extensive traces of a luxurious villa or villas, with basins, pools and mosaics; a fine alabaster vase and the exquisite mosaic of banquet preparations, now in the Louvre, came from here. Secondly, literary evidence appears to locate the proconsul's palace and the *Ager Sexti*, where St Cyprian was beheaded in 257, and the nearby *Ager Macrobii*, where he was buried, close to the shore, and Dar Saniat is the only likely location for this. Specifically, the *Ager Macrobii* is said to be near the sea and near the proconsul's palace, on the *via Mappaliensis*, next to the pools (*iuxta piscinas*, which translators have variously interpreted as either fishponds or cisterns).[45] The Acts of Maximilian say that after Maximilian's martyrdom his body was brought to Carthage for burial near Cyprian's tomb, not far from the palace, at the foot of a hill. Victor of Vita (1.5.16) adds that two churches were dedicated to Cyprian, both outside the walls of 425, one at the spot of his martyrdom and the other at his tomb. One of these could be Delattre's basilica near St Monique;[46] the other might be a building described by Renault at Falbe's point 72. Both Augustine (*Conf.* 5.8) and Procopius (*BV* 1.21.18) confirm that a basilica of St Cyprian was located on the shore outside the town, and from Augustine it is clear that it was near an anchorage. The bay of Dar Saniat is the only good anchorage north of the walls before one reaches Sidi bou Said. The locations both of Cyprian's martyrdom and of his burial, close to the palace, would seem to fit the general location of Dar Saniat, and Renault sees further support for the location of the proconsul's palace in this area in the modern name Dar Saniat, 'palace of the gardens', which he regards as an Arabic survival of the memory of the palace.

The cisterns of La Malga

On the outskirts of ancient Carthage lies one of the largest known set of reservoir cisterns of the Roman world, at the hamlet now known as La Malga (fig. 1 no. 1). The complex consists of at least 15 vast parallel barrel-vaulted chambers in mortared rubble (fig. 7).[47] No firm esti-

---

43 Falbe 1833, 42.

44 The Danish excavations at Falbe's point 90, by the shore some distance to the south (fig. 1), discovered at least 3 channels feeding cisterns (Dietz 1979, 20-23, 34-35; 1992). The published plan (138-39) omits some channels mentioned in the text, but it appears that there may have been a network of supply channels. Whether these were fed by draining galleries tapping local groundwater, or from the Dar Saniat cisterns, cannot at present be determined.

45 Acts of Cyprian; Augustine, *Conf.* 5.8.4.

46 Frend 1977, 36-37.

47 Fifteen are traceable today, but El Edrisi, writing in the 12th c., mentions 24 and Shaw, writing in the 18th c., noted 'more than twenty' (Shaw, T. 1757, 81); it seems that the number of chambers may have been reduced by destruction over the centuries. Other writers (see Audollent 1901 for a convenient collection of early reports) also give the impression that formerly more chambers were visible than are now recognisable; even allowing for variations in the perspicacity of different observers, there is some indication of a progressive decline in the number of recognisable chambers. Stanley 1786 mentions 17 chambers; Caronni 1805 vol. 2, 70 saw 20; Falbe 1833, 31 counted 15, and Temple 1835, 105-6 saw 13 plus a transverse chamber but says there originally existed more. This view is supported by the course taken by the Zaghouan aqueduct, which postdates the cisterns; it makes a series of bends before and after the cisterns, but pursues a straight course along the edge of these cisterns and for a further 70 m or so beyond the surviving 15 chambers — just far enough to accommodate 9 missing chambers to bring the

1 - Large La Malga cisterns. 1.1 Transverse chamber of cisterns.
2. - Parts of aqueduct. 2.1 - Zaghouan aqueduct. 2.2 presumed course of aqueduct. 2.3 *Castellum* excavated by Vernaz. 2.4 Branch excavated by Vernaz. 2.5 *Castellum* excavated by Ellis.
2.6 Inlet to cisterns.
3 - Small La Malga cisterns.
4 - Remains of a cistern later than aqueduct 2.
5 - Branch supplying cistern 4 or possibly cistern 3.
6 - Group of cisterns: 6.1 and 6.2 each have a settling basin at their N end. They are connected with aqueduct 2 by the channel 6.3. 6.4 is a channel feeding cisterns 6.5 and 6.6.
7 - Remains connected with the aqueduct.
7.1 - aqueduct; 7.2 and 7.3 - related structures.
8 - Complex with walls and cisterns; possibly baths?
9 - Aqueduct.
10 - Group of 3 cisterns.
11 - Tank and well; recently constructed but lower parts may be ancient.
12 Hillock with traces of cisterns and isolated blocks.
13 - Various cisterns.
14 - Various blocks. (Verité regards Falbe's point 62, near here, as "canal derrière le grand aqueduc", but it is clear from Falbe's text and map that his point 62 is simply the branch channel running past La Malga at this point, Verité's aqueduct 2.)
15 - Wall.
16 - Fragments of columns in Chemtou marble.

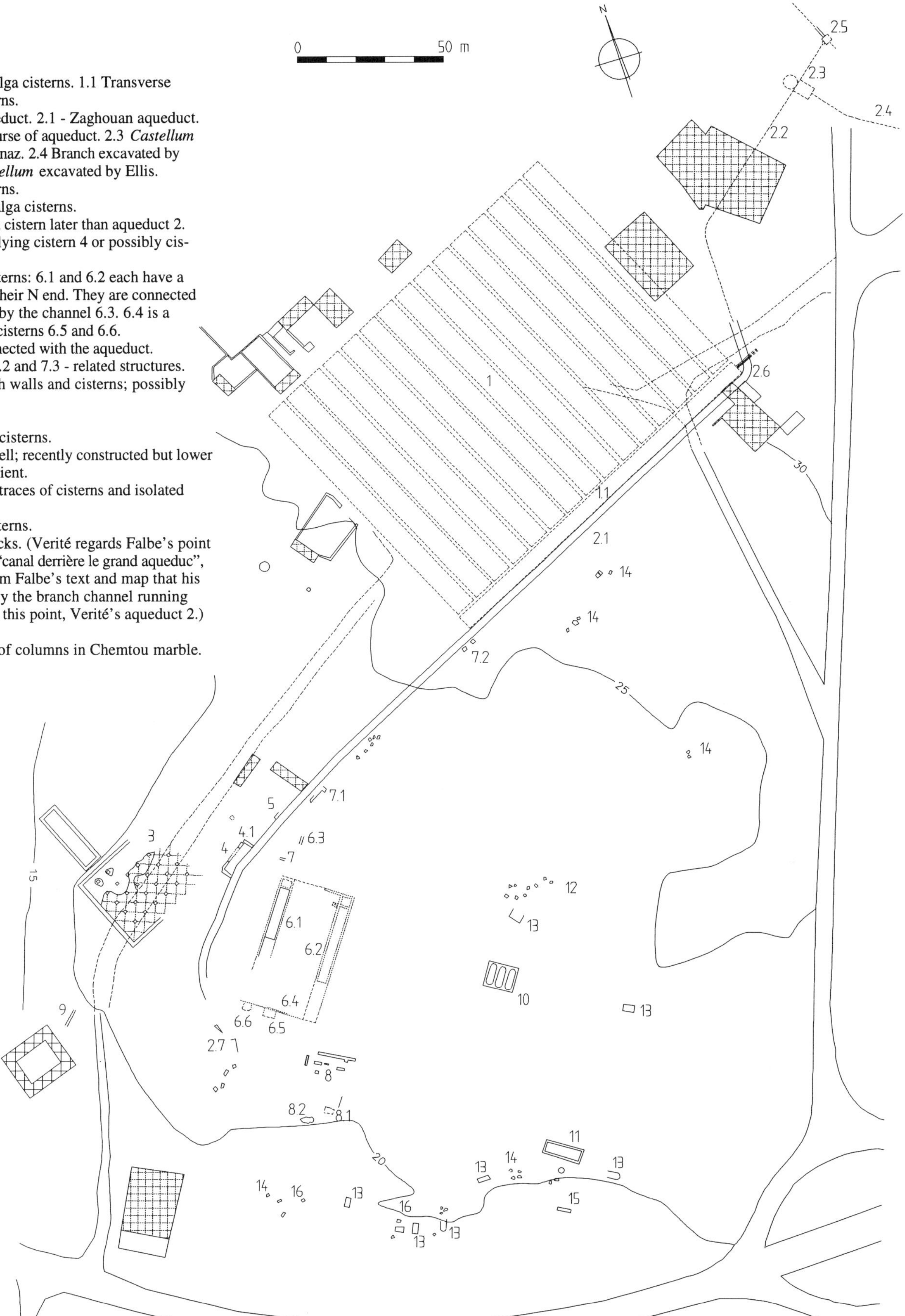

Fig. 7. Plan of the La Malga area, showing cisterns, the aqueduct from Zaghouan, and other structures (after Verité, 1989, 42 fig. 1, with additions and amendments).

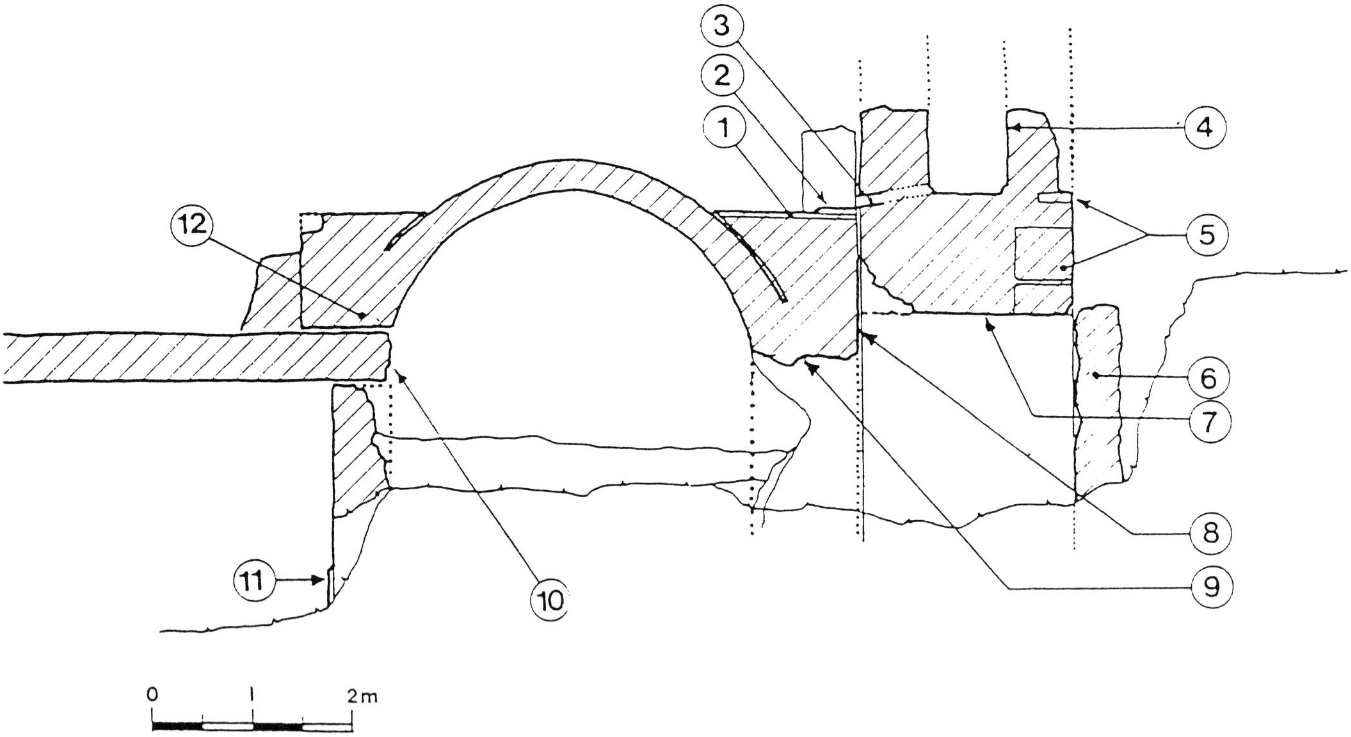

Fig. 8. Section through transverse cistern and main aqueduct in La Malga cistern complex (Verité 1989, fig. 3). 1. Waterproof mortar. 2. *Opus signinum*. 3. Terracotta pipe. 4. Waterproof lining (*opus signinum*). 5. Sandstone blocks. 6. Earth supporting wall (late?); blocks mortared with earth. 7. Intrados of aqueduct arcade. 8. Intermittent traces of plaster. 9. End wall of the cisterns, knocked through to create greater living space when cisterns were re-used as habitations (personal observation; *contra* Verité 1989 fig. 3). 10. Current state of preservation makes it unclear where the longitudinal vaults originally ended. 11. Waterproof lining curving round onto end wall. 12. Transverse vault constructed on top of the longitudinal vaults.

mates of capacity yet seem to have been made for the La Malga cisterns.[48] Excavations by A. Ennabli in one of the chambers had (by October 1997) revealed the crowns of two arches communicating with the chambers either side, at a depth of some 2 m below the vault spring and 2.80 m below the terracotta pipes draining water from the extrados of the cistern vaults. The dimensions of these arches (1.20 m wide) suggest that a further 2 m (or perhaps up to 3 m) remains to be excavated. Assuming a water depth of 4.5 m below the inlet, and using J. Verité's figures for the other dimensions (15 chambers at 7.40 m wide and 102 m long),[49] one arrives at a capacity of some 51,000 m^3. The La Malga cisterns are therefore by far the largest covered reservoirs of the ancient world before the Byzantine period: the three next largest, all from North Africa, are Cirta (30,000 m^3),[50] Zama (28,000 m^3),[51] and Bordj Djedid (20,000 m^3, sometimes erroneously said to be the largest in the ancient world[52]). Outside North Africa the Piscina Mirabilis at Bacoli (12,500 m^3) and the cisterns in the Baths of Caracalla in Rome (11,500 m^3) are among the largest.[53]

---

total up to the 24 observed by El Edrisi. Against this view, however, is the lack of visible vaults above ground level, and lack of evidence of destroyed chambers, southwest of the surviving cisterns. Only excavation could resolve the question.

48 L. Magne (1911, 4) estimated their capacity at 50,000 m^3. Although he gave no dimensions on which this was based, the calculations below suggest this estimate is probably not too far off the mark.

49 Verité 1989, 44.

50 Gsell 1901 vol. I, 269.

51 Drappier 1899, 147-48.

52 E.g., Tolle-Kastenbein 1990, 127.

53 Baths of Caracalla: Manderscheid and Garbrecht 1994, 122 and 266-67 n.497 with discussion of ear-

Verité identified several stages in the construction process of the cisterns, which he saw as falling into two main phases (fig. 8).[54] In the first phase, the walls of the longitudinal chambers (all apparently contemporary) were built up to the springing of the vault; the vaults were then added (the mortar join is very clear internally). At this level terracotta tubes placed every 5-6 m or so drained water from the extrados of the vaults (covered in *opus signinum*) into the interior. This indicates that, as was common practice, supply was supplemented by the collection of rain falling on the extrados of the vaults, although this could not have formed the main source of supply. After the longitudinal walls had been built, a transverse chamber (3.65 m wide) was added whose vault rests upon the extrados of the longitudinal vaults. The walls closing the longitudinal vaults (fig. 8, no. 11) are built up to meet the intrados of the vaults, but this is normal construction practice (found also at the other ends of the chambers) and need not imply a significantly later date than the vaults. Nevertheless, the yellowish mortar of the end walls contrasts with the greyish mortar of the longitudinal walls, and the transverse vault seals the *opus signinum* lining of the extrados of the longitudinal vaults; both these facts speak for the construction of the transverse vault being a second phase, as does its profile, more pointed than that of the longitudinal vaults. The haunches of the transverse vault were subsequently reinforced by two phases of masonry buttressing, the first also sealing the *opus signinum* covering of the extrados of the longitudinal vaults.

The Zaghouan aqueduct runs alongside the SE face of the cisterns but is clearly later than them; a narrow gap exists between the cisterns and the aqueduct, and the exterior wall of the cisterns here displays traces of plaster which show that it was exposed before the aqueduct was built; in addition the gap is so narrow that the plaster could not have been applied after the aqueduct's construction.

The fact that the cisterns pre-date the Zaghouan aqueduct raises some major questions: when were they built, and how were they supplied before the construction of the aqueduct (if, indeed, the aqueduct ever fed them at all)?[55] The outside dates for the cisterns should be the foundation of the colony in 29 B.C. and the construction of the Zaghouan aqueduct, probably in the second quarter of the 2nd c. (see below). Several factors speak for a date earlier rather than later within this span: the use of greyish mortar (similar to that of the amphitheatre) rather than the yellowish-brown mortar more characteristic of the 2nd c. A.D.; the apparent lack of sophistication in design (absence of inspection galleries; lack of a transverse chamber in the initial phase); the relative infrequency of communicating arches between chambers, suggesting structural caution; and an apparent lack of concern to make fullest use of the height at which the inlet arrived (see below), suggesting that higher parts of the town may not yet have been fully built up. The cisterns' alignment on the rural cadastration rather than the urban grid may indicate a date early in the colony's history, or it may merely associate them with rural rather than urban space, as a result of their location on the outskirts of the city (fig. 1).[56] Certainty must await further excavation; for the moment, any date between the Augustan period and the early 2nd c. seems possible, which serves to underline how little the architectural development of cistern complexes is understood.

Until recently the source of supply for the La Malga cisterns has remained a puzzle. Verité believed that the cisterns might have been fed by a local spring to the south-west, but this

---

lier erroneous estimates (up to 80,000 m^3!). Piscina Mirabilis: Tolle-Kastenbein 1990, 126-27 (her figures for the cisterns in the Baths of Caracalla and the Baths of Trajan are incorrect).

54 The following discussion draws on Verité 1989, confirmed by my own observations in 1997.

55 Verité (1989, 46) mentions terracotta pipes, later blocked, which might have communicated between the aqueduct channel and the extrados of the transverse chamber, but there is no proof that these delivered water to the *inside* of the cisterns.

56 Rakob 1974, 44.

Fig. 9. The supply channel for the La Malga cisterns at the point where it crosses the line of the aqueduct from Zaghouan, looking N. The aqueduct (running from left to right in the picture) is clearly later than the inlet channel, incorporating in its vault mortar the cover slabs of the channel. Scale: 10 cm in cm units.

would have been far too low to supply them and is nowhere near the line of the inlet.[57] The underground aqueduct in the plain near La Soukra to the west of Carthage is also at too low an elevation to have fed Carthage.[58] Rain falling on the *impluvium* created by the extrados of the vaults ran into the interior through terracotta pipes, but rain can never have filled the cisterns, acting rather to supplement a more substantial source. My investigation of the La Malga cisterns in October 1997 identified the inlet at the E corner of the cistern complex (fig. 7, point 2.6), where it had apparently been revealed by Verité's *sondage* in 1979 but not remarked on by him.[59] Here the Zaghouan aqueduct bends to follow the long side of the cistern complex and its line is crossed by a masonry channel of rectangular cross-section, lined with hard waterproof cement.[60] Three pieces of evidence show clearly that the channel pre-dates the Zaghouan aqueduct. First, although the channel passes through the aqueduct in the upper half of the aqueduct's cross-section, there is no sign of destruction of the aqueduct's side walls by a foundation trench for the channel; rather, the aqueduct walls butt directly against the channel's walls. Secondly, the mortared rubble of the aqueduct vault seals the channel's cover slabs (fig. 9). Thirdly, *opus signinum* lining on the interior of the aqueduct's channel seals the stone slab forming the base of our channel (fig. 10). Therefore this channel is indisputably earlier than the aqueduct. Its alignment coincides with the SE wall of the transverse vault of the cistern complex. It should therefore be the inlet for either the first or the second phase of the cisterns,

---

57 Verité 1989, 47.

58 The aqueduct is described by Renault, J. 1912b, 471-75 and Fornacciari 1928. It seems to have been intended for rural irrigation in the plain to the west of Carthage. (I am grateful to F. Rakob for pointing out to me that this aqueduct could not have fed the La Malga cisterns.)

59 Verité 1979, 19 merely says of this point (2.6) "parcours déterminé par sondage".

60 The channel is constructed in masonry and roofed with slabs of El Haouaria sandstone. Dimensions: channel 0.27-0.275 m wide internally by 0.49 m deep; walls 0.34-0.39 m thick.

Fig. 10. The supply channel for the La Malga cisterns where it crosses the aqueduct from Zaghouan, looking E. The channel is sealed by the vault mortar of the aqueduct, and *opus signinum* in the aqueduct channel curves round and seals the slab forming the channel base. Scale: 10 cm in cm units.

or both. Its location might suggest that the transverse chamber was constructed as a settling tank to filter water entering the cisterns, an arrangement found elsewhere in North Africa, as at Tuccabor and Djebel M'rabba.[61] It is uncertain how far the supply channel extends to the north of the cisterns; it may have tapped groundwater in the rising ground to the north of the cisterns, a spur continuing the Odeon hill to the west.[62] Alternatively, it may be connected with an underground channel ("un conduit ou égout") noted by Falbe at his point 89 on the outskirts of Sidi bou Said, on exactly the same alignment some 2.2 km further to the NE;[63] the topography would probably allow a largely underground aqueduct to extend from Sidi bou Said to La Malga (fig. 1). This may suggest that Carthage had an aqueduct of perhaps 2-3 km length before the construction of the Zaghouan aqueduct. Excavation alone could resolve the issue.[64]

The Zaghouan aqueduct

At some date in the 2nd c., Carthage's water supply was supplemented by the construction of one of the largest aqueducts of the ancient world. Running for 90 km from an elaborate spring nymphaeum at Zaghouan, its imposing arcaded structure strides across the plain of the Oued Miliane and the plain of Ariana in the approaches to Carthage, resembling, in the words of Sir Grenville Temple, "the bleached vertebrae of some enormous serpent".[65] It is comparable in

61 Drappier 1899, 136-38.

62 If indeed there is an aquifer there; I have not been able to obtain geological information on this locality, but there are no evident signs of wells.

63 Falbe 1833, 42. Falbe's map seems to indicate the channel at point 89 extending for a distance of some 220 m.

64 The putative route of such a channel lies almost directly under the road from Sidi bou Said to La Malga.

65 Temple 1835, 107.

length to the aqueduct of Cologne, but more ambitious in its engineering, with some 17 km on arcaded sections which maintain an elevation of up to 20 m across low-lying plains and include a bridge 33.65 m high and 125.78 m long over the Oued Miliane.[66] The interior dimensions of its *specus* are 0.86 m wide and 1.25-1.40 m high, and its daily delivery has been estimated at between 17,280 m^3 and 30,000 m^3, with the latest research suggesting 25,000 m^3.[67] The channel is provided with inspection shafts at intervals, and small circular settling pits are sunk into its floor. Later, the aqueduct was extended by a branch to the spring at Zucchara (Aïn Djouker) which, with two extra short feeder spurs, brought the total length of the conduit to 132 km.

The aqueduct's architecture and construction techniques have been studied in detail by F. Rakob in a series of articles.[68] Two outstanding questions, however, are the aqueduct's date and its relationship to the construction of the Antonine Baths. Rakob dates the construction of the nymphaeum complex at Zaghouan to the 160s, on the basis of its architectural decoration; the aqueduct must be earlier than the sanctuary, but by how much is unclear; in any case, the aqueduct must have taken many years, perhaps over a decade, to build.[69] It should have been complete no later than the opening of the Antonine Baths, started possibly by 146 and certainly by 159, and dedicated by 161/62.[70] It has often been assumed that the Zaghouan aqueduct is Hadrianic, a suggestion first proposed by Dureau de la Malle on the basis of several passages in the *SHA* life of Hadrian: a 5-year drought in Africa which ended with Hadrian's visit, Hadrian's general fondness for building aqueducts, and Carthage's adoption of the name Hadrianopolis.[71] Certainly the sheer scale and length of the aqueduct virtually demands an imperial benefactor, and the precise wording of the *SHA* is suggestive:

> [Hadrianus] et cum titulos in operibus non amaret, multas civitates Hadrianopolis appellavit, ut ipsam Karthaginem et Athenarum partem. Aquarum ductus etiam infinitos hoc nomine nuncupavit.
>
> (*SHA*, Had. 20)
>
> And since Hadrian did not like inscriptions on his buildings, he named many cities Hadrianopolis, as for instance Carthage itself and part of Athens. He even called countless aqueducts by this name.

Possibly a link between aqueduct construction and Carthage's adoption of the name Hadrianopolis is implied — Hadrian did build an aqueduct at Athens. Although the *SHA* is notoriously unreliable, it does provide circumstantial evidence. The story of Hadrian's visit after a 5-year drought would provide a plausible context for the aqueduct's construction if Carthage had until then been relying on cisterns to collect rain and on the La Malga cisterns, fed by ground-water whose level would have been liable to drop after a prolonged drought. Such an experience could well have prompted the safeguarding of supply by using the copious but remote water of the perennial spring at Zaghouan. Dureau de la Malle also suggested that the extension to Aïn

66 Rakob 1974, 47.

67 Hodge 1992, 279; Slim 1992, 518.

68 Rakob 1969a; 1969b; 1974; 1979b; 1983.

69 Rakob 1974, 65-70; Wilson, R. J. A. 1996, 17-18.

70 *CIL* 8 12513 appears to be the building inscription for the baths, and although usually dated to 146 could in fact date from one of several years between 146 and 159 (Ben Abdallah 1986, 254-55 no. 9). The figure for Antoninus Pius' tribunician power is missing, and in the space available the following numerals could be restored: VIIII, XIIII, XVII, XXII, giving dates of 146, 151, 154 or 159 respectively (Cagnat 1887); Wilmanns (*CIL* ad loc.) notes that [X Imp II] could also be restored in this position, which would give a date of 148. A second inscription, *AE* 1949. 27 (A.D. 161/2), refers to the decoration of the baths, but it is not certain that this relates to the original construction project; it might be a secondary refurbishment or embellishment. On the other hand, if *CIL* 8 12513 dates to 159, then the gap of 2 or 3 years between completion of the structure and dedication of the decoration would not be surprising. The latest writer on the Antonine Baths, F. Ferjaoui-Weber (1994, 38), suggests they were begun under Hadrian but gives no evidence (perhaps confusing this with the traditional dating of the aqueduct to Hadrian's reign); in the following sentence she says that construction lasted 17 years (145-162), apparently accepting the usual epigraphic dating.

71 Dureau de la Malle 1835, 136-39. Until his time the aqueduct had sometimes been considered Punic.

Djouker was Severan, on the evidence of coins of Septimius Severus (datable examples from 203 and 204) showing Astarte mounted on a lioness running along a spring issuing from a rock, and bearing the legend *indulgentia* [or *munificentia*] *Augg(ustorum) in Carthaginem*.[72] This suggests work on the aqueduct financed by a remission of taxes, and the extension to Aïn Djouker would be the only likely candidate for such work. Yet more than 160 years after Dureau de la Malle wrote, we are little closer to establishing more closely the date either of the original aqueduct or its extension.

The objection to a Hadrianic date for the initial construction of the long aqueduct has been that some scholars have preferred to see it and the Antonine Baths as part of a single construction programme, with the baths as the chief reason for the aqueduct's construction. For this there is no direct evidence: it is connected with the popular view that aqueducts were a monumental luxury designed to support a Romanised lifestyle of bathing and conspicuous consumption of water, and that their practical utility was limited.[73] Whilst there is much to commend the view that aqueducts played a vital rôle as symbols of Romanisation and expressions of civic pride, their utility should not be under-estimated — indeed, it was one of the factors which made their symbolic rôle so powerful. Although the Antonine Baths must have required extremely large quantities of water, the Zaghouan aqueduct can only be said to have created the conditions which enabled the baths to function (and even this may not be strictly true if we recall that the La Malga cisterns could have supplied them); the baths cannot on present evidence be said to have motivated the aqueduct's construction. Even if begun by Hadrian the aqueduct may not have been finished during his reign. But an examination of the Zaghouan aqueduct, the Antonine Baths, and the cisterns of Bordj Djedid shows that the baths were by no means the prime destination of the aqueduct; certain aspects of its construction — notably the height of the arcades across the Ariana plain — were determined by a need to supply other structures.

The Bordj Djedid cisterns, and the Antonine Baths

The Antonine Baths were supplied by the large cisterns of Bordj Djedid (fig. 1 no. 6), which were restored to service by the French in 1888 and still serve parts of Carthage (though now inaccessible within the grounds of the presidential palace). These cisterns occupied an entire *insula* of the street grid and were formed of a battery of huge vaulted chambers, with sets of circular shafts at both ends (fig. 11), containing about 20,000 m^3 with a depth of water of 7.23 m.[74] A surveillance gallery ran around the upper level with inspection windows into the chambers.

The outlet arrangements of the Bordj Djedid cisterns were similar to those of Dar Saniat but on a larger scale. In the SE corner of the complex was a circular chamber reached by a spiral

72 Dureau de la Malle 1835, 139-40. Caronni 1805, 73-74 took these coins to be evidence for Severan construction of the whole aqueduct. Cf. Mattingly 1975, 208-9 nos. 279-82; 218 nos 333-38; 248n.; 332 no 825 and n.; 334 no. 830; pls. 34.2-3, 35.11-14, 50.1-3.

73 Leveau and Paillet 1976; Shaw, B. D. 1984; id. 1991; Schwartz 1981, and, most strongly, Hodge 1992, 6. Cf. Wilson, R. J. A. 1996, 16-18.

74 Measurements are taken from the figures, plans and section drawings in Magne 1911. These indicate a maximum water depth of 7.23 m below a channel which, whether an inlet or an overflow, would have determined a maximum level (calculated from Magne's data for floor and gallery levels, with inflow or overflow in chamber 3 given as 2 m below the gallery floor). Calculation from Magne's figures for chamber dimensions gives a capacity of 19,880 m^3, or 20,000 m^3 in round figures. Although Magne does not himself give a figure for the capacity of the cisterns in the Roman period, this calculation accords with his statement on p. 44 that the capacity in the Roman period was less than that obtained after restoration in the late 19th c., when by raising the level of the overflow the capacity was increased to 25,200 m^3.

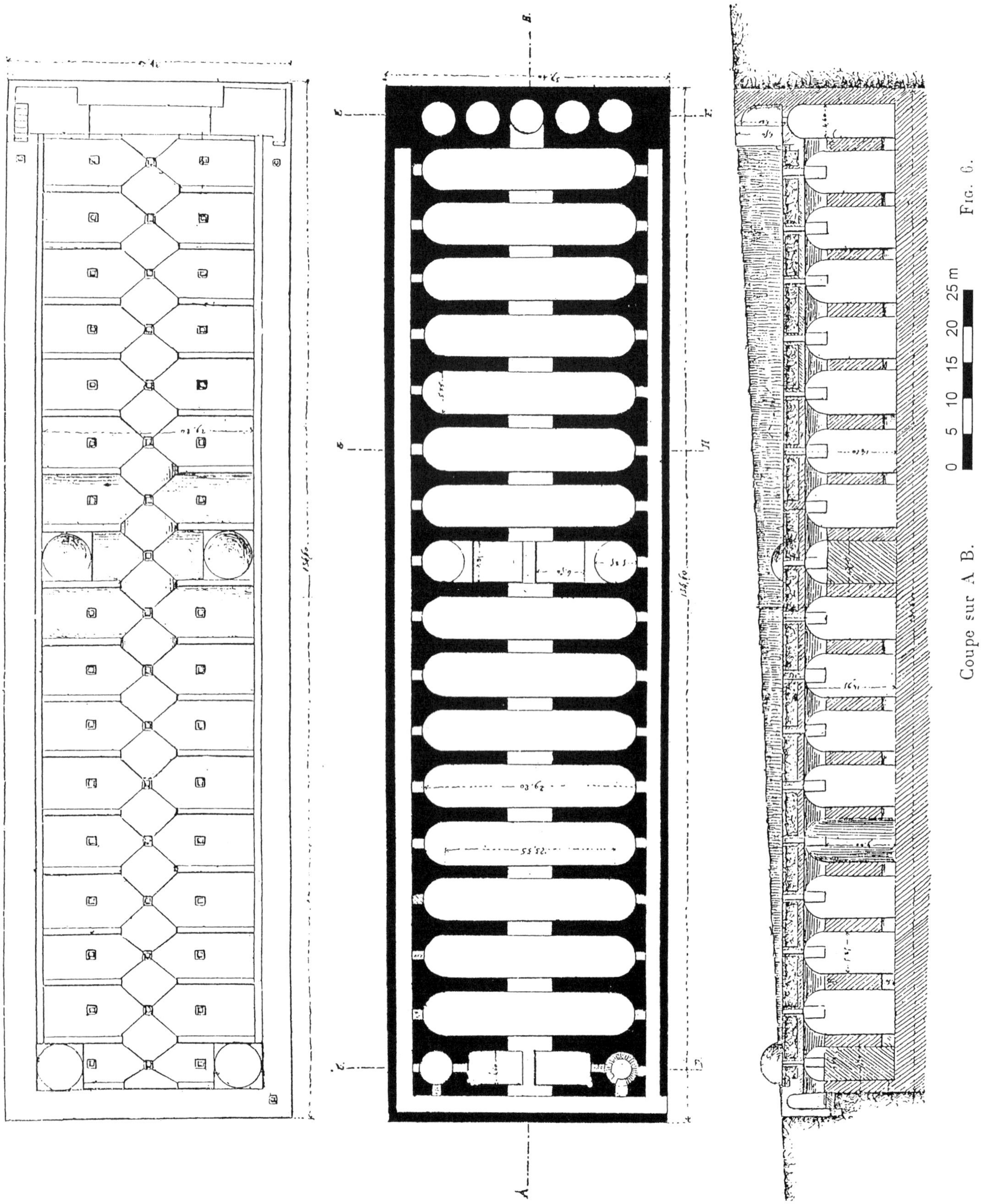

Fig. 11. Plan of the large cisterns at Bordj Djedid (after Babelon and Cagnat 1893).

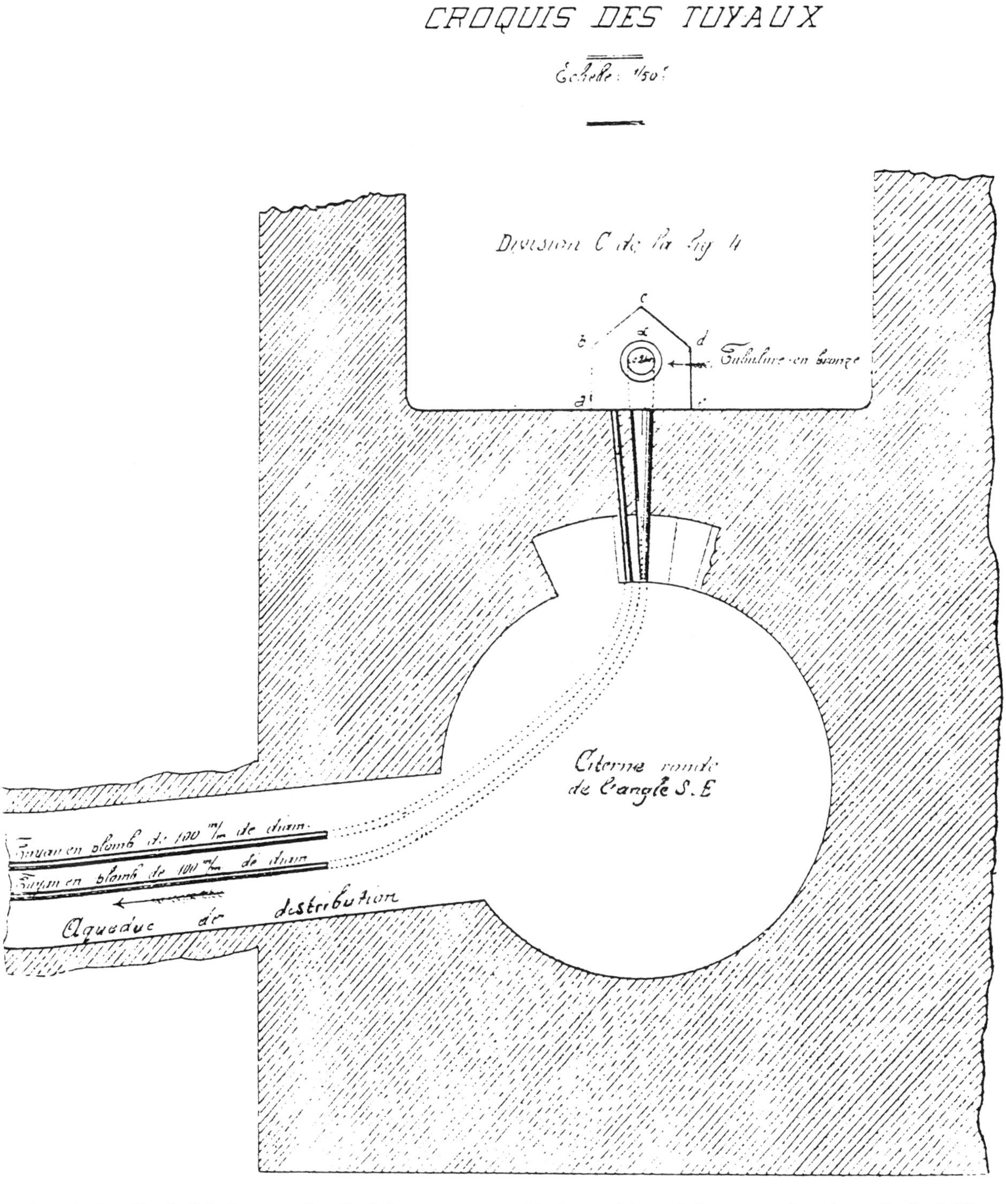

Fig. 12. Bordj Djedid cisterns: detail of the tap room, with the position of the two outlet pipes. Scale 1:50. Compare the arrangements at Dar Saniat (fig. 3) (Magne 1911, 23 fig. 5).

stair (fig. 12). At the bottom of the adjacent cistern chamber were the intakes for two lead pipes. One intake was set in a block of masonry with a bronze sheet around the opening of the pipe, grooved to take a mesh filter; the other intake was formed from a lead sheet mounted around the mouth of the second pipe and set into the wall (this and part of an exit pipe are now in the Bardo Museum).[75] Both pipes passed through the wall into the circular chamber, from

75 Vernaz 1887; du Coudray la Blanchère and Gauckler 1897, 125 no. 13.

which they left at floor level in an underground gallery. When the circular chamber was excavated in 1853, a bronze tap was apparently found *in situ* on one of the pipes, confirming the chamber's function as a tap room.[76] The outlet gallery is cut through the rock of the Bordj Djedid hill, heading towards the Antonine Baths, which at least one of the lead pipes must have fed, though not necessarily both. Overflow water ran to the street drains via a channel leading from the SW chamber, but this overflow was later suppressed.[77]

The cisterns are therefore intimately linked to the baths (despite an earlier belief that they were Punic[78]). During restoration in 1888 a brickstamp of Flavius Aper was found beneath the *opus signinum* floor lining.[79] Aper seems to have been active from A.D. 140 to 160, with datable stamps of 151 and 157.[80] No trace was found of a repair to the lining at this point, and an Antonine construction date for the cisterns as well as for the baths is logical.

The Bordj Djedid cisterns must have been supplied by an aqueduct, although Carton thought that they were originally fed by run-off from the natural depression in which they sit[81] — clearly impossible given the developed Roman city plan around them, although supply was supplemented by collecting rain that fell on the extrados of the vaults. It is likely that they were fed by a branch of the Zaghouan aqueduct but their source has still not been traced. In 1884 Vernaz followed an underground aqueduct branch which diverged from the Zaghouan aqueduct channel just north of the La Malga cisterns (fig. 1 no. 5) and which seemed to be heading for Bordj Djedid, but he was not able to trace it as far as the cisterns.

The urban distribution network

Rather, the discoveries made by Vernaz shed some light on the complexity of the intra-urban distribution network. Shortly upstream of the La Malga cisterns were arrangements for the off-take of part of the Zaghouan aqueduct's flow (fig. 7 point 2.3). In the main channel were two opposed openings in the side walls, followed by a series of holes in the E wall and then a sill across the main channel, formed by a slab pierced in its lower part. These appeared to be the remains of a system of sluices allowing regulation of distribution from the main channel into the branch which departed from the E side of the main aqueduct at right-angles. At the origin of the branch was a small chamber, its floor significantly lower than the main aqueduct's channel, such that water entering it would have been subjected to considerable turbulence. Turbulence encourages the deposition of sinter, and there were heavy sinter deposits on the floor and walls of this chamber. The chamber's N wall was pierced a few centimeters above the floor by 5 openings, for 3 lead and 2 terracotta pipes. They led into two masonry channels supplying neighbouring cisterns, and into 5 terracotta pipes parallel to the main aqueduct; their destination is unknown.[82]

The side branch was traced by Vernaz for a total of 788 m (fig. 1 no. 5). Beyond the distribution chamber was another chamber, placed above the aqueduct branch and communicating with it through an opening in the vault. Roofed with vaulting tubes, it admitted water through 3 openings in the walls; dirty deposits in the chamber and in the channel below show that this water was heavily earth-laden. Further on, a settling pit (0.65 m in diameter, 0.35 m deep) in

76 The tap was said to have been taken to the 'Musée de Vienne', which probably meant Vienne in France but might mean Vienna (Magne 1911, 22-25; cf. Tissot 1884 vol. I, 598).

77 Vernaz 1887, 26-27.

78 Audollent 1901, 251-52; Magne 1911, 47-49; Carton 1911, 493-94; Carton 1935, 83.

79 Delattre 1891, 54-55: *ex pr. Flavi Apri opus | dolia larcio* = *CIL* 15 1146, probably *a* rather than *b*. *Contra* Audollent 1901, 252, this stamp is not datable to 142; Delattre (1893b, 34-35; 1893a, 121) has confused Flavius Aper with Flavius Apricis.

80 Righini 1975, 58-59; Setälä 1977, 113.

81 Carton 1911, 494; Carton 1935, 83-84.

82 Vernaz 1887, 13-15.

the channel floor recalls those in the main channel of the Zaghouan aqueduct. Two secondary branches departed from the right-hand side of the channel. The first (0.50 m wide, 1 m high) was roofed with pitched slabs and led 4 m to an unexcavated chamber. The channel's entrance was blocked by a sill 0.50 m high and pierced with 9 openings. The second branch was 9 m long, similar in construction to the first, but it was 2 m high and equipped with an inspection shaft. It did not open directly off the channel but communicated with it by a circular hole half-way up the side wall of the aqueduct, into which was fixed a lead pipe that ran the length of the branch to a cistern (originally Punic) whose floor was covered by a sheet of lead. This branch may therefore represent an earlier conduit re-used to lay the pipe.

The aqueduct branch then continues for some distance before debouching into a vaulted chamber whose floor was roughly level with that of the aqueduct. Many nails set deeply into the walls suggest the presence of some kind of wall cladding or decoration. Access to the chamber was by means of a staircase divided in two by a central barrier, and the whole arrangement seems designed to allow water to be drawn from the chamber. The upper part of the chamber was not preserved, and it is unclear whether this was a public or a private point for drawing water. The former might be suspected if the central division of the staircase was an attempt to control the circulation of people. Such an underground point for drawing water would seem to represent a solution to the problem of making water available in the higher regions of Carthage.

Beyond this chamber the channel continued for some 100 m but close to ground level; it is in a poor state of preservation, and its trace was eventually lost. Its form in this section was peculiar: a wide barrel-vaulted gallery led from the chamber, divided into two compartments by a longitudinal wall which at its origin reached only to below the height of the vault. The left-hand compartment was closed by a transverse wall and did not communicate with the chamber; the right-hand compartment formed the continuation of the aqueduct but with reduced dimensions (0.5 x 0.5 m). Although the aqueduct's width remained constant, the left-hand gallery progressively diminished in width with distance from the chamber and finally disappeared. At the same time, the vault, originally a full semi-circle, becomes increasingly flattened. Apparently the aqueduct must have been installed in a pre-existing gallery or drain running on almost but not quite the same alignment and with a greater slope, with the result that the shallower gradient of the new aqueduct gradually intersects the vault. Given the dimensions of the gallery and the fact that the channel is at this point running under the length of *decumanus* III N, the likelihood is that a street drain was being re-used, although this raises the question of what happened to the street's drainage thereafter. Vernaz interpreted this section of the channel as an overflow from the drawing point, and concluded that the branch from La Malga under *decumanus* III N could not have fed the Bordj Djedid cisterns. Its main purpose, he thought, was to supply the point for drawing water. Around the Bordj Djedid cisterns themselves, Vernaz was unable to locate the original supply channel, finding only two successive overflows and several street drains unconnected with the cisterns.[83] However, he seems not to have excavated against the N side of the cisterns, which is where one would expect to find the inlet, as this is the end of the cisterns where the circular settling tanks were placed.

However, Ellis has excavated a distribution arrangement shortly to the north of the branch followed by Vernaz, which has a better claim to being the start of the Bordj Djedid branch (fig. 7, point 2.5). The aqueduct from Zaghouan enters a rectangular chamber on its NW side; from its SE side perhaps ran a now-destroyed channel, while from its SW side led off the channel that runs past the La Malga cisterns and feeds, *inter alia*, the branch under *decumanus* III N. Traces of some kind of gate or sluice on the La Malga channel indicate that it could be shut off. Ellis believed that the SE branch led to the cisterns of Bordj Djedid and was the major one, because it lay directly opposite the inlet to the *castellum*, while the La Malga branch left at right-

83 Vernaz 1887.

angles and at a level above the floor of the *castellum*.[84] If it could be shown that this channel did indeed lead to the Bordj Djedid cisterns as its prime destination, that would be of immense interest since, as the *castellum* is clearly integral to the original construction of the aqueduct, it would demonstrate the contemporaneity of the aqueduct, the Bordj Djedid cisterns, and the Antonine Baths, and an intended connection between them. However, this outlet is not preserved and the course of its channel has not been traced. While it is possible that it led around the N side of the city and ran under *decumanus* VI N towards Bordj Djedid, it would have to have been deeply buried (tunnelled) up to 14 m below the surface; at such depths, it would have been easier to tunnel in a staight line towards the cisterns. Alternatively, a branch from *decumanus* III N or IV N could have swung off to the north by the theatre towards the cisterns,[85] but Vernaz's excavations suggest that the branch of *decumanus* III N did not supply the Bordj Djedid cisterns.

Whatever the route of a branch supplying the Bordj Djedid cisterns, the evidence of other aqueduct branches in the city should lead us to suspect that that branch too would have had numerous side channels and derivations. It is premature to assert that the Bordj Djedid cisterns were the exclusive or even the prime destination of this channel. It is entirely possible that the distribution was regional: one branch intended to supply the urban regions of Carthage north and east of the Hill of Juno, while the La Malga branch fed areas south of the Byrsa, and Vernaz's branch under *decumanus* III N supplied some regions between the two. The existence of other undiscovered branches, of progressively decreasing capacity, is to be suspected. Viewed in this light, Ellis' suggestion of a series of distribution chambers successively subdividing flow is particularly attractive.[86]

Ellis saw his *castellum* as dividing the aqueduct's flow into two, with the primary branch leaving from the SE side to serve Bordj Djedid. Only the SW (La Malga) outlet is preserved; the SE outlet is completely destroyed, and the NE wall too has been totally robbed, although Ellis believed that as it points away from the city no outlet existed on this side.[87] However, the presumed SE outlet would actually point not towards Bordj Djedid but to the *insulae* between *decumani* III and IV N. As it would have been difficult to lay conduits under developed *insulae*, the channel would have had to change direction to run under a street. A branch going to Bordj Djedid could have left to the NE, running around the edge of the city, before tunnelling underneath *decumanus* Vl N to reach the N end of the Bordj Djedid cisterns. In my view, it is just as possible that there existed 3 outlets, to the SW, SE and NE, or 2, to SW and NE, rather than only 2 to the SW and SE. The state of preservation of the *castellum* does not allow us to decide.

A further point relates to the control of flow. A recess in the *castellum* wall by the outlet to La Malga suggests that this branch could be closed by a sluice-gate or swing gate. Ellis notes that a swing gate does not allow fine control of flow, and suggested that the gate functioned simply to close off the La Malga channel in times of shortage or when the cisterns were full, thus establishing an absolute priority of the other outlet over the La Malga channel. Other interpretations, however, are possible; as the outlet of the other channel (or channels) does not survive, it is possible that it (or they) were also equipped with gates. Although Ellis is correct to point out that, if these were swing gates, flow on an individual channel could not easily have been finely tuned, the *castellum* could still have divided the flow in a number of ways: equally between channels with all gates open, or to one channel only with the other channel(s) shut.[88] If there were three outlets, two could still have received water while the third was

84 Ellis 1996.
85 C. M. Wells, pers. comm.
86 Ellis 1996, 183.
87 Ellis 1996, 180.
88 As Hodge 1996 suggests for the *castellum* at Pompeii.

shut. A more precise allocation of priorities could have been achieved with distribution by time periods, as is commonly attested on Roman urban and irrigation systems.[89] The floor of the La Malga outlet is some 0.30 m above the floor of the *castellum*; if the putative Bordj Djedid outlet left from the level of the *castellum* floor, it would indeed have drawn more water than the La Malga channel. If, on the other hand, all outlets left at a level above the *castellum* floor, this would have helped equalise distribution between the branches if the sluice-gates were left open.

The excavations of Vernaz and Ellis help set the Bordj Djedid cisterns in the wider context of the urban water network. Despite their size, those cisterns were not the only or even the major destination of the aqueduct and could have received only a fraction of its flow. The area of the German excavations near the shore was supplied by lead pipes.[90] Private supply has also been found for the Maison de la Volière.[91] The Zaghouan aqueduct supplied the *castellum divisorium* at La Malga and its various derivations discovered by Vernaz, but it also supplied a smaller set of cross-vaulted cisterns at La Malga (capacity at least 1325 m^3) and many other structures, including baths and cisterns in the La Malga region (fig. 7, nos 6.3. 7.1 and 7.2, being derivations leading to cisterns 6.1, 6.2 and 6.4). The main channel of the aqueduct continues from La Malga towards the amphitheatre and circus, in which traces of *opus signinum* on the *euripus* bear witness to pools.[92] Beyond this it may have supplied the large cistern complexes (6,000 and 7,000 m^3) of the *turris aquaria* at Douar ech-Chott (fig. 1 no. 9), from which it seems that the suburbs near the Lake of Tunis drew their water.

The *turris aquaria* and associated installations

The nature of the *turris aquaria* itself is unclear. The name is taken from mediaeval accounts of the siege of Carthage by St Louis, which distinguish two fortifications, the *turris aquaria* named for its proximity to a group of cisterns, and the *turris salinensis*, by the salt pans. It should not be thought of necessarily as comparable with *castella divisoria* or water towers at Pompeii. It seems to have been a large structure oriented on the city plan but occupying parts of 3 *insulae*. Around the 4 sides of a central massif were 4 large underground cisterns which intersected at their extremities; their combined capacity was some 7,000 m^3. In late antiquity a set of baths was built near the SW corner, with a set of smaller cisterns apparently linked to those of the *turris aquaria*. Nearby is a bizarre and apparently unique arrangement of what is said to be a line of some 150 intercommunicating cisterns extending for 1.3 km. This seems to be the set of underground vaults marked by Falbe as point 102 (fig. 1). Each chamber measured 8.95 m x 1.72 m x 2.70 m high and communicated with its neighbours through an opening with a pointed top, 0.47 m wide and 2.35 m high. Total capacity was therefore of the order of 6,000 m^3. The chambers examined by Saumagne lacked feed pipes, and the source of supply is unknown. Although the arrangement could represent a compartmented conduit rather than a set of cisterns, the gradient is perhaps insufficient. Certainly it could not be a draining gallery because the chambers were waterproofed. The cisterns are not aligned on either the urban or the rural grid.

89 Thomas and Wilson 1994, 147.

90 Rakob in Rakob ed.. 1991, 249.

91 Ennabli 1983, 138-39. Schwartz 1981 is incorrect to assert that private houses at Carthage and Ptolemais were not fed by aqueducts.

92 Humphrey 1988, 14 fig. 3. Although it has been suggested that the amphitheatre could have been flooded for mock sea-battles (Audollent 1901, 303), there is no evidence for waterproofing of the arena and it is hard to see how the ancients could have avoided flooding the substructures — or have drained them afterwards. In general I do not believe that amphitheatre arenas were flooded, with the exception of special cases such as Mérida or Verona which have purpose-built tanks set within the arena. Cf. Coleman 1993, esp. 57-60, although I regard the basins at Mérida and Verona as probably intended to introduce an aquatic element into *venationes*, with crocodiles and hippopotami.

One end of the line appears to relate to traces of a large building by the *turris aquaria*; the other abuts ruins at Falbe's point 103 on the edge of the Lac de Tunis, so Saumagne suggested that the arrangement may have been connected with supplying ships in the port.[93]

The *turris aquaria* remains enigmatic, but it seems to have been a hydraulic complex supplying the southern districts of the city. Supply from the urban water network (whether fed originally by the La Malga cisterns or the Zaghouan aqueduct) is probable.[94]

The urban water network, and in particular the parts of it supplied by the Zaghouan aqueduct, therefore supplied numerous establishments besides the Bordj Djedid cisterns and the Antonine Baths. The height of the arcades across the Ariana plain, bringing the aqueduct past the La Malga cisterns at an elevation of *c*.27 m asl, is not explicable solely by the need to feed the Bordj Djedid cisterns (whose inlet must have been at *c*.18.4 m asl);[95] if they had been the primary goal, the arcades could have been built some 7 m lower and still have had sufficient gradient to reach Bordj Djedid, saving massive expense in construction and easing the problem of maintaining a very shallow gradient between Moghrane and La Malga. Much more likely is that the arcades were built as high as was feasible to ensure maximum distribution within the city.

Supply to the higher regions of Carthage

Water channels lined with *opus signinum* and covered with stone slabs (thus apparently not drains) have been located flowing east under *decumanus* VI N and north under *cardo* IV E at the intersection of these two streets. They relate to 5th-c. or later street surfaces and raise the question of how the water reached that part of the town. Although the elevations of the channels are not given, the street surfaces were at *c*.50 m asl, some 14 m higher than the aqueduct's entry to the town.[96] A lead pipe has been discovered under *cardo* III E on the Odeon hill, again on high ground.[97] The Maison de la Volière nearby must also have been supplied from an external source, given the scale of its nymphaeum; although elevations have not been published, it too may lie above the 35-m contour delimiting areas of the city that the Zaghouan aqueduct could have fed by gravity flow. Two possible explanations present themselves: either water was lifted artificially from an underground branch of the aqueduct to a distribution system on the Odeon hill;[98] or the same source that fed the La Malga cisterns was able to feed other parts of the Odeon hill too. Possibly the subterranean chamber for drawing water discovered by Vernaz represents another solution to the problem of making water available in parts of the city where the surface was too high to be reached by aqueduct.

---

93 Saumagne 1928.

94 Saumagne's suggestion (1928, 634, 647) that local ground-water might have played a part is unlikely: the linear cistern complex was separated from the water-table below by 1 m of impermeable clay, while if the reservoirs around the *turris aquaria* itself had penetrated the water-table, as Saumagne suggests, ground-water would have filled them to a depth of only *c*.0.9 m rather than their full depth of 5-6 m.

95 Ellis (1996) gives the elevation of the raft of stone blocks below the floor of the channel and *castellum* as 26.65 m asl. Magne (1911, 16) gives the elevation of the floor of the Bordj Djedid cisterns as 11.199 m; his fig. 2 shows an inlet or outlet, defining the maximum water level, at 18.429 m asl. (Rakob's figures for the elevation of the aqueduct channel near La Malga as *c*.36 m, and the elevation of the floor of the Bordj Djedid cisterns as 24.40 m asl [1974, 45 and 50] are incorrect.)

96 A 4th- or 5th-c. conduit was also found further west under *decumanus* N 6 in the vicinity of the Odeon: Wells and Wightman 1980, 47, 57. Cf. Garrison *et al.* 1993, 257.

97 C. M. Wells, pers. comm.

98 For the use of human and animal labour on an urban aqueduct system in Egypt, see *P.Lond* 1177; on water-lifting devices, see Oleson 1984; 1992.

A model for urban water supply?

It is sometimes noted that the aqueduct's estimated discharge and the capacity of the Bordj Djedid cisterns are roughly equal (20,000 m^3), and this is taken to show an intended link between the two.[99] Hodge argues that the cisterns held at most a day and half's discharge from the aqueduct and suggests that they were either used to supplement discharge when the aqueduct's flow diminished, or were topped up overnight to meet daytime demands which exceeded supply during daylight hours.[100] His calculations, however, ignore the fact that the Zaghouan aqueduct had to supply other structures as well; not all of its discharge can have flowed down the branch to Bordj Djedid. Assuming that the Bordj Djedid cisterns were fed by the Zaghouan aqueduct, their capacity of 20,000 m^3 represents considerably more than a day and a half's supply of the branch that fed them and implies a longer-term storage function. Under normal operating conditions, assuming that when the cisterns' outflow was opened the amount of water delivered at the inlet was sufficient to keep the water level constant, to fill up the cisterns their outflow must have been shut off or at least regulated so that less water flowed out than was flowing in. Given that Roman taps do not seem to have been designed as valves for fine control but were either in the on or off position, regulation of outflow was not achieved by setting taps in a partly open position but by varying the length of time for which an outflow tap was open or closed. This implies that supply to the Antonine Baths was shut off while the cisterns were filled up. It therefore seems to me most likely that private users, public fountains, and baths were supplied during the day, and that during the night water was impounded in the reservoirs. At this rate the reservoirs could have taken several days, perhaps even a week or two, to fill. Those reserves of water could then be drawn down in times of shortage or when inflow was diminished below the normal outflow rate or interrupted. This could have included the possibility of using such reservoirs to provide continued service for parts of the city during hours when their supply branch had been shut off, if the suggestion of regional distribution by time allocation made in relation to the *castellum* near La Malga is correct. The period of time for which such reservoirs could function as a reserve would depend on whether inflow had merely diminished below normal rates, or had been stopped completely, but a full reservoir ought to have been able to provide several days' reserve given that the capacity equalled several days' delivery through the supply branch, and this period could have been prolonged if during such times of shortage outflow was restricted to a shorter period per day than normal. Probably one of the reservoir's main uses was during the dry season, when aqueduct flow could be expected to drop and demand increase as domestic cisterns dried up. A seasonal storage pattern for such reservoirs may also be implied by the fact that large storage reservoirs of this type are generally found on aqueducts in the more arid regions of the empire (Spain, Italy, Crete, as well as North Africa) but not in wetter areas such as N Europe.

This model envisages active control and manipulation of the water supply by personnel at reservoirs and at certain branch points, distributing and redirecting water now into main channels, now into branch channels, and now into storage reservoirs. We have seen that there is good evidence for tap control rooms and surveillance galleries in North African storage reservoirs. An inscription from Ptolemais refers to *valvas* apparently in connection with an aqueduct,[101] a *castellum divisorium* from Thuburbo Minus allowed control of water distribution *via* 3 different outlets with variable settings for their sluice-gates, and one of the nymphaea at Cherchel seems to have acted as a distribution point equipped with sluice gates that created a

99 Slim 1992, 518; cf. Hodge 1992, 279.

100 Hodge 1992, 279-80.

101 *[a]edificandas et [.../...]t valvas et hydr(agogium)*. Robinson 1913, 185 no. 75. Cf. Oliverio 1936, 251 no. 32 and Kraeling 1962, 73. But *valvae* could also be the doors of a building.

variable water-level.[102] The distribution *castellum* found by S. Ellis north of La Malga was equipped with a swing gate on at least one of its outlets and almost certainly on the other(s). Generally, sluice-gates seem to have been used in open flow channels and in distribution *castella*, while taps and stopcocks were used at the exits of reservoirs and on pipelines. The pipe to the fountain 'utere felix' at Carthage was controlled by a bronze stopcock.[103] The evidence for taps, stopcocks and other control devices is widespread in North Africa and elsewhere.[104] Frontinus, speaking of the public and imperial slaves owned by the water-board at Rome, makes it clear that there were *castellarii* to operate the reservoirs at Rome:

> utraque autem familia in aliquot ministeriorum species diducitur, vilicos, castellarios, circitores, silicarios, tectores aliosque opifices ... homines in urbe circa castellorum et munera stationes opera quaeque urgebunt, in primis ad subitos casus, ut ex compluribus regionibus, in quam necessitas incubuerit, converti possit praesidium aquarum abundantium. *De Aq.* 117
>
> Both gangs are divided into several kinds of workmen: overseers, reservoir-keepers, inspectors, plasterers, tilers and other craftsmen ... The men within the city around the reservoirs and the fountains will devote their energies to any works, especially to sudden emergencies, so that a copious reserve of water can be diverted from several city regions to the one in which it is required.

Elsewhere (87 and 122) Frontinus mentions the cross-linking of fountains to two aqueducts, to guarantee supply in case one line failed, and the need to stagger repairs on Rome's aqueducts so that those still in service can cover for one under repair. Although these passages deal primarily with repairs and emergency interruptions in supply, they demonstrate an awareness of the need to store water against fluctuation in supply, and show that at Rome the technology and personnel were available to do so.

Although in recent years it has begun to be acknowledged that there was rather more regulation of flow in urban water distribution than used to be thought,[105] the model here envisaged for Carthage runs counter to the common view that Roman aqueducts ran on a principle of continuous off-take and were excessively wasteful of water. Leveau and Paillet's impressive study of the Cherchel aqueduct concluded with a couple of paragraphs assessing the aqueduct as a civic luxury, built chiefly to support a Romanised lifestyle of bathing, that played no significant rôle in urban growth. This view had a profound effect on later aqueduct studies. Several questionable beliefs contributed to this conclusion, including the supposed lack of taps on water networks (itself considered a product of technological backwardness deriving from an over-reliance on slave labour[106]), and the idea that in Cherchel "on pouvait aisément se suffire de l'eau des citernes".[107] In fact we have insufficient data on both public and private cisterns at Cherchel to know whether they alone could easily suffice; my own research in North Africa suggests that urban strategies of water supply relied on the use of all available sources — wells, cisterns for rainwater, local springs, and remote aqueduct-led springs — to ensure the best

102 Thuburbo Minus: Germain de Montauzan 1907; Fleury de Sert and Héron de Villefosse 1915; Hodge 1992, 289-90; Ellis 1996. Cherchel: *CIL* 8.2 1081 and Leveau and Paillet 1976, 125-29.

103 Carton 1935, 36.

104 For taps in general see, e.g., Kretzschmer 1960; Hodge 1992, 322-30; Jansen 1996. In North Africa bronze taps are known from Volubilis (Étienne 1960; Hassar-Benslimane 1976, 46), Banasa (Thouvenot and Luquet 1951, 58 and 59 fig. 6) and Rusicade (Ravoisié 1846, vol. 2 pl. 48), and a tap in the Museum of Constantine (anon. 1876, 291 no. 342). Stone taps are also known from North Africa: 2 marble taps from La Cherguia near Tunis and Medjez el-Bab (Renault, J. 1911, Saladin 1913), and a stone tap in the Museum of Constantine (anon. 1876, 280 no. 239).

105 Bruun 1991; Hodge 1992, 279-80.

106 A view now called into question: Wikander 1984; Greene 1990; Greene 1994.

107 Leveau and Paillet 1976, 166-67 and n. 152 bis: "les Romains ne utilisaient pas le robinet et, de la sorte, étaient contraints de garder l'eau dans une citerne ou de la laisser librement couler. C'est là une variante du couple contradictoire pénurie-gaspillage, qui a toujours été la conséquence du retard technique."

chance of riding out a dry season of unpredictable length, during which wells and cisterns were liable to run dry.[108] Although in later studies Leveau acknowledged the practical utility of aqueducts,[109] the emphasis by others has often been on their luxury rôle.[110] Support for a lack of connection between aqueducts and urban growth is sometimes adduced from chronology and from postulated links with particular sets of public baths, in both of which arguments the example of Carthage plays a large part. Shaw argues that many Roman towns in North Africa existed for some time before they received an aqueduct, while others never received one at all.[111] However, two of his chief examples do not bear this out: the Cherchel aqueduct is now thought to belong originally to the first half of the 1st c. A.D., the period of Juban expansion,[112] and although Carthage may not have acquired a long-distance aqueduct until the mid 2nd c. (unless the La Malga cisterns were fed by an aqueduct from Sidi bou Said) it did already possess the La Malga cisterns (a storage capability unparalleled in scale) and presumably therefore a piped urban supply network. Furthermore, Shaw is incorrect in several of the 6 examples he gives of towns that supposedly never received aqueducts:[113] Thapsus and Thysdrus did have aqueducts;[114] the underground channel supplying the cisterns at Bararus, which is equipped with sluice-gates, is far more likely to derive from an underground aqueduct draining an aquifer than from a putative well; and while the source of supply for the vast *exceptoria antoniniana* cisterns at Thuburbo Maius is unknown, they can hardly have been fed by local run-off.[115] Nor is it true to say that "all the urban centres along the Sahelian coast were, once again, devoid of monumental aqueducts", for Hadrumetum, Leptiminus, and Thaenae, as well as Thapsus, are known to have had aqueducts.[116] Of the towns cited by Shaw there remain only Acholla and Tiddis; Tiddis, a small satellite town of Cirta perched on a steep hill, can never have had an aqueduct, but all one can say of Acholla is that an aqueduct has not yet been found.[117] The remarkable point about Shaw's examples is that there are so few of them.

As to chronology, the argument that some towns existed for a long time without aqueducts has some validity, but is less clear cut than may at first seem. Our dating evidence for North African aqueducts is woefully incomplete;[118] of the scores of known aqueducts, only about 18 are datable with any degree of precision, a small sample on which to base conclusions. Nine date from before the middle of the 2nd c., and 9 after, but of these latter 3 are from the same site (Lambaesis), and another 3 (Thamugadi, Thugga and Cirta) are not the first aqueducts to be built in their towns (Table 1).

---

108 Wilson, A. I. 1997.
109 Leveau 1991, 158.
110 Schwartz 1981; Shaw, B. D. 1991, passim and esp. 66.
111 Shaw, B. D. 1991.
112 Leveau 1984, 61-62.
113 Shaw, B. D. 1991, 60-61, 80-82.
114 Flick 1897; Cintas, J. 1956; Foucher 1963.
115 Thuburbo Maius possessed at least one public fountain (Merlin 1912, cclxxiv-v; Poinssot, L. 1917, 115); water was also delivered under pressure to a jet fountain in the House of Bacchus and Ariadne (Lantier 1943); although the Winter and Summer Baths both have wells (Drappier 1920), the baths are of a size which seems to demand a piped supply. Such a network may well have derived from the *exceptoria antoniniana*, but in the absence of a local spring it is implausible to regard these cisterns as having functioned without some external source of supply.
116 Shaw, B. D. 1991, 81. For Hadrumetum: Gresse 1901. Leptiminus: Ben Lazreg *et al.* 1992, 300. Thaenae: Berrier and Benson 1908.
117 Acholla has at least two sets of public baths and several houses with fountain basins (Fendri 1985, 156-58; pls. IX and XIV show fountain basins), which might lead one to suspect the existence of a water-supply network (I owe this point to Roger Wilson). Study of Acholla has concentrated largely on the mosaics.
118 On the problems of dating aqueducts in general, see Wilson, R. J. A. 1996, 12-19.

Table 1: Dates of aqueduct construction
in roughly chronological order (repairs are ignored)

Site	*Date*	*Evidence*
Berenice Aqueduct C	Augustan	Lloyd 1977, 199
Caesarea	Juba II?	Leveau–Paillet 1976, 151-53; Leveau 1984, 61-62
Volubilis	60-80	Akerraz 1987
Thysdrus	*c.*80	*AE* 1991.1635
Hippo Regius	pre 150?	Use of *opus reticulatum*
Lepcis Magna	119	*IRT* 357
Carthage (Zaghouan)	Hadrianic?	SHA, *Had.* 22
Saldae	137-152	*ILS* 5795
Thamugadi	146	*AE* 1985. 875a
Verecunda	160/61	*ILS* 5752
Ammaedara	pre 160/180	*AE* 1988.119 refers to pre-existing aqueduct
Thugga (Aïn el-Hammam)	184/185	Poinssot, C. 1966. The Aïn Mizeb aqueduct (which is much shorter) and cisterns must be earlier
Thamugadi (Aquae Paludensis)	184/185	*AE* 1934.40
Bisica	180/200	*CIL* 8 23888, cf. *AE* 1991.1665
Lambaesis (Aquae Alexandrianae)	222/235	*CIL* 8 2659
Lambaesis (Aïn Cherchar)	225/236	*AE* 1942-43. 93
Lambaesis (Aqua Lu...nensis Mellariensis)	226	CIL 8 2658
Cirta	388/392	*ILAlg* 2 619. This was not Cirta's first aqueduct.

Although in many cases there is some lapse of time between a town's foundation and the construction of an aqueduct, it begins to look as if a significant number of important North African towns possessed aqueducts before the middle of the 2nd c. — and thus before the main phase of population expansion and urban growth.[119] This leaves open the possibility that aqueducts could have helped support larger and more dense urban populations than would otherwise have been possible. Indeed, it is hard to imagine that urbanisation in North Africa would have been possible on the scale achieved during the 3rd c. without them. Aqueducts provided an important supplement to the water table and roof and courtyard *impluvia.*

Although smaller baths could function by drawing water from wells alone (Sabratha, Thaenae), large installations required an aqueduct to function. It is almost certain that water from the Zaghouan aqueduct fed the Antonine Baths, but the evidence is still insufficient to say that both were part of the same plan or that the prime purpose of the Zaghouan aqueduct was to supply the Antonine Baths. Perhaps instead the aqueduct created the opportunity for the baths' subsequent construction. Such a sequence is seen at Lepcis Magna, where dedicatory inscriptions of the aqueduct built by Q. Servilius Candidus date from 119/120 (they come from the main reservoir cisterns and from the theatre, possibly associated with the fountain behind the stage[120]). These were followed by the dedication of the Hadrianic Baths in 126/7. The cisterns supplying these baths look like a subsequent addition to the large public cisterns, suggesting that supply to the baths was not part of the original scheme.[121] It is demonstrable only that large baths follow the construction of aqueducts, not that they motivate them. Nevertheless, this connection is significant; it does not invalidate points about connections between aqueducts and the popularity of bathing, but it does necessitate a slight readjustment

119 For the late 2nd and 3rd c. as the main period of population growth in North Africa, see Lassère 1977, 573-85.

120 *IRT* 357, 358, 359.

121 *IRT* 361. For a plan and sections of the cisterns, in which two phases are clearly distinguishable, see Bartoccini 1929, tav. X; Romanelli 1925, tav. VI. It is the smaller and later phase which supplied the baths. Although the construction of both the aqueduct and the baths must have lasted several years, there is a time-lag of several years between their respective completion dates, and the phasing of the cisterns suggests that the baths were not originally planned as part of the same project as the aqueduct.

of perspective. Curiously, in North African inscriptions which refer to structures served by aqueducts, such as those from Thysdrus (*ILS* 5777 = *CIL* 8 51) and Sabratha (*IRT* 117), it is public fountains and private distribution, not the baths, that are mentioned.

I do not wish to deny that aqueducts served as expressions of civic pride and of Romanisation. Indeed, I have argued elsewhere that private water connections in North Africa were employed largely for ornamental fountains and not for 'useful' purposes within the house.[122] But the opposition between utility and luxury has been drawn too starkly; aqueducts served both purposes, and the symbolic value of public fountains — from simple stone basins up to the great nymphaea such as the Severan nymphaeum at Lepcis Magna or the fountain at Cirta decorated with bronze and marble statues, a gilded inscription, and golden drinking cups[123] — was derived both from their appearance and from their value as fountains that people actually used. Too many discussions of the significance of aqueducts have lost sight of the rôle that public fountains played in providing water for that sector of the population who, for reasons such as poverty or lack of access to sufficient *impluvium* space to collect rainwater, had perforce to rely on public provision of water. One reason for overlooking this point may be that there has been so little excavation of lower-class housing in North Africa, but buildings without their own wells or cisterns did exist, such as the 'immeuble à l'apside' at Volubilis or some of the units in Regio II *Insula* 10 at Sabratha.[124]

Vandal and Byzantine Carthage, and the late history of the Zaghouan aqueduct

Evidence for the state of Carthage's water supply in late antiquity is scattered but allows a tentative picture to be sketched. The La Malga cisterns were included within the Theodosian wall, suggesting that they were still functioning. Presumably the Zaghouan aqueduct continued in service during the Vandal period, since it was cut by Gelimer while attempting to blockade Carthage in 533.[125] The Antonine Baths, however, were left to decay after the collapse of the *frigidarium* vault in the 5th c.; coin evidence, the force necessary to demolish the concrete vaults, and traces of attempted burning of the adjacent latrines combine to suggest the possibility of deliberate destruction after the Vandal capture of Carthage. Lézine notes a burnt destruction layer 10 cm thick, with a clay abandonment deposit overlying it. A hoard sealed by the burnt layer included coins from the reigns of Constans I and Constantius II up to John (425), giving a *terminus post quem* that would be consistent with the Vandal sack of 439. If so, the Antonine Baths should be added to the list of buildings, including the Theatre, Odeon and Aedes Memoriae, destroyed by the Vandals.[126] It may be to the aftermath of this that we should date the blocking of the main outlet of the Bordj Djedid cisterns, and the re-arrangement of their overflow so that it no longer went to the street drains of *cardo* XV E but now served a structure somewhat to the west.[127]

The Bordj Djedid cisterns underwent considerable alteration at a relatively late date: the former tap room was converted into a storage cistern for rainwater (fig. 13), and the service galleries were partially blocked and small rainwater cisterns dug through their floor, fed presumably from the *impluvium* formed by the extrados of the vaults of the main complex.[128] The construction of small rainwater cisterns within the large cistern complex smacks of opportunistic re-use of a largely redundant structure, and strongly suggests that supply to the main cis-

122 Wilson, A. I. 1995.

123 *CIL* 8 6982 = *ILS* 4921b.

124 Étienne 1960, 65-66; Kenrick 1986, fig. 66. The majority of units in this *insula* did have cisterns, but some did not.

125 Proc., *BV* 2.1.2.

126 Lézine *et al.* 1956. An unrecorded earthquake, however, might be a possibility.

127 Vernaz 1887, 25-27.

128 Magne 1911, 28-31.

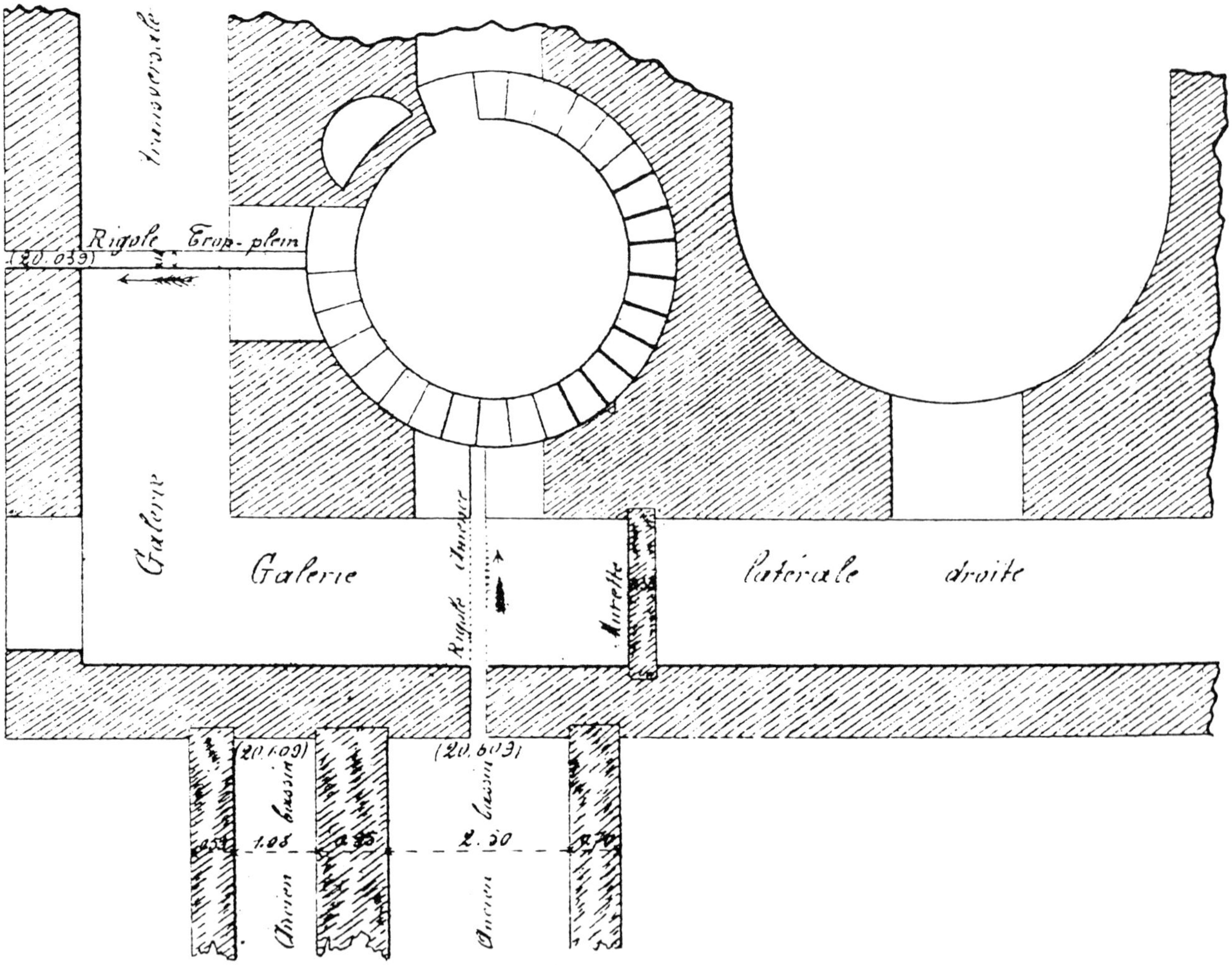

Fig. 13. Bordj Djedid cisterns: late alterations connected with converting the tap room to a collection cistern. An inlet ("rigole amenée") and overflow ("rigole trop-plein") were added to the chamber, in connection with two tanks against the external wall of the main cistern complex, and a wall ("murette") blocked the service gallery (Magne 1911, 30, fig. 7).

terns had been drastically reduced or had ceased completely. Similarly re-use, of uncertain date, is evident at La Malga in the main channel of the Zaghouan aqueduct where it runs alongside the cisterns. Here there are indications, previously unremarked,[129] that several small cisterns were constructed within the aqueduct's channel at a late date (figs. 14-17). One pair of walls, lined with waterproof mortar, clearly created a small cistern in the channel (fig. 16); the walls overlie both the waterproof lining and the sinter (lime deposits) in the aqueduct's channel, indicating a date after the aqueduct had been in use for a considerable period of time. As the cistern completely blocks the channel, it must have been constructed after the La Malga branch of the aqueduct had gone out of use. Other cisterns in the channel are traceable as pairs of cuttings visible in the channel's walls (fig. 17).[130] They truncate the waterproof lining of the *specus* and the sinter deposits and should therefore be late and broadly contemporary with each other and with the preserved cistern. The cuttings are too rough and irregularly

129 I am very grateful to A. Ennabli for permission to study the aqueduct in the area of La Malga.

130 The cuts vary between 16 and 25 cm wide, and between 13 and 24 cm deep into the thickness of the wall; their vertical extent may vary between 20 cm and the entire preserved height of the channel wall (up to 1 m).

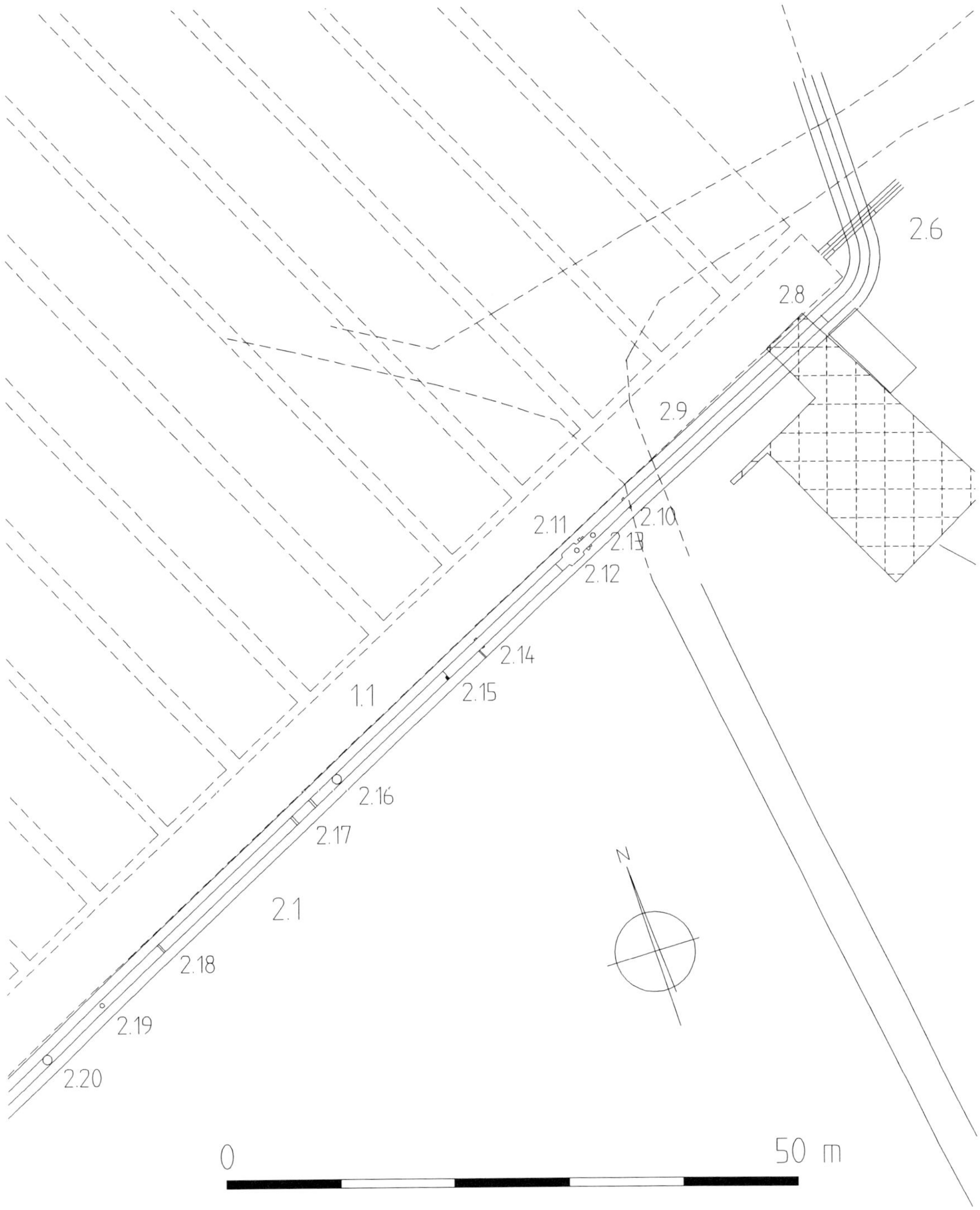

Fig. 14. Plan of late features in the aqueduct channel beside the La Malga cisterns.

2.1 and 2.6 Channel of the Zaghouan aqueduct. 2.8 Wall across channel, apparently part of cistern. 2.9 Wall of La Malga cisterns. 2.10 Pair of cuttings in aqueduct channel walls. 2.11 Pair of cuttings in aqueduct channel walls, but with traces of mortared blocking wall keyed into the cut, forming the N wall of: 2.12 chamber formed by widening the aqueduct channel; it contains original settling pit (d. 0.44 m). 2.13 Settling pit in channel floor (d. 0.44 m). 2.14 Pair of cuts in aqueduct channel walls. 2.15 Remains of mortared blocking in channel floor, with waterproof lining against it, angled up on the N side. 2.16 Circular settling tank in aqueduct channel floor (d. 0.84 m). 2.17 Cistern (2 m long) formed by blocking the aqueduct channel. 2.18 Faint traces of blocking wall with waterproof mortar against both faces. 2.19 Small settling pit in channel floor (d. 0.42 m). 2.20 Large settling pit in channel floor (d. 0.85 m).

Fig. 15. View to N along the channel of the Zaghouan aqueduct next to the La Malga cisterns, showing late cisterns constructed in the channel.

Fig. 16. Detail of one of the late cisterns in the Zaghouan aqueduct channel at La Malga (at fig. 14 point 2.17), showing how the waterproof lining of the cistern seals the lining and sinter of the aqueduct channel (foreground).

Fig. 17. Late alterations in the aqueduct channel at La Malga, to form a cistern (at fig. 14 points 2.11 and 2.12). The circular settling pit in the channel's floor is an original feature; the widening of the aqueduct channel at this point also seems to be original. After the channel fell into disuse, a cistern was constructed by building a blocking wall (now removed) keyed into the pair of cuts in the channel wall visible in the foreground; the far end of the cistern was closed by another wall (also robbed) at the point where the light coloured waterproof mortar ends towards the top of the photograph.

positioned to be grooves for sluice-gates, and some have mortared masonry blocks remaining in them, overlain with waterproof mortar. They are best interpreted as cuts to allow blocking walls across the channel to be more keyed securely into the side walls of the channel. These cisterns can only have been built after the La Malga branch had ceased functioning as an aqueduct, and they are presumably to be related to Ellis' observation of a pair of similar cuts in the La Malga branch by his *castellum*, which he suggested indicated the sealing of the channel.[131] The small capacity of these cisterns suggests a domestic function, perhaps for structures built against or near the aqueduct. A late Vandal or Byzantine date is possible, but so too is an early Arab one, as the use of *opus signinum* continued in early mediaeval North Africa.

After 533 the aqueduct was restored and continued in use during the Byzantine period, while the spring at Aïn Djouker was fortified to protect one of its sources in a period of instability. In the city, new street paving and drainage construction in the 6th and 7th c. attests to the continued upkeep of some urban services in parts at least of Byzantine Carthage, yet the picture is not

---

131 Ellis 1996, 182. Ellis' suggestion that this may be related to the Byzantine rebuilding of the Antonine Baths is interesting but not, to my mind, convincing; the Byzantine rebuilding of the Baths was on a very limited scale, and the Bordj Djedid cistern outlet may already have been sealed by this time.

uniform,[132] and it is perhaps difficult to make generalisations about civic infrastructure in this period. The drains of *cardo* XVI E near the Bordj Djedid cisterns had apparently fallen out of use some time in late antiquity,[133] and several streets were blocked by the Byzantine period.[134] Although Justinian repaired the Antonine Baths, they were on a much smaller scale than before and drew their water from two cisterns; the connection to the Bordj Djedid cisterns does not seem to have been re-instated.[135] Evidence from the German excavations indicates a re-organization of water-supply in the 6th c., possibly connected with interruption in the supply of piped water to that region of the city (although this need not necessarily imply an interruption in the Zaghouan aqueduct itself if that was still supplying other areas).[136]

With the siege of Carthage in 698 the Zaghouan aqueduct was cut again, but that was not the end of its history. Put back into service to supply Tunis in 1267, it was cut, rebuilt, cut again, and quarried for construction materials throughout the chequered history of the following centuries.[137] Late but undatable repairs to the aqueduct channel near Moghrane employed re-used inscriptions.[138] In 1859 a French proposal to put parts of the aqueduct back into service to supply Tunis was made to Mohammed Bey, and the underground sections of the aqueduct were re-used while the arcaded engineering works were supplanted by a large pressurised pipeline. This involved the destruction of the magnificent bridge across the Oued Miliane, to provide construction materials.[139] Thus the springs of Aïn Djouker and Zaghouan still provide water for Tunis, the Byzantine fort continuing to prevent unauthorised access to the Ain Djouker springs. In the 1870s the Bordj Djedid cisterns were restored, and they still function. The La Malga cisterns experienced a different kind of *Nachleben*: writers from the medieval period onwards describe them as sheltering poverty-stricken inhabitants,[140] and during the Second World War they served as homes for refugees from Tunis who had fled the danger of Allied shelling.

Conclusion

This study may be felt to have raised as many questions as it has attempted to answer. Although we have good evidence for storage and control devices on the Carthage water network, and can propose some kind of model for its functioning, we are still some way from understanding the rôle of the La Malga cisterns. Assuming they had an outlet, what structures did they serve? How often could they be filled? Which parts of the city did the La Malga cisterns serve, and how much more of the city could be served by the elevated channel of the Zaghouan aqueduct? Where does the supply line for the Bordj Djedid cisterns run, and how close is the connection between the Zaghouan aqueduct, on the one hand, and the Antonine Baths and Bordj Djedid cisterns, on the other? If nothing else, I hope that this study will point future researchers to some of the unsolved problems. We also need more data on orientations and elevations of channels. Because of the differences in distribution arrangements from those of better studied towns, such as Pompeii or Volubilis, the water supply of Carthage has the potential to enlarge our understanding of the diversity of Roman methods of supplying water.

Magdalen College, Oxford

132 Humphrey 1980 passim; ibid. 115 for drains.
133 Vernaz 1887, 25-27.
134 Ellis 1988, 8.
135 Lézine *et al.* 1956.
136 Rakob ed. 1991, 249; Humphrey 1980, 109.
137 Caillat 1873; Rakob 1979b, 37.
138 Audollent 1901, 184 n.5; *CIL* 8 887-894, 10522.
139 Caillat 1873.
140 Loth 1896. Traces of recent occupation and soot blackening from hearths may still be seen.

Bibliography

Akerraz, A. (1987) "Nouvelles observations sur l'urbanisme du quartier nord-est de Volubilis," in *L'Africa Romana* 4 (Sassari) 445-57.

Anon. (1876-77) "Catalogue du Musée Archéologique de Constantine," *Recueil de Constantine* 18, 1-307.

Audollent, A. (1901) *Carthage romaine, 146 avant J.-C. - 698 après J.-C.* (Paris).

Babelon, E. and Cagnat, R. (1893) (edd.) *Atlas archéologique de la Tunisie* 1 (Paris).

Bartoccini, R. (1929) *Le terme di Leptis* (Bergamo).

Ben Abdallah, Z. (1986) *Catalogue des inscriptions latines païennes du Musée du Bardo* (Rome).

Ben Abed-Ben Khader, A. (1987) *Corpus des mosaïques de Tunisie* II.3 (Tunis).

Ben Lazreg, N. and Mattingly, D. J. (1992) *Leptiminus (Lamta): a Roman port city in Tunisia* (JRA Suppl. 4).

Ben Lazreg, N., Mattingly, D. J. and Stirling, L. (1992) "Summary of excavations in 1990 and preliminary typology of burials," in *Leptiminus (Lamta)* 301-33.

Berger, P. (1911) *CRAI* 604-5.

Berrier, L. and Benson, L. (1908) "Fouilles à Thina (Tunisie)," *BAC* 22-58, pl. 4-8.

Blanchet, P. (1897) "Rapport sur les travaux hydrauliques des Romains dans l'arrière pays de Sfax," in P. Gauckler (ed.), *Enquête administrative sur les installations hydrauliques romaines en Tunisie* I.1 (Tunis) 25-49.

Bruun, C. (1991) *The water supply of ancient Rome: a study of Roman Imperial administration* (Helsinki).

Cagnat, R. (1887) "Note sur l'inscription des thermes de Carthage," *RA* 2, 171-79.

Caillat, P. (1873) "Extrait d'une note sur la restauration de l'ancien aqueduc de Carthage," *RA* n.s. 26.2, 292-301.

Caronni, F. (1805-6) *Ragguaglio del viaggio compendioso d'un dilettante antiquario sorpreso da' corsari, condotto in Barberia e felicamente ripatriato* (2 vols., Milano).

Carrie, J.-M. and Sanviti, N. (1979) "Le secteur B (1974-1975)," in S. Lancel (ed.), *Byrsa* 1 (Rome) 97-142.

Carton, L. (1896) "Études sur les travaux hydrauliques des Romains en Tunisie," *RevTun* 3 [12] (Octobre), 530-64.

Carton, L. (1903a) "Chronique d'archéologie nord-africaine," *RevTun* 10 [37] (Janvier) 66-85.

Carton, L. (1903b) "Chronique d'archéologie nord-africaine (suite)," *RevTun* 10 [38] (Mars) 141-62.

Carton, L. (1911) "Documents pour servir à l'étude des ports et de l'enceinte de la Carthage punique," *RevTun* 18 [90] (Novembre) 488-505.

Carton, L. (1912) "Documents pour servir à l'étude des ports et de l'enceinte de la Carthage punique," *RevTun* 19 [96] (Novembre) 560-67.

Carton, L. (1919) *CRAI* 372-76.

Carton, L. (1920) "Découverte d'une fontaine antique à Carthage," *CRAI* 258-67.

Carton, L. (1935) *Pour visiter Carthage* (Tunis).

Cintas, J. (1956) "L'alimentation en eau de Thysdrus dans l'antiquité," *Karthago* 7, 179-87.

Cintas, P. (1976) *Manuel d'archéologie punique* 2 (Paris).

Coleman, K. M. (1993) "Launching into history: aquatic displays in the early empire," *JRS* 83, 48-74.

Delattre, A.-L. (1891) "Marques de vases grecs et romains trouvées à Carthage 1888-1890," *MEFRA* 11, 53-80.

Delattre, A.-L. (1893a) "Fouilles archéologiques dans le flanc sud-ouest de la Colline de Saint-Louis," *BAC* 94-123.

Delattre, A.-L. (1893b) "Marques de vases grecs et romains trouvés à Carthage," *MEFRA* 13, 31-47.

Deneauve, J. (1977) "Fouilles françaises à Carthage (1974-1975). Les structures romaines de Byrsa. Historique des recherches," *AntAfr* 11, 51-66.

Deneauve, J. (1990) "Le centre monumental de Carthage: un ensemble cultuel sur la colline de Byrsa," in *Carthage et son territoire dans l'antiquité. Histoire et archéologie de l'Afrique du Nord, Actes du IVe colloque international* 1 (Paris) 143-55.

Dietz, S. (1979) "Description préliminaire des vestiges – datation des vestiges," in S. Dietz and S. Trolle (edd.), *Premier rapport préliminaire sur les fouilles danoises à Carthage. Les campagnes de 1975 et 1977* (København) 20-50.

Dietz, S. (1992) "Le secteur nord-est de la ville: Falbe point 90," in A. Ennabli (ed.), *Pour sauver Carthage* (Paris–Tunis) 143-49.

Drappier, L. (1899) "Rapport sur les travaux hydrauliques romains étudiés en 1898," in P. Gauckler (ed.), *Enquête administrative sur les installations hydrauliques romaines en Tunisie* I.3 (Tunis) 127-67.

Drappier, L. (1920) "Les thermes de Thuburbo Maius," *BAC* 55-75.

du Coudray la Blanchère and Gauckler, P. (1897) *Catalogue du Musée Alaoui* (Paris).

Dunbabin, K. M. D. (1978) *The mosaics of Roman North Africa* (Oxford).

Dureau de la Malle (1835) *Recherches sur la topographie de Carthage* (Paris).
Ellis, S. P. (1988) "Carthage sewers project 1986," *CEDAC Carthage* 9, 6-38.
Ellis, S. P. (1996) "Systems of water control – the evidence of some African *castellae*," in N. de Haan and G. C. M. Jansen (edd.), *Cura Aquarum in Campania* (Leiden) 179-84.
Ennabli, A. (1983) "La Maison de la Volière à Carthage: l'architecture," in *Mosaïque: recueil d'hommages à Henri Stern* (Paris) 129-45.
Eschebach, H. (1979) "Pompéi: la distribution des eaux dans une grande ville romaine," *DossPar* 38 (Oct.-Nov.) 74-81.
Étienne, R. (1960) *Le quartier nord-est de Volubilis* (Paris).
Falbe, C. T. (1833) *Recherches sur l'emplacement de Carthage, suivies de renseignements sur plusieurs inscriptions puniques inédites* (Paris).
Fendri, M. (1985) "Cités antiques et villas romaines de la région Sfaxienne," *Africa* 9, 151-208.
Ferjaoui-Weber, F. (1994) *Carthage: le parc des Thermes d'Antonin* (Tunis).
Fleury de Sert and Héron de Villefosse (1915) *BAC* clxxxi-ii.
Flick (Capitaine) (1897) "Rapport sur les travaux d'eau des Romains reconnus par la deuxième Brigade topographique de Tunisie pendant la campagne 1895 (Mokenine, Mahdia)," in P. Gauckler (ed.), *Enquête administrative sur les installations hydrauliques romaines en Tunisie* I.1 (Tunis) 55-57.
Fornacciari, C. (1928-29) "Note sur le drain romain de la Soukra," *BAC* 413-15.
Foucher, L. (1963) *Découvertes archéologiques à Thysdrus en 1961* (Tunis).
Frend, W. H. C. (1977) "The early Christian church in Carthage," in J. H. Humphrey (ed.), *Excavations at Carthage 1976 conducted by the University of Michigan* 3 (Ann Arbor) 21-40.
Garrison, M. B., Foss, P. and Wells, C. M. (1993) "A newly-discovered cryptoporticus and bath at Carthage," *JRA* 6, 251-60.
Gauckler, P. (1902) "Les fouilles de Tunisie," *RA* 3e sér., 41.2, 369-408 with pls. XV-XX.
Gauckler, P. (1904) "Lettre sur l'emplacement du camp de la première cohorte urbaine à Carthage," *CRAI* 695-703.
Gendre, F. (1907) "L'Ile de Djerba," *RevTun* 4 [66] (Novembre) 504-22.
Germain de Montauzan, C. (1907) "Rapport sur une mission scientifique en Italie et en Tunisie," *NouvArch* 15, 71-123.
Greene, K. (1990) "Perspectives on Roman technology," *OJA* 9, 209-19.
Greene, K. (1994) "Technology and innovation in context: the Roman background to mediaeval and later developments," *JRA* 7, 22-33.
Gresse, A. (1901) "Restauration de la conduite romaine de l'Oued Kharroub à Sousse," in P. Gauckler (ed.), *Enquête administrative sur les installations hydrauliques romaines en Tunisie* I.5 (Tunis) 301-10.
Gsell, S. (1901) *Les monuments antiques de l'Algérie* (2 vols., Paris).
Gsell, S. (1911) *Atlas archéologique de l'Algérie* (Alger–Paris).
Hallier, G. (1987) "Les citernes monumentales de Bararus (Henchir Rougga) en Byzacène," *AntAfr* 23, 129-48.
Hassar-Benslimane, J. (1976) "L'archéologie marocaine de 1973 à 1975," *BAMaroc* 10, 243-52.
Hodge, A. T. (1992) *Roman aqueducts and water supply* (London).
Hodge, A. T. (1996) "In Vitruvium Pompeianum: urban water distribution reappraised," *AJA* 100, 261-76.
Homolle (1894) *BCH* 18, 161-67.
Humphrey, J. H. (1980) "Vandal and Byzantine Carthage. Some new archaeological evidence," in J. G. Pedley (ed.), *New light on ancient Carthage* (Ann Arbor) 85-120.
Humphrey, J. H. (1988) (ed.) *The circus and a Byzantine cemetery at Carthage* 1 (Ann Arbor).
Jansen, G. C. M. (1996) "Die Verteilung des Leitungswassers in den Häusern Pompejis," in N. de Haan and G. C. M. Jansen (edd.), *Cura Aquarum in Campania* (Leiden) 47-50.
Kenrick, P. M. (1986) *Excavations at Sabratha 1948-1951* (London).
Kraeling, C. H. (1962) *Ptolemais, city of the Libyan Pentapolis* (Chicago).
Kretzschmer, F. (1960) "La robinetterie romaine," *RAEst* 11, 89-113.
Lachaux, J.-C. (1979) *Théâtres et amphithéâtres d'Afrique Proconsulaire* (Aix-en-Provence).
Lancel, S. (1979) "Le secteur A (1974-1975)," in S. Lancel (ed.), *Byrsa* 1 (Rome) 59-96.
Lancel, S. (1982) (ed.) *Byrsa* 2 (Rome).
Lancel, S. (1995) *Carthage: a history* (Oxford).
Lancel, S. and Morel, J.-P. (1992) "La colline de Byrsa: les vestiges puniques," in A. Ennabli (ed.), *Pour sauver Carthage* (Paris–Tunis) 43-71.
Lantier, R. (1943-45 [1951]) "Un bassin à mosaïques de Thuburbo Maius," *BAC* 280-82.
Lassère, J.-M. (1977) *Ubique populus* (Paris).

Leveau, P. (1984) *Caesarea de Maurétanie: une ville romaine et ses campagnes* (Rome).
Leveau, P. (1991) "Research on Roman aqueducts in the past ten years," in A. T. Hodge (ed.), *Future currents in aqueduct studies* (Leeds) 149-62.
Leveau, P. and Paillet, J.-L. (1976) *L'alimentation en eau de Caesarea de Maurétanie et l'aqueduc de Cherchell* (Paris).
Lézine, A., Picard, C. and Picard, G. C. (1956) "Observations sur la ruine des thermes d'Antonin, Carthage," *CRAI* 425-30.
Lloyd, J. A. (1977) "Water supply and storage systems," in J. A. Lloyd (ed.), *Excavations at Sidi Khrebish, Benghazi (Berenice)* 1 (Tripoli) 199-209.
Loth, G. (1896) review of *Le cisterne di Cartagine nel 1600, relazione di Michel Angelo Tilli, RevTun* 3 [10] 346-48.
Magne, L. (1911) "Notes sur les citernes de Carthage," *Cahiers d'archéologie tunisienne* 4, 1-60.
Manderscheid, H. and Garbrecht, G. (1994) *Die Wasserbewirtschaftung römischer Thermen. Archäologische und hydrotechnische Untersuchungen* vol. A (Braunschweig).
Mattingly, H. B. (1975) *Coins of the Roman Empire in the British Museum* 5 (2nd ed., London).
Maumené (Capitaine) (1897) "Notice sur les travaux hydrauliques exécutés par les Romains dans la partie de la Byzacène comprenant Thysdrus (El-Djem), Ruspae (Sbaïa), Caraga ou Bararus (Rougga), Justinianopolis (Chebba), Caput-Vada (Ras-Kaboudia), Acholla (El-Aalia)," in P. Gauckler (ed.), *Enquête administrative sur les installations hydrauliques romaines en Tunisie* I.1 (Tunis) 7-24.
Merlin, A. (1912) *BAC* cclxxii-x.
Montalier (Capitaine) (1903) "Travaux d'eau à l'est du Djebel Zriba," in P. Gauckler (ed.), *Enquête administrative sur les installations hydrauliques romaines en Tunisie* II.2 (Tunis) 59-64.
Oleson, J. P. (1984) *Greek and Roman mechanical water-lifting devices: the history of a technology* (Toronto).
Oleson, J. P. (1992) "The human side of Hellenistic and Roman water-lifting technology," *MittlnstWasser* 117, *Geschichte der Wasserwirtschaft und des Wasserbaus im Mediterranen Raum. Vorträge und schriftliche Beiträge zum 8. Internationalen Symposium zur Geschichte des Wasserbaus, 12. bis 20. Oktober 1991, Merida/Spanien*, 359-85.
Oliverio, G. (1936) *Il decreto di Anastasio 1° su l'ordinamento politico-militare della Cirenaica. Inscrizioni di Tocra, El Chamis, Tolemaide, Cirene* (Bergamo).
Patroni, G. (1904) "Nora. Colonia fenicia in Sardegna," *MonAntLinc* 14.1, 109-268.
Poinssot, C. (1966) "Aqua Commodiana civitatis Aureliae Thuggae," in J. Heurgon, G. Picard and W. Seston (edd.), *Mélanges J. Carcopino* (Paris) 771-86.
Poinssot, L. (1917) "Quelques inscriptions de Thuburbo Maius," *BAC* 94-130.
Rakob, F. (1969a) "Das römische Quellheiligtum bei Zaghouan in Tunesien," *ArchAnz* 3, 284-300.
Rakob, F. (1969-70b) "Le sanctuaire des eaux à Zaghouan," *Africa* 3-4, 133-74.
Rakob, F. (1974) "Das Quellenheiligtum in Zaghouan und die römische Wasserleitung nach Karthago," *RömMitt* 81, 41-89.
Rakob, F. (1979a) "Allemagne," *CEDAC Carthage* 21-29.
Rakob, F. (1979b) "L'aqueduc de Carthage," *DossPar* 36 (Oct.-Nov.) 34-42.
Rakob, F. (1983) "Die Wasserleitung von Karthago," in J.-P. Boucher (ed.), *Journées d'études sur les aqueducs romains. Tagung über römische Wasserversorgungsanlagen, Lyons, 26-28 mai, 1977* (Paris) 309-32.
Rakob, F. (ed.) (1991) *Die deutschen Ausgrabungen in Karthago* (2 vols., Mainz).
Ravoisié, A. (1846-53) *Exploration scientifique de l'Algérie pendant les années 1840, 1841, 1842. Beaux-Arts, architecture et sculpture* (2 vols., Paris).
Reddé, M. (1985) "Occupation humaine et mise en valeur économique dans les vallées du nord de la Libye: l'exemple du wadi Tlal," *BAC* n.s. 19 = *Histoire et archéologie de l'Afrique du Nord. IIe Colloque International (Grenoble, 5-9 avril 1983)* 173-82.
Reddé, M. (1988) *Prospections des vallées du nord de la Libye (1979-1980). La région de la Syrte à l'époque romaine* (Paris).
Renault, H. (1903) "Installations hydrauliques romaines de Sicca Veneria (Le Kef)," in P. Gauckler (ed.), *Enquête administrative sur les installations hydrauliques romaines en Tunisie* II.2 (Tunis) 83-103.
Renault, J. (1911) "La Cherguia: robinet-vanne antique en marbre blanc," *Cahiers d'archéologie tunisienne* 4, 105-9.
Renault, J. (1912a) "Les bassins du trik Dar-Saniat à Carthage," *RevTun* 19 [94] 346-68.
Renault, J. (1912b) "Les bassins du trik Dar-Saniat à Carthage," *RevTun* 19 [95] 471-98.
Renault, J. (1912c) "Les bassins du trik Dar-Saniat à Carthage," *RevTun* 19 [96] 543-59.
Renault, J. (1913a) "Les bassins de Trik dar Saniat," *Cahiers d'archéologie tunisienne* n.s. 1, 89-91.

Renault, J. (1913b) "Les bassins du trik Dar-Saniat à Carthage," *RevTun* 20 [97] 63-102.

Righini, V. (1975) *I bolli laterizi romani: la collezione Di Bagno* (Bologna).

Robinson, D. M. (1913) "Inscriptions from the Cyrenaica," *AJA* 17, 157-200.

Robinson, D. M. (1930) *Excavations at Olynthus* 2 (Baltimore).

Robinson, D. M. (1946) *Excavations at Olynthus* 12 (Baltimore).

Robinson, D. M. and Graham, J. W. (1938) *Excavations at Olynthus* 8 (Baltimore).

Romanelli, P. (1925) *Leptis Magna* (Roma).

Ros, K. E. (1996) "The Roman theater at Carthage," *AJA* 100, 449-89.

Saladin, H. (1913) "Un robinet de marbre trouvé en Tunisie," *BAC* 284-86.

Saumagne, C. (1928-29) "Notes de topographie carthaginoise: I, La "Turris Aquaria" (d'après les fouilles de 1926); II, Les vestiges de la colonie de C. Gracchus à Carthage," *BAC* 629-64.

Saumagne, C. (1982) "Le Metroôn de Carthage et ses abords," in S. Lancel (ed.), *Byrsa* 2 (Rome) 283-310.

Schwartz, H. (1981) "Patterns of public and private water-supply in North Africa," in J. H. Humphrey (ed.), *Excavations at Carthage 1977 conducted by the University of Michigan* 6 (Ann Arbor) 50-54.

Setala, P. (1977) *Private domini in Roman brick stamps of the Empire: a historical and prosopographical study of landowners in the district of Rome* (Helsinki).

Shaw, B. D. (1984) "Water and society in the ancient Mahgrib: technology, property and development," *AntAfr* 20, 121-73.

Shaw, B. D. (1991) "The noblest monuments and the smallest things: wells, walls and aqueducts in the making of Roman Africa," in A. T. Hodge (ed.), *Future currents in aqueduct studies* (Leeds) 63-91.

Shaw, T. (1757) *Travels or observations relating to several parts of Barbary and the Levant* (2nd ed.; 2 vols., London).

Slim, H. (1990) "Le modèle urbain romain et le problème de l'eau dans les confins du Sahel et de la Basse Steppe," in *L'Afrique dans l'occident romain, Ier siècle av. J.-C. - IVe siècle ap. J.-C. Actes du colloque ... 1987* (Rome) 169-201.

Slim, H. (1992) "Maîtrise de l'eau en Tunisie à l'époque romaine," in G. Argoud *et al.* (edd.), *L'eau et les hommes en Méditerranée et en Mer Noire dans l'antiquité de l'époque mycénienne au règne de Justinien. Actes du Congrès ... 1988* (Athènes) 513-32.

Stanley, E. (1786) *Observations on the city of Tunis and the adjacent country* (London).

Stanzl, G. (1991) "Punische Bautechniken," in F. Rakob (ed.), *Die deutschen Ausgrabungen in Karthago* 1 (Mainz) 211-14.

Stillwell, R. (1933) "Architectural studies," *Hesperia* 2, 110-48.

Stillwell, R. and Sjöqvist, E. (1957) "Excavations at Serra Orlando. Preliminary report," *AJA* 61, 151-59.

Temple, G. T. (1835) *Excursions in the Mediterranean. Part 1: Algiers and Tunis* (2 vols., London).

Thomas, R. G. and Wilson, A. I. (1994) "Water supply for Roman farms in Latium and South Etruria," *PBSR* 62, 139-96.

Thouvenot, R. and Luquet, A. (1951) "Les thermes de Banasa," *PSAM* 9, 9-62.

Thuillier, J.-P. (1982) "Le secteur nord-est de l'îlot C et les niveaux de la rue IV," in S. Lancel (ed.), *Byrsa* 2 (Rome) 61-84.

Tissot, C. (1884 and 1888) *Géographie comparée de la province romaine d'Afrique* (2 vols., Paris).

Tolle-Kastenbein, R. (1990) *Antike Wasserkultur* (Munchen).

Vann, R. L. (1981) "The architecture of the cisterns in the Michigan field," in J. H. Humphrey (ed.), *Excavations at Carthage 1977 conducted by the University of Michigan* 6 (Ann Arbor) 1-54.

Verité, J. (1979) *Citernes de La Malga: étude archéologique PNUD/UNESCO - INAA - DAT* (unpublished manuscript)

Verité, J. (1989) "Le site de La Malga à Carthage," *CEDAC Carthage* 10, 41-48.

Vernaz, J. (1887) "Note sur des fouilles à Carthage," *RA* 2, 11-27, 151-70 and pl. XIII.

Wells, C. M. and Wightman, E. M. (1980) "Canadian excavations at Carthage, 1976 and 1978: the Theodosian Wall, northern sector," *JFA* 7, 43-63.

Wikander, O. (1984) *Exploitation of water-power or technological stagnation? A reappraisal of the productive forces in the Roman Empire* (Lund).

Wilson, A. I. (1995) "Running water and social status in North Africa," in M. Horton and T. Wiedemann (edd.), *North Africa from antiquity to Islam* (Bristol) 52-56.

Wilson, A. I. (1997) *Water management and usage in Roman North Africa: a social and technological study* (D.Phil. thesis, Oxford)

Wilson, R. J. A. (1996) "Tot aquarum tam multis necessariis molibus ... Recent studies on aqueducts and water supply," *JRA* 9, 5-29.

A Roman bath-house at Bir el Jebbana: preliminary report on the excavations (1994-1997)

J. J. Rossiter

Background

Since 1994 Canadian archaeologists have been excavating a Roman bath-house at Bir el Jebbana on the western edge of Carthage.[1] The site lies about 100 m to the west of the Carthage amphitheatre, along the south side of the modern road which runs from Carthage towards Sidi Daoud (fig. 1). Excavations first took place here in the late 19th c., under the direction of Père A.-L. Delattre, who reported the discovery of a Roman villa and bath-house, as well as a number of Early Christian tombs.[2] Among the finds from Delattre's excavations were several mosaic pavements, including one, now in the Carthage Museum, which commemorates the victory of the charioteer Scorpianus (fig. 2).[3] Following the discovery of this mosaic, the building in which it was found came to be known as the "villa of Scorpianus".[4] Delattre dated the buildings, on the basis of brick-stamps, to the 2nd c. A.D.[5]

The "villa of Scorpianus" was described in early reports as "a sumptuous suburban residence".[6] The bath-house was seen as a private bath which served as a dependency of the villa. Delattre's original reports of the bath-house excavations, although brief, preserve several important details of the building's architecture. Among the features mentioned are a large bathing pool (10 m or more x 4.8 m), round at each end with a surrounding portico, and a number of associated rooms, one with a hypocausted floor.[7] Several of the rooms contained mosaics, which in some cases (not uncommonly for his day) were cut into sections so that the figured panels could be removed to the safe keeping of the museum.[8]

---

1 The excavations have been carried out by a team based at the University of Alberta, with help from faculty and students from several other Canadian universities. Regular staff have included T. Allen (administrative assistant and site supervisor), E. McDonald, M. Cassis and D. Hoyt (site supervisors), S. Copp (architect), S. Bingham (architectural assistant), B. Gerecke (artist), M. MacKinnon (faunal analysis), E. Pennefather-O'Brien (human osteology), and P. Reynolds (pottery). From the start the success of the project has owed much to the friendly support and encouragement of A. Ennabli, Conservateur du site de Carthage, and to the staff of the Musée de Carthage. Funding for the project has been provided in part by generous grants from the University of Alberta Central Research Fund (Humanities and Fine Arts Division).

2 A. L. Delattre, *Missions Catholiques* 14 (1882) 117-20; 15 (1883) 93-96, 106-8, 142-43; id., *Cosmos* 9 (1888) 298; 27 (1894) 279-80.

3 For the Scorpianus mosaic see, among others, P. Gauckler, *Inventaire des mosaïques de la Gaule et de l'Afrique* II. *Afrique Proconsulaire (Tunisie)* (Paris 1910) 273, no. 816; K. M. D. Dunbabin, *The mosaics of Roman North Africa* (Oxford 1978) 96-97. The mosaic is reproduced in colour in J. Richerson, "From the floor to the wall: mosaics from Carthage from the 4th century B.C. to the 7th century A.D.," *Minerva* 5.4 (1994) 49-53, fig.6.

4 For example: Vellard, *Carthage autrefois; Carthage aujourd'hui* (Lille 1896) 18-19; E. Babelon, *Carthage* (Paris 1896) 146-47; A. Audollent, *Carthage romaine* (Paris 1901) 191; Gauckler (supra n.3) 272.

5 A.-L. Delattre, *Saint-Louis de Carthage: musée archéoloqique* (Tunis 1893) 13; see also Gauckler (supra n.3) 274; Dunbabin (supra n.3) 97, n.31.

6 Audollent (supra n.4) 191; Gauckler (supra n.3) 272.

7 Delattre, *Missions Catholiques* 15 (1883) 106-8; Vellard (supra n.4).

8 Gauckler (supra n.3) records 5 different pavements found in the baths: *Inventaire* nos. 822-27. See also Dunbabin (supra n.3) 250, Carthage A.1a-c; K. Schmelzeisen, *Römische Mosaiken der Africa Proconsularis* (Frankfurt 1992) microfiche nos. 67.1-3.

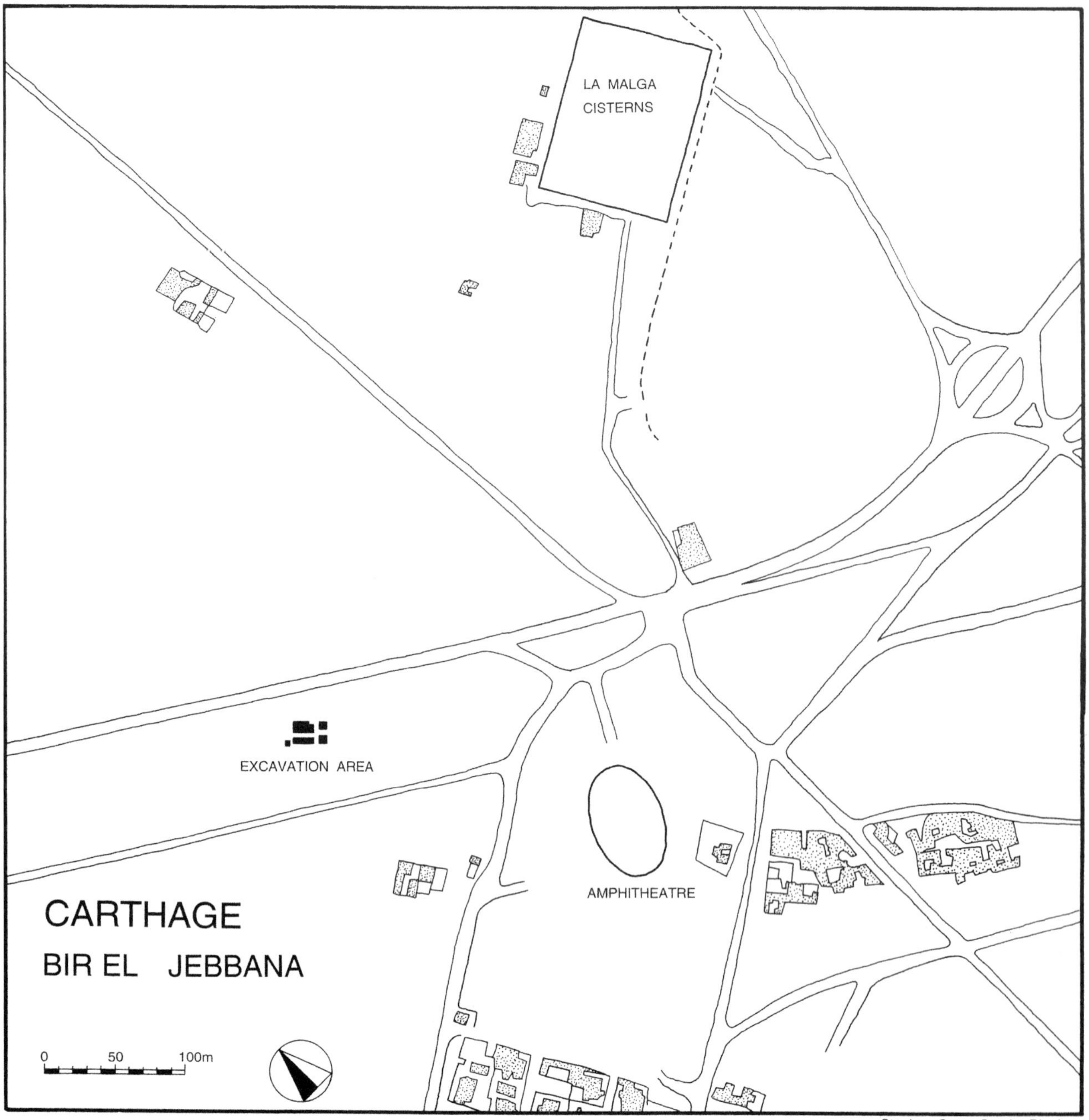

Fig. 1. Plan of region of Bir el Jebbana (S. Copp and S. Bingham).

Following completion of the excavations in 1892, most of the site was backfilled, except for the large pool which was left open and was still visible in 1896.[9] Although no plan of the buildings was ever made, a sketch of the excavation trenches appeared on Bordy's Archaeological Map of Carthage.[10] For the last hundred years the site has remained largely undisturbed, the only noteworthy activity being the reconstruction and widening of the modern road which took place in the early 1970s.

---

9 Vellard (supra n.4) 18.

10 Gauckler (supra n.3) 273: "Il n'y a pas de plan des constructions dégagées jusqu'ici, qui ne comprennent d'ailleurs qu'une partie de la villa". Bordy, *Carte archéologique et topographique des ruines de Carthage* (Paris 1900).

Fig. 2. The "Scorpianus" mosaic from Bir el Jebbana (photo author, courtesy Musée de Carthage).

The new excavations

The current project at Bir el Jebbana began in 1991 as part of a general investigation of Roman villas in the suburban zone around Carthage. In the first phase of the project a surface and magnetometer survey was conducted at the site, the results of which suggested that use of the site extended well into the post-Roman period.[11] New excavations began in 1994 with two principal aims: firstly, to learn more about the Roman buildings which Delattre had found and, secondly, to establish a clearer picture of the changing use of this suburban area during the Roman and post-Roman periods.

The main focus of the work so far has been the re-exploration of the bath-house. In the first year of excavation the round-ended pool was re-located and has since been largely uncovered (fig. 3 at P1; figs. 4-5). Both the pool and the surrounding platform remain in good condition, with much of their white mosaic paving intact. Heavy mineral deposits still cover the surface of the pool. The settings for column bases which Delattre had noted around the rim of the pool were re-examined, revealing that 6 columns once surrounded the pool, not 10 as Delattre claimed.[12] At the south end of the pool a masonry-built outflow drain (fig. 4) led through the wall.[13] A small piece of lead found in situ on the floor of this drain may represent some kind of sluice or control device. The main entrance to the pool was from the north by means of steps leading up

11 For results of the first season of work at the site, see J. J. Rossiter, "Two suburban sites at Carthage: preliminary investigations, 1991-2," *EMC/Classical Views* 12.2 (1993) 301-11; J. J. Rossiter, G. S. Hoye, T. J. Allen, "The Carthage Villas Project 1991," *CEDAC Carthage* 13 (1993) 19-22.

12 The explanation of this discrepancy may be that Delattre originally recorded "six colonnes" which later was erroneously transcribed as "dix colonnes".

13 The arrangement of the outflow drain is very similar to that found in the large bath at Jebel Oust: see M. Fendri, "Evolution chronologique et stylistique d'un ensemble de mosaïques dans une station thermale à Djebel Oust," in *La mosaique gréco-romaine* 1 (Paris 1965) 157-72.

Fig. 4. Main cold pool (P1), south steps, looking E (scale of 2.0 m).

Fig. 5. Cold pool (P1) and mosaic-paved room, looking S (scale of 1.0 m) (photos author).

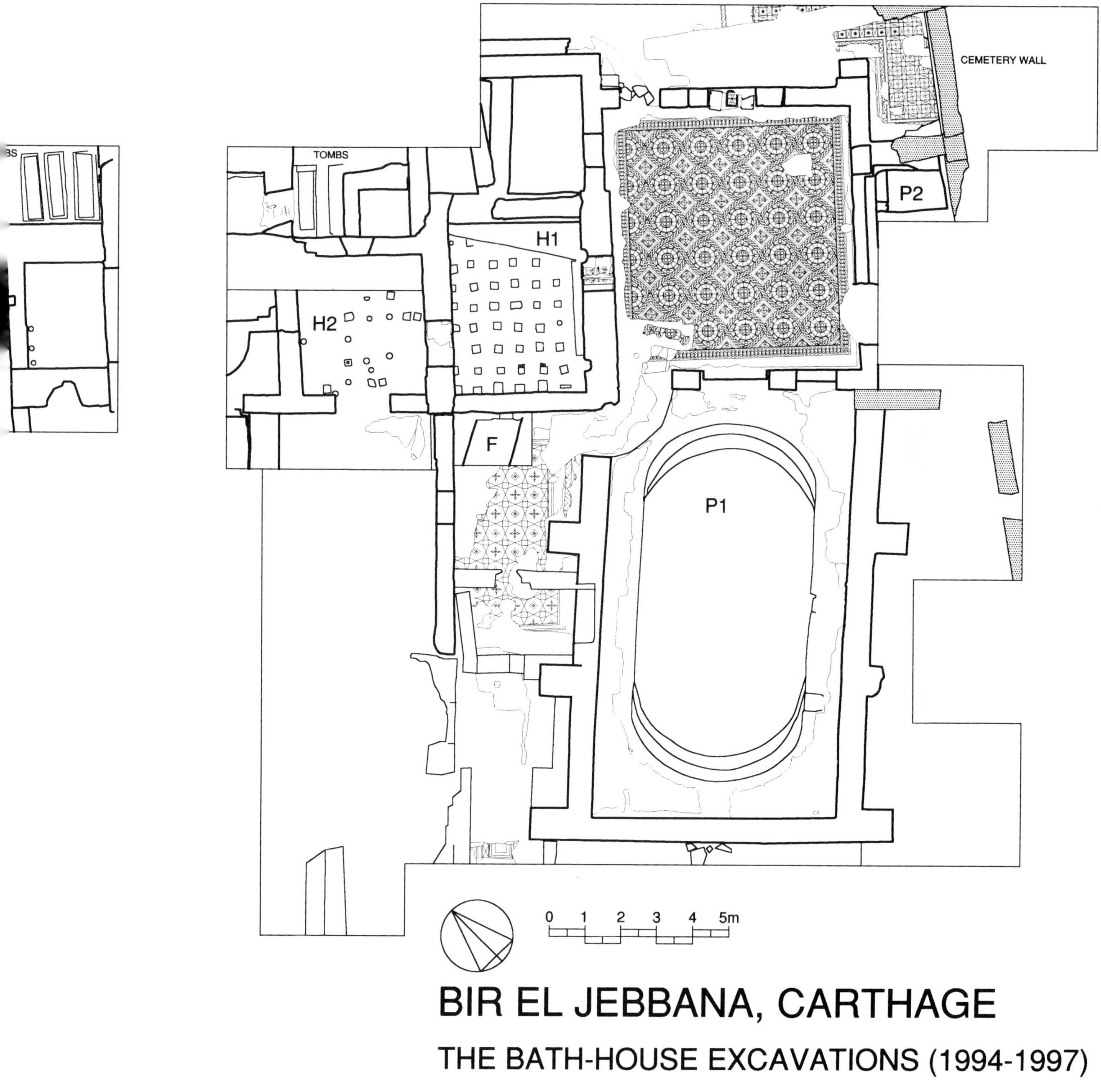

Fig. 3. Plan of the excavations of the bath-house 1994-97 (S. Copp and S. Bingham).

from a room at a lower level. This room was paved with a polychrome geometric mosaic surviving in excellent condition (fig. 5 foreground). In 1997 part of a second pool (fig. 3 at P2), rectangular in form and also paved with white mosaic, was found immediately to the east of the room with the mosaic. To the north, a doorway led into what may have been a peristyle courtyard. Owing to the proximity of the modern road, only a small part of this area could be

Fig. 6. Hypocaust (H1), looking S (scale of 0.5 m) (photo author).

excavated, but enough was revealed to indicate another geometric mosaic which overlay two large and well-preserved cisterns.

The 1997 season was devoted largely to the exploration of the heated rooms of the bath-house, which lay further to the west. In one of the doorways giving access to these rooms, a mosaic sill was found preserved under a later blocking of the doorway. The first of the heated rooms to be excavated contained a well-preserved hypocaust constructed with regular brick-built piers (fig. 3 at H1; fig. 6); fragments of at least two different mosaics were recovered here, including many pieces of a polychrome pavement with a zig-zag design.[14] Building débris inside the room included several large pieces of collapsed roofing vault and numerous vaulting tubes of varying dimensions.[15] From the same area came the head and upper torso of a small stucco figure (fig. 7), which probably formed part of the room's original interior decoration. The hypocaust was heated by a furnace located to the south (fig. 3 at F). Excavation here revealed part of the collapsed furnace chamber, built using large numbers of vaulting tubes. The blackened deposits found inside the chamber included a considerable quantity of animal bone among which were the bones from the right paw of a large brown bear (*ursus arctos*), no doubt explained by the close proximity of the Roman amphitheatre.[16]

---

14 For the latter: Schmelzeisen (supra n.8) 347 Schemata no. 021.01. Fragments of another geometric pavement with a design similar to Schmelzeisen 351 schemata 034.06 were present.

15 Dimensions range from 130 mm to 280 mm (length). The largest are a good deal larger than any of the examples on display in the Carthage Museum, for which see S. Storz, *Tonröhren im antiken Gewölbebau* (Mainz 1994); cf. R. J. A. Wilson, "Terracotta vaulting tubes (*tubi fittili*): on their origin and distribution," *JRA* 5 (1992) 97-129, whose catalogue of sites includes the "Villa of Scorpianus" at Carthage.

16 The faunal material from the site is being studied by M. MacKinnon who provides the following: the en-

Fig. 7. Stucco figure found in H1 (B. Gerecke).

Immediately to the west of the first heated room, the remains of a second hypocausted room were found (fig. 3 at H2). Here the hypocaust piers were in the form of hollow ceramic tubes, round in section at the bottom and square at the top. The tubes were perforated on the top and sides by round or oval-shaped ventilation holes (fig. 8). On top of each of these tubes were placed three square bricks which acted as supports for the paving tiles of the floor. More than a dozen iron T-clamps and numerous fragments of *tegulae* found in the room provided evidence for cavity walling. Some of the *tegulae* had holes drilled through them indicating the manner in which they were held in place by the T-clamps.

The most striking feature of the construction of the hypocaust is the use of tubular *pilae* in place of the more usual stacked bricks. Although parallels can be cited from Italy and the European provinces, this is, to the best of my knowledge, the first example of this method of hypocaust construction which has been found in Roman Africa.[17] Adam points to the use of similar ceramic *pilae* in a number of early bath-houses in southern Campania, suggesting that this method of support was abandoned by the late 1st c. A.D. in favour of brick-built *pilae*.[18] Blake,

---

tire set of metatarsals and tarsals, as well as 12 of the 15 phalanx bones, were recovered. The missing bones appear to derive from one digit of the paw.

17 For tubular *pilae* in general, see J.-M. Degbomont, *Hypocaustes* (2nd ed., Liège 1984) 104-5; G. Brodribb, *Roman brick and tile* (Gloucester 1984) 94-95.

18 J.-P. Adam, *Roman construction* (English ed., London 1994) 267.

Fig. 8. Tubular *pilae* and floor collapse in hypocaust (H2), looking S (scale of 0.5 m) (photo author).

however, identifies several examples of tubular *pilae* found in bath buildings around Rome, all said to be of Hadrianic date.[19]

Dating

The evidence so far gathered points to two major phases of development of the bath-house. Initial construction of the building appears to have taken place around the middle of the 2nd c. A.D. At this date the principal features of the bath building were laid out: the cold rooms and pools on the east side of the complex, the heated rooms to the west; the building clearly extended further to the north where an open courtyard may have existed. The 2nd-c. date is supported by small amounts of pottery retrieved from contexts below the build-up for the floor in the hypocaust room and from foundation levels to the south and east of the main pool.[20] Further dating evidence is provided by new finds of brickstamps. As noted earlier, Delattre reported finding a number of 2nd-c. brickstamps. These included 10 brickstamps dating to the year A.D. 126, which were found on bricks used to construct a drain below the "Scorpianus" mosaic.[21] The latest excavations have produced several more brickstamps, the most complete being found on one of the floor-tiles in the room with the tubular hypocaust pilae. It was a circular brickstamp with the name T. Statilius Maximus, probably the consul of 115, or possibly

19 M. E. Blake and D. T. Bishop, *Roman construction in Italy. From Nerva through the Antonines* (Philadelphia 1973) 114-15.

20 Pottery from contexts 96, 116, 453, 1371 and 1653 included a range of forms dating from the mid to late 2nd c. Study of the pottery is being conducted by P. Reynolds who has kindly supplied this information.

21 Delattre, *Bull. d'Hipp.* 21 (1886) 218; *CIL* VIII.3 22632.7, 17 and 52; cf. H. Bloch, *I bolli laterizi e la storia edilizia romana* (Rome 1968) 260, no.89.

Fig. 9. West room with octagon mosaic, looking S (scale of 0.5 m) (photo author).

his son who was consul in 144.[22] The same room also yielded part of a rectangular brickstamp with the name M. Publicius Sedatus, another early 2nd-c. brickmaker whose bricks have been found elsewhere in Carthage.[23] While these brickstamps provide only a *terminus post quem* for the construction of the bath-house (or at least of part of it) a Hadrianic or early Antonine date for the building seems a strong likelihood.

22 The inscription reads: [F]ort[unati | Stat]ili Maximi op(us); cf. Bloch (ibid.) 181; M. Steinby, *La cronologia delle figlinae doliari urbane dalla fine dall' età repubblicana fino all'inizio del III secolo* (Rome 1976) 28-29; J. P. Bodel, *Roman brick stamps in the Kelsey Museum* (Ann Arbor 1983) 57.

23 The inscription reads: [M. Publ]ici [Sedati | teg(ula)] Ton(neiana). For similar brickstamps from Borj Jedid in Carthage: *CIL* VIII.3 22632.29; cf. *CIL* XV 637; M. Steinby, *Lateres signati ostienses* I (Rome 1978) no. 542; Bloch (supra n.21) 35, 56.

In the early 3rd c. the bath-house underwent major rebuilding. At this time one of the two heated rooms, that to the east (fig. 3 at Hl), was remodelled. The doorway in its E wall was blocked in, as was the stoke hole in the S wall. The furnace was put out of use and the hypocaust was filled in with a considerable amount of redeposited débris to make a solid floor level over which a new mosaic was laid. At the same time the room to the north of the large pool was redecorated with new marble veneer and a new mosaic. The geometric mosaic found in this room (fig. 5), with a design of rosettes set in a curvilinear grid, belongs to this second phase of building.[24] This phase also involved the construction of at least one new room to the south of the original heated rooms, in the area where the furnace chamber had stood. To build this room the furnace chamber was destroyed and the buttresses on the W side of the large pool were reduced to pavement level. At the N end a quarter-round corridor was constructed to provide access between the remodelled north room and the new room to the south. The latter was decorated with a blue and white geometric mosaic with a design of octagons and triangles (fig. 9).[25] An early 3rd-c. date for the rebuilding of the bath-house is provided by late 2nd/early 3rd c. pottery found in the infilling of the hypocaust and in levels underlying the octagon mosaic.[26]

Current evidence suggests that the bath-house began to fall into disuse in the 4th c. The earliest indication of change is provided by a number of late 3rd-c. coins found in tombs cut into the north rooms of the bath-house.[27] While the presence of these coins cannot be used to date the tombs closely, it would seem unlikely that the burials belong much later than the mid 4th c. Modifications to the south part of the building also point to a change in function. The room with the octagon mosaic was partitioned by a series of late walls, and a crude masonry bench was built in one of the newly-created spaces. Finds from the latest levels in this part of the site included more than 50 fragmentary glass vessels and dozens of worked bone hairpins.[28] Eventually these rooms too were abandoned and used for burials. As the fabric of the building began to decay, burials continued to be placed over the ruins of the collapsed building. Pottery and coins from contexts associated with the burials were consistently of the mid 4th to early 5th c.[29] By the time Carthage fell to the Vandals in 439, the urban topography of this part of the city had changed significantly. By then the area of the baths lay outside the line of the

---

24 Cf. Schmelzeisen (supra n.8) 378, schemata no. 124.01 and Fullmotive Typ 7a/7g E1.1, 11a/19c E6a.1. The pavement was first discovered by Delattre and is included in Gauckler's catalogue (supra n.3) 275, no. 823. A comparable mosaic from Borj Jedid in Carthage is dated by Duval to the 3rd or 4th c.: N. Duval and A. Lezine, "Nécropole chrétienne et baptistère souterrain à Carthage," *CahArch* 10 (1959) 80, fig. 5; cf. A. and M. Levi, *Itineraria picta* (Rome 1967) fig. 93.

25 For the basic pattern see Schmelzeisen (supra n.8) 372 schemata no. 098.16. For the rosette motifs, ibid. Fullmotive Type 1.2, 7a.3. See also K. M. D. Dunbabin, "Mosaic of octagons," *Cahiers des Etudes Anciennes* 10 (1979) 13-23 for discussion of a similar mosaic found elsewhere in Carthage. Dunbabin notes that the "octagon and triangle" pattern of this mosaic is found over a long period in North Africa, beginning in the 2nd c. The Bir el Jebbana example would seem to belong somewhere in the middle of the series. For a much later (7th c.) example from Carthage, see M. Alexander in S. T. Stevens, *Bir el Knissia at Carthage: a rediscovered cemetery church* (JRA Suppl. 7, 1993) 138-40.

26 The relevant contexts are nos. 1100-09 (hypocaust infill) and 1608-11 (furnace collapse), containing mainly late 2nd-c. pottery, with some possible early 3rd-c. material; none of the deposits dates later than *c.*250 (information thanks to P. Reynolds).

27 Tomb F272b to the north of H2 contained two barbarous radiates: cf. T. V. Buttrey and B. Hitchner, "The coins" in J. H. Humphrey, *Excavations at Carthage conducted by the University of Michigan* vol. 4 (Ann Arbor 1978) 107-8.

28 Compare the large number of worked bone objects, including hair-pins, found at the nearby circus site: V. J. Hutchinson and D. S. Reece, "A worked bone industry at Carthage," in J. H. Humphrey (ed.), *The circus and a Byzantine cemetery at Carthage* (Ann Arbor 1988) 549-94.

29 Context nos. 166, 171, 175, 179, 188, 194, 218, 219.

newly constructed Theodosian Wall, the line of which is thought to have passed just to the west of the nearby amphitheatre.[30]

Before the end of the 4th c. a cemetery enclosure was constructed to the east of the disused bath-house. Part of the west wall of this enclosure, standing to its full height of 2 m, was excavated in 1994. Excavation inside the enclosure revealed more than 30 burials, some marked by mosaic panels, others by architectural fragments taken from the bath-house. A number of fragmentary inscriptions were also found, some re-used. Finds from the tombs included coins, pieces of worked bone, and occasional bronze objects such as rings and bracelets, ranging in date between the late 4th and late 6th c.

The excavations also produced new evidence for post-Roman activity in areas to the east and west of the baths. To the east, in an area of heavily disturbed stratigraphy, the remains of several late walls were located in association with significant amounts of 5th-6th c. pottery and coins. A trial trench dug *c.*50 m to the west of the main pool revealed modest remains of a building flanking a narrow paved alley. Pottery from within the core of the paving suggested an early Byzantine date for the deposition of the latest road surface here.

Provisional interpretations

The late 19th-c. reports of the excavations at Bir el Jebbana identified the site as a rich Roman villa with an associated private bath-house.[31] The picture emerging from the current excavations, however, suggests that this view of the Roman buildings needs to be revised. Our conclusions to date can be summarized as follows:

1. The scale and construction of the bath-house suggest that it was a public bath-building, not a private villa-bath.
2. What was originally thought to be a separate Roman villa was probably part of the bath complex.
3. The bath complex was first constructed in the mid 2nd c., and later modified and partly rebuilt during the Severan period

Several factors point to the conclusion that the Bir el Jebbana baths were public. One is the scale of the main pool. Its dimensions and design correspond closely to those of a number of other public bath-houses in Roman Africa. Parallels include the cold water pools of the Large North Baths at Hippo Regius and of the Large Baths at Cherchel.[32] Comparisons such as these suggest that the Bir el Jebbana bath may extend well beyond the limits of the area excavated. It is certain that more of the complex lies to the north, close to the modern road. This is where many of the bath-house features excavated by Delattre must lie buried. Of the different parts of the building which have now been re-explored, only the large pool and the room immediately to the north can be securely linked to Delattre's excavations. The latest excavations of the two hypocaust rooms and of the room with the octagon mosaic showed clearly that these areas of the bath-house had not been previously disturbed. The hypocaust found by Delattre, therefore, and the other mosaic-paved rooms which he mentions in his reports lie elsewhere, confirming the considerable extent of the complex.

A second reason for believing that this was a public building is the number of brickstamps recovered. Brickstamps are not common in Roman Africa and where they do occur they are found

---

30 On the line of the Late Roman City Wall, see H. R. Hurst and S. P. Roskams, *Excavations at Carthage: The British Mission* 1.1. *The Avenue du Président Habib Bourguiba. Salammbo* (Sheffield 1984) 30-41. The foundations of a possible gate tower were found just west of the amphitheatre in the late 19th c.: A.-L. Delattre. "Inscriptions de Carthage VI, La Malga," *MEFR* 12 (1892) 258-60.

31 E.g., Audollent (supra n.4) 191: "maison somptueuse avec .... thermes et piscine pour les bains"; Gauckler (supra n.3) 274: "thermes privés dépendant de la villa de Scorpianus".

32 F. Yegül, *Baths and bathing in classical antiquity* (Cambridge 1992) 201-2, 230-32, figs. 220 and 265.

most often in the fabric of bath houses, particularly public baths. In Carthage most of the other recorded examples come from Borj Jedid and the Hill of Juno, both sites of bath-houses, and from the Antonine Baths.[33]

The issue of the so-called "villa" remains unresolved. So far the excavations have produced no clear evidence of a villa, and a close study of the early excavation reports shows that even at the time of Delattre's excavations there was some doubt about how to interpret the Roman buildings: while Vellard could speak confidently of a Roman villa, Delattre himself in his early reports referred only to the excavation of a Roman bath-house.[34] Similar inconsistencies are found in references to the original context of the "Scorpianus" mosaic. Gauckler says that the mosaic came from the *oecus* of the villa, but according to Delattre the mosaic was found in one of the rooms of the bath-house.[35] The fact that the room which it decorated contained a brick-built drain suggests that Delattre was correct, and it is likely that all the building remains found by Delattre belonged to baths. Thus the villa seems to have been a mistaken invention resulting from a failure to recognize the true scale of the bath complex.

Early interpretations of the "Scorpianus" mosaic also need to be revised. Gauckler, for example, argued that the small figures shown in the roundels which frame the central tableau of the charioteer represent farmers ("personnages champêtres") engaged in various rural activities.[36] This is certainly wrong. What are shown here are a number of additional circus figures, judges and other officials associated with the awarding of prizes, whose inclusion on the mosaic reinforces the central image of victory in the circus and gives the whole pavement a strong thematic unity. Race horses and circus scenes were a favourite theme of mosaic art in Roman Africa, especially Carthage; for the similar inclusion of a circus motif in the decorative scheme of a public bath-house we need look no further than the nearby Antonine Baths, where excavation yielded fragments of a mosaic pavement showing circus horses and athletes together.[37]

Compared to many other cities of Roman North Africa, the number of public bath buildings which have been identified and excavated in Carthage is small. Apart from the Antonine Baths, which stand in a class of their own, the only other major bath building that has come to light was found in the late 19th c. in the grounds of the Carmelite Convent on the Hill of Juno.[38] Other public baths are attested in ancient sources, but these cannot be securely linked to archaeological discoveries.[39] In recent years a number of small-scale bathing establishments have been excavated, notably a small "private" villa-bath excavated by the Swedish Mission off the Avenue de l'Amphithéâtre, and part of a bath building, including a hypocaust, found during excavations by Trinity University on the Hill of the Odeon.[40] In contrast to these, the building at Bir el Jebbana is the first example of a mid-sized public bathing establishment that

33 For brickstamps from bath sites at Carthage: *CIL* VIII.3 22632.14, 26, 65, 87, 89, 98, 105. The relative rarity of stamped bricks in Roman construction in North Africa is commented on by T. Helen, *Organization of Roman brick production in the 1st and 2nd centuries A.D.* (Helsinki, 1975) 18.

34 Vellard (supra n.4) 18.

35 Gauckler (supra n.3); Delattre (supra n.21).

36 Gauckler (supra n.3) 273.

37 G. Ch. Picard, "Observations sur la ruine des Thermes d'Antonin à Carthage," *CRAI* 1956, 426; Dunbabin (supra n.3) 102, n.57. For other race-horse mosaics in North African baths see Dunbabin 94 (Oued-Athménia) and 101 (Sidi Abdallah).

38 Audollent (supra n.4) 304-5; A. Lézine, *Architecture romaine d'Afrique* (Tunis 1962) 45-55.

39 E.g., the Baths of Gargilius referred to by Saint Augustine, *Gesta Conlationis Carthaginiensis* I.1; S. Lancel, *Actes de la conférence de Carthage en 411*, I (Sources chrétiennes 144, Paris 1972) 50-53.

40 C. G. Styrenius and B. Sander, "Byrsa: la villa aux bains" in A. Ennabli (ed.), *Pour sauver Carthage* (Paris/Tunis 1992) 151-54; M. B. Garrison, P. Foss, C. M. Wells, "A newly-discovered crypt and bath at Carthage," *JRA* 6 (1993) 251-60.

has been investigated in detail. It occupied a prominent location beside a main road, the *decumanus maximus,* on the western outskirts of Carthage and was close to the city's major recreational facilities. Bordy's map shows vestiges of another bath building located on the opposite side of the *decumanus maximus,* close to the La Malga cisterns.[41] Whether or not these baths depended directly on the La Malga cisterns for their supply of water is not known. The discovery in 1997 of two (possibly more) large cisterns under the northern part of the Bir el Jebbana complex provides the only evidence so far for on-site water storage. That this area of the city, alongside a major road and close to one of the city's main gates, should have attracted a high density of baths is consistent with patterns of Roman urban development noted elsewhere.[42]

Department of History and Classics, University of Alberta

41 The site is marked on the map as "Ruines de Thermes". Surprisingly, Audollent (supra n.4) does not seem to mention this building, which today lies on the site of the new Phénix de Carthage restaurant. See J. Verité, "Le site de la Malga à Carthage," *CEDAC Carthage* 10 (1989) 41-48, no. 8.

42 Cf. D. W. Reynolds, "The lost architecture of Rome: insights from the Severan plan and the Regionary Catalogues," *Expedition* 39.2 (1997) 15-24.

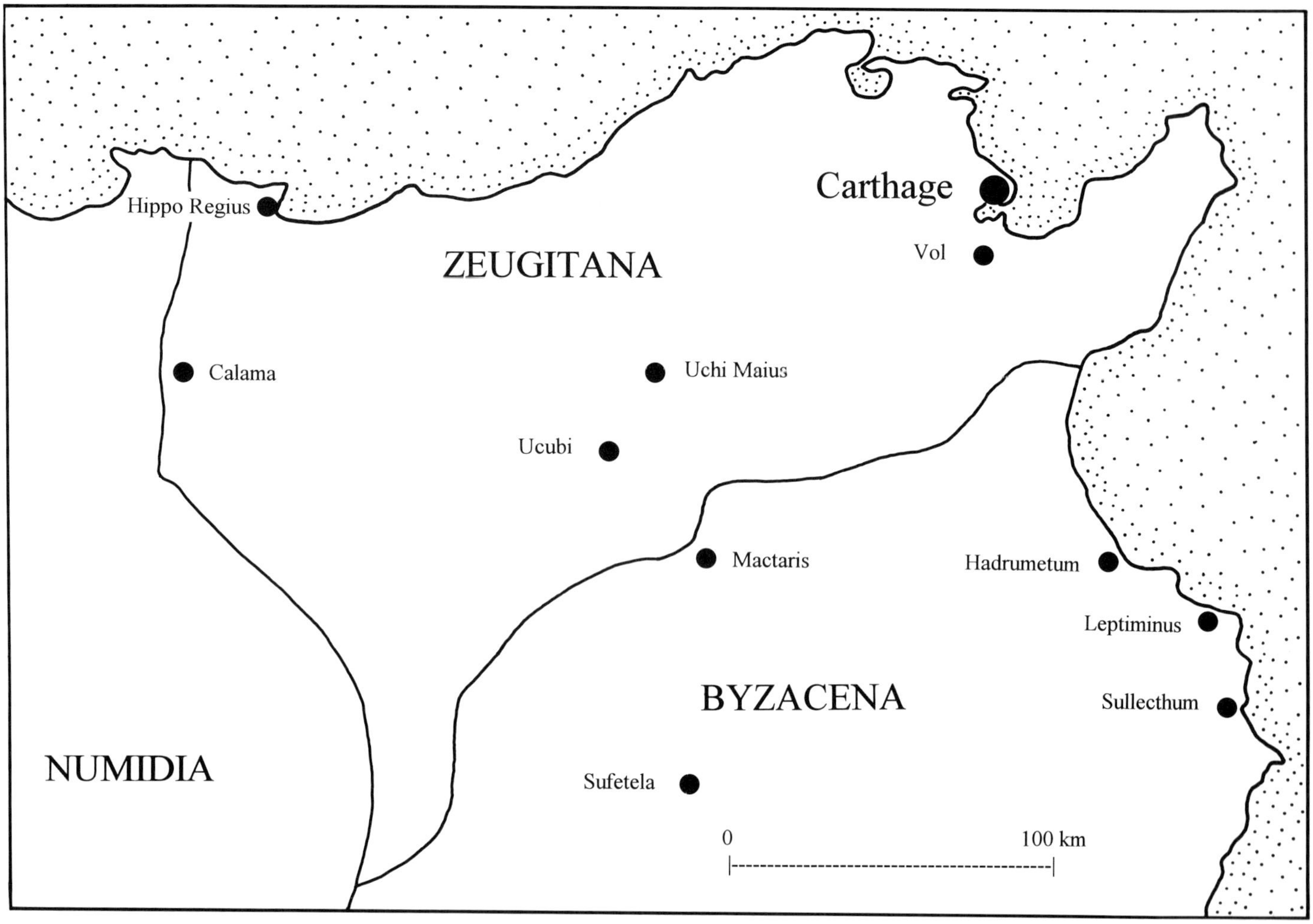

Map showing locations of provinces and settlements mentioned in the text.

The mobilization of state olive oil in Roman Africa: the evidence of late 4th-c. *ostraca* from Carthage

J. T. Peña

1. INTRODUCTION[1]

Excavations carried out in 1911 by the Direction des Antiquités de Tunisie on the Ilôt de l'Amirauté recovered a group of at least 32 Latin *ostraca* concerned with the reception and weighing of state olive oil at Carthage over a portion of the year A.D. 373.[2] Immediately upon their discovery Cagnat and Merlin published a brief article that reported transcriptions of 10 of these documents, their goal being to bring these extremely interesting, if somewhat problematic, texts to the attention of other specialists.[3] The remaining documents in the group they judged insufficiently legible to warrant publication, and they have never been reported in the literature. In the years since Cagnat and Merlin's publication, the Ilôt de l'Amirauté *ostraca* have received scant notice and they have yet to be the subject of any detailed analysis.[4] This is regrettable, as they represent a unique source of information regarding the state's involvement in the mobilization (i.e., the collection and transport to points of consumption) of foodstuffs in the period subsequent to the fiscal and administrative reforms carried out under Diocletian. This essay aims to redress the situation by first describing the documents and then discussing their implications for our understanding of the state's involvement in the mobilization of oil in the province of Zeugitana during the later 4th c.[5]

As this study will reveal, these documents constitute an important supplement to the evidence provided by legal sources, oil amphoras, and archaeological remains in the oil-producing regions of Roman North Africa, and their analysis provides important new insights into several aspects of state involvement in the mobilization of African oil, including the methods employed for its collection, transport, weighing, and packaging, the organization of the administrative bureaucracy responsible for conducting and overseeing oil mobilization operations, and

---

1 It may be useful to single out certain of the conventions employed below. All dates are A.D. All linear measurements are expressed in centimeters. The words amphora/amphoras are used to denote containers, while *amphora/amphorae* are used to denote the unit of volumetric measure. The conversions of *sextarii/amphorae* of olive oil to (Roman) pounds (lbs), kilograms (kg), and liters (l) presented below are based on the following set of assumptions:
1. The Roman pound was equal to 327 g;
2. The *sextarius* was equal to 0.546 l, hence one *amphora* was equal to 26.2 l (i.e. 48 x 0.546 l);
3. The density of Roman olive oil was equal to 0.91;
4. The Romans considered 1 *sextarius* of olive oil to be equal to 1.5 lbs.
For the density of oil, see Viedebantt 1912, 432, where it is stated that this varies from 0.91 to 0.93 as a function of several factors (e.g., quality of oil, temperature). At a density of 0.91-0.93, 1 kg of oil would have had a volume of 1.08-1.09 l. In a trial carried out to confirm these values, I determined that at room temperature 1.5 l of commercially distributed Bertoli olive oil from Italy weighs 1.37 kg, for a density of 0.913. I therefore assume a density of 0.91 and employ a factor of 1.1 to convert kilograms to liters of oil. For the assumption that 1 *sextarius* of oil was considered to weigh 1.5 lbs, see Hultsch 1864-66 [1971], 208, ll.15-16; 223, l.26; 239 l.11; 241 l.13; 247 l.11; 251 l.2.

2 For the figure of 32 *ostraca*, see below. Cagnat 1911, ccxxxviii, reporting on their discovery, refers simply to a "série considérable de tessons de poterie."

3 Cagnat and Merlin 1911. The 10 documents treated in this publication are *AE* 1912 nos. 61-70.

4 I am aware of only a small number of passing references to the Ilôt de l'Amirauté *ostraca*, including Cagnat 1916, 257; Pavis d'Escurac 1976, 196; Hurst 1979, 39, 46-47; *PLRE* 103, 607; Bagnall *et al.* 1987, 278-81; Salama 1987, 157; Hurst 1994, 111, 114; Mattingly and Hitchner 1995, 183.

5 This essay thus makes no effort to address various palaeographic, linguistic, and onomastic issues raised by the *ostraca*.

the geography, calendar, and scale of the operations. Further, since much of the oil referred to in the *ostraca* was probably destined for the supply of the city of Rome, the results of this analysis also enhance our understanding of the state's rôle in the provisioning of the *urbs*. As will be shown, the oil to which the documents refer was collected under two distinct initiatives, one probably the general land tax, the other perhaps a supplement to it. The oil was transferred in oilskins and amphoras from collection districts in Zeugitana and perhaps also Byzacena to Carthage, where it was placed in storage at a facility under the control of the provincial administration of Zeugitana that was probably known as the *conditorium Zeugitanum*. It was eventually transferred to a weighing facility, where it was weighed and shifted to amphoras for export by men termed *centenarii*, who probably belonged to a group of functionaries known as *mensores olei*, and then it was consigned to the imperial fisc. Both the *conditorium Zeugitanum* and the weighing facility can probably be identified with known structures located on the Ilôt de l'Amirauté. The amounts of oil referred to in the documents suggest that the oil raised under these two initiatives might have provided 10-40% of the oil disbursed by the state each year to the populace of Rome. Of particular interest from an archaeological point of view is the fact that 5 of the 7 different types of oil containers mentioned in the *ostraca* can be identified more or less securely with specific amphora classes, shedding light on how African oil amphoras were used during the period of the Late Empire.

This essay is divided into 5 sections. The first, 'Description', offers detailed descriptions of the *ostraca*. It is followed by 'Contextualization', which discusses background information essential for the analysis of the documents. The third section, 'Reconstruction,' undertakes to reconstruct the specific operations to which the *ostraca* refer. This is followed by 'Interpretation', which endeavors to fit the information provided by the *ostraca* into a broader context, considering their implications for our understanding of state involvement in the mobilization of oil in Africa during the later 4th c. The final section, 'Conclusions', briefly reviews the principal inferences drawn in the preceding sections. The analysis presented here depends in large part on detailed considerations of numerical data that can be gleaned from the *ostraca*. In the interest of sparing readers the obligation to wade through large amounts of onerous detail, the more complex discussions of this sort have been relegated to a series of 4 appendices placed at the end, the more important conclusions reached in them being summarized in the main text.

Acknowledgements

In composing this essay I have benefitted from the assistance of several individuals, and I would like to express my appreciation to R. Bruce Hitchner, who generously undertook the final editing of the finished manuscript, saving me from several errors. S. Dyson, H. Hurst, D. J. Mattingly, E. Shapiro Peña, and C. R. Whittaker read earlier versions, offering numerous helpful comments on matters of content and structure. A. Ennabli and H. Hurst generously granted me permission to examine the *ostraca*; the latter hosted me at Churchill College Cambridge during a visit undertaken for this purpose and arranged for the production of the photographs published here. T. Gagos and L. Koenen offered advice regarding several textual problems, and D. McGuire clarified several problems regarding the Latin of the documents. Finally, E. Fentress provided several helpful bibliographical references.

2. DESCRIPTION

This section first discusses the evidence for the archaeological context in which the *ostraca* were recovered and describes the methods employed for their study. It then presents detailed descriptions of the documents.

Archaeological context

Little can be said about the archaeological context in which the *ostraca* were recovered.[6] H. Hurst, who since 1974 has directed excavations at Carthage in the area of the Circular Harbor, including the Ilôt de l'Amirauté, has attempted to identify their find-spot by combining information contained in the published accounts of the Ilôt de l'Amirauté excavations of 1908-11 with an analysis of the remains visible on the island at the time that he began his own research there.[7] On the basis of this information he was able to establish only that the *ostraca* must have been recovered within a small triangular area situated in the NE quarter of the open court that occupied the central part of the island during the late Roman period. The only other relevant observation that can be made is that, from the analysis of the documents, it seems clear that they must have been either lost or discarded as a group in antiquity.

Study methods

This subsection begins with a brief account of the genesis of the present study. The author originally undertook an analysis of the texts of the 10 *ostraca* published by Cagnat and Merlin, assuming that the *ostraca* themselves were no longer available for study. Unknown to him, however, the entire group of documents (except, apparently, one) had recently been located in the collections of the Musée National du Bardo, from which they were transferred to the Musée de Carthage. A. Ennabli, Conservateur en Chef du Site de Carthage, immediately brought the recovery of the *ostraca* to the attention of Hurst and subsequently arranged for their transfer on temporary loan to Cambridge University, Hurst's institution, so that he might study them in connection with his work in the area of the Circular Harbor. Upon learning of the author's interest in the *ostraca*. Hurst invited him to undertake a more comprehensive examination of the entire group. The author accordingly arranged to spend several days working with the *ostraca* at Cambridge in August of 1997. The aims of the work undertaken during this period were to produce a physical description of *ostraca*, check the transcriptions of the 10 published documents, and, to the extent possible, produce transcriptions of the unpublished documents. Not surprisingly, the results of this work allowed me to expand and modify my original study of the 10 published *ostraca* in several significant regards.

The group of *ostraca* examined at Cambridge included 9 of the 10 *ostraca* published by Cagnat and Merlin, together with 22 additional *ostraca*. No. 4 (= Cagnat and Merlin 1911 no. 3) was not apparently among the group of *ostraca* transferred from the Musée du Bardo and its current whereabouts remains unknown. The surfaces of all 31 of the *ostraca* examined were to some greater or lesser degree covered by a calcareous incrustation which had formed during their period of deposition and significantly obscured the text. In a few cases it was evident that at some point — presumably during the period immediately following excavation in 1911 — an attempt had been made to remove this calcareous layer by mechanical means, apparently by scrubbing with a stiff brush, resulting in the destruction of a portion of the underlying text. One of the published *ostraca* (No. 14) was broken in the period since 1911 and the detached fragment lost, while one of the unpublished *ostraca* (No. 30) appeared once to have had a joining fragment re-attached with glue, but it is now broken off and lost.

In most cases the preservation of the texts was so poor that it proved impossible to produce workable transcriptions from the *ostraca* without recourse to special measures. These consisted of bathing the surfaces of the *ostracon* with distilled water dispensed from a spray bottle, which had the effect of radically enhancing the legibility of the texts without producing any apparent degradation of the ink. Facsimiles of the texts, which served as the basis for transcriptions, were prepared from the wet *ostraca*. Both a magnifying glass (8x) and a low-power binocular microscope with a zoom lens (8-40x) were employed for the examination of

---

6 For the published accounts of their recovery, see Cagnat and Merlin 1911, 514; Cagnat 1911, ccxxxviii.

7 Hurst 1979, 38 fig. 8, 39.

certain problematic characters. Even with the aid of these measures, however, it sometimes proved impossible to read characters recorded by Cagnat and Merlin in 1911, and it would thus appear that in many cases the documents have experienced significant deterioration since the time of their excavation. While the transcriptions published by Cagnat and Merlin proved to be generally reliable, it was possible to correct or supplement their readings in a few instances. The texts of the unpublished *ostraca* could be read with varying degrees of success. While in a few cases significant portions of a text proved to be readily legible, more often than not it was possible to discern only extremely faint traces of the characters. Even in cases of this kind, however, it was sometimes possible to recognize strings of characters that belonged either to numerals or to formulae known from one or more of the more readily legible *ostraca*. Despite the poor legibility and/or the brevity of many of the texts, it was possible to recognize several distinct hands and, in some instances, to identify two or more texts apparently produced by the same individual. More accurate and complete readings of several of the texts could no doubt be obtained through the use of methods not available to the author, including the examination of the *ostraca* under ultraviolet light and the evaluation of photographic images of the texts produced using infra-red film.

General physical characteristics

All 31 of the *ostraca* examined by the author were produced from sherds of African amphora.[8] They displayed the light red to red (Munsell range 10R-2.5YR 5-6/6-8) quartz/quartz-limestone fabric characteristic of African amphoras, and in a few instances one surface of the *ostracon* bore the pale yellow to very pale brown salt scum which frequently occurs on the exterior surface of these containers.[9] In several cases one surface also bore the vertical smoothing facets that occur on the exterior of the middle and lower portions of many classes of African amphora.

At least 25 of the 31 *ostraca* were produced using what appears to have been a sherd cut to a more or less standardized size and shape, here referred to as a 'shield-shaped blank'. The shape of these blanks is roughly rectangular, with long, straight sides and short, curved ends (cf. fig. 8 below). In several instances the short, curved ends trend upward from left to right, imparting a parallelepiped shape to the blank. In other cases the long sides grade more gradually into the short ends, resulting in a shape that more closely approximates an oval. In every case the blank is bowed to a more or less pronounced degree, most often along the axis of the short, curved ends, reflecting the curve in the wall of the parent amphora. Complete examples range in size from 14.0 high by 8.5 wide to 23.0 high by 13.5 wide, with most blanks ranging between 0.9 and 1.2 cm thick.

Blanks were normally cut with their long axis aligned with the vertical axis of the parent amphora, no doubt because this minimized the amount of curvature in the available writing surface. The final stages of the manufacturing process appear to have involved the removal of chips by means of blows delivered from the side of the sherd's interior surface. This presumably reflects the desire to keep the exterior surface as smooth as possible, since this was the preferred writing surface. Given the care involved in the preparation of these blanks, it seems likely that, rather than being manufactured on the spot as needed, they were cut well beforehand, the functionaries responsible for the record-keeping operations keeping a supply of pre-cut blanks on hand.

The surfaces on which the documents were written were either the light red/red color of the parent amphora's fabric or, less often, the pale yellow-pale brown of its exterior salt scum. The texts on all 32 *ostraca* are in Latin, written in New Roman Cursive script, with the occasional use of capitals, using what appears to be a standard dark ink. As already noted, the convex exterior surface of the blank was the preferred writing surface, presumably because this was somewhat flatter than the concave interior surface.[10] In the vast majority of cases, texts located on the exterior surface of the blank have their lines oriented along the blank's short axis. There is, by contrast, no clear pattern to the disposition of texts located on the interior surfaces of blanks, some having their lines oriented along the short axis, others along the long axis.

These shield-shaped blanks can be grasped firmly and comfortably in the palm of the hand, with the fingers folded over one of the long sides, the opposite long side wedged against the heel of the hand, and the

8 The term African amphora is here used to indicate transport amphoras produced in the areas corresponding to the provinces of Zeugitana and Byzacena. For a recent overview of African amphoras of the late imperial period, see Freed 1995.

9 For African amphora fabrics and this salt scum, see Fulford and Peacock 1984, 14, 17-18, 263-64.

10 Of the 16 *ostraca* bearing a text on one side only, 14 have it on the exterior surface, while only two have it on the interior surface.

Fig. 1. Hand grasping shield-shaped *ostracon* (No. 13). Fig. 2. Reconstructed file of 4 shield-shaped *ostraca*.

thumb folded around the curved transition between the upper part of this side and the adjacent short, curved side (fig. 1). The functionaries who composed these texts could thus have held the blank securely in one hand while writing out the text with the other.

The manufacture of blanks to a standardized size and shape and the orientation of texts in a uniform manner were presumably undertaken with a view to facilitating the archiving of the *ostraca*.[11] Since the *ostraca* are able to be 'nested', it would have been possible to arrange a chronological series of documents into a neat, compact stack, and then set the whole upright in a box or basket in the manner of a card file (fig. 2). Since most of the texts are headed with the date, it would have been a simple matter for a functionary who wished to consult the file to flip through the series of documents until reaching the one or more *ostraca* that were of interest to him. The author has seen a shield-shaped blank of this kind (devoid of any text) among the materials recovered in a 4th-5th c. dump deposit excavated on the Palatine Hill,[12] and it would thus appear that this method of record-keeping was also employed at Rome.[13]

The *ostraca*

The *ostraca* can be divided into two distinct groups on the basis of the content of their texts. The first, termed Group 1, consists of 6 *ostraca* that are invoices documenting the receipt of shipments of oil containers brought to Carthage by ship. The second, termed Group 2, consists of 17 *ostraca* that are inventories recording amounts of weighed and unweighed oil housed at two different facilities, one an oil-weighing facility, the other a storehouse. The remaining 9 *ostraca* preserved too little writing to permit them to be assigned to one group or the other with confidence.

---

11 For the methods employed for the storage of *ostraca*, see Wilcken 1970, 19.

12 The deposit in question is among those uncovered in the course of the joint Soprintendenza Archeologica di Roma/American Academy in Rome excavations on the NE slope of the Palatine Hill (Hostetter *et al.* 1994). The author is in charge of the study and publication of the pottery from this project.

13 While *ostraca* are exceedingly rare outside Egypt (as are Latin *ostraca* in general), this should presumably be attributed to factors of preservation; see Marichal 1992, 5. For a survey of known Latin *ostraca* of 3rd-c. or earlier date, see Marichal 1992, 3-4.

The two groups of *ostraca* will be presented in separate sections. Each section includes individual descriptions for the several *ostraca* in the group, followed by a discussion of the general structure and content of the documents. Appendix 1 presents brief descriptions of the 9 unassigned *ostraca*.

Within each section the descriptions of the *ostraca* are arranged in the order in which the documents were produced, with undatable documents placed at the end. Each catalogue description begins with information pertaining to the shape, degree of completeness, and dimensions of the blank. Height (H.) refers to the length of the blank along the vertical axis of the parent amphora, while width (w.) refers to its length along the parent amphora's horizontal axis. Thickness (th.) records the maximum and minimum values for the thickness of the blank. This information is followed by an exposition of the one or two texts on the *ostracon*, including a reconstructed text and a translation. Where an *ostracon* bears a text on both surfaces, the text with the earlier date is presented as the *recto* and that with the later date as the *verso*. The exposition of each text begins with an indication of the surface of the blank on which it is located (i.e., whether on the surface that corresponds to the interior or the exterior of the parent amphora), the orientation of the lines of the text with respect to the vertical axis of the parent amphora, and the hand responsible for its production. For orientation, the symbol ↕ is used to indicate that the lines of the text are oriented parallel to the vertical axis of the parent amphora, while the symbol ↔ is used to indicate that they are oriented parallel to its horizontal axis. The 8 different hands recognized are numbered from 1 to 8. Readers should be advised that the expansions, reconstructions, and translations of the texts draw heavily on inferences reached in Sections 4 and 5 of this essay. The discussion that would usually be included in an apparatus is deferred to the section that follows.

The group 1 ostraca

The 6 *ostraca* assigned to Group 1 can be broken down into two subgroups, the first, termed Subgroup 1A, consisting of 5 documents (Nos. 1-5), and the second, Subgroup 1B, consisting of a single document (No. 6). As noted, the Group 1 *ostraca* are invoices that record quantities of containers of olive oil delivered to Carthage by sea. The 5 *ostraca* assigned to Subgroup 1A have the same format, with both a *recto* and a *verso* document, the date of the former preceding that of the latter by anywhere from one to 4 days. In the two instances (Nos. 2 and 3) in which it is possible to evaluate the hands responsible for producing the two texts on a single *ostracon*, it is evident that they were composed by two different individuals. The *recto* appears to be a set of working notes that documents in an abbreviated fashion the results of the inspection of a shipment of containers, recording the date, the name of the shipper who delivered the containers, the number of containers delivered, and the number rejected. It was presumably composed at the moment that the shipment of containers was first received by a group of state functionaries, who were perhaps known as *mensores olei*. The *verso* appears to be a formal invoice composed at the time that the state accepted possession of the shipment of containers from the shipper, drawing on the information contained in the *recto*. It was apparently composed by a functionary known as a *mensor olei Fori Karthaginiensis*, perhaps when the group of containers was consigned at the *conditorium Zeugitanum*, an oil storage facility referred to in the documents of Group 2. In addition to the date and the name and title of the functionary responsible for composing the document, the *verso* records the information regarding both the identity of the shipper and the number of containers delivered and rejected that is recorded in the *recto* document, the type and provenience of the containers in the shipment, and additional information of an uncertain nature, perhaps comprising an indication of the facility to which the containers were consigned. The single *ostracon* assigned to Subgroup 1B bears a single text consisting of two distinct records composed on different dates, each of which is more or less identical to a Subgroup 1A *recto* text. This *ostracon* presumably functioned in a fashion similar to that of the Group 1A *recto* documents, recording the results of the inspection of two shipments of oil containers so that it would be possible to compose formal invoices for their receipt similar to the Group 1A *verso* texts at some later date. The fact that it was produced over three months later than the latest dated Group 1A document suggests that the differences in its structure are due to some change in the methods employed for record-keeping.

CATALOGUE DESCRIPTIONS

1. (= *AE* 1912 no.64; Cagnat and Merlin 1911 no. 4)
Complete shield-shaped *ostracon*. H.: 14.5; w.: 11.2; th.: 0.6-0.8. Subgroup 1A.

Recto
Exterior surface ↔; *Hand 1*

III Nonas Feb(ruarias) n̶(avicula)
Ianuari f(ero?) CCXV r̶(eprobo) V

Verso
Interior surface ↔; *Hand ?*

pos(t) cons(ulatu)s
mod[esto et arinthei]
pri[die Nonas Feb(ruarias)
traces of 2 lines
]ịtimit
traces of 1 line

Translation
3 days before the Nones of February [= *Feb. 3*]
Boat of Januarius
I receive 215. I reject 5.

Following the consulships of Modestus and Arintheus
The day before the Nones of February [= *Feb. 4*]
Name of oil measurer attached to the Forum at Carthage
Name of shipper and numbers of oil containers received and rejected

2. (= *AE* 1912 no.62; Cagnat and Merlin 1911 no. 2)
Complete irregularly-shaped *ostracon;* H.: 13.0; w.: 12.5; th.: 0.8. Subgroup 1A.

Recto
Interior surface ↔; *Hand 2*

XVI [k(a)l(endas) mart(ias)] n̶(avicula) [cilindri
f(ero) CCVIỊỊ r(eprobo)Ṿ[III

Verso
Exterior surface ↕; *Hand 3*

pos(t) cons(ulatu)s
modesto et arinthei
XIIII K(a)l(endas) mart(ias) felix mensor olei fori
karthag(iniensis) suscepimus per nav(i)c(u)la(m)
cilindṛị caproreses centenaria
levia ducenta X̣ṃḷ }c̣ et m(ensore?) ol(e?)i
p̣ẹṭṛo reprob(ata sunt?) octo
C̣ọṇ (ditorium?)· ẓ(eugitanum?)

6. Xml}c: This is presumably the corruption of some number.

Translation
16 days before the Kalends of March [= *Feb. 14*]
Boat of Cilinder
I receive 208. I reject 8.

Following the consulships of Modestus and Arintheus
14 days before the Kalends of March [= *Feb. 16*]
Felix, oil measurer attached to the Forum at Carthage
We received via the boat of Cilinder 200 .... Caproreses light centenaria, and 8 were rejected by the oil measurer Petrus.
Zeugitana storehouse

Fig. 3 (top). *Ostracon* No. 3, *recto*.

Fig. 4 (below). *Ostracon* No. 3, *verso*.

3. (= *AE* 1912 no.61; Cagnat and Merlin 1911 no. 1)
Complete irregularly-shaped *ostracon.* H.: 13.5; w.: 12.5; th.: 0.5-0.8. Subgroup 1A.

Recto
Interior surface ↔; Hand 4; fig. 3

XV kal(endas) martias ꞃ(avicula) felicis
f(ilius?)xe ri f(ero?) CCVIII ꞅ(eprobo) XIII
2 large flourishes

Verso
Exterior surface ⇕ ; Hand 3; fig. 4

pos(t) cons(ulatu)s
modesto et arinthei
XIIII [k(a)l(endas) mart(ias)] felix mens[or]
olei [fori kar]thag(iniensis) sus[ce]pimus
per nav(i)c(u)la(m) felicis X[eri?] c(a)pro
reses centenaria levia ducenta
et octo et reproba(ta sunt?) t[re]decim
c̣ọṇ(ditorium?) • ẓ(eugitanum?)

Translation
15 days before the Kalends of March (= *Feb. 15*)
Boat of Felix, son of Xerus
I receive 208. I reject 13.

Following the consulships of Modestus and Arintheus
14 days before the Kalends of March (= *Feb. 16*)
Felix, oil measurer attached to the Forum at Carthage
We received via the boat of Felix, son of Xerus, 208 Caproreses light centenaria, and 13 were rejected.
Zeugitana storehouse

4. (= *AE* 1912 no.63; Cagnat and Merlin 1911 no. 3)
Ostracon not available for examination. Subgroup 1A

Recto
Orientation? Hand?

] Nonas mar[t(ias) ꞃ(avicula) repos]t[i]*
traces of 1 line

1. Repos]t[i]*: Cagnat and Merlin: Feli]c[is.

Verso
Orientation? Hand?

pos(t) cons(ulatu)s
modesto et arinthei
III Nonas mar(tias) felix mensor olei fori
karthag(iniensis) s[u]s[ce]pim[u]s p[e]r nav(i)c(u)la(m)
reposti cap[ro]res[es levia?] centenaria
[d]ucenta decem et [reprobata?] s(unt?) oct[o omn?]e tulit
ta[bul?]arius m(ensorum?) ol(e?)i.ad.

Translation
3, 4, 5, or 6 days before the Nones of March [= *March 2, 3, 4, or 5*]
Boat of Repostus
Numbers of oil containers received and rejected

Following the consulships of Modestus and Arintheus
3 days before the Nones of March [= *March 5*].
Felix, oil measurer attached to the Forum at Carthage
We received via the boat of Repostus 210 Caproreses light centenaria, and 8 were rejected.
The registrar of the oil measurers took all to ....

Fig. 5. *Ostracon* No. 6.

5. (Previously unpublished)
Complete shield-shaped *ostracon*. H.: 10.5; w.: 12.0; th.: 1.1-1.2; salt scum on exterior surface. Subgroup 1A.

Recto
Interior surface ⇕; *Hand 4?*

III Idus april(es) Erṭoriọt[
.............CC r(eprobo) VIII
.....

Verso
Exterior surface ⇕ ; *Hand ?*

1 line missing?
m[odesto et arinthei
v[
XVII K[al(endas) Mai(as)] felix m[ensor]
[olei fori] ḳ [arthag(iniensis)] sus[cepimus]
traces of 5 lines

Translation
3 days before the Ides of April (= *April 11*)
Boat of Ertoriot...
I receive 200. I reject 8.
....

Following the consulships of Modestus and Arintheus....
17 days before the Kalends of May (= *April 15*)
Felix, oil measurer attached to the Forum at Carthage
Name of shipper and numbers of oil containers received and rejected

6. (Previously unpublished)
Irregular sherd that may preserve none of original edges of *ostracon*. Pres. H.: 7.5; pres. w.: 10.5; th.: 0.7-1.3. Subgroup 1B.

Interior surface ⇕; *Hand ? fig. 5*

XI Kal(endas) augustas n(avi)c̣(u)ḷạ
felic(i)s X̣[e]ri ψ̣ I ƀ(zacenae?) [
VI Kal(endas) augustas n̸(avicula) [
ƀ(zacenae?) CXLIIII ɍ(eprobo) IIII

Translation
11 days before the Kalends of August (= *July* 22)
Boat of Felix Xerus
Four-centenaria containers: 1; Byzacena containers:....; *Number of containers rejected*
6 days before the Kalends of August (= *July* 27)
Boat of ...
Byzacena containers: 144; I reject 4.

Structure and content

All 5 *ostraca* assigned to Subgroup 1A preserve their dates more or less intact, showing that the series was produced for shipments of oil containers that reached Carthage over a period of time beginning no later than February 3, 373, and extending at least through April 11 of that year. The 4 *recto* documents for which the hand can be identified were produced by three different individuals. These are designated Hands 1, 2, and 4, and correspond to the *ostraca* as follows: Hand 1 (No. 1 *recto*), Hand 2 (No. 2 *recto*), and Hand 4 (Nos. 3 *recto* and 5 *recto*?). The two *verso* documents for which such a determination could be made (Nos. 2 *verso* and 3 *verso*) appear to have been written by Hand 3. Two of the 4 documents available for examination were produced on shield-shaped blanks (Nos. 1 and 5), while the other two (Nos. 2 and 3) appear to have been produced using irregular sherds. These last two documents were initiated on consecutive days (February 14 and 15), and it thus seems possible that the group of functionaries responsible for composing the *recto* texts exhausted their supply of pre-cut blanks at this time, employing more casually prepared sherds for the production of these records.

The *recto* documents consist of 3 elements:
Element 1: the date.
Example - No. 1, l.1: *III Nonas Feb*
This element consists of the month and the day only, with no indication of the year.

Element 2: the name of the owner/operator of the ship that delivered the group of oil containers.
Example - No. 1, ll.1-2: *n̶ Ianuari*
This element, preserved more or less intact only in Nos. 1 and 3, consists of a barred 'n', followed by a *cognomen* in the genitive. In No. 3, the only case in which the corresponding *recto* and *verso* documents are more or less complete, this name, Felix, matches that of both the presumed author of the *verso* document (the *mensor olei Fori Karthaginiensis*), and that of the shipper who delivered the oil containers, who is also named in the *verso* document. That here this name refers to the latter individual is suggested by two observations:

1) Since the hand of the *recto* is different from that of the *verso*, the *mensor olei Fori Karthaginiensis*, the apparent author of the *verso*, was probably not involved in the transaction recorded in the *recto* and presumably not named in this document.
2) Since the *verso* is probably an expanded version of the *recto*, we would expect the name of the shipper to be indicated somewhere in the *recto* document.

The phrase which immediately follows this name in No. 3 *(f x̣ẹri)* is problematic. It should perhaps be interpreted as an irregular rendering of the shipper's filiation, presumably included due to the fact that there was more than one shipper with the name Felix, with the father's *cognomen* perhaps to be restored as Xerus.[14] By analogy with this document the name of the shipper indicated in No. 4 *verso* can be restored in this location in No. 4 *recto*, although doing so requires an emendation to the text as reported by Cagnat and Merlin. The barred 'n'

14 The *cognomen* Xerus is presumably a variant of Serus, a name attested twice in inscriptions from North Africa: *CIL* VIII 1703 (Sicca Veneria); *CIL* VIII 17173 (Thubursicum Numidarum). For similar substitutions of x for s in initial position, see *CIL* VIII 9072; *CIL* VIII 17607.

that precedes the name in this element is presumably an abbreviation for *navicula*, the word used to refer to the delivery ship in the *verso* documents. In No. 5 the barred 'n' appears to have been omitted.

Element 3: a summary of the results of the reception/inspection of the group of oil containers.
Example - No. 3, l.2: *f CCVIII ꝛ XIII*

This element consists of an 'f' followed by a number between 200 and 215, then a barred 'r' followed by a number between 5 and 13. In No. 3 these numbers almost certainly match those recorded in Element 3 of the *verso* document for the number of oil containers received and the number rejected; thus it appears all but certain that this element reports the same information. The barred 'r' that precedes the second number is almost certainly an abbreviation for some form of the verb *reprobare* (to reject), the word used to indicate rejection in the *verso* documents. The interpretation of the 'f' that precedes the first number is more problematic. While it is most likely an abbreviation for some form of the verb *ferre* (in its meaning of to receive), it may represent either a sign standing for the specific type of oil container included in the shipment or an abbreviation for the name of this container type. That this did serve to indicate a specific container type is suggested by the fact that in analogous contexts the sole Subgroup 1B *ostracon* presents a sign and a ligature of two letters both used in the Group 2 documents to indicate specific container types. If the 'f' did represent a specific container type, then it would appear to have been a sign rather than an abbreviation for that type's name, since in the cases of Nos. 2 and 3 it can be shown that the containers in question were known as *centenaria levia*. As discussed below (this section), however, the evidence suggests that, during the period of the year in which the Subgroup 1A *ostraca* were produced, the shipments of oil being delivered to Carthage by sea consisted entirely of containers of this one type, and it may thus have been unnecessary to indicate the specific container type when reporting the results of an inspection. The letters 'f' and 'r' are accordingly interpreted here simply as abbreviations for *fero* (I receive) and *reprobo* (I reject).

The Subgroup 1A *verso* documents consist of 4 elements:

Element 1: the date.
Example - No. 2, ll.1-3: *pos conss/ modesto et arinthei/ XIIII Kl mart*

This element consists of an irregular and ungrammatical formulation that is used to indicate a date in the postconsulship of Modestus and Arintheus (373) in the 4 documents in which it is preserved (Nos. 1-4).[15] The expected form would be *post consulatum Modesti et Arinthei*,[16] and the expansion of the formula employed here is problematic. While the expansion of *conss* as *cons(ulatu)s* seems the best solution, the second 's' may indicate *cons(ulibu)s*, retaining the ablative from the standard formula for consular dates, or *cons(ulatum)*, the doubling of the letter alluding to the fact that there were two ex-consuls. As already noted, the date given ranges from 1 to 4 days later than that of the corresponding *recto* document.

Element 2: the name and title of the presumed author of the document.
Example - No. 2, ll.3-4: *felix mensor olei fori / karthag*

In the 4 documents in which this element is preserved (Nos. 2-5), it consists of the *cognomen* Felix in the nominative, followed by the title *mensor olei fori Karthag(iniensis)* (oil measurer attached to the Forum at Carthage).

Element 3: an account of the results of the reception/inspection of the group of oil containers.
Example - No. 3, ll.4-7: *sus[ce]pimus per navcla felicis X[eri] cpro/reses centenaria levia ducenta/ et octo et reproba t[re]decim*

---

15 See Bagnall *et al.* 1987, 278-81.
16 See Bagnall *et al.* 1987, 65-66.

In the 3 documents in which this element is preserved (Nos. 2-4), it first records the reception of a quantity of items (*c.*200) termed *caproreses centenaria levia,* via the *navicula* (boat) of an individual whose name is given in the genitive. This is followed by an indication of the number of these items rejected. Olive oil was commonly measured in terms of *centenaria,* or hundredweights (cwt.), in the Roman world, and it thus seems likely that the *caproreses centenaria levia* were oil containers of some sort.[17] *Caproreses* is a toponym that presumably refers to the locale or district where the containers and/or the oil that they held originated (see Section 5). While the term *centenarium leve* might have been employed to refer to empty *centenaria* that were being brought to Carthage for filling, the apparent association of the groups of *centenaria levia* mentioned in Nos. 2 and 3 with containers assigned a standard oil weight value of 100 lbs. in No. 7 (see below) would appear to exclude this possibility.[18] It would thus appear that the containers in question were termed *levia* due to the fact that they were capable of holding somewhat less than 100 lbs. of oil. While this portion of the text is not preserved in No. 1 *verso,* it seems likely that the containers referred to in this document were likewise *caproreses centenaria levia,* since the earliest appearance of an oil container type other than the *centenarium leve* occurs only in No. 9, dated March 9. No. 5 may also have documented a shipment of *caproreses centenaria levia,* although the later date of this document suggests an increased probability that these containers were of some other type. The verb used in this element, *suscipere,* is that employed to denote the reception of tax payments. It is rendered in the first person plural of the perfect tense, with the subject perhaps to be understood as the members of the organization (perhaps *corpus*) of the *mensores olei* (see Section 5). The verb employed to denote rejection, *reprobare,* is abbreviated, with the form indeterminable. The occurrence of a letter 's' in a damaged section of this element in No. 4, however, suggests that it may have been *reprobata sunt,* the perfect passive. In No. 2 this element should perhaps be expanded to indicate that a *mensor olei* by the name of Petrus was responsible for the inspection of the shipment.

Element 4: additional information of an uncertain nature.

Nos. 2 and 3 conclude with a 4th element consisting of a string of letters of problematic reading that should perhaps be transcribed as *con•z.* If this reading is correct, this would appear to be an abbreviation for the name of the oil storage facility referred to in several of the Group 2 *ostraca* as the *conditorium Zeugitanum* (see below, this section). If so, this element probably served to indicate the facility where the shipment of containers was received. No. 4 concludes with a fourth element that should perhaps be restored and expanded to indicate that a *tabularius mensorum olei* (registrar of the oil measurers) conveyed all of some set of items, presumably the *caproreses centenaria (levia?)* to which the document refers, to some location. This may perhaps have been the oil weighing facility, the existence of which can also be inferred from the Group 2 documents (see below).

Subgroup 1B consists of a single *ostracon,* No. 6. This document, which bears a text on one side only, is fragmentary and it is unclear whether it was produced on a shield-shaped blank or an irregular sherd. The text consists of two distinct records, one produced on July 22, the other on July 27. Each of these is nearly identical to one of the Subgroup 1A *recto* texts, differing only in the way in which they introduce the figure for the quantity of containers received. The first record lists two quantities of containers, one introduced by a designation here transcribed *ψ,* and the other by a designation here transcribed *b̸*. The second record, which was added directly below the first, lists only a single group of containers, in this case introduced by the *b̸* designation. In the Group 2 documents, the first of these two designations and a variant of the

17 For the *centenarium* and its use as a standard module for the measuring of olive oil, see Oxé 1940.

18 If the identification of Caproreses with the area of the Montes Caprarienses, south of Calama (Guelma), is correct, it too would seem to preclude this possibility, as it seems highly improbable that empty amphoras would have been transported to Carthage from so great a distance. For the identification, see Section 5.

second are employed to indicate oil container types other than the *centenarium leve* (see below), and they were presumably used for this same purpose here. This *ostracon* would thus seem to record the results of the inspections of two shipments of containers, the second of which was received 5 days after the first. It was presumably used as the basis for the production of two documents analogous to the Subgroup 1A *verso* texts.

The group 2 *ostraca*

The 17 *ostraca* assigned to Group 2 can be divided into three groups, the first, here termed Subgroup 2A, consisting of two *ostraca* (Nos. 7-8), the second, here termed Subgroup 2B, consisting of 13 *ostraca* (Nos. 9-21), and the third, here termed Subgroup 2C, consisting of two *ostraca* (Nos. 22-23). The Group 2 *ostraca* are inventories that record quantities of oil processed by a body of oil weighers and the overall amount of oil being held at two facilities, one that served for the weighing of oil, and the other for its storage. The three subgroups show no overlap of dates, and would appear to represent distinctive, though broadly similar, forms of record-keeping that were employed during different portions of a single administrative year. The two Subgroup 2A *ostraca* bear both a *recto* and a *verso* text. No. 7 *recto* records the date, quantities of oil containers being held at the storage facility, and an estimate for the total weight of this oil. The *recto* text of No. 8 is largely illegible. In both No. 7 and No. 8 the *verso* text records the date, amounts of oil weighed by several oil weighers, a summation of these figures, and, in the case of No. 7, a number that probably refers to a quantity of oil containers being held at the weighing facility. The 13 *ostraca* assigned to Subgroup 2B all appear to have a more or less identical format, differing from one another only in matters of detail. Each of these *ostraca* bears a single document that records the date, a list of amounts of oil weighed by one or more oil weighers, a summation of these figures, a list of quantities of various types of oil containers being held first at the weighing facility and then at the storage facility, and, finally, an estimate for the total weight of the oil being held at the two facilities. The two *ostraca* assigned to Subgroup 2C are fragmentary and difficult to interpret. The more complete of the two, No. 22, consists of three distinct records, each made on a different date, that consist of entries for groups of oil containers and weighed oil, together with a summation of weighed oil or an estimate for the total weight of oil. In all likelihood these are tallies of amounts of oil being held at the weighing facility. No. 23 appears to contain multiple records consisting of entries listing groups of oil containers and estimates for the total weight of oil, and may perhaps be a similar document.

Since none of the Group 2 *ostraca* is dated to the year, it cannot be excluded that some or all of these documents were produced in some year other than 373, the year in which the Subgroup 1A *ostraca* were produced. That all 17 *ostraca* were produced in 373, however, is suggested both by the overlapping of their dates at the level of the month with those of the Group 1 *ostraca* and by the fact that all of these documents appear to have been either discarded or lost together. In addition, as will be discussed below (this section), circumstantial evidence suggests that a group of oil containers recorded in No. 7 subsumes groups of containers referred to in two of the Subgroup 1A *ostraca* (Nos. 2 and 3). It thus seems almost certain that this *ostracon* was also produced in 373.

CATALOGUE DESCRIPTIONS

7. (*AE* 1912 no.65; Cagnat and Merlin 1911 no. 5)
Complete shield-shaped *ostracon*. Broken into two pieces since 1911, with small chip bearing first two words of *verso* l.7 lost. H.: 19.5; w.: 11.0; th.: 0.9-1.1; salt scum on exterior surface. Subgroup 2A.

Recto

Interior surface ↔; Hand 5; fig. 6

Vol Cal(assini)	K(e)N^{T}(enaria)	X
[C]aprorenses	K(e)N^{T}(enaria)	dCVII

Fieri K(e)N^{T}(enaria) CCCXIIII r CCLIIII
et erunt in condit(orio)
in ḍ (ie) XIIII K[al(endas) Mar(tias)]
[K(e)N^{T} dCCCC]XXXI
Fieri in condit(orio)
ʃ ∞CLXXXV

Verso

Exterior surface ↔; Hand 5; fig. 7

XIII Kal(endas) Mar(tias) ad Octob(rem)

7 Maurus	P̶	XXXV
7 Ianuarianus	P̶	LV
7 Felix	P̶	$\overline{\text{VIII}}$CCXXVI
7 Vindemialis	P̶	CCC
7 Victor Mercur(ialis)	P̶	$\overline{\infty\infty}$XCVII
7 Augustalis	P̶	$\overline{\infty}$cCCXCVIII
7 Maioricus	P̶	$\overline{\infty\infty}$XCVII
7 Marianus	P̶	IIIIdCLXXVII
7 Primus	P̶	$\overline{\text{IIII}}$dCLX
7 Murc̣	P̶	$\overline{\text{III}}$CCCCXXV
7 Evasius	P̶	∞dCCCLXXII
7 Restutus	P̶	$\overline{\text{IIII}}$XXII
7 Victorinus	P̶	$\overline{\infty}$dCCXCIIII

Fieri N(umero) 7 CCCL P̶ LXXVIII
Vol Calassini Ḳ LXXVI

Translation

Vol Calassini:	10 centenaria
Caprorenses:	607 centenaria
To do:	314 centenaria; 254 cwt.

And there were in the storehouse
14 days before the Kalends of March (= *Feb. 16*)
931 centenaria.

To do, in the storehouse
Total cwt.: 1,185

13 days before the Kalends of March (= *Feb. 17*), for the period through October

Centenarius	Maurus	35 lbs.
Centenarius	Ianuarianus	55 lbs.
Centenarius	Felix	8,226 lbs.
Centenarius	Vindemialis	300 lbs.
Centenarius	Victor from Ad Mercurium	2,097 lbs.
Centenarius	Augustalis	1,398 lbs.
Centenarius	Maioricus	2,097 lbs.
Centenarius	Marianus	4,677 lbs.
Centenarius	Primus	4,660 lbs.
Centenarius	Murc	3,425 lbs.
Centenarius	Evasius	1,872 lbs.
Centenarius	Restutus	4,022 lbs.
Centenarius	Victorinus	1,794 lbs.
Number to do:	350 cwt.	78 lbs.
Vol Calassini:	76 centenaria	

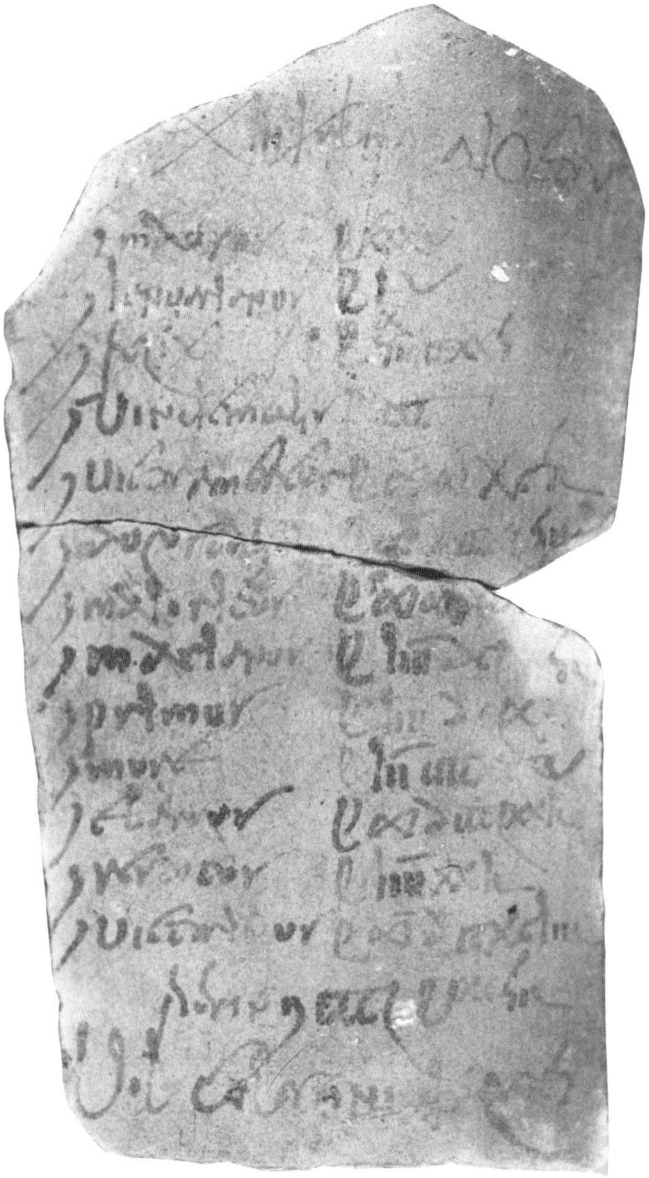

Fig. 6. *Ostracon* No. 7, *recto*.

Fig. 7. *Ostracon* No. 7, *verso*.

8. (Previously unpublished)
Lower portion of shield-shaped *ostracon*. Pres. H.: 15.5; w.: 15.0; th.: 0.7-1.2; salt scum on exterior surface. Subgroup 2A. Similarities to No. 7 suggest that this was probably produced around the same time as this other document.

Recto?
Interior surface ↔; Hand 5?

] ̣n m ̣[
]n c[
traces of 2 lines
]r. 7 XLXXXỊ Ị.

Verso?
Exterior surface ↔; Hand 5?

7̣ [Ꝑ
7 Obbaḷ ụ ṣ [Ꝑ
7 mẹ trị ạ nus Ꝑ VIIICCCÇ XX̣

7	lạmpạ dius	Ꝑ	$\overline{III}$CC
7	marinus	Ꝑ	$\overline{VII}$dCCCḶ XVIII
7	ṭ uṭ us	Ꝑ	∞CCCC
7	....	Ꝑ	......
7	ḷ ị ṿ ị ạ ṇ ụ s	Ꝑ	∞d[
7	...n.	Ꝑ	∞̣.[
7	ḅ	Ꝑ	[
7	n....an(u)s ..XV.	Ꝑ	IIIIC̣ C̣ XIIII
7	...du.us	Ꝑ	$\overline{II}$ X̣
7	Ig nu....	Ꝑ	$\overline{IIII}$CC
	F(ieri) $\overline{N}$(umero)	7 $\overline{CCCC}$ XLII Ꝑ XCIII	

Translation

....

... Total cwt.:	40	33-34 lbs.

Date.

One or more entries for oil weighers?

Centenarius	....	.....	lbs.
Centenarius	Obbalus	.....	lbs.
Centenarius	Metrianus	8,420	lbs.
Centenarius	Lampadius	3,200	lbs.
Centenarius	Marinus	8,868	lbs.
Centenarius	Tutus	1,400	lbs.
Centenarius	....	.....	lbs.
Centenarius	Livianus	≥1,500	lbs.
Centenarius	...n.	≥1,000	lbs.
Centenarius	B.....	.....	lbs.
Centenarius	N....anus...	4,214	lbs.
Centenarius	...du.us	≥2,010	lbs.
Centenarius	Ignu....	4,200	lbs.
Number to do:	442 cwt.	93	lbs.

9. (*AE* 1912 no.66; Cagnat and Merlin 1911 no. 6)

Upper portion of shield-shaped *ostracon*, preserving entire text. H.: 12.0; w.: 10.5; th.: 0.7-0.8. Subgroup 2B.

Exterior surface ↔; *Hand 6*

VII Idus mart(ias) ad octob(re)ṃ
7 felix 1/ XXXIII Ꝑ LXIIII
l} XXXIIII Ꝑ LXIII
Inpletu(r) Vol as(copae) a ƀ(zacena?) $\overline{N}$(umero) XXI 1/ XXXIIII
[fieri] In condit(orio) Ẓ(eugitano?) a(mphorae?) g(emellariae?) $\overline{N}$(umero) CLXVII
as(copae) a b(yza?)c̣ ẹ (na?) $\overline{N}$(umero) VI
l} CCCCXIII Ꝑ XX

Translation

7 days before the Ides of March (= *March 9*), for the period through October

Centenarius Felix:	33 cwt.	63 lbs.
Total cwt.:	34	63 lbs.

Being filled:

Vol: number of Byzacena oilskins	21
Cwt. weighed oil	34

To do, in the Zeugitana storehouse:

number of twin amphoras	167
number of Byzacena oilskins	6

Total cwt.:	413	20 lbs.

10. (Previously unpublished)
Lower portion of shield-shaped *ostracon*. Pres. H.: 12.0; w.: 10.5; th.: 1.0. Subgroup 2B. Figures in text suggest that this was produced after No. 9 and before No. 11.

Exterior surface ↔; Hand 7

[7 1/] XV[
[7] 1/ III Ꝑ XC̣[
[7 u]s 1/ XVIII P̣ V
[7]vus 1/ XIII Ꝑ XXV
1} CCXXII Ꝑ VII
Inplẹ ṭu(r) Vol as(copae) a ƀ(zacena?)
N̄(umero) CXXXVIII 7 C̣C̣XXIIII
fieri in conḍ[it(orio) Z(eugitano?) a(mphorae?) g(emellariae?) N̄(umero)] CLXVII
traces of one line
1} dC[ ] Ꝑ XXX̣X̣ [

Translation

Date

Several entries for oil weighers

Centenarius	15-19	cwt.	0-99	lbs.
Centenarius	3	cwt.	90-99	lbs.
Centenarius ....us	18	cwt.	5	lbs.
Centenarius ....vus	13	cwt.	25	lbs.
Total cwt.	222		7	lbs.

Being filled:
Vol: number of Byzacena oilskins 138
Cwt. weighed oil 224

To do, in the Zeugitana storehouse:
number of twin amphoras 167
Additional entries for oil containers in storehouse

Total cwt.: 600-999 40-49 lbs.

11. (Previously unpublished)
Complete shield-shaped *ostracon*. H.: 14.0; w.: 8.5; th.: 1.0-1.1; salt scum on exterior surface. Subgroup 2B.

Exterior surface ↔; Hand 8

In Idus mart(ias) (ad) Octọ(b)ṛ(em)
7 augrinus[ ]C. C̣C̣ VI
7 Victor utumm(ensis?)... C̣C̣ XXV
7 Iọṃunpṛịs[II[ICC]CCV
f(ieri) 1/ XXXVIII Ꝑ XXXVỊ
Inpl(e)ṭụ(r) Vọḷ[
.c(a)p(rorenses?)[
Sunt. . . . In[
a(mphorae?) g(emellariae?) ẹt ƀ(zacenae) N(umero) dXIIII 1} ∾XVIII Ꝑ XX

Translation

On the Ides of March (= *March 15*), for the period through October

Centenarius Augrinus	... 206 lbs.
Centenarius Victor from Uthumae	... 225 lbs.
Centenarius Iomunpris	3,405 lbs.

To do: 38 cwt. 36 lbs.

Being filled:
Vol: ....
Caprorenses: ...

There are *in the Zeugitana storehouse*		
twin amphoras		
Byzacena containers	514	
Total cwt.:	1,018	20 lbs.

12. (Previously unpublished)
Complete shield-shaped *ostracon*. Dimensions not recorded. Orientation of sides slightly out of perpendicular with respect to vertical axis of vessel. Subgroup 2B.

Exterior surface ↔; Hand 8?

]Kạl april(es) Aḍ [Oct(obrem)
7[ ]rt..[ ]XXX
7 ....[ ]X̣X
7 ......[ ] . [
traces of 8 more lines

Translation

1-17 days before the Kalends of April [*March 16-31*], for the period through October

Centenarius	..rt....	≥30 lbs.
Centenarius	....	≥20 lbs.
Centenarius	....	... lbs.

One or two entries for oil weighers?
Total weight of weighed oil
Entries for oil at weighing facility
Entries for oil containers at storehouse
Estimate for total weight of oil

13. (*AE* 1912 no.68; Cagnat and Merlin 1911 no. 8)
Complete shield-shaped *ostracon*. H.: 17.0; w.: 11.0; th.: 0.9-1.4. Subgroup 2B.

Exterior surface ↔; Hand 7; fig. 8

VII Idus april(es) ad oct(obrem)
7 Flabianus l/ X
7 Felix ab Ucubi l/ VII Ꝑ XL
7 Peregrinus l/ XIIII Ꝑ XC
7 Felix ab [....]c l/ X Ꝑ XCII
7 doi..anus l/ CXI Ꝑ XXXV
l} CLIIII Ꝑ LVII
Inpletu(r) Vol as(copae) a ƀ(zacena?) N̄(umero) XXI et
o(lei?) R(omae?) c(anon?) as(copae) N̄(umero) CLXI et macrinenses
as(copae) a ƀ(zacena?) N̄(umero) VI 7̶ CLVI
fieri In condit(orio)Z̩(eugitano?) ạ(mphorae?) g(emellariae?) N̄(umero) CLXVII et K(e)N^T(enaria) L fisci
et de N(umero) tebelbucitan qz
as(copae) a ƀ(zacena?) N̄(umero) CCC et K(e)N^T(enaria) L
de N̄(umero) vol as(copae) a ƀ(zacena?) N̄(umero) ∞̄dXIIII
et o(lei?) R(omae?)c(anon?) as(copae) N̄(umero) CCLXXII et K(e)N^T(enaria) ∞̄XCI
et macrine(n)ses as(copae) a ƀ(zacena?) N̄(umero) VI
l} V̄C̄C̄L̄X̄ V Ꝑ L

Translation

7 days before the Ides of April (= *April 7*), for the period through October

Centenarius Flabianus	10 cwt.	
Centenarius Felix from Ucubi	7 cwt.	40 lbs.
Centenarius Peregrinus	14 cwt.	90 lbs.
Centenarius Felix from ..c	10 cwt.	92 lbs.
Centenarius Doi..anus	111 cwt.	35 lbs.
Total cwt.:	154	57 lbs.

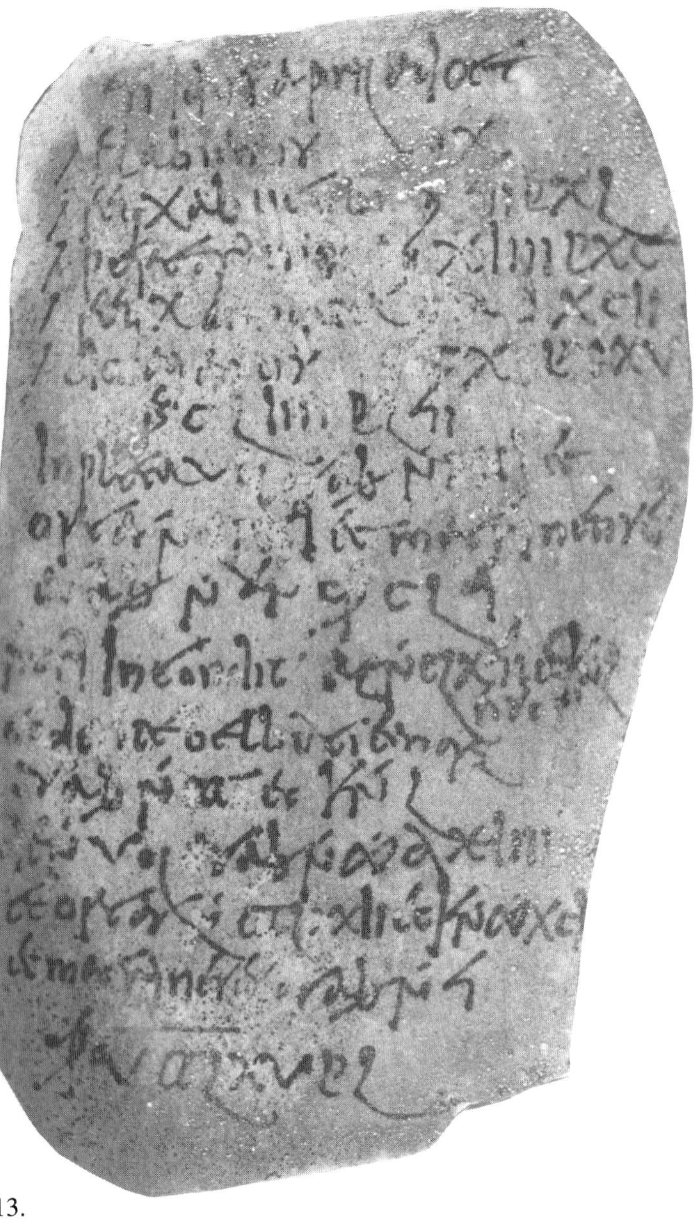

Fig. 8. *Ostracon* No. 13.

Being filled:				
Vol: number of Byzacena oilskins		21		
Rome oil levy: number of oilskins		161		
Macrinenses: number of Byzacena oilskins		6		
Cwt. of weighed oil	156			
To do, in the Zeugitana storehouse:				
Fisc: number of twin amphoras		167;	centenaria	50
Tebelbucitan qz: number of Byzacena oilskins		300;	centenaria	50
Vol: number of Byzacena oilskins		1,514		
Rome oil levy: number of oilskins		272;	centenaria	1,091
Macrinenses: number of Byzacena oilskins		6		
Total cwt.:	5,265	50 lbs.		

14. (*AE* 1912 no.69; Cagnat and Merlin [1911] no. 9)
Fragment of shield-shaped (?) *ostracon*. Pres. H.: 14.0; w.: 12.0; th.: 0.8-1.1. Subgroup 2B. Portion of sherd containing lower left-hand portion of text (ll.16-19) broken off since 1911 and now missing.

Exterior surface ↔; Hand 7

VI Idus april(es) ad oct(obrem)

7	donatilus	1/ XII	Ꝑ	L
7	Victorianus	1/ VII	Ꝑ	XV
7	Vanosus	1/ XIIII	Ꝑ	XIIII
7	fi[...]r	1/ XLVII	Ꝑ	LXV
7	Ka[....]ius	1/ XXIIII		
7	ar[....]us	1/ XXIII	Ꝑ	LIII
7	victor	1/ XLVI	Ꝑ	LX
7	Romanus	1/ LVII	Ꝑ	X

l} CCXXXII Ꝑ LXVII

Inpletu(r) macrinenses as(copae) a ƀ(zacena?) N̄(umero) XLVIIII
et K(e)N^{T}(enaria) CXX ạf̣ṛ l } CCXXXV
fieri In condit(orio)Ẓ(eugitano?) ạ(mphorae?) g(emellariae?) N̄(umero) CLXVII et K(e)N^{T}(enaria) L Fisci
et tebelbucitan qz as(copae) a ƀ(zacena?) N̄(umero) CCC et K(e)N^{T}(enaria) L 7̶
et macrinenses as(copae) a ƀ(zacena?) N̄(umero) [VI] et K(e)N^{T}(enaria) CXX
et Vol as(copae) a b(zacena?) N̄(umero) ∞d[XIIII et
o(lei?)R(omae?)c(anon?) as(copae) N̄(umero) CCC[XCI
et K(e)N^{T}(enaria) [∞XCI
l} [V̄CCCCI Ꝑ XXXV

Translation

6 days before the Ides of April (= *April 8*), for the period through October

Centenarius Donatilus	12 cwt.	50 lbs.
Centenarius Victorianus	7 cwt.	15 lbs.
Centenarius Vanosus	14 cwt.	14 lbs.
Centenarius Fi...r	47 cwt.	65 lbs.
Centenarius Ka....ius	24 cwt.	
Centenarius Ar....us	23 cwt.	53 lbs.
Centenarius Victor	46 cwt.	60 lbs.
Centenarius Romanus	57 cwt.	10 lbs.
Total cwt.:	232	67 lbs.

Being filled:					
Macrinenses: number of Byzacena oilskins		49;	centenaria	120	*afr*
Cwt. of weighed oil	235				
To do, in the Zeugitana storehouse:					
Fisc: number of twin amphoras		167;	centenaria	50	
Tebelbucitan qz: number of Byzacena oilskins		300;	centenaria	50	*qs*
Macrinenses: number of Byzacena oilskins		6;	centenaria	120	
Vol: number of Byzacena oilskins		1,514			
Rome oil levy: number of oilskins		391;	centenaria	1,091	
Total cwt.:	5,401	35 lbs.			

15. (Previously unpublished)

Lower portion of shield-shaped *ostracon*. Pres. H.: 15.0; pres. w.: 11.0; th.: 1.0-1.1. Subgroup 2B. Figure in line 17 suggests produced after No. 14.

Exterior surface ↔; Hand 8?

7 [
7 M[
7 v[
7 [
1/ XXXX IIII Ꝑ LIII
Inpleṭụ(r) Vol aṣ(copae) ạ ƀ(zacena?) N(umero) XXX[
] . XIII[ ]LX̣X[
].tebeḷḅucit[an qz] ḶXIII

fi[e]r[i in condit(orio)Z(eugitano?)
traces of circa 7 lines
1} VIII[ ]X̣ Ᵽ I[

Translation
Date
One or more oil weigher entries

Centenarius		... lbs.
Centenarius M.....		... lbs.
Centenarius V.....		... lbs.
Centenarius		... lbs.
Total cwt.	44	53 lbs.

Being filled:

Vol: Number of Byzacena oilskins	30-39
Number of containers	>14
Number of containers	>70
Tebelbucitan qz: *Number of containers*	63

To do, in the Zeugitana storehouse:
Entries for oil containers in storehouse

Total cwt.:	7,030-9,080	1-4 lbs.

16. (*AE* 1912 no.67; Cagnat and Merlin 1911 no. 7)
Complete shield-shaped *ostracon*. H.: 17.5; w.: 12.0; th. 0.9-1.2. Subgroup 2B.
Exterior surface ↔ ; *Hand 7*

VII Kal(endas) mai(as) ad oct(obrem)
7 quintus 1/ V Ᵽ LX
7 victorianus 1/ XX Ᵽ LXVII
7 bilossus ab occhi 1/ II
7 tzelica 1/ X Ᵽ XX
1} XXXVIII Ᵽ XLVII
Inpletu(r) Vol as(copae) a ƀ(zacena?) N̄(umero) XXII 1/ XXXVIII Ᵽ LXXV
Fieri In condit(orio) Ẓ(eugitano?) a(mphorae?)g(emellariae?) N̄(umero) CLXVII et K(e)N^{T}(enaria) LXII fisci
et tebelbucitan qz as(copae) a ƀ(zacena?) N̄(umero) CCCCXLVI
et K(e)N^{T}(enaria) LXV et macrinenses
as(copae) a ƀ(zacena?) N̄(umero) LV et K(e)N^{T}(enaria) CCLXXXV
et Vol as(copae) a ƀ(zacena?) N̄(umero) $\overline{\infty\infty}$CLVI
o(lei?)R(omae?)c(anon?) as(copae) N̄(umero) dCCLVII K(e)N^{T}(enaria) ∞CCXXXII
1} $\overline{\text{VII}}$dCCCLỊI Ᵽ LXXV

Translation
7 days before the Kalends of May (= *April 25*), for the period through October

Centenarius Quintus	5 cwt.	60 lbs.
Centenarius Victorianus	20 cwt.	67 lbs.
Centenarius Bilossus from Occhi	2 cwt.	
Centenarius Tzelica	10 cwt.	20 lbs.
Total cwt.:	38	47 lbs.

Being filled:

Vol: number of Byzacena oilskins		22	
Cwt. of weighed oil	38		75 lbs.

To do, in the Zeugitana storehouse:

Fisc: number of twin amphoras		167;	centenaria 62
Tebelbucitan qz: number of Byzacena oilskins		446;	centenaria 65
Macrinenses: number of Byzacena oilskins		55;	centenaria 285
Vol: number of Byzacena oilskins		2,156	
Rome oil levy: number of oilskins		757;	centenaria 1,232
Total cwt.:	7,852	75 lbs.	

17. (Previously unpublished)
Upper portion of shield-shaped *ostracon*. Pres. H.: 13.0; pres. w.: 13.0; th.: 1.0. Subgroup 2B.
Exterior surface ↔ *; Hand ?*

Ṿl Kal(endas) ṃạị (as) ạḍ oct(o)ḅ(re)ṃ
con 1/ XXVIỊ [Ꝑ]XVIỊ
iṛ icạṛ . mu . 1/ XVIII Ꝑ LXV
. . . . us 1/ XXI Ꝑ II
ḳ . . ụas 1/ XXI Ꝑ LXX
]s[ ]X Ꝑ LII
]l} [Ꝑ VI
]f(i)eri[ ]. . . CL[
]KN^{T} LXII f(i)s[ci
]XV[
trace of 1 line

Translation
6 days before the Kalends of May (= *April 26*), for the period through October

Con......	27 cwt.	17 lbs.
Iricr.mu.	18 cwt.	65 lbs.
...us	21 cwt.	2 lbs.
K.uas	21 cwt.	70 lbs.
.......s	≥10 cwt.	52 lbs.
Total cwt.	≥99	6 lbs.

To do, *at the Zeugitana storehouse*:
Fisc: number of containers ≥150; centenaria 62
Provenience: number of containers ≥15
Additional entries for oil containers in storehouse

Estimate for total weight of oil

18. (*AE* 1912 no.70; Cagnat and Merlin 1911 no. 10)
Complete shield-shaped *ostracon*. H.: 23.0; w.: 13.5; th.: 0.9-1.2. Subgroup 2B.
Exterior surface ↔ ; *Hand 7*

[Pri]d(ie) Nonas Mai(as) ad Oct(obrem)
[7]inus 1/ VIIII Ꝑ XCIIII
[7] 1/ XIII Ꝑ XLII
[7] 1/ VII Ꝑ LXVI
[7]nus 1/ IIII Ꝑ LXXXVII
7 Victor a Serve 1/ V Ꝑ XVIII
7 Felix 1/ V Ꝑ XIIII
7 Inventus 1/ XXXV Ꝑ LXII
7 Victor a Nobis 1/ XXVII Ꝑ XVIII
l} CXI Ꝑ XI
Inpletu(r) Vol as(copae) a ƀ(zacena?) N̄(umero) LXVIII 1/ CXI
Ꝑ X
Fieri in condit(orio)Z(eugitano?) ψ N̄(umero) CLXXXIIII
[et a(mphorae?)g(emellariae?) N(umero) C]LXVII K(e)N^{T}(enaria) LXII fisci
Et Tebelbucit(an qz) as(copae) a ƀ(zacena?) N̄(umero) CCCCXLVI
et K(e)N^{T}(enaria) LXV [Macrinenses]
as(copae) a ƀ(zacena?) LV et K(e)N^{T}(enaria) CCLXXXV
Vol as(copae) a ƀ(zacena?) N̄(umero) ∞ ∞CCLXXV
o(lei?)R(omae?)c(anon?) as(copae) N̄(umero) dCCLVII K(e)N^{T}(enaria) ∞CCXXXII
l} VIIIdCCCII Ꝑ LXXV

Translation
The day before the Nones of May (= *May 6*) for the period through October

Centenarius	..........inus	9 cwt.	94 lbs.
Centenarius		13 cwt.	42 lbs.
Centenarius		7 cwt.	66 lbs.
Centenarius	.............nus	4 cwt.	87 lbs.
Centenarius	Victor from Serve	5 cwt.	18 lbs.
Centenarius	Felix	5 cwt.	14 lbs.
Centenarius	Inventus	35 cwt.	62 lbs.
Centenarius	Victor from us	27 cwt.	18 lbs.
Total cwt.:		111	11 lbs.

Being filled:

Vol: number of Byzacena oilskins	68	
Cwt. of weighed oil -	111	10 lbs.

To do, in the Zeugitana storehouse:

Fisc: number of four-centenaria containers:	184;	number of twin amphoras 167;	centenaria	62
Tebelbucitan qz: number of Byzacena oilskins	446;		centenaria	65
Macrinenses: number of Byzacena oilskins	55;		centenaria	285
Vol: number of Byzacena oilskins	2,275			
Rome oil levy: number of oilskins	757;		centenaria	1,232
Total cwt.:	8,802	75 lbs.		

19. (Previously unpublished)
Complete shield-shaped *ostracon*. H.: 17.5; w.: 16.0; th.: 1.0-1.3. Subgroup 2B. While the figures in l.15 suggest that this was produced after No. 11 and before No. 13, those in ll.12-14 are difficult to reconcile with this interpretation, raising the possibility that this dates to after No. 18.
Exterior surface ↕ . *Hand ?*

traces of 11 lines
]XIIII
]CCCLXV
e]t K(e)N^{T}(enaria) dCCC[
l} $\overline{\text{IIII}}$ CCCCLXXVIII Ꝑ LXỊỊỊ

Translation
Date

One or more entries for oil weighers
Total weight of weighed oil
Entries for oil at weighing facility

Entries for portion of oil containers at storehouse

Number of containers:	≥14	
Number of containers:	≥365	
Rome oil levy: - number of oilskins ....;	centenaria:	800-999
Total cwt.:	4,478	63 lbs.

20. (Previously unpublished)
Complete shield-shaped *ostracon*. H.: 21.0; w.: 15.0; th.: 0.9-1.4; salt scum exterior surface. Subgroup 2B. Date uncertain.
Exterior surface ↔; *Hand 8?*

... [ ]...ad Octo(b)r(em)
traces of 1 line
7 Nị [
7 [
7 [
7 [
7 [

traces of 1 line
I[n]p̣[etu(r) Voḷ [
........[ ]XXX[
f(i)eri . . [
K . [
traces of 3 lines

Translation
Date, for the period through October
Centenarius Ni.... ... lbs.
Centenarius .... lbs.
Centenarius .... lbs.
Centenarius .... lbs.
Total cwt. .... lbs.

Being filled:
Vol:
Entry for weighed oil at weighing facility

To do, at the Zeugitana storehouse:
Entries for oil containers at storehouse

Estimate for total weight of oil

21. (Previously unpublished)
Upper portion of shield-shaped *ostracon*. Pres. H.: 7.0; pres. w.: 11.5; th.: 1.1-1.2. Subgroup 2B. Date uncertain.
Exterior surface ↔ *; Hand ?*

traces of one line
7]XXX . Ị̣Ị̣]
7 [
7 k[
7 m]
7 [

Translation
Date

Centenarius ...... ≥30 lbs.
Centenarius .... lbs.
Centenarius K[.... .... lbs.
Centenarius M[.... .... lbs.
Additional entries for oil weighers?
Total weight of weighed oil

Entries for oil at weighing facility

Entries for oil containers at storehouse

Estimate for total weight of oil

22. (Previously unpublished)
Lower portion of shield-shaped *ostracon*. Pres. H.: 15.0; w.: 13.5; th.: 1.2-1.5. Subgroup 2C.
Exterior surface ↔ *; Hand ? fig. 9*

Nav.sco....[
. Iu. as(copae) a b(yzacena) Xd[
III Kạ l(endas) Iun̄(ias) N[
ψ N(umero) LXII l/ CCXVII Ꝑ LXXX[
as(copae) a ƀ(zacena?) N̄(umero) CLXX l/ ÇÇ XXX VIII Ꝑ L[
l} dXVI Ꝑ LX̣Ṿ
prid(ie) K(a)l(endas) Iun̄(ias) fieri ψ N(umero) LX̣XIII l/ÇÇ [ ]XV
Ꝑ X̣X̣X̣

Fig. 9. *Ostracon* No. 22.

Insṭ (ans?) . dCCCXXX .[
VIII Idus Iun̄(ias) fieri as(copae) a b̸(zacena?) N̄(umero) CLX . [
....[ ]. l/ CXLII ỊỊỊỊ
]C̣C̣C̣ XXX[
Insṭ (ans?) l} ∞C̣C̣Ḷ XṾỊ

Translation

....

....Byzacena oilskins:	490-499				
3 days before the Kalends of June (= *May 30*)					
Number of....					
Number of four-centenaria containers	62;	cwt.:	217	lbs.:	80-89
Number of Byzacena oilskins	170;	cwt.:	238	lbs.:	50-89
Total cwt.:			516	lbs.:	65
The day before the Kalends of June (= *May 31*)					
To do:					
Number of four-centenaria containers	73;	cwt.:	235-415	lbs.:	30
Present: *total cwt.*:			830		
8 days before the Ides of June (= *June 6*)					
To do:					
Number of Byzacena oilskins	160...				
	...;	cwt.:	142	*lbs.:*	4
			≥330...		
Present: Total cwt.:			1,266		

23. (Previously unpublished)
Lower portion of shield-shaped *ostracon*. Pres. H.: 17.0; w.: 14.5; th.: 1.0-1.1; salt scum on exterior surface. Subgroup 2C? Date uncertain.
Exterior surface ↔; *Hand ?*

traces of 3 lines
f̣ i ẹ r i[
ḷ } ∞ Ᵽ̣ III
f̣ i e [ri
traces of 1 line
f̣ i ẹ ṛ (i) [
traces of 1 line
]XIIII . l} LXIII
]N(umero) XIIII ...XCVII
et Vol as(copae) a ƀ(zacena) N̄(umero) dLXIIII eṭ K(N^T) .. LXXỊỊ
l} ∞dCCLXXXII Ᵽ XXXV

Translation
.....
To do...
Total cwt.: 1,000 3 lbs.

To do...
.....
To do......
....14
Total cwt.: 63

............Number *of containers* - 14 97
Vol: Number of Byzacena oilskins - 564; centenaria - ≥72
Total cwt.: 1,782 35 lbs.

Structure and content of the documents of group 2

The discussion of the Group 2 documents commences with Subgroup 2B, as this is the most readily comprehensible of the three subgroups. Each of the 13 *ostraca* assigned to this subgroup was produced using a shield-shaped blank and bears a single text on the exterior surface. Eight preserve their dates more or less intact. If, as argued above, all date to the same year, then on the basis of these eight we can infer that the series of Group 2 documents was produced over a period beginning no later than March 9 and extending at least through May 6. For 10 documents it was possible to make some judgement as to the identity of the hand. These were produced by three different individuals, designated Hands 6, 7, and 8, with the breakdown as follows: Hand 6 (No. 9), Hand 7 (Nos. 10, 13, 14, 16, and 18), and Hand 8 (Nos. 11, 12?, 15?, and 20?).

The texts of the 5 complete documents in this subgroup (Nos. 9, 13, 14, 16, 18) consist of three elements:

Element 1: the date.
Example - No. 16, line 1:
VII Kal mai ad oct
This element includes the day and the month on which the document was composed, with no indication of the year, terminating with the notation *ad Octobrem* (through October), presumably a reference to the end of the administrative year to which the documents pertain.

Element 2: a list of entries recording names of oil weighers and amounts of oil attributed to them, followed by a summation of these figures.

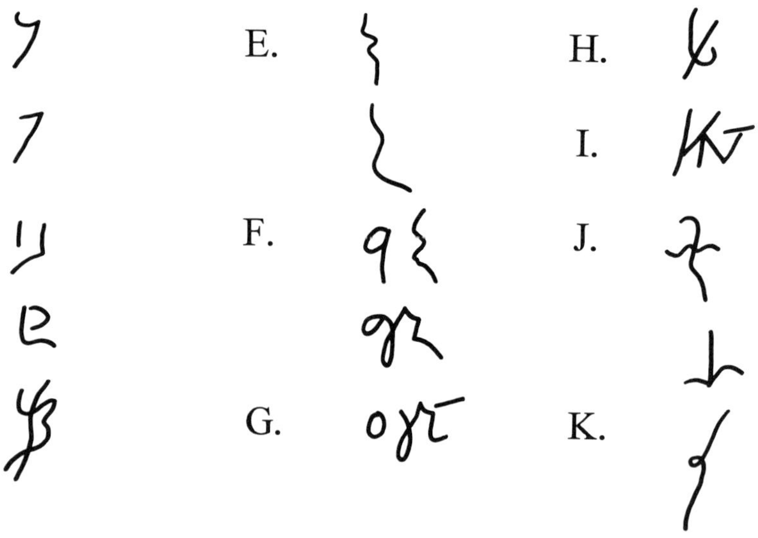

Fig. 10. Examples of special/problematic characters appearing in the *ostraca.*
A: Sign in Subgroup 2A and 2B documents translated as *centenarius* (two variants).
B: Sign in Subgroup 2A and 2B documents standing for cwt.
C: Ligature of P and L in Subgroup 2A and 2B documents standing for *pondo librae.*
D: Sign in Subgroup 2A and 2B documents standing for sum of cwt.
E: Final element in heading in Subgroup 2B documents transcribed *fieri inconditZ* (two variants).
F: Second element in provenience/ownership designation in Subgroup 2B documents transcribed *Tebelbucitan qz* (two variants).
G: Provenience/ownership designation in Subgroup 2B documents transcribed *oRc.*
H: Probable ligature of b and y in container type designation in Subgroup 2B documents transcribed *as a b.*
I: Container type designation consisting of ligature of K, N, and T in Subgroup 2A and 2B documents transcribed *KN^T.*
J: Sign of uncertain nature standing for container type with 400-lb. capacity in Subgroup 1B, 2B, and 2C documents transcribed *ψ* (two variants).
K: Figure in Number 7 *recto*, line 8, transcribed *f*.

Example - No. 16, lines 2-6:

7 quintus	*l/ V*	*P. LX*
7 victorianus	*l/ XX*	*P. LXVII*
7 bilossus ab ochi	*l/ II*	
7 tzelica	*l/ X*	*P. XX*
l} XXXVIII P. XLVII		

This element first presents a list of from one to 8 entries. These consist of the sign 7 (fig. 10.A), followed by a man's *cognomen* in the nominative, and then two numbers, the first introduced by the sign here transcribed l/ (fig. 10.B), and the second by the sign here transcribed P. (fig. 10.C). Centered at the bottom of the list are two more numbers, the first introduced by the sign here transcribed l} (fig. 10.D), and the second by the sign P.. By adding the numbers in these entries it is possible to establish that the sign l/ represents 100 of the P. units and that the number at the bottom of the list is the sum of the figures, with l} thus representing the sum of the l/ units.[19]

---

19 It seems that there are errors of transcription and/or addition in two of the 5 documents: in No. 9 the figure 33 cwt. and 63 lbs. is transcribed as 34 cwt. and 63 lbs.; in No. 18 figures that total 109 cwt. and 1 lb. are added to yield 111 cwt. and 11 lbs. These may not, in fact, be errors, but rather a deliberate effort to bring the cwt. of oil figure into line with the number of 100-lb. capacity containers filled in the course of weighing operations on the day in question, as Appendix 4 argues.

The sign Ꝑ, apparently a ligature of P and L, almost certainly stands for *pondo librae* (pounds in weight).[20] The sign l/ would thus appear to stand for *centenaria,* or cwt., and the sign l} for the sum of *centenaria*. Since, as earlier noted, the Romans commonly weighed olive oil in modules of 100 lbs., it seems a reasonable assumption that these entries record amounts of oil attributed to each of the individuals on the list on or up through the day on which the document was composed.

The sign here transcribed 7, used to introduce the individuals included in the Element 2 lists, is that normally used to denote men holding the military rank of *centurio*. Given the nature of these documents, however, it seems highly improbable that this sign was being employed for this purpose, and we should consider some alternative reading.[21] The most plausible interpretation is suggested by the text of Vegetius, who, writing in the late 4th c., notes that in his day the title *centurio* had been replaced by that of *centenarius*.[22] Since the men in these entries weighed out *centenaria* of oil into containers also known as *centenaria* (see Section 4.3 and Appendix 4), it seems reasonable to suggest that they too were known as *centenarii,* and that the compilers of these documents employed the *centurio* sign to refer to them.

Element 3: a list of entries recording quantities of oil containers or the weight of weighed oil being held at an oil weighing facility and a storage facility, followed by an estimate for the total weight of this oil.

Example - No. 16, lines 7-14:

Inpletu Vol as a ƀ N̄ XXII l/ XXXVIII Ꝑ LXXV
Fieri In conditẒ ag N̄ CLXVII et KN^{T} *LXII fisci*
et tebelbucitan qz as a ƀ N̄ CCCCXLVI
et KN^{T} *LXV et macrinenses*
as a ƀN LV et KN^{T} *CCLXXXV*
et Vol as a ƀ N ∞̄∞̄CLVI
oRc as N dCCLVII KN^{T} *∞CCXXXII*
l} V̄ĪĪdCCCLII Ꝑ LXXV

This element first presents a list of from 4 to 9 entries that record either a quantity of weighed oil or a quantity of oil containers. These are grouped under two headings, here transcribed *inpletu* and *fieri inconditZ*. The first of these was probably an abbreviated form of *inpletur,* the third person singular, present passive form of *inplere* (to fill). As will be shown below, the nature of the headings that appear under this entry together with the probable reading of the second heading both support this assumption.

The second heading begins with *fieri,* the present, passive infinitive of *facere* (to do). This is followed by the preposition *in* (in) and then a string here transcribed *conditZ*. The first 6 letters in this string are apparently an abbreviation for the ablative form of the word *conditorium* (storehouse), with the final letter an abbreviation for some modifying adjective. The reading of this letter is problematic. In 3 of the 5 documents in which it is preserved (Nos. 9, 14, and 18) it resembles a large, stylized letter 'z', while in the other two (Nos. 13 and 16) it is rendered as a wavy line most closely resembling the Greek letter 'ξ' (fig. 10.E). In the latter two documents it does not match examples of the letter 'z' that occur elsewhere in the text. In light of these observations it appears likely that the sign in question was intended as a capital

20 The pounds referred to in these documents were apparently the standard Roman pound of 12 ounces/327 g. For the use of the short pound of 10 ounces/272.5 g for the measuring of oil in the Roman and Byzantine world, see Oxé 1940, 133-34, 146-49; Schilbach 1970, 115-16, 179-81.

21 The possibility that the individuals named in these entries were, in fact, *centuriones,* with the associated weight figures corresponding to amounts of oil either issued to them as rations or consigned by them at a storage facility, is precluded by the analysis of these figures presented in Appendix 4.

22 *Mil.* 13: *centuriones qui nunc centenarii vocantur* (*centuriones,* who are now termed *centenarii*).

'z'.[23] If so, the most plausible suggestion is that this is an abbreviation for *Zeugitanum*, the adjectival form of the name of the province for which Carthage served as administrative seat, and this heading is accordingly expanded as *fieri in condit(orio) Z(eugitano)*.

The understanding of these two headings depends upon the interpretation of the various entries that occur under them, as considered in Section 4. To anticipate the conclusions regarding the interpretation of the two headings reached there, it is evident that the entries under the *inpletu* heading refer both to the weighed oil recorded in Element 2 of the same document and to containers of unweighed oil. Those under the *fieri inconditZ* heading, on the other hand, refer to containers of both weighed and unweighed oil, with the latter representing the lion's share of the total. The first heading would thus appear to refer to oil being held at a facility dedicated to the weighing of oil, with the weight of oil entry carried down from Element 2 representing oil for which the weighing process had already been completed at the time that the document was composed, while the entries for the groups of oil containers represent containers of oil that had yet to be weighed. The second heading appears to refer to containers of oil being held at a storage facility, the bulk of which was destined for transfer to the weighing facility for weighing. In light of these conclusions, the *inpletu* heading is here translated as 'being filled', while the *fieri inconditZ* heading is translated as 'to do, in the Zeugitana storehouse'.

Table 1 (see p. 174) presents synopses of the various entries in this element for the Subgroup 2B documents together with equivalent entries from the Subgroup 2A and Subgroup 2C documents. Readers will find it helpful to refer to this table for the discussion that follows, and should note that the numbers assigned to the entries in this table are henceforth employed to refer to the entries.

With the exception of the last entry under the *inpletu* heading, all entries in this element are made up of three different components, here termed the provenience/ownership designation, the container type designation, and the quantity of containers figure. There are 5 different provenience/ownership designations attested, including *fisci*, Tebelbucitan qz, Macrinenses, Vol, and *oRc*. The first of these, *fisci*, apparently indicates oil that was property of the imperial fisc. The next three, Tebelbucitan qz, Macrinenses, and Vol, are toponyms, and presumably indicate the locales or districts where the oil originated. The correct reading of the second element of the designation transcribed Tebelbucitan qz (fig. 10.F) is problematic. In No. 7, line 13 and No. 14, line 14 this element appears to read either *qz* or *orz*, while in No. 16, line 9 it appears to consist of a 'q' followed by a character that is either a stylized 'z' or a 'ξ'. The reading of the second letter in the last of the 5 designations, here transcribed *oRc* (fig. 10.G), is also problematic. In the 4 instances in which this designation has been recognized in the Group 2 ostraca, the letter has a loop that extends well below the line. Elsewhere in the Group 2 ostraca this feature is matched only by the initial letter in the name Romanus in No. 14, line 9, and it would thus appear that the letter in question is a capital 'r'. The shortness of this designation, coupled with the presence of what appears to be an upper case letter in the central position, suggests that it is most likely to be an abbreviation for a term consisting of either two or three words. The interpretation of these designations is considered in Section 5.

There are 5 different container type designations attested in the Element 3 entries, here transcribed *ag, as a ƀ, as,* KN^T*, and ψ.* As discussed in Section 4 and Appendix 3, these are signs or abbreviations that represent distinct types of oil containers. The final character in the *as a ƀ* designation is apparently a ligature of b and y (fig. 10.H). In No. 11, Entry 5, as well as in No. 6, Records 1 and 2, this designation is rendered simply as *b* , while in No. 9, Entry 4 it appears as *as a bic, as a bec,* or perhaps *as a bce.* The KN^T designation is clearly a ligature of 'K', 'N',

23 For the interpretation of similar signs in the 3rd-c. Golas ostraca as possible examples of the letter z, see Marichal 1992, 36-37.

and 'T' (fig. 10.I). The nature of the *ψ* designation, which consists of a vertical stroke crossed by a wavy line (fig. 10.J) remains unclear, although it would appear to be a sign rather than an abbreviation for a name.

The quantity of containers figures that are associated with all of these designations save the KN^T are always preceded either by the sign *N* or its barred version, $\overline{N}$. This is apparently an abbreviation for *numero* (in number), and presumably served to indicate that the figure that followed referred to a quantity of oil containers rather than to cwt. of oil. In a slight variation, No. 13, Entry 6 is introduced by *de N* and Entry 7 by *de* $\overline{N}$. The KN^T container type does not appear to have required this marker since, as will be shown below, it was assigned a standard weight value of 100 lbs., making it the equivalent of a cwt. figure.

The 3 entry components described above are combined in specific ways to formulate 3 distinct types of entries. These entry types, here termed Types 1-3, are structured as follows:

Type 1:
Example - No. 18, lines 13-14:
ψ N CLXXXIIII/[et ag N C]LXVII KN^T *LXII fisci*
- (optional) container type designation *ψ* and quantity of containers figure;
- container type designation *ag* and quantity of containers figure;
- (optional) container type designation KN^T and quantity of containers figure;
- provenience/ownership designation *fisci*.

Type 2:
Example - No. 16, lines 9-10:
tebelbucitan qz as a ƀ $\overline{N}$ *CCCCXLVI et* KN^T *LXV*
- provenience/ownership designation Tebelbucitan qz, Macrinenses, Vol, or also perhaps Caprorenses;
- container type designation *as a ƀ* and quantity of containers figure;
- (optional with Tebelbucitan qz, Macrinenses, and also perhaps Caprorenses provenience/ownership designations) container type designation KN^T and quantity of containers figure.

Type 3:
Example - No. 16, line 13:
oRc as $\overline{N}$ *dCCLVII* KN^T *∞CCXXXII*
- provenience/ownership designation *oRc;*
- container type designation *as* and quantity of containers figure;
- (optional) container type designation KN^T and quantity of containers figure.

There is one additional type of entry, here termed Type 4, structured as follows:

Type 4:
Example - No. 16, line 7:
l/ XXXVIII Ᵽ LXXV
- cwt. sign, sum of cwt. sign, or crossed *centenarius* sign;
- a figure that corresponds either to the number of 100 lb. capacity containers used to hold the oil involved in the weighing operations recorded in Element 2, or a rounded version of the figure for sum of weighed oil recorded at the bottom of this element (see Appendix 4).

There are specific patterns to the ways in which these 4 entry types appear under each of the two headings. In 5 of the 8 documents (Nos. 9, 10, 14, 16, and 18) in which the *inpletu* section of Element 3 is preserved more or less complete, the heading is followed by two entries, first a Type 2 entry, then a Type 4 entry. In the 4 of these 5 documents in which the *fieri inconditZ* section is preserved more or less intact (Nos. 9, 14, 16, and 18), the entries, which vary in number from two to six, always follow the same order with respect to type, beginning with a Type 1 entry, followed by one or more Type 2 entries, and then a Type 3 entry. In cases where there is more than one Type 2 entry, these always follow the same order with respect to provenience/ownership designation, with Tebelbucitan qz coming first, followed by Macrinenses, and then Vol.

No. 13, which also preserves both sections of this element intact, diverges from this scheme in that it has two Type 2 entries and one Type 3 entry under the *inpletu* heading, and does not respect the order noted above for the presentation of entries, inserting the Type 3 entry under both the *inpletu* and the *fieri inconditZ* headings between two Type 2 entries. No. 11, while fragmentary, appears to contain two Type 2 entries under the *inpletu* entry, while introducing the *fieri in conditZ* section by means of some divergent formula. No. 15, also fragmentary, again appears to contain two Type 2 entries under the *inpletu* entry, with a Vol entry preceding one for Tebelbucitan qz. No. 17, again only partially preserved, appears to lack an *inpletu* section. Other than this there are only minor departures from the formats here described for both the structure and ordering of the entries under the *inpletu* and *fieri inconditZ* headings.[24]

Element 3 concludes with an entry consisting of two numbers, the first introduced by the sum of cwt. sign and the second by the lbs. sign.

Example - No. 16, line 14:

l} $\overline{VII}$*dCCCḶII P̶ LXXV*

These figures evidently represent an estimate for the total weight of the oil referred to in the entries that appear under the *inpletu* and *fieri inconditZ* headings. This estimate must have been derived by assigning a standard weight value to the various container types, multiplying the quantity of containers figures in the several entries by the appropriate value, and then adding the products. As discussed below, the content of No. 7 *recto* strongly suggests that the *KN^T* container type was assigned a value of 100 lbs. for this purpose. Since four of the Subgroup 2B documents (Nos. 9, 13, 16, and 18) preserve intact both the full set of oil container entries and the figure for the estimate for the total weight of oil, it is possible to treat these sets of numbers as polynomial equations and solve for the standard weight values assigned to the other 4 container types. A detailed description of this operation is presented in Appendix 2. The results suggest that the compilers of these 4 documents (and presumably also the other Group 2 documents) employed the following standard weight values for the various container types attested:

as a ₱ :	75 lbs.
KN^T:	100 lbs.
ag:	215 lbs.
ψ	400 lbs.
as:	505 lbs.

The two *ostraca* assigned to Subgroup 2A, Nos. 7 and 8, were each produced using a shield-shaped blank and bear both a *recto* text and a *verso* text. In No. 7 the two texts were produced on February 16 and 17, both apparently by the same hand, here designated Hand 5. Both the *recto* text and the *verso* text of No. 8 are only partially legible, and in neither case is a date preserved. It appears possible, however, that both were produced by the same hand as that responsible for No. 7. The blanks on which Nos. 7 and 8 were produced are indistinguishable from one another in fabric and surfacing, and it appears highly likely that both derive from the same parent amphora. In light of the similarities between Nos. 7 and 8 at the level of

24 Nos. 9 and 11 omit provenience/ownership designations for the entries under the *fieri inconditZ* heading. In the latter document the *oRc* provenience/ownership designation in Entry 4 is apparently placed after the number of containers figure. No. 14 appends the strings *afr (or afs)* and *qs* following the quantity of containers figures for *KN^T* in Entries 1 and 4, respectively. These may be abbreviations for *amphorae* and *quadrantales*, although it is unclear how these would function in this context.

format, hand, and blank, it seems a fair assumption that both were produced during the same part of the year, presumably before the initiation of the Subgroup 2B series of documents.

Since No. 8 *recto* is largely illegible, the analysis of the *recto* texts in Subgroup 2A must be based entirely on No. 7 *recto*. Lines 1-3 of this text each record an entry that refers either to a group of oil containers or to a quantity of weighed oil:

Vol Cal	*KN^T*	*X*
[C]aprorenses	*KN^T*	*dCVII*
Fieri KN^T CCCXIIII r CCLIIII		

Entry 1 consists of the provenience/ownership designation Vol Cal followed by the container type designation KN^T and a figure for the quantity of containers. This provenience/ownership designation is apparently the abbreviated form of the Vol Calassini designation that appears in the corresponding *verso* text, which is in turn presumably the full form of the Vol designation that occurs in several of the Subgroup 2B documents. Entry 2 has a similar format, consisting of the provenience/ownership designation Caprorenses, presumably the same as the Caprorenses of the *verso* documents of Nos. 2-4,[25] followed by the container type designation KN^T and a figure for the quantity of containers. The fact that the provenience/ownership designations in these two entries are both toponyms, one or both of which is the same as one of the toponymic designations attested in the Subgroup 2B *ostraca*, suggests that they should probably be regarded as equivalent to the Type 2 entries in these other documents. Entry 3 departs from this format, consisting of the word *fieri* followed by the container type designation KN^T and a figure for the quantity of containers, then a letter 'r' and a second figure. The interpretation of this entry will be considered below.

The next three lines, ll. 4-6, record an amount of items of some sort in a *conditorium*, presumably the *conditorium Zeugitanum* of the Subgroup 2B *ostraca*, on a particular date:

et erunt in condit(orio)
in ḍ XIIII K[
]XXXI

The date should presumably be restored to read 14 days before the Kalends of March, one day earlier than the date of the corresponding *verso* document. The fragmentary number in line 6 should probably be restored to read 931, equal to the number of KN^T registered in the three entries in lines 1-3. This figure would thus appear to be a summation of the number of this type of container in the storehouse on the given date. If so, the entries in lines 1-3 must refer to oil containers and/or weighed oil being held at the *conditorium*.

This document then concludes in lines 7-8 with a second summation of items being held in the *conditorium*:

Fieri in condit(orio)
ʆ ∞CLXXXV

The figure in line 8, which is introduced by a letter or sign here transcribed ʆ (fig. 10.K), is equal to the number of KN^T listed in the three entries in lines 1-3 (or the figure of 931 restored for line 6) plus the figure introduced by letter 'r' in line 3. It would thus appear to be a summation of the items listed in Entries 1-3, with the items introduced by 'r' treated as equivalent to the KN^T. The interpretation of the character used to introduce this summation is problematic. Most likely it is a stylized *centenarius* sign used — as it is in the associated *verso* document — to represent sum of cwt., the figure in this line thus being an estimate for the number of cwt. of oil then being held at the storage facility. If this assumption is correct, then both the KN^T and items introduced by the letter r in lines 1-3 must have been assigned a standard value of 100 lbs., with the 'r' presumably representing cwt. of weighed oil.

---

25 See No. 13, lines 9 and 17 for the analogous variants Macrinenses/Macrineses.

Crucial to the understanding of No. 7 *recto* and to the larger interpretation of the *ostraca* is the observation that the 607 Caprorenses KN^T in No. 7 *recto*, Entry 2 correspond more or less to the number of containers in three shipments of *Caproreses centenaria levia* as documented in the Group 1A *ostraca*. Given the fact that No. 7 *recto* was very probably composed on the same day as No. 2 *recto* and No. 3 *recto*, it seems a reasonable assumption that the shipments of 200 and 195 *Caproreses centenaria levia* which the latter two documents record as accepted on this date represent about two-thirds of the containers recorded in this entry. If so, the balance, equal to 212 *Caprorenses centenaria levia*, presumably belonged to a third such shipment accepted on this date. On the basis of this assumption we may venture two further inferences:

1) The container type for which KN^T was the abbreviation was either identical to the *centenarium leve* container type or subsumed it.
2) Entry 2 in No. 7 *recto*, and also presumably Entry 1, which has an identical structure, represent oil containers received at the storage facility on the day the document was composed.

In light of the second of these inferences, it would appear that No. 7 *recto*, Entry 3 records the stocks of oil being held at the *conditorium Zeugitanum* prior to the arrival of the shipments recorded in Entries 1 and 2.

While No. 8 *recto* is largely illegible, its length (5 lines) and the fact that it appears to conclude with an estimate for cwt. and perhaps also lbs. of oil are compatible with the assumption that it was similar to No. 7 *recto*. The latter point also lends support to the assumption that the final figure in No. 7 *recto* represents an estimate for the total weight of oil rather than some other sort of figure (e.g., a summation of quantities of containers).

The *verso* texts of the two Subgroup 2A *ostraca* consist of two elements:

Element 1: the date.

In No. 7 *verso*, the sole case in which the beginning of the text is preserved, this element employs the same format as that used in Element 1 of the Subgroup 2B documents.

Element 2: a list of entries recording names of oil weighers and amounts of oil ascribed to them, followed by a summation of these figures.

In both *ostraca* these oil weigher entries are similar to those which appear in Element 2 of the Subgroup 2B documents, differing from these only in that the weight figures listed after each name are presented as a single number introduced by the lbs. sign rather than a compound number consisting of a cwt. figure and a lbs. figure.[26] In both cases there are more *centenarius* entries than are attested in any of the surviving Subgroup 2B documents — 13 in No. 7 and 13 or more in No. 8. The following summations of these figures differ from those in Element 2 of the Subgroup 2B documents in that the two figures are preceded by the phrase *fieri N(umero)* (with the first word abbreviated *f(ieri)* in No. 8 *verso*), while the cwt. figure is introduced by the *centenarius* sign rather than by the sum of cwt. sign. Of some interest is the use of the word *fieri* in these two documents to indicate oil that had already been weighed rather than oil that required weighing, as appears to have been the practice in the Subgroup 2B documents.

No. 7 *verso* contains a third element consisting of a single entry comprised of the provenience/ownership designation Vol Calassini followed by what appears to be a letter 'K' and then a figure. Given the fact that the Vol Calassini provenience/ownership designation appears in association with the KN^T container type in the associated *recto* document, it seems a fair assumption that the letter 'K' was here employed to indicate containers of this type. If so, this entry would appear to be analogous to the oil container entries that occur under the *inpletu*

26 In No. 7 *verso* figures that total 346 cwt. and 58 lbs. are summed to yield 350 cwt. and 78 lbs. For the argument that the cwt. figure is not an error, but a deliberate effort to bring this number into line with the number of 100-lb. capacity containers filled in the course of weighing operations, see Appendix 4.

heading in Element 3 of the Subgroup 2B documents, representing containers of unweighed oil being held at the weighing facility.

Taken together, the *recto* text and the *verso* text on the Subgroup 2A *ostraca* appear to constitute a record similar, if not comparable in every respect, to a Subgroup 2B document. No. 7 is the earliest document in the series of Group 2 *ostraca*. As will be discussed in Section 5, oil handling operations at Carthage were probably suspended from October through February due to restrictions on sailing, and it may be that the compilation of No. 7 marked the initiation of oil processing operations for the year 373. The arrival of the large number of containers recorded in Entries 1 and 2 of the *recto* document may have triggered the resumption of activity, commencing with the compilation of an inventory of the oil in storage at the *conditorium Zeugitanum*, followed one day later by the beginning of weighing operations.

The only *ostracon* that can be assigned to Subgroup 2C with certainty is No. 22. The text of this document, produced on a shield-shaped blank, is highly fragmentary and its interpretation remains problematic. The preserved portion consists of a record of an uncertain nature that contains an entry of some sort for 490-99 *as a ƀ*. This is followed by three additional records produced on three different dates, May 30, May 31, and June 6, each of which presents one or more entries recording what would appear to be partially weighed consignments of oil.

The three records each consist of two elements:

Element 1: the date.
This element includes the day and the month on which the record was composed, with no indication either of the year or of the terminus of the administrative period.

Element 2: a list of entries, each of which includes a quantity of oil containers figure and a quantity of weighed oil figure, followed by a problematic figure that may be either the sum of weighed oil or the estimated weight of oil.
Example - No. 22, Record 1, lines 4-6:
ψ N LẊII l/ CCXVII Ɽ LXXX[
as a ƀ N̄ CLXX l/ C̣C̣ XXX VIII Ɽ L[
l} dXVI Ɽ LX̣Ṿ

This element first presents a list of from one to three entries, introduced in Records 2 and 3 by the word *fieri*. Each entry consists of two figures, the first representing a group of oil containers and the second a quantity of weighed oil. Each oil containers figure is comprised of either the ψ or the *as a ƀ* container type designation followed by an N, here again presumably an abbreviation for *numero*, and then a number. Each weighed oil figure consists of two numbers, the first introduced by the cwt. sign and the second by the lbs. sign. This element concludes with a figure, introduced in Records 2 and 3 by the abbreviation *Inst* (or possibly *Insc*). This is comprised either of two numbers, as in Record 1, with the first introduced by the sum of cwt. sign and the second by the lbs. sign, or, as in Records 2 and 3, of a single number, which in Record 3 is introduced by the cwt. sign.

The presence of weighed oil figures and the absence of any reference to the *conditorium* suggests that these three records represent oil being held at the weighing facility. The existence in Record 1 and also apparently in Record 3 of multiple entries pairing quantity of oil container figures with weighed oil figures is a feature of considerable interest. One possibility is that the weighed oil figures in these entries represent the oil held in the associated group of containers. Alternatively, the oil containers and the weighed oil together may have constituted a single consignment of oil. If the former, one would expect there to be a consistent ratio of lbs. of oil to container type. While the entries are too fragmentary to permit the evaluation of this possibility, the values obtained when dividing the weighed oil figures in the two entries in Record 1 by the associated number of containers figures, *c.*350 lbs. for the ψ and *c.*140 lbs. for the *as a ƀ*, do not accord with the values obtained for these two container types on the basis of the

Subgroup 2B documents, as discussed in Appendix 2. Various other considerations suggest that this is not the nature of the relationship between the two figures in these entries.[27] That the latter interpretation — that is, that the containers and the weighed oil together constituted a shipment — is the correct one is suggested by the fact that the amount of oil represented by the 170 *as a þ* and 23,850-23,889 lbs. of weighed oil (*c*.36,600-36,639 lbs. of oil) in the second entry in Record 1 is more or less equal to the amount of oil that would have been held in the group of 490-99 *as a þ* (*c*.36,750-37,425 lbs. of oil) that appears in the problematic portion of the document immediately preceding this record. On the basis of this observation it appears likely that the entry in question represents a partial weighing of this group of containers.

The final figure in each of the three records is problematic. It would not appear to be an estimate for the total weight of oil represented in that record because multiplying the figures for the quantity of containers by their standard weight values and adding the resulting products to the figures for weighed oil in Records 1 and 2 yields an incompatible result. In Records 2 and 3, on the other hand, these figures may be compatible with values obtained by adding the amount of weighed oil recorded in that record to the final figure from the preceding record. Interesting in this regard is the fact that the fragmentary figure preserved in the penultimate line of Record 3 can be restored as 830, equal to the final figure in Record 2.[28] If this restoration is correct, then this line would appear to represent the carrying down of the final figure from the previous record for the purpose of the summing operation. If this was how the final figures in these two records were derived, then it appears that one of the functions of this document was to add the amounts of oil weighed over the period of time represented by all three records. The *Inst* abbreviation that precedes the final figures in Records 2 and 3 remains enigmatic. It is here expanded as an abbreviation for *Instans* (present).

While the information embodied in this document would have been analogous to that contained in the *inpletu* section of the Subgroup 2B *ostraca*, No. 22 does not contain data regarding the amount of oil weighed by individual oil weighers, as appear in Element 1 of these other documents, and it may be that the production of this *ostracon* reflects some modification to the record-keeping system that was instituted between the date of the latest dated Subgroup 2B document (May 6) and that of the composition of the earliest preserved record that it contains (May 30).

No. 23 is similarly fragmentary and problematic. This document appears to contain at least three distinct records that conclude with either a summation of weighed oil or an estimate for the total weight of oil. The final two lines of the last of these records consists of a standard Type 2 entry and an estimate for the total weight of oil figure as represented in Element 3 of the Subgroup 2B documents. Thus, while No. 23 may have served a somewhat analogous function to No. 22, it clearly differs from this other document in certain fundamental respects.

---

27 The fact that the two figures in question, 140 and 350, are round figures, with the former exactly 2.5 times the size of the latter, raised the suspicion that these might, in fact, have been the standard weight values employed by the compilers of the Group 2 documents when calculating their estimates for total weight of oil. Two trials undertaken to evaluate this possibility, however, indicated that this was almost certainly not the case. In the first trial, substituting these values in the complete Subgroup 2B documents and solving for the *ag* and *as* yielded inconsistent values for these two container types. In the second trial, multiplying the figure for the number of ψ in Record 2 by 350 yielded a result that was incompatible with the range of values possible for the fragmentary cwt figure preserved in that entry.

28 This figure might, on the other hand, be restored as 330, equal to the sum of the *as a þ* registered in Records 1 and 3.

3. CONTEXTUALIZATION

In order to reconstruct the operations represented in the *ostraca* and to interpret them, it is essential to make extensive use of information concerned with two distinct topics:

1) The methods employed by the state for the mobilization of oil in the province of Zeugitana during the late 4th c. and the rôle that Carthage played in these operations;
2) The procedures employed for the weighing and bottling of oil in the province of Baetica during the 1st to 3rd c.

While extended discussions of both topics are already available in the literature, their consideration from the point of view of the analysis and interpretation of our *ostraca* leads to several new observations. It is thus essential to review both here in some detail.

Carthage and the mobilization of state oil in Zeugitana

During the late 4th c., state oil was presumably brought to Carthage for two purposes:

1) distribution to persons resident in the city;
2) export through the city's port in connection with state supply initiatives aimed at the provision of foodstuffs to persons residing elsewhere.

Regarding the distribution of oil to residents of Carthage, we have no evidence that there was ever any initiative for the regular supply of state oil to the general populace of that city, either during the late 4th c. or at any other time.[29] There were, however, several categories of imperial functionaries, soldiers, and state slaves resident at Carthage during the late 4th c. who would have been entitled to receive *annonae* (rations), and a certain amount of state oil must have been brought to the city in order to provide for these entitlements. Among those who might have received such rations we may list the following:

1) functionaries attached to the staffs of the *vicarius Africae* (the chief administrative official for the Diocese of Africa), the *proconsul Africae* (the governor of the Province of Zeugitana), and the *praefectus annonae Africae* (the official in charge of handling the state-owned grain and oil that was shipped overseas from the Diocese of Africa);[30]
2) functionaries and state slaves attached to the *gynaeceum* (state cloth manufactory) located at Carthage;[31]
3) functionaries attached to the office of the *res privata* in Carthage;[32]

---

29 For the evidence for state involvement in the supply of food to Carthage during the late empire, see Durliat 1990, 382-89.

30 For the provision of rations in kind to the staffs of provincial governors during the period in question, see *CTh* 1.22.4 (383) and the discussion in Neri 1976, 114-20. For the *officium* of the *vicarius Africae* see *Not.Dig.Occ.* 20, and for that of the *proconsul Africae*, see *Not.Dig.Occ.* 18. We can perhaps gain some idea of the number of rations that would have been issued to the staffs of these two officials from *CJ* 1.27.1.13, 22-39, a law of 534 that specifies the organization of the staffs to be maintained by the *praefectus Africae* and the 7 provincial governors under his jurisdiction. The *praefectus Africae* was to be served by a staff of 396 functionaries, who were entitled to draw a total of 496 *annonae*. Each of the provincial governors was granted a staff of 50. While there is no mention of the number of rations issued to the staffs of the latter, if the proportion of *annonae* to functionaries was roughly equivalent to that attested for the staff of the *praefectus Africae*, we might expect that the number came to *c.*60-65 rations.

31 This was operated by the *sacrae largitiones*. Since both *CTh* 4.6.3.5 (336) and 11.1.24 (395) make reference to this establishment, it seems a fair assumption that it was in operation in 373.

32 This office was presumably responsible for overseeing the management of all imperial properties located within the diocese. Little is known about the administrative organization responsible for the management of imperial properties in Africa during the late empire; see Jones 1964, 412-14. For earlier periods, see Pflaum 1960-61, 380-85; Millar 1977, 179 n.30.

4) soldiers in the military unit that served as the garrison of Carthage;[33]
5) various other categories of imperial functionaries, state slaves, and soldiers, who were more or less permanently stationed at Carthage, including state slaves attached to the *cursus publicus* (state post), *agentes in rebus* (special agents), and other troops on detached duty.

While we have no way of developing an accurate estimate for the number of oil rations that were issued to the individuals in these categories, a plausible guess is that the total may have come to somewhere between 2,000 and 4,000. Although we possess no information regarding the size of the rations, two 6th-c. papyri indicate that at that time troops stationed in Egypt were provided with oil rations that came to between 0.75 and 0.92 *amphorae* (54-68 lbs./17.7-22.2 kg/19.4-24.5 l) per year.[34] If we take these figures as a guide, we can estimate that somewhere in the neighborhood of 100,000-275,000 lbs. (32,700-89,900 kg/36,000-99,000 l) of state oil might have been brought to Carthage each year in order to provide rations for state workers residing there.[35] The upper end of this range is well below the amount of oil documented in our *ostraca* for either of the two distinct oil mobilization initiatives represented, not to mention the amounts that can be extrapolated for these for the course of the entire administrative year (see Section 5), and we may thus conclude that the bulk of this oil was probably being shipped through the port at Carthage in connection with one or more state initiatives concerned with the supply of persons residing elsewhere.

Two such supply initiatives warrant consideration: the *annona militaris*, the mobilization of foodstuffs for the provisioning of military units, and the *annona urbis*, the mobilization of foodstuffs for the supply of the populace of the city of Rome. Of interest with regard to the first is a law of 401 which, while absolving the inhabitants of Zeugitana from tax levies aimed at the provisioning of troops stationed outside Africa, confirms their responsibility to support troops located within the boundaries of the diocese.[36] The implication is that on some occasions prior to this ruling the taxpayers of the province had been required to provide for troops stationed outside of Africa. Olive oil was a regular component of the military ration, and the obligation for the inhabitants of Zeugitana to provide supplies for units stationed both outside Africa and in some of the more distant parts of the diocese may well have involved the shipment of oil through the port at Carthage. The volume of this oil remains impossible to estimate. The military units were probably limited to those belonging to the regular field army, since during this period *limitanei* (border troops) were expected to obtain their rations from the region within which they were stationed.[37]

Our most important evidence regarding the use of African oil for the *annona urbis* during the period in question comes from a letter of Symmachus written during his tenure as *praefectus urbi*

---

33 See Cagnat 1913 [1975] 214-15 for the Carthage garrison during the late empire. I have not been able to consult Le Bohec *et al.* 1980. The Carthage garrison during this period may have consisted of one of the urban cohorts, as during the 2nd and 3rd c. While the latest mention of the urban cohorts occurs in an inscription dating to the period 317-337, Chastagnol 1960, 255 suggests that they were probably not disbanded until some point between 357 and 384, most likely during the period 368-379. Each of these units would probably have consisted of either 1,000 or 1,500 men; see Robinson 1992, 185.

34 *P.Oxy.* 1920 and 2046, indicating oil rations of either one-tenth or one-eighth *sextarius* per day depending upon rank; see Jones 1964, 629 n.44, 1261-62. For the inference that *P.Beatty Panop.* 2.245-249 implies a monthly oil ration of one-eleventh *sextarius* per day for soldiers stationed in Egypt during the period 298-300, see Duncan-Jones 1990, 109-10.

35 The true figure may well have been considerably smaller, as in many instances rations in kind may have been commuted to payments in cash.

36 *CTh* 11.5.1, issued to the *proconsul Africae*. See also in this connection *CTh* 12.6.28, issued to the same official in the same year. For the mobilization of food supplies for the military units stationed in Africa, see Cagnat 1913 [1975] 310-34.

37 See in this regard *CTh* 7.4.15 (369), issued to the *praefectus praetorio Orientis*. For Africa, see *CTh* 11.1.11 (365), issued to the *vicarius Africae*.

(chief administrative officer of the city of Rome), which probably extended from June/July 384 to January/February 385.[38] In the letter Symmachus asks Valentinian II to aid in the resolution of an impending crisis in the urban oil supply.[39] Noting that the oil shortage was the result of the import of insufficient stocks and that there was at that time no shortage in the amount of grain on hand, he states that the *praefectus annonae* had sent *brevia* (summaries) indicating the tenuous nature of the supply situation to the office of the *praefectus praetorio* (the chief administrative officer of the praefecture) in the customary fashion, apparently to no effect. He indicates that the ongoing *praebitio diurna* (daily issue) threatened to exhaust the remaining stocks, and urged the emperor to prod the *iudices Africani* (governors of the provinces in Africa) regarding the need to send additional amounts of oil to the *horrea* (storehouses) at Rome.

While Symmachus may have been overstating the case somewhat in order to ensure timely action on the part of the emperor, his assertion that the impending exhaustion of the supply of state oil at Rome threatened the *victus plebis* (sustenance of the populace) would seem to indicate that a substantial portion of the city's population depended upon the state for the supply of its oil requirements. His request that the emperor press the *iudices Africani* to send additional oil in order to avert the crisis suggests that Africa was a major source of the state oil made available to the inhabitants of Rome at this time. This inference is certainly supported by the evidence of amphoras from Rome, which indicates that throughout the course of the 4th c. the provinces of Zeugitana and Byzacena were the city's main sources of supply.[40] Africa also provided the bulk of the state grain shipped to Rome at this time for the production of *panis gradilis*, the bread made from state grain that was made available to the populace of Rome,[41] and it seems a fair assumption that Carthage, as the administrative capital of the diocese and a major port located near important grain and oil production areas, was one of the principal ports of embarcation for both of these *species fiscales* (state-owned goods).

The oil provided to Rome's inhabitants at this time was probably made available through programs of free distribution and sale. The *praebitio diurna* to which Symmachus refers should probably be understood as a free distribution, from which we can infer that a significant portion of the city's populace received state oil *gratis* on a daily basis during the period in question.[42] According to the textual sources, the regular distribution of state oil at Rome began under Septimius Severus (193-211).[43] We have no indication of either the number of people qualified to receive this ration or the amount that they received at any point during the history of this initiative. It is not implausible to assume, however, that the set of recipients was the same as that qualified to receive rations of state grain/bread and/or pork. Tengstrom estimated that during the second half of the 4th c. the number of recipients of bread probably came to between 100,000 and 200,000 individuals,[44] while a law of 419 would seem to indicate that in that year a total of 120,000 pork rations were distributed at Rome.[45] With respect to the size of oil

---

38 *Rel.* 35. For the supply of state olive oil to Rome, see Pavis D'Escurac 1976, 188-201; Manacorda 1976-77, 555-63; Durliat 1990, 48-51; Sirks 1991, 388-91; Peña (forthcoming).

39 While the letter is headed *DDD. NNN.* (to the three co-regents), Symmachus' correspondence with the imperial administration during his tenure as *praefectus urbi* would have been directed to Valentinian II; see Barrow 1973, 15.

40 Whitehouse *et al.* 1982, 75, 80; Carignani *et al.* 1986, 38-41; Martin 1989, 476-78; Carignani and Pacetti 1989a; 1989b; Hostetter *et al.* 1994, 159; Peña (forthcoming).

41 For the argument that Egypt had ceased to be a major source of state grain for the supply of Rome prior to the revolt of Domitius Alexander in 308, see Sirks 1991, 199-200. Sardinia apparently remained a significant source of supply into the 5th c.

42 See in this regard *CTh* 14.17.7 (372), issued to the *praefectus urbi*, which abolished the practice of selling *annona* (including *panis ceteraque* [bread and other items]) to *populares*.

43 *SHA*, *Sev.* 18.3; *Alex. Sev.* 22.2.

44 Tengstrom 1974, 84-85.

45 *CTh* 14.4.10, issued to the *praefectus praetorio*. For this passage, see Barnish 1987, 162-63.

rations, we are told that this was reduced under Elagabalus (218-22) and then restored to its full measure under Severus Alexander (222-35).[46] While the sources are not entirely clear, oil distributions appear to have been reinstituted under Aurelian,[47] the implication being that they were discontinued at some point between the accession of Severus Alexander and the murder of Aurelian (i.e., between 222 and 275). If so, this probably occurred amidst the political and economic crises of the 250s and 260s. While it is not known whether free distributions of oil continued without interruption from the time of Aurelian until Symmachus' tenure as *praefectus urbi*, it is worth noting that the provisions for the distribution of *panis gradilis* were altered from time to time during the second half of the 4th c., it being distributed *gratis* during some periods and at other times sold at an officially determined, possibly subsidized price.[48]

That state oil was also sold to the urban populace of Rome on a regular basis during the 4th c. can be inferred from what is known about a group of facilities known as *mensae oleariae* (olive oil counters). The *Notitia Urbis Romae* and *Curiosum Urbis Romae*, two mid-4th c. compilations that list the various kinds of structures within the city, indicate that there were 2,300 of these facilities.[49] The only other reference to the *mensae oleariae* in the sources occurs in a law of 328, which is concerned with establishing rules governing the alienation of their ownership.[50] Since this ruling is addressed to the *praefectus annonae*, we may infer that these facilities served in some way for the distribution of state oil. It is evident from the provisions of this law that there was concern on the part of the state that individuals might speculate in the buying and selling of *mensae oleariae*. From this we can deduce that their operation was a potentially profitable undertaking. It is hard to see how this could have been the case had they served exclusively for the disbursing of free oil rations. It thus appears likely that they also functioned in some fashion as retail outlets. This presumably involved the sale of state oil to those not eligible for free distributions and/or to those who wished to buy additional oil above the amount of their ration. The inclusion of this law in the *Codex Theodosianus* indicates that these facilities continued to operate at least through the 430s.

The oil that the state raised in Zeugitana during the late 4th c. for the supply of its functionaries based at Carthage, for military units stationed both within and without the boundaries of Africa, and for the inhabitants of Rome may have been obtained by as many as three distinct methods:

1) the collection of oil as tax in kind from landholders under the *iugatio* or *capitatio terrena* (land tax);
2) the collection of oil as rent in kind from the tenants of imperial lands;
3) the purchase of oil from private owners either on the free market or through programs of *coemptio* (compulsory purchase).

Of these three methods, the first would clearly have been an important source of the oil distributed under these initiatives. Whether significant amounts of oil were also raised by means of the second and third methods remains uncertain.

46 *SHA*, *Alex. Sev.* 22.2.

47 *Chron. 354* (148) states that Aurelian *panem oleum et sal populo iussit dari gratuite* (commanded that bread, olive oil, and salt be given to the people gratis), presumably meaning that he reinstituted oil distributions. That oil distributions were made during the reign of Aurelian is also indicated by *SHA*, *Aur.* 48.1, which states that olive oil, bread, and pork were already being distributed to the urban populace at the time that Aurelian conceived an initiative for the free distribution of wine.

48 *CTh* 14.17.5 (369) institutes a shift from the sale of a specified amount of state bread to the free distribution of a different specified amount of bread, while *CTh* 14.19.1 (398) institutes or confirms the sale of state bread at a mandated price. *CTh* 14.15.1 (364) does not provide any information regarding the basis on which state bread was distributed to the urban populace, *contra* Rickman 1980, 207.

49 Nordh 1949, 106.9-10.

50 *CTh* 14.24.1.

From the time of the reforms of Diocletian, obligations under the land tax were levied against *possessores* (landholders) in terms of kind, even if it was often possible to commute these to payments in cash, with the various classes of foodstuffs and other items raised under this tax termed *species annonariae*. Subsumed under the land tax were various levies that were used to raise foodstuffs for the *annona militaris* and the *annona urbis*. The latter initiative was supported by a levy known as the *canon urbis Romae*, which eventually came to consist of 4 distinct taxes, termed the *canon frumentarius*, *canon olei*, *canon vinarius*, and *canon suarius* (the grain, oil, wine, and pork levies, respectively). The *canon frumentarius* appears to have been collected mainly within Africa and the sub-diocesan administrative district of Italia *suburbicaria*, the *canon olei* mainly within Africa and perhaps also the Diocese of Hispania, and the *canon vinarius* and *canon suarius* mainly within Italia *suburbicaria*. The *canon frumentarius* and also apparently the *canon olei* were administered by the office of the *praefectus annonae*, who was by the 4th c. an administrative subordinate to the *praefectus urbi*. The *canon vinarius* and *canon suarius* were apparently administered by officials known as the *rationalis vinorum* and the *tribunus Fori Suarii*, respectively, both of whom were also directly subordinate to the *praefectus urbi*.[51]

That the *praefectura annonae* was in some way involved in the mobilization of oil from Africa Proconsularis as early as the middle decades of the 2nd c. is indicated by a dedication from Hispalis (Seville) dating to the period 161-69 that honors a Sex. Iulius Possessor, who had served as *adiutor praef(ecto) annon(ae) ad oleum Afrum et Hispanum recensendum item solamina transferenda item vecturas naviculariis exsolvendas* (assistant to the *praefectus annonae* for the auditing of African and Spanish olive oil, the same for the conveyance of supplies, the same for the paying of shippers for carriage).[52] The sources, however, tell us exceedingly little regarding the *canon olei*. It receives explicit mention just once, in a law of 397, where it is referred to as the *frumenti vel olei urbicarius canon*,[53] and the year in which it was introduced remains uncertain. That *possessores* in Zeugitana were obliged to pay part of their tax in the form of oil from as early as 315 is, however, suggested by a law issued in that year, which specified the modalities for the payment of multiple *species*, one no doubt grain and another quite plausibly oil.[54] The fact that Symmachus, as *praefectus urbi*, had in 384 appealed first to the *praefectus praetorio Illyrici Italiae et Africae* for help in the resolution of the impending shortage of state oil at Rome may be taken as evidence that what he had in mind was the imposition of a *superindictio* (extraordinary tax levy) to the land tax, more specifically perhaps to the *canon olei*, since this official, alone of the *praefecti praetorio*, enjoyed the right

---

51 For these two officials, see *Not.Dig.Occ.* 4.9-10.

52 *CIL* II 1180. For the varying interpretations of the office referred to in this inscription, see Le Roux 1986, 252-58. Perhaps indicative of state involvement in the mobilization of African oil from two to three decades earlier is an inscribed statue base from Rome (*CIL* VI 1620) dating to *c.*140, dedicated to a C. Iunius Flavianus, *praefectus annonae*, by a group whose name can be restored as *[mercat]ores frumenta[rii et olearii] Afrari* (African grain and oil merchants). Also worth mentioning in this regard is the fact that *Dig.* 13.7.43.1 (Scaevola), dating to the second half of the 2nd c., refers in the hypothetical to the requisition for the *annona* of *cullei* (large skin containers with a notional capacity of *c.*20 *amphorae*) by a *centurio missus ex officio annonae* (centurion sent from the office of the *annona*). While containers of this kind might in theory have been used for the transport of either oil or wine, there is no evidence that the *praefectura annonae* was ever responsible for the mobilization of the latter *species*, and this passage would thus appear to indicate that during the period in question this branch of the imperial administration was involved in the collection of oil at or near its point of production. Whether this was a regular activity, and whether it was carried out in Africa Proconsularis, Baetica, or some other part of the empire, remains unclear.

53 *CTh* 14.15.3. While the term *canon* is used in *SHA Sev.* 23.3 in reference to the urban grain and olive oil supplies in the year 211, this may well be a late 4th-c. anachronism; see Herz 1988, 157.

54 *CTh* 11.1.2, addressed to Aelianus, *proconsul Africae*. See also *CTh* 12.6.9 (368), which refers to customary procedures for the collection of more than one *species annonaria* in Africa.

to impose a surcharge of this kind without obtaining the prior approval of the emperor.[55] That the *canon olei* already existed by roughly this time is also suggested by a law of 386, which provided for the cancellation of all debits registered in the *kalendarii* (account books) maintained in connection with the *arca olearia* (oil chest), an account that presumably served for the deposit of tax oil and/or commutation payments made under the *canon olei*.[56]

We are fairly well informed about the procedures employed for the levying and collection of the land tax in Africa.[57] The process began with the office of the *praefectus praetorio Italiae et Africae* (or the *praefectus praetorio Illyrici Italiae et Africae* during those portions of the 4th c. when Illyricum also formed part of the prefecture), which employed extant census data to determine the amount of tax owed by each province under the *indictio* (overall tax levy) for the coming year.[58] A *delegatio* (tax assessment) was sent to provincial governors, specifying the amount which that province owed for each of the several *species annonariae* and the rate at which each of the various units of assessment was to be taxed. Assessments were levied against lands held by private individuals, imperial lands, and imperial or municipal lands occupied by tenants farming under emphyteutic legislation.[59] A law of 355 states that in Africa collection of the tax was supported by the *rectores* (provincial governors), *praefecti annonae* (presumably meaning both the *praefectus annonae* and the *praefectus annonae Africae*), and *rationales*.[60] The *rectores* were presumably responsible for translating the *delegatio* into a *delegatio particularis* (detailed tax assessment), which established the overall amounts owed by each circumscription for the various *species annonariae* and determined the assessments for individual properties, specifying the units of measure in which these were to be paid.[61] The *rationales* arranged for the payment of the assessments levied against imperial lands.[62] The *praefecti annonae*, as will be discussed below, were concerned with coordinating the export of the *species annonariae* raised under the tax.

The collection of tax payments in Africa was the responsibility of *susceptores* (tax receivers). These were men nominated by the various *ordines* (town councils) from among their members, who undertook this service as a *munus* (public duty).[63] While in Italia *suburbicaria* there were separate bodies of *susceptores* for the collection of pork and wine known respectively as *suarii* and *susceptores vini*,[64] it is uncertain whether in Africa there was an analogous division of responsibilities between bodies of *susceptores* charged with the collection of grain and oil. Perhaps relevant to the question is a law of 369 issued to the *praefectus praetorio Illyrici Italiae et Africae*, which specifies percentage figures for the *epimetra* (surplus payments intended to cover wastage) to be paid to *susceptores*, listing rates for *aridi* (dry foods, i.e., grain), wine, and pork, while making no mention of oil.[65] This may perhaps be evidence that a single body of men was responsible for the collection of both grain and oil, with the *epimetra* to be rendered in the form of just the first of these two *species annonariae*. Alternatively, it might be argued

---

55 See in this regard *CTh* 11.16.8 (357), issued to Taurus, *praefectus praetorio Italiae et Africae*.

56 *CTh* 12.11.2. There were also an *arca frumentaria* and an *arca vinaria*, though not, apparently, an *arca suaria*.

57 For the land tax in Africa during the late empire, see Déléage 1975, 227-53; Tengstrom 1974, 14-25.

58 For the rôle of the office of the *praefectus praetorio* in the taxation process, see Jones 1964, 454-56.

59 For imperial lands, see *CTh* 11.7.8 (355); 11.7.11 (365). For emphyteutic lands, see *CTh* 11.19.3 (364).

60 *CTh* 11.7.8.

61 *CTh* 11.1.3 (336).

62 *CTh* 11.7.11 (365).

63 *CTh* 12.6.9 (368).

64 The *suarii* were the reformulated *collegium suariorum*, which since the early empire had been responsible for the provision of pigs for sale on the urban market; see Belli Pasqua 1995, 260-62.

65 *CTh* 12.6.15. See also *CTh* 12.6.21 (386), addressed to the *praefectus praetorio Orientis*, which lists *epimetra* for these same three classes of *species annonariae* while omitting any provisions for oil.

that due to the stability of oil the wastage rates for oil collected as tax in kind were so low as to obviate the need for the payment of *epimetra* to the men who served as *susceptores olei.*

A law of 386 pertaining to the eastern empire required that bronze or wood *modii, sextarii* and weights be set up at *civitates* and *mansiones* (way stations), apparently the locales where the collection of taxes took place, so that taxpayers might more readily determine the correct amount that they owed.[66] There may well have been similar arrangements within Africa,[67] with the *sextarii* and perhaps also the weights employed for measuring payments made in the form of oil.[68] A law of 375 indicates that there were *horrea fiscalia* (state storehouses) at some or all of the local collection centers, specifically forbidding the storage of anything other than *frumentum* (grain) at these facilities.[69] The failure of this law to make any allowance for the storage of oil is puzzling, although the term *frumentum* may perhaps have been used here in a general sense to refer to both grain and oil, particularly if the two were collected by a single body of *susceptores.*

From at least the 360s, *possessores* in Africa paid their annual assessment in three installments, each of which covered a 4-month period.[70] The arrangement of these periods across the year can be inferred from a law of 412 addressed to the *proconsul Africae* that required one-third of the tax owed for privately-held lands and one sixth of that owed for emphyteutic lands to be paid after the Kalends of March, with the remainder due after the Kalends of July.[71] The tax year for private lands would thus appear to have begun on November 1, the trimesters covering the periods November-February, March-June, and July-October.[72] For emphyteutic lands, on the other hand, this ruling and another law of 364 indicate that the tax year began on January 1.[73] The requirement in this law that private landholders consign their payments for the final trimester (or, in the case of emphyteutic landholders, for the final 6 months of the tax year) in advance presumably stemmed from the fact that *species annonariae* collected any later than August or September could not be exported until the following year due to the suspension of navigation during the winter months.

Important evidence regarding administrative aspects of the levying of the land tax in the provinces of Zeugitana and Byzacena at this time is provided by the so-called *Règlement Fiscal de Carthage* (henceforth *Règlement*).[74] This document, which should probably be assigned to the years 368-75, is a compilation of several surcharges to the *praestatio annonaria* (*annona* payment) for some portion of the Diocese of Africa that were enacted over a period of time extending from the reign of Constantine to that of Valentinian I. It may perhaps have been drawn up in connection with a more vigorous approach to the collection of taxes in the western empire that Zosimus assigns to the early 370s.[75] The text can be partially reconstructed from fragments belonging to at least 5 different copies inscribed in stone, all of which were recovered

66 *CTh* 12.6.21. See also *CTh* 12.6.19 (383).

67 See Tengstrom 1974, 21-23 for a discussion of the literature regarding this question.

68 See in this connection *CIL* VIII 9666, a dedication for *mensurae oleariae* from Cartenna, in Mauretania Caesariensis. For other *mensae ponderariae* from Africa, see Cagnat 1905; Albertini 1920; Tengstrom 1974, 22-23.

69 *CTh* 12.6.16. For these storehouses, see Tengstrom 1974, 18-19.

70 *CTh* 11.1.16 (367); 12.6.27 (400); see also *CTh* 11.7.11 (365), for imperial lands. Earlier in the 4th c. payments were made on a monthly basis; see *CTh* 11.1.2 (313).

71 *CTh* 11.7.19.

72 The tax year in Egypt, the other great provider of grain for the *annona*, began on July 1, while for several other provinces the date was September 1; see Jones 1964, 456.

73 *CTh* 11.19.3.

74 For the text of this document together with an interpretative essay, see Saumagne 1950. For critical comments on Saumagne's treatment, see Sirks 1991, 150-54.

75 Zos. 4.16.

at Carthage.[76] The only two of the surcharges included in this document for which the names have been preserved are termed *limitis nomine* (on behalf of the *limes*) and *naviculariorum nomine* (on behalf of the *navicularii*), the former presumably earmarked for the support of border troops, the latter for the support of state shippers.[77] One of the surcharges for which the name is not preserved was directed specifically at the province of Byzacena. The formula used to determine the amount of payment due varies from surcharge to surcharge, but generally consists of set amounts of grain levied against units of assessment in terms of *modii*, *sextarii*, and *cyathi*. In the case of two surcharges the rate was predicated on the time of payment, with a lower rate specified for payments made between the Kalends of November and the last day of March. This provision, clearly intended as an inducement for landholders to render payment during the course of the first tax trimester, was presumably designed to guarantee that sizeable amounts of tax grain would be available for export at the re-opening of navigation in April. It further indicates that obligations under these specific surcharges could to some extent be paid at a time of the taxpayer's choosing.

One copy of the *Règlement* includes an annexed table containing lists of toponyms that are presumably the names of tax circumscriptions.[78] These toponyms, of which as many as 27 may be attested in the surviving fragments of the table, appear to be arranged in alphabetical order within geographical groupings. While all of the toponyms that can be matched to a known locale lie within the province of Zeugitana, it cannot be excluded that some of those for which the location cannot be determined were located in other provinces, Byzacena in particular, since one of the tax surcharges listed in the main body of the *Règlement* was directed at this province. The circumscriptions to which the toponyms refer are of three different types: those explicitly identified as *fundi* (estates); those of unspecified type that can be shown to be *civitates* (municipalities), with their names given in the form of an ethnic; and those of a third type introduced by the term *pars territori* (subdivision of the territory? tax contribution from the territory?), which may perhaps correspond to tribal groups rather than to fixed geographical areas.

We may now turn to the second of the three methods by which the state may have mobilized oil in Zeugitana: the collection of oil as rent in kind from the tenants of imperial lands. In this case, it seems possible that a significant amount of the oil produced on the vast imperial holdings in Zeugitana was directed towards the support of state supply initiatives.[79] The only coherent body of evidence that we possess regarding the methods employed for the working of imperial land in Zeugitana derives from a group of inscriptions dating to the 2nd and early 3rd c. from several locales within the central Bagradas (Medjerda) valley.[80] These inscriptions indicate that in this region imperially-owned lands were worked by tenant farmers under the terms of a *lex Manciana*, which provided for a sharecropping arrangement under which long-term tenants tendered one-third of their produce to estate managers known as *conductores*.[81] The latter operated under 5-year rental agreements, presumably paying to the *patrimonium* (i.e., the pre-Diocletianic privy purse) some fixed amount drawn from the rent in

---

76 A single fragment of a copy of the *Règlement* found at Kairouan, not a Roman settlement, was presumably carried there from Carthage in post-Roman times.

77 On the number of distinct surcharges named in this law I follow Sirks 1991, 150-54.

78 For the discussion of these toponyms, see Saumagne 1950, 129-32; Salama 1987, 78.

79 From *CTh* 11.28.13 (422) it can be inferred that at that time the *res privata* owned roughly 18.5% of the land in Zeugitana and 15% of that in Byzacena; see Jones 1964, 415-16. While the confiscation of the vast African holdings of Gildo and Stilicho in the years around 400 probably saw a substantial increase in the amount of land in imperial hands, the privy purse no doubt controlled a significant portion of the prime agricultural land in these two provinces from well before this time.

80 For the most recent study of these inscriptions and a discussion of the previous literature, see Kehoe 1988.

81 For a summary of the provisions under the *lex Manciana*, see Kehoe 1988, 69-70, 139-40.

kind that they received from the tenant farmers. Some of these inscriptions detail inducements offered to tenants to bring additional land under cultivation. Among these are provisions aimed at promoting the planting of olive orchards, and it is clear that olives were a significant crop on these estates.[82] We have no way of judging how widespread the application of the *lex Manciana* was on imperial lands in the province at this time, nor the extent to which it was replaced by other arrangements during the course of the 3rd and 4th c. The Albertini Tablets, a group of records from the area along the Byzacena-Numidia border east of Capsa, however, indicate that provisions of the *lex Manciana* were observed on some privately-owned lands in this region during the period 493-96,[83] and it may be that sharecropping arrangements of the sort prescribed in this law remained a significant approach to the working of imperial land in Africa down to the end of Roman rule.

With regard to the modalities employed for the payment of rent for imperial lands, a law of 366 indicates that tenants were entitled to make payments at times of their own choosing, turning these over to *rationales* in up to three installments per year.[84] In the western empire, responsibility for collecting payments must have been shifted from the *rationales* to the offices of the provincial governors at some time between the issuing of this law and 392, since a law of 398 indicates that this duty was transferred from the provincial governors back to the *rationales* at some point during the reign of Valentinian II (375-92).[85]

We possess no clear evidence regarding what was done with the oil raised in the form of rent in kind on imperial lands in Zeugitana either prior to or after the reforms of Diocletian. Perhaps the most informative evidence in this regard is provided by a fragmentary epitaph from Rome probably dating to the period *c.*222-30 that preserves the *cursus* (sequence of offices) of an unidentified individual who appears to have specialized in administrative posts concerned with the logistics of supply.[86] Among this man's offices was that of *procurator ad olea conparanda per regionem Tripolitanam* (superintendent for the collection of olive oil in the *regio Tripolitana* [i.e., the Tripolitanian administrative district of the *patrimonium*]).[87] From the name of this post it appears likely that it involved the bulking of oil produced on imperial estates, presumably for export.[88] Whether this entailed the collection of oil paid as rent in kind or a program of purchase from imperial tenants, or perhaps both, however, remains unclear. More generally, Kehoe has argued that the provisions of the *lex Manciana* make best sense if we assume that they reflect an interest on the part of the state in generating surplus crops for export, concluding that much of the produce paid as rent by imperial tenants in the central Bagradas valley probably found its way to the populace of Rome.[89] Similarly, Ørsted assumes that the *conductores* who managed imperial estates in Africa conveyed the oil raised as rent in kind to ports, where they consigned it to agents known as *conductores quattuor publicorum Africae*, who arranged for its export.[90] Thus, while the specific mechanism or mechanisms employed remain unclear, it seems reasonable to assume that during the 2nd and 3rd c. a substantial amount of oil produced on imperial holdings in the area that would later

---

82 For these provisions, see Kehoe 1988, 42-43.

83 For a recent overview of the literature on the Albertini Tablets and a discussion of their implications for our understanding of African oleoculture, see Mattingly 1989.

84 *CTh* 5.15.20, issued to the *comes sacrarum largitionum*.

85 *CTh* 1.11.2. See Jones 1964, 414, 1166 n.7.

86 *AE* 1973 no.76. For discussions of this inscription, see Manacorda 1976-77, 543-55, 581-82; di Vita-Evrard 1985, 145-46.

87 For the identification of the *regio Tripolitana* as an administrative district of the *patrimonium*, see di Vita-Evrard 1985, 152-56.

88 Mattingly 1994, 55 suggests that its creation may have been linked with the introduction of free distributions of state oil at Rome.

89 Kehoe 1988, 12-20, 163-77.

90 Ørsted 1992, 827-29.

become Zeugitana was mobilized in the form of rent in kind, presumably for export in connection with one or more state supply initiatives. Whether this practice would have continued into later periods remains uncertain, although the institution of an oil levy under the land tax at some point during the late 3rd or 4th c. would presumably have diminished the need to employ oil produced on imperial lands for this purpose.

It is unclear whether the state ever had recourse to the purchase of oil in Africa, either on the free market or through *coemptio*.[91] We do know, however, that when Hymetius, *pronconsul Africae* from 366 to 368, sold state grain slated for the supply of Rome to inhabitants of Carthage in order to relieve a food crisis, he waited until the shortage had passed and then used the funds realized from these sales to buy replacement grain at one-third the price.[92] It thus seems possible that similar arrangements may sometimes have been employed by the state for the acquisition of oil. Recourse to practices of this kind might have proven advantageous in that it would have provided the state with the ability to adjust the volume of the stores at its disposal in light of the availability of supplies on the market, annual variations in the productivity of imperial estates, or interruptions to the regular supply system due to weather, revolts, and the like.

The grain and oil acquired in Africa by the state that were destined for export had first to be moved from the local collection centers to ports of embarcation for transfer to merchant ships. The administrative operations connected with the export of *species annonariae* required the participation of representatives of both the provincial administration and the imperial fisc, and the formally recognized ports of embarcation may thus have been relatively few in number.[93] State grain and oil may have been taken to these ports over land or conveyed to trans-shipment (i.e., intermediate) ports, where they were shifted to coasting vessels, which would then bear them over the final leg of the journey to the port of embarcation. There were presumably state storehouses located at both the trans-shipment ports and the ports of embarcation.[94] In Zeugitana, state *horrea* are attested at Carthage, Utica, and perhaps also Hippo Regius (Annaba/Bône),[95] and in Numidia, at Rusicade (Skikda/Philippeville).[96] There were also presumably facilities of this kind at one or more ports in Byzacena, with Hadrumetum (Sousse), Leptiminus (Lamta), and Sullecthum (Salakta) the most likely candidates. It is unclear whether we should imagine these to have been general purpose storage facilities or warehouses employed exclusively for the storage of either grain or oil.[97]

---

91 The only reference to state purchase of oil known to me is Cass., *Var.* 12.22 (537/538), which concerns the *coemptio* of oil in Histria under the Ostrogothic Kingdom. State purchase of oil would presumably have been more common during the 5th c. than the 4th, since the practice of commuting obligations in kind under the land tax to cash payments appears to have become more widespread from the late 4th c.; see Jones 1964, 460, 629-30.

92 For a discussion of this episode, see Durliat 1990, 386-87.

93 *CTh* 8.5.16 (363) indicates that in the province of Sardinia *species publicas* were brought overland to *diversi portus* (several ports). This may, however, refer both to trans-shipment ports and to ports of embarcation.

94 For these storehouses, see Tengstrom 1975, 32-34; Cagnat 1916, 262-64; Cagnat 1913 [1975] 311-17.

95 *Amm.* 28.1.17, in recounting the sale of state grain to the inhabitants of Carthage by Hymetius, indicates that the grain in question was being stored in *horrea*, presumably state storehouses at Carthage. *CIL* VIII 24654 may also refer to a *horreum publicum* at Carthage. For *horrea Augustae* at Utica, see *CIL* VIII 13190. An inscription from Hippo Regius, datable to the last decade of the 2nd c. or first two decades of the 3rd, mentions a man who may have been a *conscriptor horreorum Hippone Regio*; see Pavis d'Escurac 1976, 140. This apparently refers to one or more warehouses employed for the storage of produce from imperial lands.

96 *CIL* VIII 19852 (364-75).

97 See *Not.Const.* 6.13 for *horrea olearia* at Constantinople.

We have little evidence regarding the means whereby state grain and oil were transported from the collection centers to the ports of embarcation. Tengstrom has made the argument that it is this very lack of evidence that points to the use of the *cursus publicus* and, specifically, the *cursus clabularius* (state wagon post).[98] The evidence, however, is not so tenuous as Tengstrom asserted. A law of 363, addressed to the *praefectus praetorio Illyrici Italiae et Africae*, after abolishing the state post horse service in the province of Sardinia, continues on to state *Sane angariarium cursum submoveri non opportet propter species publicas quae ad diversos portus deferuntur* (of course it is necessary not to discontinue the heavy wagon post on account of the *species publicas* that are transported down to the several ports).[99] Given Sardinia's well-established rôle as an important grain-producer, it seems certain that the *species publicae* referred to included grain, much of which was presumably destined for the supply of Rome.[100] We thus have evidence for use of the *cursus clabularius* for the transport of a *species annonariae* in at least one province in the Prefecture of Illyricum, Italia, and Africa, and there is no reason to doubt that this was the general practice throughout the prefecture. There is only scant evidence that the *cursus publicus* ever operated river-boats or sea-going vessels, and it seems likely that any transfers of state grain and oil from trans-shipment ports to ports of embarcation involved the use of private vessels hired on a contractual basis or vessels operated within the context of a *munus*.[101] A law of 336 reveals that in Hispania *susceptores* consigned *species* directly to the *navicularii* (state shippers), indicating that the former accompanied shipments as far as the ports of embarcation.[102] Whether this was also the case in Africa remains unclear. Several laws dating to the second half of the 4th c. refer to the use of the *cursus clabularius* for the transport of goods termed *species largitionales* and the like, and there is no reason to doubt that the produce of imperial estates was also moved to trans-shipment ports and/or ports of embarcation by means of the public post.[103]

The *cursus publicus* probably employed a variety of different conveyances for transporting *species fiscales* over land. These may have included carts termed *birotae*, which were drawn by a team of three mules and limited by law to a maximum load of 200 lbs.; medium-sized wagons termed *raedae*, which were drawn by a team of 8 mules in summer and 10 in winter and limited to a maximum load of 1,000 lbs.; and heavy wagons known as *angariae*, which were drawn by

---

98 See Tengstrom 1974, 29-32, which considers the problem strictly with reference to state grain, followed by Rickman 1980, 120-21; Kehoe 1988, 12 n.23; Sirks 1991, 147.

99 *CTh* 8.5.16.

100 For Sardinian grain production during the empire, see Rowland 1984; id. 1990.

101 On the operation of water craft by the *cursus publicus*, see Holmberg 1933, 68-71. The only possible evidence for this occurs in *CTh* 8.5.48 (386), addressed to the *praefectus praetorio Orientis*. The transport of grain raised as tax in kind down the Nile to Alexandria was accomplished by a variety of arrangements, including boats hired on short- and long-term contracts, and boats operated within the context of liturgical obligations; see Sirks 1991, 194-95; Lewis 1983, 167-68, 178. See *Dig.* 49.18.4 (Ulpian) for reference to a rescript of 2nd- or early 3rd-c. date providing for the requisition of *naves* belonging to veterans for unspecified state service.

102 *CTh* 13.5.8, addressed to the *comes Hispaniarum*.

103 *CTh* 8.5.13 (362), addressed to the *praefectus praetorio Illyrici Italiae et Africae*, refers to *species largitionales*; *CTh* 8.5.18 (364), addressed to the same official, refers to *largitionum species transmittendas necessarias*; *CTh* 8.5.20 (364), addressed to the *comes rerum privatarum*, refers to *ad transferendas largitionum res necessarias*; *CTh* 8.5.40 (382), addressed to the *praefectus praetorio Orientis*, refers to *transmissio largitionalium titulorum*; *CTh* 8.5.48 (386), addressed to the *praefectus praetorio Orientis*, refers to gold and silver belonging to both the *sacrae largitiones* and the *privatae largitiones*. *CTh* 8.5.33 (374), addressed to the *proconsul Africae*, provides an indication of the other uses to which the *cursus publicus* was put in this province at the time that the *ostraca* from the Ilôt de l'Amirauté were composed, granting this official the right to issue post warrants for the purpose of moving military clothing across both his and other provinces for supplying troops, and implying that bullion was also transported by this means.

two pairs of oxen and allowed to carry a maximum load of 1,500 lbs.[104] The *cursus publicus* also appears to have provided both pack horses and donkeys on some occasions.[105]

Upon arrival at one of the ports of embarcation the *species annonariae* apparently were consigned to the office of the *praefectus annonae Africae*.[106] This official, first attested in 314, was subordinate to the *praefectus praetorio Illyrici Italiae et Africae* rather than to the *vicarius Africae*, presumably because the work of his office required close co-ordination with that of the *praefectus annonae* and because the *proconsul Africae*, in whose province much of the grain and oil was collected, was not subordinate to the *vicarius Africae*.[107] Our only evidence regarding the activities of his office comes from a law of 365, which required *tabularii* (registrars) from both the office of the *praefectus annonae Africae* and that of the *praefectus urbi* to report *quid transmissum, quid pervectum sit* (what has been passed on, what has been delivered) to the office of the *vicarius Africae* so that there might be a clear accounting of the processes of *transmissio* and *pervectio*.[108] The first of these terms presumably refers to the transfer of *species annonariae* from the possession of *susceptores* to representatives of the *praefectura annonae Africae*, while the second refers to their conveyance from Africa to Rome and their subsequent consignment to representatives of the *praefectura annonae*, which, as noted above, formed part of the *officium urbanum* at this time. It would thus appear that the *praefectura annonae Africae* assumed possession of the various *species annonariae* collected in Africa from provincial tax authorities, presumably at the ports of embarcation.

We know nothing regarding the administration of the state storehouses at the ports of embarcation.[109] It would appear, however, that the provincial administrations retained a degree of control over at least some portion of the grain and oil stored in these facilities. Thus, at some point between 366 and 368, Hymetius, as *proconsul Africae*, was able to commandeer state grain destined for export to Rome that was apparently being stored in *horrea fiscalia* at Carthage, while in 384 Symmachus requested Valentinian I to pressure the *iudices Africani* rather than the *praefectus annonae Africae* regarding the need to send additional amounts of state oil to Rome.

---

104 On the types of vehicles and the number and type of draft animals employed with each, see *CTh* 8.5.8 (357), addressed to the *praefectus praetorio Italiae et Africae*; *CTh* 8.5.11 (360), addressed to the *praefectus praetorio Orientis*. On the maximum limits for these vehicles, see *CTh* 8.5.8 (357), addressed to the *praefectus praetorio Italiae et Africae*; *CTh* 8.5.17 (364), addressed either to a provincial governor or vicar in the western empire; *CTh* 8.5.30 (368), addressed to the *praefectus praetorio Galliarum*; *CTh* 8.5.28 (368), addressed to the *praefectus praetorio Illyrici Italiae et Africae*; *CTh* 8.5.47 (385), addressed to the *praefectus praetorio Orientis*. *CTh* 8.5.28 specifies that the maximum cargo loads established for Gaul should be applied in Illyricum and Italia, while making no mention of Africa. This raises the possibility that there were special provisions of some sort for Africa.

105 For *agminales* (pack horses), see *CTh* 8.5.3 (326), addressed to the *praefectus praetorio Orientis* and 8.5.6 (354), addressed to the *agens vicariam prefecturam*. For *asini* (donkeys), see *CTh* 8.5.38 (382?) addressed to the *praefectus praetorio Illyrici Italiae et Africae*.

106 For this official, see Pavis d'Escurac 1976, 142-44.

107 Also worth noting in this regard is the fact that, while the *vicarius Africae* and the several provincial governors in Africa did not enjoy the power to issue the warrants that provided access to the *cursus publicus*, the *praefectus praetorio* did. See *CTh* 8.5.12 (362), and *CTh* 8.5.14 (362) for the rôle of the *praefectus praetorio* in the administration of the *cursus publicus* in the Prefecture of Illyricum, Italia, and Africa.

108 *CTh* 11.1.13 (365), addressed to the *vicarius Africae*.

109 Tengstrom 1974, 20-21, 34 suggests that the *praepositi horreorum* mentioned in several texts in the *Codex Theodosianus* (7.4.1 [325]; 12.1.49 [361]; 12.6.5 [365]; 12.6.8 [365]; 12.6.24 [397]) were responsible for the administration of these facilities. The fact that these texts tie the methods employed for the selection of these functionaries to those used for the selection of *susceptores*, however, suggests that they were responsible for the administration of the state storehouses located at the local collection centers rather than the storehouses located at the ports of embarcation.

The ships employed for the transport of state oil and grain to overseas destinations from Africa were operated by *navicularii*, ship owners charged with the task of carrying *onera fiscalia* (state cargoes) as a *munus* or *functio*. These individuals, referred to variously as the *navicularii africani, afri, per Africam*, or *intra Africam*,[110] were organized into a *corpus*.[111] Upon taking on a cargo, *navicularii* were issued *relatoriae*, bills of lading that attested to both the quantity and quality of the *species annonariae* that had been entrusted to them.[112] A law of 380 regularized the calendar for the *corpus naviculariorum* that served Africa, requiring its members to accept state cargoes from the beginning of April to the beginning of October, while setting the sailing season to run from the Ides of April to the Ides of October.[113] This statute also abolished a $2^{1}/_{2}$% allowance that prior to that time had been awarded to these shippers *ex hibernis oneribus* (for winter cargoes).[114] The issuance of this law suggests that prior to 380 state cargoes were sometimes carried outside the sailing season that it prescribed and that disputes of some sort had arisen between the *navicularii* and the state regarding these operations. A law of 397 required the *navicularii* to ship one-third of the *urbanus canon* at the opening of the sailing season.[115] This ruling, together with the inducements for early payment contained in some of the surcharges included in the *Règlement*, suggest that the need to restock the storehouses at Rome with grain and oil belonging to the state as soon as possible following the re-opening of navigation was a matter of concern to the state, and it may well be that prior to 380 the office of the *praefectus annonae Africae* brought pressure to bear on the *navicularii* to recommence operations during the first half of April or perhaps even as early as March.[116]

The weighing and bottling of Baetican oil

From the evidence of amphoras it is clear that from the early 1st c. to at least the middle of the 3rd c. the province of Baetica provided a large share of the oil consumed by the populace of Rome, as well as by Roman military units stationed along the Rhine frontier, in Britain, and along some parts of the Danube frontier.[117] The methods employed for the weighing and bottling of this oil can be reconstructed in considerable detail, and appear to have several

---

110 *CTh* 13.5.10 (364); 13.9.3 (380); 13.5.36-37 (412); 11.2.8 (414).

111 For this *corpus*, see Sirks 1991, 146-92.

112 Sirks 1991, 123, 156.

113 *CTh* 13.9.3, addressed to the *navicularii afri*.

114 It appears that *navicularii* were normally awarded a flat percentage of the state cargo that they carried. This share, known as the *modum centesimarum*, was set at 4% for the *corpus naviculariorum Orientis*; see *CTh* 13.5.7 (334). The size of the share awarded to the *navicularii Africani* is not known; see Sirks 1991, 157-58.

115 *CTh* 13.5.27 (April 15, 397), addressed to the Senate and People. The assertion in Sirks 1991, 147 n.8, 156 that this law originated as a temporary measure enacted to offset shortages caused by the revolt of Gildo must be incorrect, as this uprising did not commence until the fall of 397; see *PLRE* 396.

116 Vegetius, *Mil.* 4.39 places the outside limits for navigation at March 10 and November 10. Illustrative of the state's concern to force early sailings even after the issue of this law is *CTh* 13.5.34 (410), addressed to the *praefectus praetorio Illyrici Italiae et Africae*, which established penalties against both magistrates and shippers on occasions when *navicularii* remained in port *sub praetextu hiemis* (under the pretext that it was winter) when fair winds were blowing. An episode related by Paulinus of Nola, *Ep.* 49, which describes a case of Sardinian *navicularii* being compelled to transport cargoes during the winter of 408-409, indicates that even after the issuance of the law of 380 *navicularii* might be forced to deliver cargoes during the winter when there was a food crisis at Rome. For a discussion of this episode, see Rougé 1986 and, on winter sailing in general, see Rougé 1952.

117 For Rome, see Blázquez Martínez *et al.* 1994, 137, 140-42. For military units along the Rhine frontier, see Remesal Rodríguez 1986. While stamps and *tituli picti* on Dressel 20 amphoras indicate that some of this oil originated in the vicinity of Castulo, in the province of Tarraconensis, the vast bulk appears to have been produced in the province of Baetica, and oil from southern Spain is here referred to as Baetican for ease of discussion.

points of correspondence with the procedures employed for the weighing and bottling of state oil at Carthage.[118]

The main source of evidence regarding the procedures employed for the weighing and bottling of Baetican oil is the complex set of stamps and *tituli picti* that occur on the Dressel 20, the class of amphora that served for the export of the oil produced in this province. To date, over 80 production sites for the Dressel 20 amphora have been identified in the Baetis/Singilis (Guadalquivir/Genil) drainage, the heartland of oil production in Baetica, for the most part clustered along the banks of these two rivers.[119] From the stamps that regularly occur on the handles of Dressel 20 amphoras it is evident that from at least the middle of the 2nd c. these facilities were known as *figlinae*, and that most were owned by private individuals.[120] In some instances, however, stamps indicate that *figlinae* were imperial possessions, and in one case a group of three appears to have passed from private ownership into the hands of the emperor, and then been transferred to the control of a state agency of uncertain nature known as the *Kalendarium Vegetianum*.[121]

The weighing and bottling of the oil appears to have occurred at facilities known as *portus* situated either at or in the vicinity of the *figlinae*. It is unclear whether the term *portus* should be understood as simply referring to the fact that these facilities were river ports, or rather to the fact that they functioned as *portus* in the legal sense, that is, enclosures that served for clearing goods across a customs boundary.[122] The oil was presumably brought to the *portus* from the estate where it was produced in a skin container of some sort,[123] here referred to as a primary container. In the course of the weighing procedure it was transferred to a Dressel 20 amphora, here termed a secondary container, in which it was transported overseas. Several aspects of the weighing/bottling procedure can be inferred from the *titulus pictus* (henceforth *titulus*) that appears on the neck and shoulder of this class of amphora. This consists of 4 standard components generally referred to using the letters alpha through delta.[124] Three of these, the alpha, gamma, and delta, are directly related to the weighing/bottling process, and on the basis of these the procedure can be reconstructed as follows:

1) The empty amphora was weighed to the pound and the resulting figure written on the vessel's neck (alpha *titulus* component).
2) The amphora was filled with oil and then weighed a second time.
3) The empty weight of the amphora was subtracted from the gross weight of the amphora plus the oil, and the resulting figure, equal to the net weight of the oil, recorded on the vessel's shoulder well below the alpha *titulus* component (gamma *titulus* component).
4) The amphora was sealed with a stopper.

---

118 For recent overviews of the topics discussed in this subsection, see Mattingly 1988, 38-44; Blázquez 1992; Rodríguez-Almeida 1993; Liou and Tchernia 1994; Funari 1994.

119 For the distribution of sites producing Dressel 20 amphoras, see Remesal Rodríguez 1982, 67 Abb. 30; 1983, 116 fig. 1; Blázquez Martínez *et al.* 1994, 136 fig. 24.

120 Mayet 1986; Rodríguez-Almeida 1993, 100; Liou and Tchernia 1994, 137-49.

121 The three *figlinae* are the *figlinae Barb( ), Cepariae*, and *Grumensae*; see Mayet 1986, 300-3. Tchernia and Liou 1994, 147-48 argue that these may have passed from imperial to private ownership rather than the other way around. For the *Kalendarium Vegetianum*, see Manacorda 1977; Remesal Rodríguez 1996.

122 For the latter, see *Dig*. 50.16.59 (Ulpian): *portus apellatus est conclusus locus quo importantur merces et inde exportantur* (a *portus* is an enclosed area into which goods are imported and subsequently exported).

123 Rodríguez-Almeida 1993, 100 supposes that this involved the use of *cullei* mounted on wagons. Loyzance 1986, 281 envisages the use of *utres* (small skin containers) carried on the backs of mules.

124 For the *tituli* on the Dressel 20 amphora, see Blázquez Martínez *et al.* 1994, 36-37; Rodríguez-Almeida 1989a, 26-30; Rodríguez-Almeida 1993, 100-3; Liou and Tchernia 1994. Two additional *titulus* components, known as epsilon and theta, sometimes appear on these amphoras.

5) A certification of the operation was written obliquely on the vessel's shoulder to the right of the alpha and gamma *titulus* components in the vicinity of one of the vessel's handles (delta *titulus* component). The format of this certification shows substantial change from the mid-1st to the mid-3rd c. At different moments it included some or all of the following items of information: a crossed 'R', probably standing for *recensitum*, indicating that the container had been processed, the name of the administrative district or locale where the oil was bottled, the weight of the oil in the container, the type and/or estate of origin of the oil together with a number of uncertain significance, the names of individuals presumably connected with the processing and documenting of the oil, and the consular date.

While the figure for the weight of oil recorded in the gamma *titulus* component ranges from a low of 162 to a high in the 230s, and some of the weight of oil figures recorded in the delta *titulus* component are as high as 275, in roughly one-third to one-half of the known cases the weight of oil figures associated with these containers is 216. It would thus appear that this number represented a standard module for the packaging of Baetican oil.[125]

The weighing/bottling procedure appears to have been undertaken by men termed *diffusores olearii*.[126] Their presence in the Baetis/Singilis Valley is attested in two inscriptions of probable 2nd-c. date, one from Astigi (Écija), the other from Oducia (Tocina), a town located on the left bank of the Baetis, roughly 30 km upstream from Hispalis.[127] These functionaries are also mentioned in at least two, and more likely three inscriptions from Rome, all epitaphs, and all again of probable 2nd c. date. The first belongs to a D. Caecilius Onesimus, who, in addition to working as a *diffusor olearius ex Baetica*, served as a *viator apparitor Augustorum* (adjutant to the emperors for issuing legal summonses).[128] The second epitaph is to a C. Sentius Regulianus, who is styled *eques Romanus, diffusor olearius ex Baetica, curator eiusdem corporis, negotiator vinarius Lugdunensis canabis consistens, curator et patronus eiusdem corporis, nauta Araricus, patronus eiusdem corporis, patronus sevirum Lugduni consistentium* (Roman equestrian, *diffusor olearius*, *curator* of the *corpus* of the same, wine merchant from Lugdunum [Lyon] established in the Canabae district, *curator* and *patronus* of the *corpus* of the same, sailor on the Arar River, *patronus* of the *corpus* of the same, *patronus* of the *seviri* established at Lugdunum).[129] The third and last epitaph is to a Caecilia Helias from her husband, Domitius Abscantus, who is termed *lictor curiatus, fusor olearius* (curial *lictor, diffusor(?) olearius*).[130]

Both the nature of the activities carried out by the *diffusores olearii* and the locus of their operations have been the subject of dispute among scholars. With regard to the first point, opinion has been divided as to whether the job title *diffusor olearius* should be understood as 'oil transvaser' (i.e., one who transfers oil from one container to another) or 'oil distributor.' Linguistic considerations strongly suggest that the former interpretation is, in fact, the correct one,[131] and it thus seems likely that *diffusores olearii* were involved in the bottling of oil rather than in its transport and/or marketing. The inscriptions mentioning *diffusores olearii* found at Astigi and Oducia demonstrate that these men were active in the Baetis/Singilis

125 For the range of values recorded in this *titulus* component, see Martin-Kilcher 1987, 152-53, 155 Abb. 86. For the frequency of the occurrence of the figure 216, see n.233.

126 For reviews of the evidence regarding *diffusores olearii*, see Le Roux 1986, 258-63; Loyzance 1986, 280-83; Liou and Tchernia 1994, 134-37. On the meaning of this phrase, see below.

127 *CIL* II 1481; *AE* 1984 no.528.

128 *AE* 1980 no.98.

129 *CIL* VI 29722 = *ILS* 7490.

130 *CIL* VI 1885. The assertion in Loyzance 1986, 281-82 that *diffusores olearii* are also attested at Arelate (Arles) and Lugdunum is unconvincing, as it is based on a highly conjectural expansion of a single inscription from each of these two towns (*CIL* XII 714; *CIL* XIII 10029 no. 115 [misleadingly cited as *CIL*, XIII 3, II, 115]).

131 Loyzance 1986, 280-81.

valley, where their work presumably involved the transfer of oil from the oilskins (in which it was brought to the *portus*) to Dressel 20 amphoras. It thus seems likely that the individuals whose names appear in the delta *titulus* component in association with the figure for the lbs. of oil held in the amphora were *diffusores olearii*. Less clear is whether *diffusores olearii* also played some rôle in the re-bottling of Baetican oil upon its arrival at Rome. The attestations of these men in the three inscriptions from Rome by no means demonstrate that they participated in oil-bottling operations there,[132] and all three of the men held posts other than that of *diffusor olearius* that may have occasioned their relocation to the *urbs*. The use of the qualifier *ex Baetica* in two of these inscriptions may, in fact, have served to underscore the fact that the men in question carried out their oil bottling activities not at Rome but in Baetica. The only alternative is to assume that there was a body of oil bottlers based at Rome composed of men from Baetica who were specialized in the re-bottling of oil from their home province. This seems highly implausible, and we should probably assume that the inscriptions from Rome refer to men who were based in Baetica. If this inference is correct, we may also infer that the men who worked as *diffusores olearii* in Baetica were organized into a *corpus*.

The fourth *titulus* component on the Dressel 20 amphora, the beta, appears on the lower part of the vessel's neck, between the alpha and the gamma components. While it cannot be proven that this component was produced after the alpha and gamma components,[133] it seems highly likely that it was, and it may be that it was added only at the time that the amphora was trans-shipped from a river barge to a merchantman for export, presumably at Hispalis.[134] In *tituli* dating to the period before *c*.200 this component bears the name of one or more private individuals in the genitive. In several cases these individuals can be identified with persons elsewhere termed *navicularius*, *mercator olei Hispani* (oil trader from Hispania), *negotiator olearius ex Baetica* (oil merchant from Baetica), and *diffusor olearius ex Baetica* (oil transvaser from Baetica).[135] With the exception of the *diffusores olearii*, who, as we have seen, were responsible for the weighing and bottling of oil, these individuals appear to have been involved in some way with the transport overseas of the oil. They presumably assumed either possession or ownership of the oil either at the *portus* or, if this *titulus* component was produced at Hispalis, at the port of embarcation.

The assemblage of Dressel 20 amphoras from Monte Testaccio, the massive mound of discarded oil amphoras in the Emporium district of Rome, displays an interesting series of changes in the beta *titulus* component over the course of the first half of the 3rd c.[136] These changes may be summarized as follows:

1) The names of the co-emperors Septimius Severus and Caracalla appear, apparently replacing those of the private individuals who had previously appeared in this *titulus* component (presumably the emperors' names were introduced at some point between 198 and 205, continuing through 205).
2) The name of Geta, made co-regent in 205, appears along with those of Severus and Caracalla (presumably 205-11).
3) The designation *fisci rationis patrimoni provinciae Baeticae* (of the account of the office of the privy purse of the Province of Baetica) appears, probably substituting for the name of the emperor Caracalla (at least 217-29, and probably through the 250s/260s).[137]

132 *Contra* Le Roux 1986, 261-62.

133 Rodríguez-Almeida 1993, 103.

134 Remesal Rodríguez 1986, 22.

135 For reviews of the evidence regarding these individuals, see Le Roux 1986, 258-63; Rodríguez-Almeida 1989b; Liou and Tchernia 1994, 134-37.

136 For a discussion of these changes, see Rodríguez-Almeida 1980, 282-87; Rodríguez-Almeida 1989a, 35-37; Blázquez 1992, 184; Blázquez Martínez *et al.* 1994, 38; Remesal Rodríguez 1996.

137 For the translation of this designation, see Remesal Rodríguez 1986, 105-06.

4) The designation *fisci rationis patrimoni provinciae Tarraconensis* (of the account of the office of the privy purse of the Province of Tarraconensis) appears (presumably introduced at some point after 217, perhaps in 235, and probably continuing through the 250s/260s).
5) The names of private individuals reappear (230, probably continuing through the 250s/260s).

Despite the unusual wealth of information offered by the stamps and *tituli* on the Dressel 20 amphora, it has remained difficult to work out the specific set of arrangements that lay behind the mobilization, bottling, and export of the oil carried in these containers. From the content of the delta *titulus* component, it would seem fair to infer that the weighing/bottling operations documented in these texts were undertaken and/or supervised by some branch of the state administrative system. That the oil bottled according to these procedures was for the most part mobilized in connection with state initiatives for the supply of the urban populace and the military is further suggested by the fact that the bulk of the Dressel 20 amphoras that bear this *titulus* have been found either at Rome, at trans-shipment ports in southern Gaul, or in the environs of an army camp. State activity of this sort would thus seem to have begun at least by the 40s, when the full form of the *titulus* first appears.[138]

In all likelihood, the branch of the state administrative system responsible for mobilizing Baetican oil was the *praefectura annonae*.[139] The previously mentioned dedication to Sex. Iulius Possessor demonstrates that this branch of the imperial administration was involved in the mobilization of Baetican oil from at least the 160s, while an inscribed statue base from Rome dating to *c.*147 that records a dedication by the *negotiatores olearii ex Baetica* (oil merchants from Baetica) to their *patronus*, M. Petronius Honoratus, a man who had formerly served as *praefectus annonae* (probably during the period *c.*144-46), strongly suggests that the participation of the *praefectura annonae* began at least two decades earlier.[140] Whether this oil was raised as tax in kind or through a purchase program of some sort, however, remains unclear.[141] Studies of the assemblages of Dressel 20 stamps from military sites along the Rhine frontier and from Monte Testaccio have shown that distinct areas within the Baetis/Genil drainage were responsible for the supply of specific military zones and the *urbs* over circumscribed periods of time,[142] a pattern that may be viewed as compatible with either approach.

The exact nature of the rôle played by the private individuals named in the beta *titulus* component also remains unclear. On the one hand, they may have bought the oil — presumably from the state, although possibly from producers — undertaking to convey it to designated destinations, where they would sell it either to the *praefectura annonae* or to the military.[143] Alternatively, they may have enjoyed a more limited rôle, simply assuming responsibility for

---

138 For the appearance of the standard Dressel 20 amphora *titulus* by at least the early 40s, see Rodríguez-Almeida 1980, 277-80, 287; Blázquez 1992, 176-77.

139 Rodríguez-Almeida 1993, 99 n.16 suggests that bottling operations were conducted by the imperial fisc, perhaps working on behalf of the *praefectura annonae*. Remesal Rodríguez 1986, 22, in contrast, surmises that the delta *titulus* component may have been a fiscal control connected with the levying of the *portorium* (customs tax). For criticisms of this view, see Le Roux 1986, 250 n.13; Liou and Tchernia 1994, 151 n.10. Mattingly 1988, 44 suggests that local municipal authorities may have conducted bottling operations during the 1st c., with responsibility for this then shifting to the *praefectura annonae*. Keay 1988, 101 is non-committal, simply stating that "the filling, sealing and exporting of oil amphorae were... carefully monitored by imperial authorities in Baetica."

140 *CIL* VI 1625.

141 For the assumption that this oil was raised by the *praefectura annonae* under an unspecified initiative, see Le Roux 1986, 263-64. Blázquez 1992, 176 suggests that Baetican oil was mobilized by a range of different means, including taxation, gift, and purchase.

142 Remesal Rodríguez 1986, 74-76; Blázquez 1992, 175-77, 186; Blázquez Martínez *et al.* 1994, 142-43, 146.

143 Liou and Tchernia 1986, 136-37 assume that these individuals operated entirely within a free-market context.

the transport of state-owned oil to a designated destination under the terms of a contract. The substitution of these *privati* by the Severans that is documented in these *tituli* probably reflects the assumption of responsibility for the transport of Baetican oil to Rome by the *ratio privata,* that is, the private estate of the emperor. The timing of this development suggests that it may have been linked to the initiation of the program of free oil distributions at Rome.[144] With the death of Caracalla in 217, this responsibility would appear to have been absorbed by the *ratio patrimoni,* the bureau of the privy purse.[145] It was then apparently allowed to revert, at least in part, to private merchants in or shortly before 230. This step may have formed part of a program aimed at increasing the level of oil imports that is linked to the restoration of the full oil ration under Severus Alexander.

The system for the mobilization of Baetican oil reflected in the Dressel 20 *titulus* appears to have been discontinued at some point during the first half of the 260s. The latest known *titulus* on a Dressel 20 amphora is one from Monte Testaccio that bears a consular date indicating Gallienus as sole regent, putting it no earlier than 261 and possibly as late as 266.[146] While the precise set of circumstances that precipitated this change remains uncertain, the most plausible suggestion is that the transfer of Hispania's allegiance from the emperor at Rome to the breakaway Imperium Galliarum at some point between 260 and 264 led to the discontinuation of the state-sponsored system for the mobilization of Baetican oil.[147]

144 Note, however, that our main source regarding free oil distributions under Septimius Severus, *SHA, Sev.* 18.3, appears to link the initiation of this program with the pacification of hostile tribes that had been threatening Tripolitania. This raises the possibility that some real or anticipated expansion in the production of Tripolitanian oil may have enabled the state to begin free oil distributions at Rome.

145 The transfer of the *figlinae Barb( ), Cepariae,* and *Grumensae* from private hands first to imperial control and then to the *Kalendarium Vegetianum* is more or less synchronous with, and closely parallels, these developments in the beta *titulus* component, suggesting that the state may also have made an effort to assume a higher profile in the bottling of Baetican oil during the first two decades of the 3rd c.

146 Rodríguez-Almeida 1989a, 112, no. 119.

147 For the chronology of the Gallic Empire, see Lafaurie 1975.

4. RECONSTRUCTION

By combining the information contained in the Group 1 and Group 2 *ostraca* with the evidence discussed in the preceding section it is possible to achieve a detailed reconstruction of certain aspects of the operations involved in the handling of state oil at Carthage from early February to late July of the year A.D. 373. Three distinct aspects of operations are amenable to reconstruction:
1) the progress of operations
2) modalities for the transport and consigning of oil
3) modalities for the weighing of oil.
The inferences that can be drawn with regard to each of these topics are not only of interest in their own right but constitute much of the basis for the general interpretation of the documents presented in Section 5.

The reconstructions presented here depend upon sets of inferences in three areas:

1. The capacity and nature of the 7 container types:

The abbreviations employed for the names of the 5 container types referred to in the Group 2 *ostraca*, together with the standard weight values assigned for calculating estimates for total weight of oil, can be used to determine both the nature and capacity of each container type. Similar determinations can also be made for the *centenarium leve* and *ƀ* container types referred to in the Group 1 *ostraca*. Appendix 3 presents a detailed analysis of this evidence. The results, which are summarized in Table 8, can be characterized as follows. The designation KN^T was used to refer to amphoras that had a capacity of *c*.95-100 lbs. (31.1-32.7 kg/34.2-36.0 l) of oil. It was almost certainly an abbreviation for *kentenarium*, presumably a variant of the term *centenarium*. The term *centenarium leve* was probably used to refer to amphoras of this same size. The bulk of these containers were probably large examples of the class of amphoras that archaeologists refer to as the Keay 25 amphora (fig. 11.B). The designation *ag* was used to refer to amphoras that held *c*.216 lbs. (*c*.70.6 kg/77.7 l) of oil, an amount equal to 3 *amphorae* or 2 *metretes*. It was probably an abbreviation for *amphora gemellaria* (twin amphora). These containers most likely belonged to the class of amphoras that archaeologists refer to as the Keay 35 amphora (fig. 11.C). The designation *ψ* was probably used to refer to amphoras that held *c*.400 lbs. (*c*.130.8 kg/143.9 l) of oil, an amount equal to 4 *centenaria*. The name to which this designation referred remains enigmatic. These containers were probably examples of the class of amphoras that archaeologists refer to as the wide-bodied Keay 35 amphora (fig. 11.D). The designation *as* was used to refer to oilskins with a capacity of *c*.504 lbs. (164.8 kg/182.7 l) of oil, an amount equal to 7 *amphorae*. It was presumably an abbreviation for *ascopa* or *ascopera*, both being Latinizations of the Greek ἀσκὸς (skin bag). Finally, the designation *as a ƀ* was used to refer to oilskins that held either *c*.72 lbs. (23.5 kg/26.1 l) of oil, an amount equal to one *amphora* or, less probably, 75 lbs. (24.5/27.0 l) of oil. The first two letters of this designation presumably stood for *ascopa/ascopera*, with the remaining portion perhaps standing for *a byzacena* (from Byzacena). While the designation *ƀ* may simply have been a variant of the *as a ƀ* designation, there is some evidence to suggest that it was used to refer to amphoras, presumably also with a capacity of either 72 or, less probably, 75 lbs. of oil. If so, the bulk of these containers were probably small examples of the Keay 25 amphora (fig. 11.A). This designation presumably stood for *byzacena*.

2. The nature of the groups of oil containers registered in Type 1, Type 2, and Type 3 entries:

The pronounced structural difference in the Subgroup 2B documents between, on the one hand, the Type 1 entries (i.e., those associated with the *fisci* provenience/ownership designation), and, on the other, the Type 2 and Type 3 entries (i.e., those associated with the 4 topographic provenience/ownership designations and the *oRc* provenience/ownership designation, respectively) suggests that the functionaries who composed these documents recognized some basic distinction between the stocks of oil to which these entry types referred. The most obvious infer

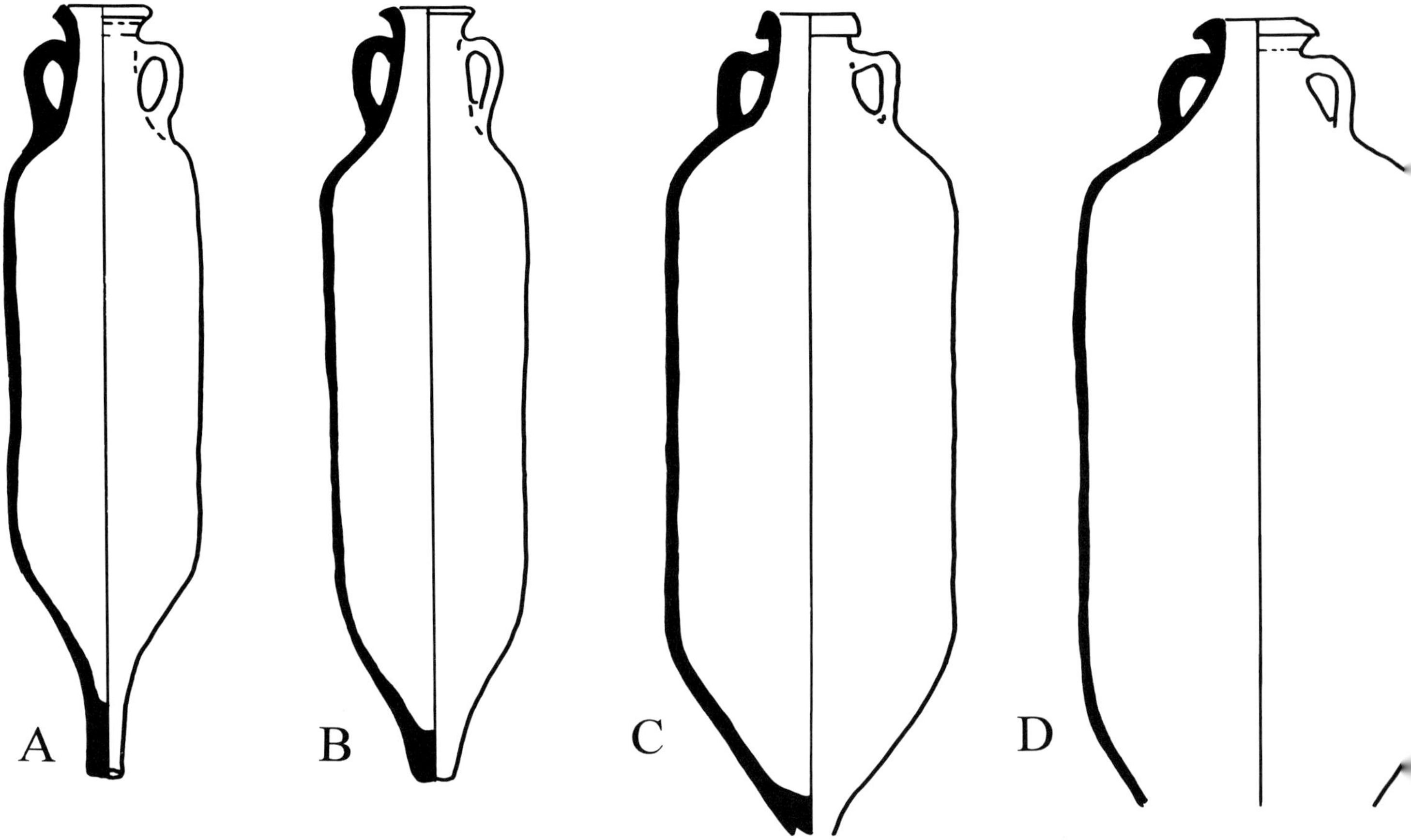

Fig. 11. Profile drawings of examples of amphora classes that may correspond to container types recorded in the *ostraca*. Scale 1:10.
A: Small example of the Keay 25 amphora (= Freed 1995, 182 fig. 1.3); maximum capacity *c.*27.0 l or 75 lbs. of oil; possible example of the ꝑ container type.
B: Large example of the Keay 25 amphora (= Carandini and Panella 1977, 258 fig. 20); maximum capacity 35.1 l or 98 lbs. of oil; probable example of the *KN*^{T}*/centenarium leve* container type.
C: Large example of the Keay 35 amphora (= Freed 1995, 183 fig. 2.2); maximum capacity *c.*80.2 l or 223 lbs. of oil; probable example of the *ag* container type.
D: Example of the wide-bodied Keay 35 amphora (= Freed 1995, 183 fig. 2.1); est. maximum capacity *c.*148 l or 412 lbs. of oil; probable example of the ψ container type.

ence to be drawn from the evidence is that, while the oil associated with the Type 1 entries was owned by the fisc, that associated with the Type 2 and Type 3 entries either did not belong to the fisc or, if it did, was not at that time in its possession. Several additional observations can be brought to bear on the question of the nature of the difference between these two stocks of oil:

1) While Type 2 entries regularly appear and a Type 3 entry on one occasion appears under the *inpletu* heading, Type 1 entries never appear under this heading.
2) The analysis of No. 7 *recto* suggests that entries that are the equivalent of Type 2 entries were used to register newly-arrived shipments of oil containers recorded in the Group 1 documents.
3) Type 2 and Type 3 entries are both regularly (if not exclusively) associated with oil container types that are best interpreted as oilskins, whereas Type 1 entries are always associated with oil container types that are best interpreted as amphoras.
4) The analysis of the individual oil weigher entries in the Group 2 documents suggests that weighing operations involved the transfer to amphoras of oil brought to Carthage in oilskins (see Appendix 4).

In light of these observations, the most plausible interpretation of the distinction noted here is that the oil to which these documents refer passed into the possession of the fisc as part of the weighing operation, with Type 2 and 3 entries used to refer to unweighed oil and Type 1 entries used to refer to oil that had already been weighed. This interpretation may receive support from the evidence regarding the procedures employed for the mobilization of state oil in Baetica, since the addition of the delta *titulus* component to the weighed and sealed Dressel 20 amphora may well have represented the moment at which the *fiscus* took formal possession of the oil. The principal difficulty with this inference lies in the fact that the heading for the groups of containers being held at the storage facility is prefaced with the word *fieri*, implying that the oil being held at this facility had yet to be weighed. If the interpretation of No. 7 *recto* presented above is correct, however, it would appear that *fieri* was used in a general sense to refer to the oil being held at the storage facility (perhaps because the overwhelming bulk of it was, in fact, unweighed), and that quantities of weighed oil were sometimes placed in storage there. This inference appears to be the most likely explanation of the patterning evident in the Group 2 documents, and the remainder of this analysis is based on the assumption that it is correct.

3. The composition of oil shipments:

In some cases it is possible to identify groups of containers registered in the *ostraca* that probably represent distinct shipments of oil. While the presence of such shipments is self-evident in the case of the Subgroup 1A *ostraca*, they also can be recognized in the Group 2 documents in some instances. In the case of the *fieri inconditZ* heading in the Subgroup 2B documents, the oil container entries for each provenience/ownership designation display a pattern of continuous increase from one document to the next. It seems a fair assumption that each of these increases represents the reception of one or more newly arrived shipments of containers at the storage facility, or the transfer there of one or more groups of containers previously held at the weighing facility. Thus, by comparing the numbers of containers of a specific provenience/ownership designation and type in two consecutive documents, it is possible to identify groups of containers that may represent one or more new shipments. In contrast with the oil container entries under the *fieri inconditZ* heading, those under the *inpletu* heading display no apparent pattern from one document to the next. Since the container entries listed under this heading do not appear to represent groups of containers transferred from the storage facility, it seems a fair assumption that they are newly arrived shipments of oil received at some point subsequent to the composition of the last previous document, presumably on or shortly before the date on which the document in question was composed.

Logically, the groups of oil containers identified in this manner may represent one of four different things:

1) one or more complete shipments of oil containers;
2) a portion of one or more such shipments, with the remaining portion of the shipment or shipments received at the other facility;
3) a portion of one or more such shipments, with the remaining portion of the shipment or shipments received at the weighing facility, weighed, and perhaps transferred to some third location;
4) some combination of the preceding.

While the interpretation of No. 7 presented above suggests that in some instances the groups of containers listed under the *inpletu* entry may represent the third of these four possibilities, certain regularities in the numbers of containers in entries listed under the *inpletu* entry and in the figures obtained when calculating the difference between analogous entries listed under the *fieri inconditZ* in two consecutive documents suggest instances of either the first or the second possibility.

TABLE 1.

Entries for weighed oil, groups of containers of weighed and unweighed oil and the estimate for total weight of oil for dated/datable Group 2 documents.

ENTRY	WEIGHED OIL	OIL CONTAINERS				
		ψ	ag	as a ƀ	as	KN^T
A. No. 7 r.						Date: ? 16.2
in condit						
1. Vol Calassini						10
2. Caprorenses						607
3. unidentified	25,400					314
TOTAL	25,400					931
Estimated weight oil: 118,500						
B. No. 7 v.						Date: 17.2
(inpletu)						
1. Vol Calassini						76
2. weighed	35,078					
TOTAL	35,078					76
C. No. 8 v.						Date: *c.* 17.2
(inpletu)						
1. weighed	44,293					
TOTAL	44,293					
D. No. 9						Date: 9.3
inpletu						
1. Vol				21		
2. weighed	3,400					
fieri inconditZ						
3. fisci?			167			
4. Vol?				06		
TOTAL	3,400					
Estimated weight oil: 41,320						
E. No. 10						Date: ? >9.3 - <15.3
inpletu						
1. Vol				133		
2. weighed	22,207					
fieri inconditZ						
3. fisci?			167			?
X.- Y? unknown				?	?	?
TOTAL	22,207		167	≥138	?	?
Estimated weight oil: 60,040-99,049						
F. No. 11						Date: 15.3
inpletu						
1. Vol				?		?
2. Caprorenses?						?
3. weighed	3,836					
fieri inconditZ						
4. fisci?			?			?
5. Vol?				514		
TOTAL	3,836		?	≥514		?
Estimated weight oil: 101,820						
H. No. 13						Date: 7.4
inpletu						
1. Vol				21		
2. oRc					161	
3. Macrinenses				06		
4. weighed	15,600					
fieri inconditZ						
5. fisci			167			50
6. Tebelbucitan qz				300		50
7. Vol				1,514		
8. oRc					272	1,091
9. Macrinenses				06		
TOTAL	15,600		167	1,847	433	1,191
Estimated weight oil: 526,520						

I. No. 14						Date: 8.4
inpletu						
1. Macrinenses				49		120
2. weighed?	23,500					
fieri inconditZ						
3. fisci			167			50
4. Tebelbucitan qz				300		50
5. Macrinenses				?06		120
6. Vol				?1,514		?0
7. oRc					?391	?1,091
TOTAL	23,500		167	?1,869	?391	?1,431
Estimated weight oil: ?500,960						

J. No. 15						Date: ? >8.4
inpletu						
1. Vol				30-39		
X.-Y. unknown				?	?	?
2. Tebelbucitan qz				?		?
3. weighed	4,453					
fieri inconditZ						
X.-Y. unknown			?	?	?	?
TOTAL	4,453		?	≥30-39	?	?
Estimated weight oil: 703,001-908,004						

K. No. 16						Date: 25.4
inpletu						
1. Vol				22		
2. weighed	3,875					
fieri inconditZ						
3. fisci			167			62
4. Tebelbucitan qz				446		65
5. Macrinenses				55		285
6. Vol				2,156		
7. oRc					757	1,232
TOTAL	3,875		167	2,679	757	1,644
Estimated weight oil: 785,275						

L. No. 17						Date: 26.4
inpletu						
1. weighed	≥9,906					
fieri inconditZ						
2. fisci			?167			62
X.-Y? unknown		?		?	?	?
TOTAL	≥9,906	?	?167	?	?	≥62
Estimated weight oil: unknown						

M. No. 18						Date: 6.5
inpletu						
1. Vol				68		
2. weighed	11,110					
fieri inconditZ						
3. fisci		184	167			62
4. Tebelbucitan qz				446		65
5. Macrinenses				55		285
6. Vol				2,275		
7. oRc					757	1,232
TOTAL	11,110	184	167	2,844	757	1,644
Estimated weight oil: 880,275						

N. No. 22						
inpletu?						Date: 30.5
1. unknown	?6,000	?		?		?
2. unidentified	21,780 -21,789	62				
3. unidentified	23,850 -23,889			170		
TOTAL	?51,665	≥62		≥170		?
inpletu?						Date: 31.5
4. unidentified	23,530 -41530	73				
TOTAL	?31,500	73				
inpletu?						Date: 6.6
5. unidentified	?			160		
6. unknown	14,200 -14,299	?		?		?
TOTAL	?43,600	?		≥160		?

TABLE 2

Weight/percent of oil by provenience/ownership designation by facility as recorded in Group 2 documents.

Figures based on data in Table 1 and values derived using standard weight values for container types as determined in Appendix 2. Rate of change figures represent mean daily change in amount of oil held at storage facility since previous document in which both date and estimate for total weight of oil are intact.

PROVENIENCE/ OWNERSHIP	WEIGHING FACILITY		STORAGE FACILITY	
	LBS.	%	LBS.	%
A. No. 7 r.	Date: ? 16.2			
weighed (fisci?)			25,400	21.4
unidentified			31,400	26.5
Vol			1,000	0.8
Caprorenses			60,700	51.3
TOTAL	-	-	118,500	100.0
B. No. 7 v.	Date: 17.2			
weighed	35,078	82.2		
Vol	7,600	17.8		
TOTAL	42,678	100.0	-	-
C. No. 8 v.	Date: ? ca. 17.2			
weighed	44,293	100.0		
TOTAL	42,678	100.0	-	-
D. No. 9	Date: 9.3			
weighed	3,400	68.3		
fisci?			35,905	98.8
Vol	1,575	31.7	?450	1.2
TOTAL	4,975	100.0	36,355	100.0
RATE OF CHANGE	21 days		-3,911 lbs./day	
E. No. 10	Date: ?>9.3-<15.3			
weighed	22,207	68.2		
fisci?			≥36,905	-
Vol	10,350	31.8	?	-
Other			?	-
TOTAL	32,557	100.0	36,905 -66,492	-
F. No. 11	Date: 15.3			
weighed	3,836	-		
fisci?			?≥36,905	-
Vol	?	-	?38,550	-
Caprorenses?	?	-		
TOTAL	>3,836	-	?≥75,455	-
RATE OF CHANGE	6 days		+10,083 lbs./day	
G. No. 13	Date: 7.4			
weighed	15,600	15.8		
fisci			40,905	9.6
Tebelbucitan qz			27,500	6.4
Macrinenses	450	0.4	450	0.1
Vol	1,575	1.6	113,550	26.5
oRc	81,305	82.2	245,644	57.4
TOTAL	98,930	100.0	428,049	100.0
RATE OF CHANGE	23 days		+18,465 lbs./day	
H. No. 14	Date: 8.4			
weighed	23,500	60.0		
fisci			40,905	8.1
Tebelbucitan qz			27,500	5.5
Macrinenses	15,675	40.0	?12,450	2.5
Vol			?113,550	22.7
oRc			?306,555	61.2
TOTAL	39,175	100.0	?500,960	100.0
RATE OF CHANGE	1 day		?+72,911 lbs./day	
I. No. 16	Date: 25.4			
weighed	3,875	70.1		
fisci			42,105	5.4
Tebelbucitan qz			39,950	5.1
Macrinenses			32,625	4.2
Vol	1,650	29.9	161,700	20.7
oRc			503,214	64.6
TOTAL	5,525	100.0	779,594	100.0
RATE OF CHANGE	18 days		+19,53C lbs./day	
J. No. 18	Date: 6.5			
weighed	11,110	68.5		
fisci			117,651	13.6
Tebelbucitan qz			39,950	4.6
Macrinenses			32,625	3.8
Vol	5,100	31.5	170,625	19.8
oRc			503,214	58.2
TOTAL	16,210	100.0	864,065	100.0
RATE OF CHANGE	11 days		+ 7,697 lbs./day	
K. No. 22 Record 1	Date: 30.5			
weighed	?51,655	-		
unidentified	≥37,550	-		
TOTAL	?≥89,205	-	-	-
L. No. 22 Record 2	Date: 31.5			
weighed	?31,500	-		
unidentified	29,200	-		
TOTAL	?60,700	-	-	-
M. No. 22 Record 3	Date: 6.6			
weighed	?43,600	-		
unidentified	≥12,000	-		
TOTAL	?≥55,600	-	-	-

The progress of operations

On the basis of the information provided by the Group 1 and Group 2 *ostraca* it is possible to reconstruct the progress of operations at the two facilities, including the reception of newly arrived shipments of oil, the transfer of oil containers and weighed oil from one facility to the other, the weighing of oil, and the transfer of weighed oil to some third location. It should be noted that as the Subgroup 2B *ostraca* would appear to indicate that between March 9 and May 6 it was not the practice to transfer oil containers from the storage facility to the weighing facility, the following reconstruction assumes that no such transfers occurred during this period. In order to follow the complicated narrative of the reconstruction readers may find it helpful to refer to Tables 1-5.

Table 1 summarizes the entries for weighed oil and groups of oil containers and the estimate for the total weight of oil at the two facilities for each of the Group 2 *ostraca*.

Table 2 converts the figures in Table 1 to weight figures by multiplying them by the standard weight figures derived in Appendix 2, grouping the entries by facility and provenience/ownership designation. It also records the rate of change in the amount of oil being held at the storage facility since the previous document.

Table 3 summarizes oil weighing activity on a document by document basis, indicating the amount of oil weighed, the percent of the total amount of weighed oil attested in the documents represented by this amount, the number of oil weighers involved, and the mean lbs. of oil weighed per weigher.

TABLE 3

Oil weighing activities attested in Group 2 documents

DOCUMENT	DATE	LBS. WEIGHED	PERCENT TOTAL	NUMBER WEIGHERS	LBS. per WEIGHER	NUMBER WORK GROUPS	LBS. per WORK GROUP
No. 7 r.	17.2	34,658	11.4	13	2,666	8	4,332
No. 8 r.	?	44,293	14.6	≥13	≤3,407	?	-
No. 9	9.3	3,363	1.1	1	3,363	1	3,363
No. 10	?	22,207	7.3	>4	<5,552	?	-
No. 11	15.3	3,836	1.3	3	1,279	1	3,836
No. 13	7.4	15,457	5.1	5	3,091	3	5,152
No. 14	8.4	23,267	7.7	8	2,908	5	4,653
No. 15	?	4,453	1.5	≥4	≤1,113	?	-
No. 16	25.4	3,847	1.3	4	961	1	3,847
No. 17	26.4	≥9,906	3.3	5	≤1,981	?	-
No. 18	6.5	10,901	3.6	8	1,362	3	3,637
No. 22	30.5	?51,655	17.0	-	-	-	-
	31.5	?31,400	10.4	-	-	-	-
	6.6	?43,600	14.4	-	-	-	-
TOTAL	110 days	≥302,843	100.0	-	-		-

Table 4 presents a list of minimum oil inputs to the two facilities (i.e., transfers of oil to either facility from some third location) as inferred from both the Group 1 and Group 2 documents. It includes information regarding the date of the transfer, the facility to which the transfer was made, the entries on the basis of which the transfer was identified, the provenience/ownership designation of the oil, the number of containers involved, and the weight of the oil as calculated using the standard weight values derived in Appendix 2.

Table 4

Minimum oil inputs to two facilities as inferable from Group 1 and Group 2 documents

ENTRIES column indicates entries on basis of which inferred input is based (see discussion in text).
Figures in WEIGHT OIL column calculated using standard weight values derived in Appendix 2.
Abbreviations: N = Number; PROV/OWN = provenience/ownership designation; Teb = Tebelbucitan qz; Mac = Macrinenses; Cap = Caprorenses; uni = unidentified; by = *as ab*; KNT = KN^T.
Number of Vol by is underestimated by 21 due to fact that group of containers recorded in No. 9, Entry 1 is deducted twice.

DATE	FACILITY	ENTRIES	PROV/ OWN	NUMBER CONTAINERS	WEIGHT OIL
4.2	storage	No.1	Cap?	210 KNT	21,000
<16.2	storage	No.7r.3a-No.1	uni	104 KNT	10,400
<16.2	storage	No.7r.3b	uni	?254 KNT/ ?118/119 ag	25,400
16.2	storage	No.7r.2	Cap	607 KNT	60,700
16.2	storage	No.7r.1	Vol	10 KNT	1,000
<17.2	weighing	No.7v.1	Vol	76 KNT	7,600
<17.2	weighing	No.7v.2	uni	?	34,658
c.?17.2	weighing	No.8.1	uni	?	44,293
5.3	weighing?	No.4	Cap	202 KNT	20,200
>16.2-9.3	weighing	No.9.1	Vol	21 by	1,575
>16.2-9.3	storage	No.9.4	Vol?	6 by	450
>9.3-14.3	weighing	No.10.1-?No.9.1	Vol	≥117 by	≥8,775
>9.3-14.3	weighing	No.10.2	uni	?	22,207
>9.3-15.3	weighing	No.11.2	Cap?	?	?
>9.3-15.3	weighing	No.11.3	uni	?	3,836
>10.3-15.3	storage	No.11.5-?No.9.1-?No.9.4-?No.10.1	Vol	≥349 by	≥26,175
>15.3-7.4	storage	No.13.6	Teb	300 by+ 50 KNT	27,500
>15.3-7.4	weighing	No.13.3	Mac	6 by	450
	storage	No.13.9	Mac	6 by	450
>15.3-7.4	weighing	No.13.2	oRc	161 as	81,305
	storage	No.13.8	oRc	272 as+ 1,091 KNT	246,460
>15.3-7.4	storage	No.13.7-No.11.5	Vol	1,000 by	75,000
8.4	weighing	No.14.1	Mac	49 by+ 120 KNT	15,675
	storage	No.14.5	Mac	120 KNT	12,000
8.15	weighing?	No.5	unk	192 ?KNT	?19,200
>8.4-25.4	storage	No.16.4-No.14.4	Teb	146 by+ 15 KNT	12,450
>8.4-25.4	storage	No.16.5-No.14.1-No.14.5	Mac	45 KNT	4,500
>8.4-25.4	weighing	No.16.1	Vol	22 by	1,650
	storage	No.16.6-No.14.6	Vol	642 by	48,150

>8.4-25.4	storage	No.16.7-No.14.7	oRc	?366 as+ ?141 KNT	198,930
26.4	storage	No.17.1-?No.16.1	uni	-	≥8,256
>25.4-6.5	weighing	No.18.1	Vol	68 by	5,100
	storage	No.18.6-No.16.6	Vol	119 by	8,925
>25.4-6.5	weighing	No.18.3-?No.17.1	uni	-	?63,694
>6.5-30.5	weighing	No.22.1/2/3	uni	62 ψ + 1 0 2 by+weighed	?≥84,115
31.5	weighing	No.22.4-No.22.1/2/3	uni	37 ψ + weighed	?≥23,150
>31.5-6.6	weighing	No.22.5	uni	160 by +weighed	?≥41,400
≥27.7	?	No.6.1	uni	?1 ψ + ? by	?
≥27.7	?	No.6.2	uni	140 by	?10,500

Table 5

Oil outputs from two facilities inferable from Group 1 and Group 2 documents

TOTAL 1 excludes entry in second row under >8.4-25.4.

DATE	WEIGHT
>16.2-9.3	≥211,000
9.3-7.4	≥21,043
7.4-8.4	15,457
>8.4-25.4	22,067
	?19,200
TOTAL 1	≥269,567
TOTAL 2	≥288,767

Table 5 presents a list of minimum oil outputs from the two facilities (i.e., transfers of oil from either facility to some third location) as inferred from both the Group 1 and Group 2 documents, including the date of the transfer and the amount of oil involved.

February 3/4:

A shipment of 215 containers, most likely Caprorenses *centenaria levia*, is delivered to Carthage by coasting vessel on February 3, with 210 containers (*c.*21,000 lbs. of oil) accepted. The shipment is consigned on the following day, probably to the weighing facility.

February 14-16:

A shipment of 208 Caprorenses *centenaria levia* is delivered to Carthage by coasting vessel on February 14, with 200 (*c.*20,000 lbs. of oil) accepted. A second shipment of 208 Caprorenses *centenaria levia* is delivered on the following day, with 195 (*c.*195,000 lbs. of oil) accepted. Both shipments are consigned on February 16, apparently to the weighing facility.

The estimated weight of oil at the storage facility on this date is 118,500 lbs. Already in storage there are 314 KN^T (*c.*31,400 lbs. of oil) of unspecified provenience/ownership (probably including the containers accepted on February 3/4) and 254 cwt. (25,400 lbs.) of weighed oil. If these cwt. were *fisci* oil, data for March 9 suggest that it may have been held in *c.*118/119 *ag*. A group of 607 Caprorenses KN^T (*c.*60,700 lbs. of oil) and another group of 10 Vol KN^T (*c.*1,000 lbs. of oil) are consigned to this facility on this date. The former presumably consists of three shiploads of containers, including the two documented as consigned on this day, plus a third for which documentation is lacking. The 10 Vol KN^T may represent either a shipment consigned in its entirety to this facility on this date, or a portion of a larger shipment, the bulk of which is attested at the weighing facility on the following day.

February 17:

At the weighing facility, 34,658 lbs. of oil (11.4% of total weighed oil) are processed by 13 weighers. This activity may represent the initiation of weighing operations for the administrative year, following their suspension the preceding October. Also present are 76 Vol *KN*^{T} (*c*.7,600 lbs. of oil), bringing the total amount of oil at this facility to *c*.42,258 lbs. These containers may represent either an entire shipment received at the weighing facility on this day or a portion of such a shipment, with the balance represented by the weighed oil and/or the 10 Vol *KN*^{T} received at the storage facility on the previous day.

At unknown date (probably around this same time) 44,293 lbs. of oil (14.6% of total weighed oil) are processed at the weighing facility by at least 13 weighers.

March 2/3/4-5:

A shipment of 210 Caprorenses *centenaria levia* is delivered to Carthage by a coasting vessel on either March 2, 3, or 4, with 202 (*c*.20,200 lbs. of oil) accepted. The shipment is consigned on March 5, probably to the weighing facility.

March 9:

The estimated weight of oil at the two facilities is 41,320 lbs. At the weighing facility, 3,363 lbs. of oil (1.1% of total weighed oil) are processed by a single weigher. Also present are 21 Vol *as a ℔* (*c*.1,575 lbs. of oil). At the storage facility there are 167 *ag* (*c*.35,905 lbs. of oil) and 6 *as a ℔* (*c*.450 lbs. of oil), both of unknown provenience/ownership. Reference to later documents suggests that the former are almost certainly *fisci*, while the latter are likely to be Vol.

The two groups of *as a ℔* may represent individual shipments, or may constitute a single shipment, perhaps together with the weighed oil. Whatever the case, these containers must have been delivered to Carthage and consigned to their respective facilities after February 16. The weighed oil may be oil newly arrived since February 16-17, or may represent oil registered at either of the two facilities on these dates.

The oil held in the group of *ag*, which presumably consists of weighed oil, does not appear to correspond to the 34,568 lbs. of oil weighed on February 17, as the weight of oil figures for individual oil weighers in No. 7 *verso* cannot be reconciled with a group of 167 *ag* (see Appendix 4). The figures yield an average of only 207.0 lbs. of oil per container, well below the 215/216 lbs. that one would expect. The oil in these containers may, on the other hand, subsume the 25,400 lbs. of weighed oil already present on February 16. If so, and if the oil attested on the earlier date was held in 118/119 *ag*, this would suggest that a group of 48/49 *ag* of *fisci* oil was transferred from the weighing facility to the storage facility at some point after that date.

While some of the *c*.250,171 lbs. of oil registered at the two facilities on earlier dates may be subsumed under the *c*.35,905 lbs. of *fisci* oil at the storage facility and/or the 3,363 lbs. of weighed oil, the remainder, at least *c*.211,000 lbs., must have been transferred to some third location by this date.[148] As a result, the amount of oil at the storage facility decreases at a rate of 3,911 lbs. per day from February 16 through March 9.

Apparently between March 9 and March 15.

The estimated weight of oil at the two facilities falls between *c*.69,000 and 99,949 lbs. At the weighing facility, 22,207 lbs. of oil (7.3% of total weighed oil) are processed by at least 4 weighers. Also present are 138 Vol *as a ℔* (*c*.10,350 lbs. of oil). While the situation at the storage facility is unclear, it is evident that the number of *fisci ag* remains unchanged since March 9.

The 138 Vol *as a ℔* at the weighing facility may constitute an entire shipment or may form part of a shipment along with the weighed oil. Since this group may include the 21 Vol *as a ℔* registered at this facility on March 9, no more than 117 of these containers (*c*.8,775 lbs. of oil) need have been delivered to Carthage and consigned to this facility after March 9.

March 15:

The estimated weight of oil at the two facilities is 101,820 lbs. At the weighing facility, 3,836 lbs. of oil (1.3% of total weighed oil) are processed by three weighers. Also present are an unknown number of Vol containers (probably *as a ℔*, although possibly *KN*^{T}) and perhaps a group of Caprorenses containers (very

---

148 This figure comes to *c*.167,000 lbs. of oil if one omits No. 8 *verso* due to the conjectural nature of its dating.

probably KN^T). At the storage facility there are an unknown number of *ag* and 514 *as a ƀ* (*c*.38,550 lbs. of oil), both of unknown provenience/ownership. Since *ag* are attested only with the *fisci* provenience/ownership designation, it appears virtually certain that the former group contains *fisci* oil. Since there are 167 *fisci ag* registered at the storage facility on both March 9 and April 7, it seems all but certain that this is also the number of these containers at this facility on this date. The fact that 1,514 Vol *as a ƀ* are registered at the storage facility on April 7 suggests that the latter group consists entirely of Vol containers. If so, the 6 unidentified *as a ƀ* registered at this facility on March 9 — unless transferred to some third location in the interim — must also be Vol.

The group of Vol containers at the weighing facility and the group of 514 unidentified *as a ƀ* at the storage facility may each constitute an entire shipment, or they may represent portions of a single shipment, perhaps together with the weighed oil. Since the former group may include the 21 Vol *as a ƀ* registered at the weighing facility on March 9, none of the containers in this group need have been delivered to Carthage or consigned to this facility after that date. Similarly, since the latter group may include the 21 Vol *as a ƀ* registered at the weighing facility on March 9 and the 6 unidentified *as a ƀ* registered at the storage facility on this same date, no more than 508 and perhaps as few as 487 of these containers (*c*.36,525 - 38,100 lbs. of oil) need have been delivered to Carthage after this date. Further, since this group may also include the 138 Vol *as a ƀ* registered at the storage facility on an unknown date between March 9 and March 15, as few as 349 of these containers (*c*.26,175 lbs. of oil) may have been delivered to Carthage after this date.

April 7:

The estimated weight of oil at the two facilities is 526,520 lbs. At the weighing facility, 15,457 lbs. of oil (5.1% of total weighed oil) are processed by 5 weighers. Also present are 21 Vol *as a ƀ* (*c*.1,575 lbs. of oil), 6 Macrinenses *as a ƀ* (*c*.450 lbs. of oil), and 161 *oRc as* (*c*.81,305 lbs. of oil). At the storage facility there are increases of 50 KN^T of *fisci* oil (*c*.5,000 lbs. of oil) since March 9, and 300 *as a ƀ* and 50 KN^T of Tebelbucitan qz oil (*c*.27,500 lbs. of oil), 1,000 Vol *as a ƀ* (*c*.75,000 lbs. of oil), 6 Macrinenses *as a ƀ* (*c*.450 lbs. of oil), and 272 *as* and 1,091 KN^T of *oRc* oil (*c*.246,460 lbs. of oil) since March 15, for an overall increase of 13,507 lbs. of oil per day at this facility since the first of these dates.

The 21 Vol *as a ƀ* at the weighing facility and the probable group of 1,000 Vol *as a ƀ* newly consigned to the storage facility may each constitute an entire shipment, or they may represent portions of a single shipment, perhaps together with the weighed oil. Since the former group may include the unknown number of Vol containers registered at the weighing facility on March 15, none of the containers in question need have been delivered to Carthage or consigned to this facility after that date. The probable group of 1,000 Vol *as a ƀ* newly consigned to the storage facility presumably represents containers delivered to Carthage and consigned to this facility since March 15. The groups of 6 Macrinenses *as a ƀ* at both the weighing facility and the storage facility presumably represent a single shipment of 12 delivered to Carthage after March 15 that was divided into two halves, with one of these consigned to the weighing facility and the other to the storage facility. The Tebelbucitan qz containers represent oil delivered to Carthage and consigned to the storage facility since March 15.

The groups of *oRc* containers at the weighing facility and the storage facility likewise represent oil delivered to Carthage and consigned to these facilities since March 15. The specific numbers of containers in these two groups raise the possibility that all of this oil belongs to a single shipment of immense proportions. The weight of the oil being held in the group of 161 *as* at the weighing facility (*c*.81,305 lbs.) is almost exactly one-quarter of the combined amount of *oRc* oil received at the two facilities (*c*.327,765 lbs.), while the amount of *oRc* oil being held in KN^T (*c*.109,100 lbs.) is almost exactly one-third of the total.[149] These observations suggest that the groups of *oRc* containers consigned to the two facilities belong to a single shipment that was made up in such as way as to have one-third of the total packaged in amphoras and two-thirds in oilskins. Upon the arrival of this shipment at Carthage the responsible functionaries apparently decided to divide it into two parts, directing one-quarter to the weighing facility and the other three-quarters to the storage facility. The exceptionally large size of this shipment is presumably the reason it was divided between the two facilities.

The increase of *c*.5,000 lbs. in the amount of *fisci* oil indicates that at least *c*.21,043 of the 26,043 lbs. of oil weighed on March 9, March 15, and the unknown date between those two days has been transferred to some third location.

---

149 One-quarter of 327,765 is 81,941 (+ 636 lbs., or 0.8%), while one-third is 109,255 (+ 155 lbs., or 0.1%).

April 8:

The estimated weight of oil at the two facilities, while not known, can be reconstructed as *c.*540,135 lbs. (see below under this date) At the weighing facility, 23,267 lbs. of oil (7.7% of total weighed oil) are processed by 8 weighers. Also present are 49 *as a ƀ* and 120 KN^T of Macrinenses oil (*c.*15,675 lbs. of oil). The situation at the storage facility is only partially clear. While there is no change in the numbers of *fisci* and Tebelbucitan qz containers since the previous day, there are increases of 120 KN^T (*c.*12,000 lbs. of oil) and also possibly an unknown number of *as a ƀ* from Macrinenses, and anywhere from 28 to 127 *as* and perhaps also an unknown number of KN^T of *oRc* oil. It is unclear whether there is any increase in the numbers of Vol containers.

The fact that both the weighing facility and the storage facility register the presence of a recently consigned group of 120 Macrinenses KN^T suggests that the increases in Macrinenses oil at the two facilities represent a single shipment delivered to Carthage since the previous day. If this assumption is correct, this shipment, which would consist of 240 KN^T and at least 49 *as a ƀ* (*c.*27,675 lbs. of oil), was split in two upon arrival at Carthage, with half of the amphoras and some or all of the *as a ƀ* consigned to the weighing facility and the remaining containers consigned to the storage facility. Data from April 25 suggest that this shipment probably contained just the 49 *as a ƀ* documented at the weighing facility.

The amount of weighed oil is far less than the amount of unweighed *oRc* oil registered at the weighing facility on the previous day. It thus seems likely that the oil weighed on this day consists of all of the unweighed Vol and Macrinenses oil plus some portion of the *oRc* oil registered at the weighing facility on that day. This assumption is compatible with the data for April 25, which suggest that the increase in Macrinenses *as a ƀ* at the weighing facility between April 7 and April 25 consists entirely of the 49 such containers registered at the weighing facility on April 8. If we assume that the 23,267 lbs. of weighed oil includes all of the oil contained in the combined 27 *as a ƀ* (*c.*2,025 lbs. of oil) of Vol and Macrinenses oil at the weighing facility on the previous day, only *c.*21,242 lbs. of *oRc* oil can have been weighed on this day. This is almost the exact equivalent of 42 *as* (*c.*21,210 lbs. of oil), or roughly one-quarter of the 161 *as* recorded on the previous day. This suggests that the functionaries in charge of weighing operations may have decided to process one-quarter of the group of *oRc* containers and shift the remaining three-quarters (119 *as* containing *c.*60,095 lbs. of oil) to the storage facility. This would bring the number of *oRc as* at the storage facility to 391 (*c.*197,455 lbs. of oil), a figure compatible with the range of possible values for this day.[150] The fact that these containers are shifted from the weighing facility to the storage facility without processing the day after their consignment raises the possibility that they were originally consigned to the weighing facility due to congestion at the storage facility resulting from the extremely large size of the shipment. We may surmise that as soon as the 272 *as* consigned to the storage facility were stowed, the bulk of the containers consigned to the weighing facility are transferred there.

The lack of any increase in the amount of *fisci* oil indicates that the 15,457 lbs. of oil weighed on the previous day are transferred to some third location either on this day or at the end of the previous day.

April 11-15:

A shipment of 200 containers of unknown provenience/ownership, most likely *centenaria levia*, is delivered to Carthage by a coasting vessel on April 11, with 192 (presumably *c.*19,200 lbs. of oil?) accepted. The shipment is consigned to one of the two facilities on April 15. The fact that this shipment does not appear to be present at the storage facility on April 25 suggests that it is probably consigned to the weighing facility.

April 25:

The estimated weight of oil at the two facilities is 785,275 lbs. At the weighing facility, 3,847 lbs. of oil (1.3% of total weighed oil) is processed by 4 weighers. Also present are 22 Vol *as a ƀ* (*c.*1,650 lbs. of oil). At the storage facility, 12 KN^T (*c.*1,200 lbs. of oil) have been added to the amount of *fisci* oil. The number of containers of Tebelbucitan qz oil has been increased by 146 *as a ƀ* and 15 KN^T (*c.*12,450 lbs. of oil), that of Vol oil by 642 *as a ƀ* (*c.*48,150 lbs. of oil), and that of *oRc* oil probably by 366 *as* and 141 KN^T (*c.*198,930 lbs. of oil) since April 8. The amount of Macrinenses oil has been increased by 49 *as a ƀ* and 165 KN^T (*c.*20,175

150 The restoration suggested here could not be evaluated against the *ostracon* as the relevant portion is now missing. It should be noted, however, that the facsimile published by Cagnat and Merlin shows a small space between the preserved portion of this figure and the break at the edge of the blank, raising the possibility that this portion of the text is not compatible with the figure *CCC[XCI*, as suggested here.

of oil) since April 7, with the increase in the amount of oil at this facility since this date coming to 19,530 lbs. per day.

The increases in numbers of Tebelbucitan qz and *oRc* containers represent shipments delivered to Carthage and consigned to the storage facility after April 8. The 22 Vol *as a ꝑ* at the weighing facility and the group of 642 Vol *as a ꝑ* newly consigned to the storage facility may each constitute an entire shipment, or they may represent portions of a single shipment, perhaps together with the weighed oil. The increase in the numbers of Macrinenses containers presumably represents the transfer from the storage to the weighing facility of 49 *as a ꝑ* and 120 KN^T after April 8 and the delivery to Carthage and consignment to the storage facility of 45 KN^T after this same date.

The increase of 1,200 lbs. in the amount of *fisci* oil indicates that of the 23,267 lbs. of oil weighed on April 8, *c.*22,067 lbs. has been transferred to some third location. The analysis of the weight of oil figures for individual oil weighers in No. 14 suggests that the 12 *fisci* KN^T that represent this increase may be containers of oil weighed on April 8 (see Appendix 4). If the assumption that the group of 192 containers consigned on April 15 consists of KN^T is correct, then it would appear that some or all of the *c.*19,200 lbs. of oil in this shipment was also transferred to some third location prior to this date.

April 26:

The situation at both facilities is unclear. At the weighing facility, more than 9,906 lbs. of oil (3.3% of total weighed oil) are processed by 5 weighers. Since there were only 22 *as a ꝑ* of unweighed oil (*c.*1,650 lbs. of oil) at this facility on the previous day, at least *c.*8,256 lbs. of oil must be consigned to this facility on this day. Since there would appear to be no containers of unweighed oil at this facility, all of the newly consigned oil must be weighed. At the storage facility, the number of KN^T and also perhaps *ag* of *fisci* oil remain unchanged since the previous day.

May 6:

The estimated weight of oil at the two facilities is 880,275 lbs. At the weighing facility, 10,901 lbs. of oil (3.6% of total weighed oil) are processed by 8 weighers. Also present are 68 Vol *as a ꝑ* (*c.*5,100 lbs. of oil). At the storage facility, while there are no changes in the quantities of containers of Tebelbucitan qz, Macrinenses, and *oRc* oil with respect to April 25, there are increases of 119 Vol *as a ꝑ* (*c.*8,925 lbs. of oil) and 184 ψ (*c.*73,600) of *fisci* oil, for an increase of 7,665 lbs. of oil per day at this facility since that date.

The 68 Vol *as a ꝑ* at the weighing facility and the 119 Vol *as a ꝑ* newly consigned to the storage facility may each constitute an entire shipment, or they may represent portions of a single shipment, perhaps together with the weighed oil. All of these containers were presumably delivered to Carthage and consigned to their respective facility after April 25, with the weighed oil delivered and consigned after April 26.

Since the increase of *c.*73,600 lbs. in the amount of *fisci* oil may include the 9,906 plus lbs. of weighed oil registered on April 26, this amount represents the delivery to Carthage, consignment to the weighing facility, processing, and transfer to the storage facility of perhaps no more than *c.*63,694 lbs. of oil since April 26.

May 7 through October:

We possess no information regarding the situation at the storage facility for the period after May 6. While we thus do not know what portion of the unprocessed oil being held at this facility on this date (*c.*746,414 lbs.) is transferred to the weighing facility, processed, and then transferred to some third location before the presumed close of operations at some point in October, the fact that there are only modest amounts of weighed and unweighed oil documented at the storage and weighing facilities at the beginning of the administrative year in February suggests that most or all of this oil is transferred to some other location.

May 30:

At the weighing facility there are three consignments of containers of unknown provenience/ownership, each of which is partially weighed. One consists of 62 ψ and 21,780-21,789 lbs. of weighed oil (*c.*46,580-46,589 lbs. of oil) and another of 170 *as a ꝑ* and 23,850-23,889 lbs. of weighed oil (*c.*36,600-36,639 lbs. of oil). While no data are available regarding the third consignment, the fact that the total amount of oil weighed on this day may be 51,665 lbs. (17.0% of total weighed oil) suggests that it may include *c.*6,000 lbs. of weighed oil. Since the only ψ containers on hand at either facility on May 6 are *fisci*, if the assumption that *fisci* oil has already been weighed is correct, then the first of these consignments must represent oil delivered to Carthage and consigned to this facility since that date. By extension, the other two consignments would also presumably consist of newly delivered and consigned oil. Since the second consignment may, however, include the 68 Vol *as a b̸* registered at this facility on May 6, the newly delivered and consigned oil may come to no more than 102 *as a b̸* and 23,850-23,889 lbs. of weighed oil (*c.*31,500-31,539 lbs. of oil).

May 31:

At the weighing facility, between 23,530 and 41,530 lbs. of oil are weighed. The true amount may be *c.*31,500 lbs. (10.4% of total weighed oil). Also at the weighing facility are 73 ψ (*c.*29,200 lbs. of oil) of unknown provenience/ownership designation. It is not certain that these containers and the weighed oil represent a single consignment, as do similar entries on the previous day and on June 6. It thus seems possible that some or all of the 62 ψ and 170 *as a b̸* of unweighed oil registered at this facility on the previous day are subsumed under these figures. Thus, no more than 15,180 - 33,180 lbs. of the oil at this facility need have been delivered to Carthage and consigned to this facility since the previous day. If the amount of weighed oil is, in fact, *c.*31,500 lbs., then the figure for the minimum amount of newly consigned oil would come to *c.*23,150 lbs. If so, the newly arrived consignment of oil must have included at least 37 ψ.

June 6:

At the weighing facility there are two consignments of containers of unknown provenience/ownership, each of which is partially weighed. One consists of 160 *as a b* (*c.*12,000 lbs. of oil) and an unknown quantity of weighed oil, the other of an unknown quantity of an unknown container type and 14,204 lbs. of weighed oil. The total amount of oil weighed on this day may be *c.*43,600 lbs. (14.4% of total weighed oil), suggesting that the figure for the amount of weighed oil in the first consignment may be *c.*29,400 lbs. Unless the 170 *as a b̸* of unweighed oil registered at this facility on May 30 were retained through to this date without being registered on May 31, it would appear that the oil in the first consignment was delivered to Carthage and consigned to this facility since the latter date. Since the second consignment may consist partly or entirely of the 73 ψ of unweighed oil registered at this facility on May 31, none of this oil need be newly delivered to Carthage and consigned to this facility since that date.

July 22:

A shipment of 1 ψ (*c.*400 lbs. of oil) and an unknown number of b̸ of unknown provenience/ownership designation is delivered to Carthage by coasting vessel, with an unknown number accepted. This shipment apparently is not received at one of the two facilities until July 27 or later.

July 27:

A shipment of 144 b̸ of unknown provenience/ownership designation is delivered to Carthage by coasting vessel, with 140 accepted (*c.*10,500 lbs. of oil). This shipment is apparently received at one of the two facilities on the same day as the shipment documented for July 22.

Modalities for the transport and consigning of oil

The Subgroup 1A *ostraca* suggest that from early February until at least the middle of April it was standard practice to deliver consignments of *c.*200-215 *centenaria levia* of Caprorenses oil to Carthage by vessels termed *naviculae*. If the identification of Caprorenses with the area of the Montes Caprarienses is correct (see Section 5), it seems likely that these ships took on their consignments of oil at Hippo Regius, near the western border of Zeugitana, some 260 km sailing distance to the west of Carthage. No. 6, the sole document in Subgroup 1B, provides evidence for a distinctly different set of practices during the later part of July, with the delivery to Carthage by *navicula* of consignments consisting of ψ and/or b̸, one of which included 144 of the latter container type. The group of 138 Vol *as a b̸* registered at the weighing facility in No. 10, Entry 1 at an undetermined date between March 9 and March 15 may perhaps represent another such consignment. If so, this would indicate that consignments of this sort were reaching Carthage as early as the second week of March. It might also be taken as evidence that the unidentified consignment in No. 6 consisted of Vol oil.

As previously noted, since the *cursus publicus* does not appear to have operated water craft on a regular basis, it seems likely that the men who operated these vessels were private individuals working either under contract or within the context of a *munus*. Whether or not they belonged to the *corpus* of the *navicularii africani* is unclear. The fact that the Felix Xerus of No. 3 *recto* and *verso*, composed on February 15 and 16, may appear again in No. 6, Record 1, composed on July 22 is a point of some interest, as it suggests that these individuals had an ongoing rôle in oil transport operations and, since the oil in the consignments referred to in these two documents may have originated at different locations, that they were perhaps based at Carthage.

Since *centenaria levia* would have had a gross weight of *c.*45 kg (see Appendix 3), the vessels employed for these operations must have had a burden on the order of at least 10 metric tons. Since we have no idea whether these consignments represented the sole cargo carried on these runs, however, it is unclear whether this figure represents the maximum capacity of these ships. Of the 1,041 containers delivered in the 5 consignments documented in the Subgroup 1A *ostraca*, 42, equal to 4% of the total, were rejected upon their arrival at Carthage. If this was the normal wastage rate for these voyages, it may be that *centenaria levia* were made up into consignments of *c.*208 containers in the anticipation that roughly 200 of these holding approximately 20,000 lbs. of oil would reach Carthage with their contents intact. In the one shipment in No. 6 for which the relevant figures are preserved, 4 containers out of a consignment of 144 ℔ were rejected upon their arrival at Carthage. If the inference that the ℔ held one *amphora*/*c.*72 lbs. of oil is correct, then it would appear that the latter consignment may have been made up so as to provide for the safe arrival of 139 containers holding *c.*10,000 lbs. of oil, here again providing for a wastage rate in the range of 4%.[151]

Certain aspects of the modalities employed for the reception of consignments of oil containers delivered to Carthage by sea can be inferred from the Group 1 *ostraca*. Upon the arrival of a *navicula*, a functionary, who perhaps bore the title *mensor olei*, inspected the consignment of containers that it carried. At the conclusion of the inspection the inspector (or perhaps an assistant) recorded the basic facts of the operation in an abbreviated fashion on either a shield-shaped blank or an irregular sherd. Since it does not appear to have been the practice in the Roman world to perform a *degustatio* (tasting) at the time that oil containers changed hands (presumably because oil, unlike wine, was stable over the short term and not subject to spoiling),[152] this inspection may have involved nothing more than a perusal of the containers as they lay in the ship's hold in order to identify any that had lost their contents through breakage or leakage while at sea. Interestingly, in three of the five instances in which we know the number of containers rejected in one of the consignments of 200 or more *centenaria levia* delivered to Carthage by sea, the figure in question is 8. This raises the possibility that in some cases in which the wastage rate was actually lower than 4% the inspector rejected a quantity of containers equal to 4% of 200, presumably retaining the surplus oil either for himself or for the organization of the *mensores olei*.

Within anywhere from 1 to 5 days or more after this inspection, a second functionary, known as a *mensor olei Fori Karthaginiensis*, produced a document that recorded the consignment of the group of containers at the storage facility or, perhaps in some cases, at the weighing facility. He also presumably at this time issued a receipt to the shipper that reproduced more or less the same information.[153] This transaction presumably represented the moment at which the organization of the *mensores olei* took formal possession of the oil. Where we have this document it is an expanded form of the inspection document executed on the reverse of the same sherd, drawing on the information contained in the earlier document. In all 4 instances in which the name of this second functionary is preserved, it is a certain Felix, and it may be that a

---

151 The figures are as follows: 139 x 72 = 10,008; 0.96 x 144 = 138.2.

152 For the practice of *degustatio* in the context of the consignment of *ampullae* (small amphoras) of wine paid as tax in kind at Rome under the *canon vinarius*, see *CIL* VI 1785. For *degustatio* in connection with the sale or legacy of wine in general, see Frier 1983, 278-82. The legal sources suggest no such arrangements for oil.

153 These receipts would have been analogous to the *securitates* that were issued to *navicularii* by the *praefectura annonae* upon off-loading fiscal cargoes at Ostia/Portus; see Sirks 1991, 156-57.

single man was responsible for recording all such transactions. That two or more consignments of containers received and inspected on different days were sometimes accepted on the same day is illustrated by Nos. 2 and 3. This suggests that on some occasions groups of containers were retained at or near the place where they had been inspected, presumably either on board the ship or at quayside, for a period of up to several days. This practice may be explained in three different ways. One possibility is that it required this amount of time to arrange for the transfer of the containers from the harbor to the facility where they were to be received. Another is that the functionaries in charge of these operations preferred to wait until a minimum number of containers had built up at the harbor before undertaking the transfer/consignment procedure. The third could be that the *mensor olei Fori Karthaginiensis* was available to perform his part of the transaction only on certain days.

While the Group 1 documents relate exclusively to shipments of oil brought to Carthage by sea, various considerations make it appear highly likely that a significant portion of the oil referred to in the Group 2 *ostraca* reached the city over land. Among these we may list the locations of the Tebelbucitan qz and Macrinenses proveniences, which may well have lain in the interior of Byzacena (see Section 5), the small size of some oil shipments, and the apparent use of very large oilskins as transport containers. More generally, the fact that the major oil-producing regions of Zeugitana lay inland and were connected to Carthage by an excellent road system, coupled with the availability of the *cursus publicus* for transport operations, makes it seem likely that a significant portion of the oil referred to in these documents reached the city over land. The absence of any Group 1 *ostraca* pertaining to oil shipments over land can be explained in two different ways. On the one hand, it may be that, since the transport of tax oil over land to Carthage was accomplished by means of the *cursus publicus*, with *susceptores* accompanying the shipments, the oil in these shipments never left the possession of the administrative entity responsible for its collection, obviating the need for an inspection/reception procedure such as that carried out for shipments of tax oil conveyed to Carthage by private shippers. Alternatively, the lack of any such documents can perhaps be attributed to some systematic difference in the way that those records were produced. Shipments over land might, for example, have been inspected at a different facility (situated at one of the city's customs gates?) that employed a perishable recording medium such as papyrus or *tabellae ceratae* (wooden tables with wax-filled writing insets) rather than potsherds,[154] or, if potsherds were employed, the resulting *ostraca* might have been archived in an office located in some other part of the city.

With regard to transport over land, since the maximum bearing capacity of a pack mule would have been on the order of 90-120 kg, it seems likely that it would have been possible to transport balanced pairs of *centenaria levia*/*KN*^{T}, *as a ƀ*, or *ƀ* by mule. (see Appendix 3) The *as* and the *ψ*, on the other hand, would have been much too heavy to transport by mule, and, if sent over land, these container types must have been moved by wagon. Since the *ag* is associated exclusively with the *fisci* designation, it appears unlikely that it served as a primary container, and is thus irrelevant to these considerations. The fact that the *as* had a capacity of 7 *amphorae*, equal to just slightly more than 500 lbs. of oil, suggests that the use of this container type was intended to permit the convenient and efficient loading of oil onto *raedae* and *angariae*, the two classes of heavy wagons operated by the *cursus publicus*, which, as previously noted, were permitted maximum loads of 1,000 and 1,500 lbs., respectively. If so, we would expect that containers of this type were made up into consignments that were multiples of either 2 or 3 containers. If the inference that state oil was packaged with these considerations in mind (along with the assumption that when functionaries of the *cursus publicus* made up cargoes of oil for *raedae* and *angariae* they discounted the weight of the containers) is correct,

---

154 For the use of *tabellae ceratae* for harbor-side record-keeping by officials of the *praefectura annonae* at Portus and by customs officials at Massilia (Marseille), see France and Hesnard 1995.

we might also expect that, when moved by wagon, *centenaria levia*/KN^T were made up into consignments consisting of multiples of 10 and/or 15 containers, and *as ab* into consignments consisting of multiples of 14 or 21 containers.[155]

Several groups of containers registered in the Group 2 documents at both the weighing facility and the storage facility correspond to these expectations. Most interesting in this regard are the groups of 21 Vol *as a ƀ* attested in No. 9, Entry 1, and No. 13, Entry 1, and perhaps also the group of 22 such containers attested in No. 16, Entry 1. The group of 45 Macrinenses KN^T that appears to have been consigned to the weighing facility at some point between April 8 and 25 may represent a shipment carried by 3 *angariae*. The group of 146 *as a ƀ* and 15 KN^T that appears to have been consigned to this facility between these same two dates may represent a shipment transported by a single *angaria* for the KN^T and 7 *angariae* for the *as a ƀ* (with one container lost to wastage?). Also perhaps worth noting are the groups of 49 *as a ƀ* and 120 KN^T and 120 KN^T of Macrinenses oil registered in No. 14, Entries 1 and 5. Here the groups of KN^T may represent loads transported either by 10 *raedae* or 8 *angariae*, while the *as a ƀ*, even though not evenly divisible into groups representing either 1,000 or 1,500 lbs. of oil, might represent loads transported aboard 2 *raedae* and 1 *angaria*. Finally, the groups of 6 *as a ƀ* registered in No. 9, Entry 4 and No. 13, Entries 3 and 9 may represent consignments carried by a string of three pack mules. If these inferences are correct, the frequency with which shipments of this kind are attested in the Group 2 documents suggests that the wastage rate associated with transport over land was substantially lower than that for marine transport.

Also worthy of mention at this point are the two groups of 161 *as* and 272 *as* and 1,091 KN^T registered in No. 13, Entries 2 and 8, which appear to have constituted a single shipment. If the assumption that *as* would have been unsuitable for marine transport is correct, the conveyance of these groups of containers to Carthage must have involved a train of something like 217 *raedae* or 145 *angariae* (or some combination of these two wagon types) for the *as*, and a large number of additional wagons (*c.*109/110 *raedae*, 72/73 *angariae*, or some combination of these) and/or *c.*546 pack mules for the KN^T. Of interest is the fact that the numbers of *raedae* and *angariae* posited for the *as* and the number of *angariae* posited for the KN^T are one more than values that elsewhere figure prominently in the oil mobilization operations documented in the *ostraca*,[156] perhaps an indication of their integrated nature.

Modalities for the weighing of oil

As discussed in Section 2, Element 2 of the Subgroup 2A and 2B documents consists of a series of entries consisting of the name of a man apparently termed a *centenarius* and a figure representing a weight of oil. These entries, here referred to as individual oil weigher entries, named men who were presumably responsible for the weighing of the oil. That some or all of these men were *mensores olei* is suggested by three points:

1) the job responsibilities implied by the title *mensor olei*;
2) the fact that the Felix who is the presumed author of the Group 1 *verso* documents may well be the same individual as a Felix who apparently enjoyed a position of prominence among the group of *centenarii*, as indicated by the fact that a Felix probably appears twice among the lists of these men, is the only weigher listed in No. 9, and is attributed with an unusually large amount of oil in No. 7 *verso*;
3) the fact that both the Group 1 and the Group 2 documents were apparently stored and discarded together, as this suggests they were produced by a single body of functionaries.

---

155 For the possibility that the presence of groups of 21 *as a ƀ* was due instead to considerations linked to weighing operations, see Appendix 4.

156 The number of *sextarii* in a *metretes* and the lbs. of oil in the *as a ƀ* is 72; 144 equals the number of *sextarii* in the *ag*; 216 equals the lbs. of oil in the *ag*.

The 15 *ostraca* in Subgroups 2A and 2B contain a minimum of 81 individual oil weigher entries. The name of the weigher is preserved more or less intact in 46 of these. As discussed in Appendix 4, the Felix appearing in No. 7 *recto*, Entry 3 is likely the same man as the Felix in No. 9, Entry 1. However, the Felix in No. 18, Entry 6 is presumably a different man, perhaps the same individual as either the Felix ab Ucubi or the Felix ab ....c who appears in No. 13, Entries 2 and 4, respectively. The Victor in No. 14, Entry 7 may be the same man as the Victor Mercur(ialis) in No. 7 *verso*, Entry 5, the Victor Utumm(ensis) in No. 11, Entry 2, or the Victor a Serve or the Victor a Nobis in No. 18, Entries 5 and 8, respectively. Finally, the Victorianus in No. 14, Entry 2 may well be the same individual as the man of this name appearing in No. 16, Entry 2. Thus, since 4 men may appear twice in these lists, the 46 entries for which the name of the weigher is intact may represent no more than 42 different weighers. The small number of repeat appearances by these men suggests, however, that the pool of workers from which they were drawn was, in fact, considerably larger than this.

From the names of the *centenarii* (which are predominantly of Roman origin) it would appear that these men were free individuals of modest social standing. While the Victor a Nobis (i.e., 'from us'), in No. 18, Entry 8, was presumably from Carthage, some of these men hailed from elsewhere in Zeugitana and perhaps in at least one case from outside the province. Victor Utumm(ensis) in No. 11, Entry 2 presumably came from Uthumae, a settlement apparently located in the environs of Sicilliba (Bordj Alaouine), *c.*45 km SW of Carthage.[157] Bilossus ab Ochi in No. 16, Entry 3 probably originated at Uchi Maius (Henchir Douamis), a town situated *c.*15 km WNW of Thugga (Henchir Dougga), in south-central Zeugitana,[158] while Felix ab Ucubi in No. 13, Entry 2 probably hailed from Ucubi (Henchir Kaoussat), a town located *c.*20 km ENE of Sicca Veneria (Le Kef), in the same general part of the province.[159] It may be worth noting that the region in which these last two towns were located was at that time an area of intensive olive cultivation. Victor Mercur(ialis) in No. 7 *verso*, Entry 5 may perhaps have come from one of the 4 settlements in Zeugitana known as Ad Mercurium, one located on Cap Bon, one situated *c.*35 km SW of Carthage, one lying 20 km NE of Theveste (Tipassa), and the last 15 km WNW of this same town.[160] Alternatively, Mercurialis may be simply a second *cognomen*. The identity of the home town of the Victor a Serve(?) listed in No. 18, Entry 5 is uncertain, although this may perhaps be a corruption of Sertei (Kherbet Guidra), a town located in Mauretania Sitifensis, roughly 50 km WNW of Sitifis (Sétif).[161]

From the analysis of the weight of oil figures in the individual oil weigher entries it is possible to draw several inferences regarding the specific procedures employed in weighing operations and the organization of the labor force involved. A detailed analysis of these entries is presented in Appendix 4, with the relevant data summarized in Tables 9 and 10. The discussion that follows draws in substantial measure on this analysis. The weight figures reported in these entries indicate that oil transported to Carthage in oilskins was transferred to sets of secondary containers consisting of amphoras, including KN^T, and also presumably both *ag* and *ψ*, as part of the weighing procedure. This oil was probably weighed using the transvasing method employed for Baetican oil, an amphora intended for use as a secondary container being weighed empty, filled with oil either to its maximum effective capacity or to the requisite weight module, and then re-weighed, the former figure then being subtracted from

157 Lancel 1991, 1528.

158 For the identification of Occhi with Uchi Maius, see also Salama 1987, 157. The town in question may have been Uchi Minus, however, the precise location of which remains unknown.

159 While the Ucubi referred to might conceivably have been Ucubis (Espejo), a town near Corduba (Córdoba), in the upper valley of the Baetis, it seems unlikely that this was the case.

160 For these locales, see Miller 1916 [1964] 907, 923, 931, 934. The compiler of this document presumably employed the adjectival form of the name due to the fact that it began with the word *ad*.

161 Lancel 1991, 1460.

the latter in order to determine the weight of the oil that had been transferred to the amphora. It is uncertain whether this was also the procedure employed for the weighing of oil transported to Carthage in amphoras. The only plausible alternative is that the various examples of each amphora type were so consistent in their efficiency ratio that the weighers were able to weigh unopened primary container amphoras and then subtract an estimated value for the weight of the container, the oil then being exported in the same container in which it had been conveyed to Carthage. It seems unlikely, however, that this method would have provided the degree of precision required in these operations, in which oil was weighed to the pound. It thus appears likely that the transvasing method was also employed for weighing this oil.

The balances used in weighing operations must have had a capacity of at least *c.*170 kg if they were able to accommodate a filled ψ, which probably had a gross weight of roughly this amount (see Appendix 3). They may have resembled a balance shown in a 3rd-c. mosaic from a tomb at Hadrumetum, which depicts the weighing of what appear to be metal ingots being unloaded from a boat.[162] This apparatus appears to consist of a heavy wooden beam slung from a wood tripod *c.*2 m high with a rectangular pan suspended from a metal hook at either end. One man is shown adjusting two ingots on one of the pans while gesturing to a man positioned at the other, who appears to be adding weights to it. In lieu of a pan on one end, the balances used for oil-weighing operations were probably fitted either with a set of hooks from which amphoras could be suspended by their handles, or a ring-shaped support into which it was possible to set the three different sizes of amphoras attested in the *ostraca*.

In several cases it appears that anywhere from two to as many as 6 of the weighers listed in adjacent entries were organized into work groups. Both work groups and unassociated weighers appear to have been issued sets of amphoras, presumably empty secondary containers, at the outset of the day's operations. In several instances the number of containers received was equal to a multiple of 12 or one less than a multiple of 12, suggesting that it was common practice to distribute these amphoras by the dozen. In the case of some of the two-man work groups, the allotment of amphoras was divided up between the two men before the initiation of weighing operations. These containers were then presumably weighed, filled with oil from primary containers, and re-weighed, the figure for the cumulative weight of oil for the set of amphoras then being attributed to the weigher to whom the containers in question had been assigned. In other instances, including all of the work groups that contained three or more weighers, it appears that a different approach was employed for the crediting of weighed oil, with the two or more men in the group being attributed a base share corresponding to a certain number of cwt. (quite possibly prior to weighing operations), with credit for a small residual amount of oil being divided up among some or all of the men in the group according to various arrangements.

If the analysis of the weight of oil figures for individual oil weighers presented in Appendix 4 is correct, the amounts of oil attributed to work groups and unassociated weighers in any one document range from a low of 1,092 lbs. to a high of 11,620 lbs., a factor of over 10.6 times. If these figures represent amounts of oil processed in the course of a single day, then some of the larger figures attributed to individual weighers appear problematic, most notably the 11,135 lbs. assigned to Doi..anus in No. 13, Entry 5. If, for purposes of illustration, we assume that oil weighers labored continuously for 10 hours on a typical work day, then Doi..anus, who is attributed with enough oil to have filled 112 KN^T, must have processed one container of oil every 5.4 minutes, or 11.2 containers per hour. This rate seems excessive, and raises the suspicion either that some of the larger figures reflect work done over a period of more than one day or that the weigher in question received credit for oil weighed on more than one balance, the extra balances being operated by men whose names do not appear in the list. If the latter, we

162 Casson 1971, fig. 191.

may wish to attribute the variability in these figures to differences in the number of workers subsumed under each entry.

It is unclear how it was determined which oil weighers were to be called in for duty on any particular day. The fact that the lists of weighers in Nos. 13 and 14 and No. 16 and 17, in both instances pairs of documents composed on consecutive days, have no names in common, however, suggests that the group of weighers was changed on a daily basis. The fact that the weighers who probably appear more than once do not occur in association with the same men further suggests that there were not fixed panels of weighers who were engaged as a group. Similarly, if the Victorianus in No. 14, Entry 2 is the same individual as the man of that name in No. 15, Entry 2, then it would also appear that the composition of work groups might change.

The amount of oil weighed on any one day varies from low of 3,363 to high of 44,293 lbs. (or perhaps 51,655 lbs.), with the largest amounts registered in the *ostraca* falling towards the beginning and the end of the period for which we possess documentation. Of considerable interest is the fact that on four dates between March 15 and April 25 — all of the days over this span of time for which we possess documentation, save the unknown date on which No. 15 was produced — the number of KN^T involved in oil processing operations appears to have been equal either to a multiple of 39 or to a multiple of 39 plus one (see Table 10). Also perhaps worth noting in this regard is the fact that the number of KN^T involved in operations on February 17 was equal to a multiple of 39 minus one, while the amount of oil apparently weighed on May 30 is compatible with the processing of a number of KN^T equal to a multiple of 39 plus one or two.[163] The most plausible explanation for this pattern departs from the observation that in some instances the groups of private individuals involved in the collection and transport of *species annonariae* were granted allowances equal to one-fortieth or 2.5% of the consignment entrusted to them. Most notable in this regard is the one-fortieth allowance that up through A.D. 380 was granted to *navicularii* who serviced the Africa-Portus route for the carriage of winter cargoes.[164] In light of this fact, it seems possible that operations at the weighing facility were organized around lots consisting of 40 containers, with one container from each lot set aside as an allowance of some sort, these containers and the oil that they held not being registered in the documents that recorded weighing activities.[165] The use of the 400 lb. capacity *ψ* alongside the 100 lb. capacity KN^T may also hint at the handling of oil in lots equal to 40 cwt., as may the conveyance of oil to Carthage in consignments consisting of 200 *centenaria levia*. While the allowance in question may have been that granted to the *navicularii* for the carriage of winter cargoes, the fact that this practice extended through April 25 and perhaps even later suggests that this was probably not the case. An attractive alternative is that this was an allowance awarded to the oil weighers.

Our documentation is too fragmentary to allow us either to infer the frequency of weighing operations or to determine whether these were carried out in accordance with a regular schedule of some sort. Suggestive in this regard, however, is No. 22, which documents oil weighing activity on May 30, May 31, and June 6. If this document records all weighing activity carried out during the period in question, then we may infer that oil was not processed on a daily basis. The fact that, for 6 of the 11 dates for which oil weighing is attested, activity is also attested for either the previous day or the following day may indicate that operations were compressed into periods of two or more consecutive days, followed by periods of inactivity.

---

163 Perhaps *c.*31,400 pounds, equal to *c.*314 KN^T. 8 x 39 = 312.

164 *CTh* 13.9.3 (380). See also *CTh* 12.6.21 (386), addressed to the *praefectus praetorio Orientis*, which grants a one-fortieth allowance to *susceptores* for barley.

165 If this inference is correct, and if the inference that the weighed oil recorded in No. 14 consisted of the oil held in all 27 *as a* ♭ and 42 of the 161 *as* registered in No. 13 is also true, then the containers set aside in this way must have been empty, to be filled with oil not included in the oil weight figures recorded in the Group 2 documents.

If we assume that the amount of oil that appears to have been weighed on May 30, 51,655 lbs., represents the maximum processing capacity, then the weighing of the *c.*746,000 lbs. of unweighed oil at the storage facility on May 5, the last date for which we possess such information, would have required a minimum of 14-15 days of work. At the mean rate for the 10 days for which we possess certain figures, 16,628 lbs. per day, this figure comes instead to nearly 45 days of work. Assuming that operations continued through to October 1, we may infer that it was necessary to process unweighed oil shifted from the storage facility to the weighing facility at least one day in ten, and perhaps as often as one day in every three for the period after May 5. Since, as No. 22 appears to indicate, large oil shipments continued to reach Carthage during the period after May 5, it must have been necessary to carry out weighing operations on a substantially more frequent basis than these figures suggest.

If the inferences drawn above regarding the nature and capacity of the various container types are correct, and if the *fisci* designation was indeed used to designate weighed oil that had already been transferred to secondary containers, then we can estimate that *c.*one-half of the oil referred to in these documents reached Carthage in oilskins, one-quarter in amphoras, and the remaining one-quarter in containers of uncertain type.[166] While there is no way of gauging the extent to which these figures are representative of operations at Carthage over the course of the entire year, they do indicate that weighing operations required large numbers of empty amphoras to serve as secondary containers. A substantial portion of these containers was presumably manufactured specifically for this purpose somewhere in the vicinity of Carthage. While there is little firm evidence regarding amphora production in the environs of the city during the period in question, the small amount available demonstrates that at least two classes of certain or possible oil amphoras were manufactured there at this time, the Keay 25, which, as argued in Appendix 3, probably subsumes most or all of the containers denoted by the *centenaria levia*/*KN*^{T} and perhaps also the ƀ designations, and the Keay 26 (*spatheion*), which is smaller than any of the container types referred to in the documents.[167] It is also possible that the entity responsible for weighing operations re-used empty amphoras that had originally served to bring oil or other liquids to Carthage for sale on the local market.

In the documents at our disposal there are but four instances in which amphoras are attested at the weighing facility (No. 7 *verso*, Entry 1, No. 14, Entry 1, and No. 22, Entries 2 and 4),[168] and, as discussed above, it appears likely that in the second of these cases the group of containers in question was transferred to the storage facility without weighing. All other containers attested at the weighing facility are oilskins. This suggests that when shipments of oil arrived at Carthage most or all of the amphoras and a portion of the oilskins were directed to the storage facility for warehousing, while the remaining oilskins were sent to the weighing facility for processing. This practice may well have been determined by the relative robustness and re-use values of these two different kinds of containers. All things being equal, amphoras, as rigid, stable containers, were probably superior to oilskins for the long-term storage of oil. At the same time, oilskins were probably far more efficient (in terms of liter of content to kilogram

166 These figures were derived by multiplying the container figures in the last row of Table 6 by their respective standard weight values.

167 The only amphora workshop of the late 4th c. that has been discovered to date in the Carthage area is an establishment that was revealed in the course of construction work at Ariana, *c.*12 km west of the city. The remains of this workshop were examined by Panella, who observed wasters belonging to *Africano* 1B, Keay 25, and Keay 26 amphoras; see Panella 1982, 174, 177, 179. The presence of examples of the *Africano* 1B suggests that production probably began at this location no later than the early 4th c. The apparent absence of the Keay 26 from any of the operations documented in the *ostraca* from the Ilôt de l'Amirauté may perhaps suggest a *terminus post quem* for the introduction of this class.

168 No. 11, Entry 2 might also refer to *KN*^{T}.

of container) and far more expensive than amphoras,[169] and for these reasons they appear to have been treated as re-usable containers to an extent that amphoras were not.[170] It may thus have been advantageous to concentrate on the processing of oil transported to Carthage in oilskins during the earlier part of the administrative year, so that the containers of this kind that were emptied in the course of weighing operations could be returned to the local collection districts for re-use during the course of the same year.[171]

---

169 Some idea of the relative values of oilskins and amphoras may be gleaned from the *Edictum de Pretiis* (301). In Entry 15.98 (Giacchero ed. [1974]) the price for a *lagoena s(extariorum) vi[ginti quattuor?]* (24 *sextarius* jug) is set at 12 *denarii*, while in Entry 10.14 the price for an *uter olearius primae formae* (first quality oilskin) is set at 100 *denarii*. While there is no indication of the size of the *uter* referred to, it would need to have a capacity of 200 *sextarii* ([100/12] x 48), roughly 1.4 times the volume of the *ag*, for the cost to capacity ratio to equal that of the *lagoena*. It may be worth noting in this regard that *Edictum de Pretiis* Entry 9.1a lists 100 *denarii* as the price for *formae caligares maximae* (one pair of large shoes). The manufacture of an oilskin with a capacity of 200 *sextarii* would have involved appreciably more raw material than a pair of sandals (low grade leather in both cases), and probably required an equivalent amount of labor, if not substantially more, suggesting that the *uter* in question was considerably smaller than this. For the use of *cullei* as security for a loan, implying that they had significant value, see *Dig.* 13.7.43.1 (Scaevola).

170 *Dig.* 33.6.3 (Ulpian) draws a distinction between amphoras and *utres/cullei*, ruling that while the former passed to an heir along with legated wine, the latter did not. This suggests that wineskins had a significantly greater re-use value than amphoras. Also interesting in this regard is the fact that *Edictum de Pretiis* Entry 10.15 lists a price of 2 *denarii* for *in utrem mercedem diurnam*, which Giacchero interprets as a daily rental rate for an *uter*.

171 See *CIL* VIII 24654 for a *corarius* (leather worker) associated with what is perhaps a *publicum horreum* at Carthage. Might this man have been employed reconditioning oilskins in preparation for their re-use?

5. INTERPRETATION

In light of the information presented in the preceding sections it is possible to advance to a more general interpretation of the *ostraca*. The discussion is here directed towards 5 distinct topics:

1) the identification of the one or more oil mobilization initiatives under which the oil referred to in the documents was collected;
2) the identification of the specific administrative contexts within which the operations reflected in the documents were carried out;
3) the calendar of operations at the two facilities referred to in the documents;
4) the location and physical nature of the two facilities referred to in the documents;
5) the broader implications of the documents for our understanding of the state's rôle in the mobilization of African oil.

It is possible to draw fairly secure inferences regarding each of the first three of these areas, and on the basis of these to develop a reasonably satisfactory interpretation of the operations to which the *ostraca* refer. With regard to the location and physical nature of the two facilities to which the documents refer, it is possible to identify them, if only conjecturally, with known structures on the Ilôt de l'Amirauté. The broader implications of the *ostraca* are somewhat uncertain, due in large part to the partial nature of the available information.

The identification of the oil mobilization initiatives

We may draw on several forms of evidence to identify the possible initiatives under which the oil referred to in the *ostraca* was mobilized. These include the natures of the various provenience/ownership designations, the absolute amounts of oil attested for each of these, and the size and timing of both oil inputs and oil outputs. Table 6 provides a summary of oil inputs by provenience/ownership designation, while Table 7 converts these data to three different forms, including their equivalents in kilograms, estimates for the hectares of olive orchard that might have been required to produce these quantities of oil,[172] and an estimate for the number of people whose yearly oil requirement could have been met by these quantities of oil.[173] Needless to say, much of the evidence on which this analysis is based is fragmentary and must be employed with caution.

As will be shown, the evidence strongly suggests that the oil associated with the 4 toponymic provenience/ownership designations (Tebelbucitan qz, Macrinenses, Vol Calassini, and Caprorenses) was raised under one oil mobilization initiative, here referred to as Initiative 1, while that associated with the *oRc* provenience/ownership designation was raised under a different initiative, here referred to as Initiative 2. At the same time, the fact that on April 8 oil raised under both of these initiatives appears to have been processed and recorded under a single figure for sum of weighed oil indicates that the two formed part of one, larger oil mobilization program.

As previously observed, the 4 topographic provenience/ownership designations presumably refer to districts within which the oil associated with them originated. While it cannot be excluded that oil was raised under Initiative 1 in one or more additional districts not named in the surviving documents, this would appear to be unlikely. All 4 of these locations may proper-

---

172 The figure employed to derive this estimate is 110 kg of oil per ha. This a regional average for production in N Tunisia in modern times reported in Mattingly 1994b, 98 Table 3. The derivation of meaningful average productivity figures for olive cultivation is a highly problematic undertaking; see Mattingly 1994b, with special reference to Tunisia. The data derived on the basis of the figure used here should be understood as extremely crude estimates.

173 The figure employed here to derive this estimate is the figure 20 l per person per year adopted by Mattingly for the Roman empire in general; see Mattingly 1988, 34.

TABLE 6
Minimum oil inputs by provenience/ownership designation
as inferable from Group 1 and Group 2 documents.

PROV/OWN	NUMBER CONTAINERS					WT. OIL	PERCENT
	ψ	*ƀ*	*as a ƀ*	*as*	KN^T		
Tebelbucitan qz			446		65	39,950	3.0
Macrinenses			61		285	33,075	2.5
Vol Calassini			2,365		86	184,975	13.8
Caprorenses					1,019	101,900	7.6
oRc				799	1,232	526,695	39.4
unidentified	99	140	262		296	99,350	7.4
unidentified					?	351,009	26.3
TOTAL	99	140	3,134	799	2,983	1,336,954	100.0

TABLE 7
Minimum oil inputs by provenience/ownership designation expressed in terms of kg,
with estimates for number of ha of olive orchard required to produce that amount of oil
and number of annual individual oil requirements that could have been met by much oil.
See text for conversion figures employed to derive these figures.

PROV/OWN	KG	HA ORCHARD	INDIVIDUAL REQUIREMENTS
Tebelbucitan qz	13,064	119	719
Macrinenses	10,816	98	594
Vol Calassini	60,487	550	3,327
Caprorenses	33,321	303	1,831
oRc	172,229	1,566	9,463
unidentified	147,267	1,338	8,092
TOTAL	437,184	3,974	24,024

ly be characterized as obscure, in the sense that they are not well attested in the surviving epigraphic and textual sources. The most valuable sources for the identification of the first three are the lists of Catholic and Donatist bishops that appear in the *Gesta Conlationis Carthaginiensis Anno 411* and the *Notitia Provinciarum et Civitatum Africae* of 484.[174] Tebelbucitan qz should perhaps be identified as a district corresponding to the bishopric of the *plebs Tubulbacensis* that is mentioned in both of these works, the latter placing it in the province of Byzacena.[175] The element qz remains enigmatic, although it presumably stood for a second term that served to further qualify the location.[176] Macrinenses, rendered in the form of

174 For the texts of these works, see Lancel 1974, and Petschenig 1881 [1967], 115-34, respectively.

175 For this identification, see Cagnat and Merlin 1911, 522. Lancel 1991, 1502 makes note of it without offering any judgement as to its validity.

176 The only plausible candidate in either the *Gesta Conlationis Carthaginiensis Anno 411* or the *Notitia*

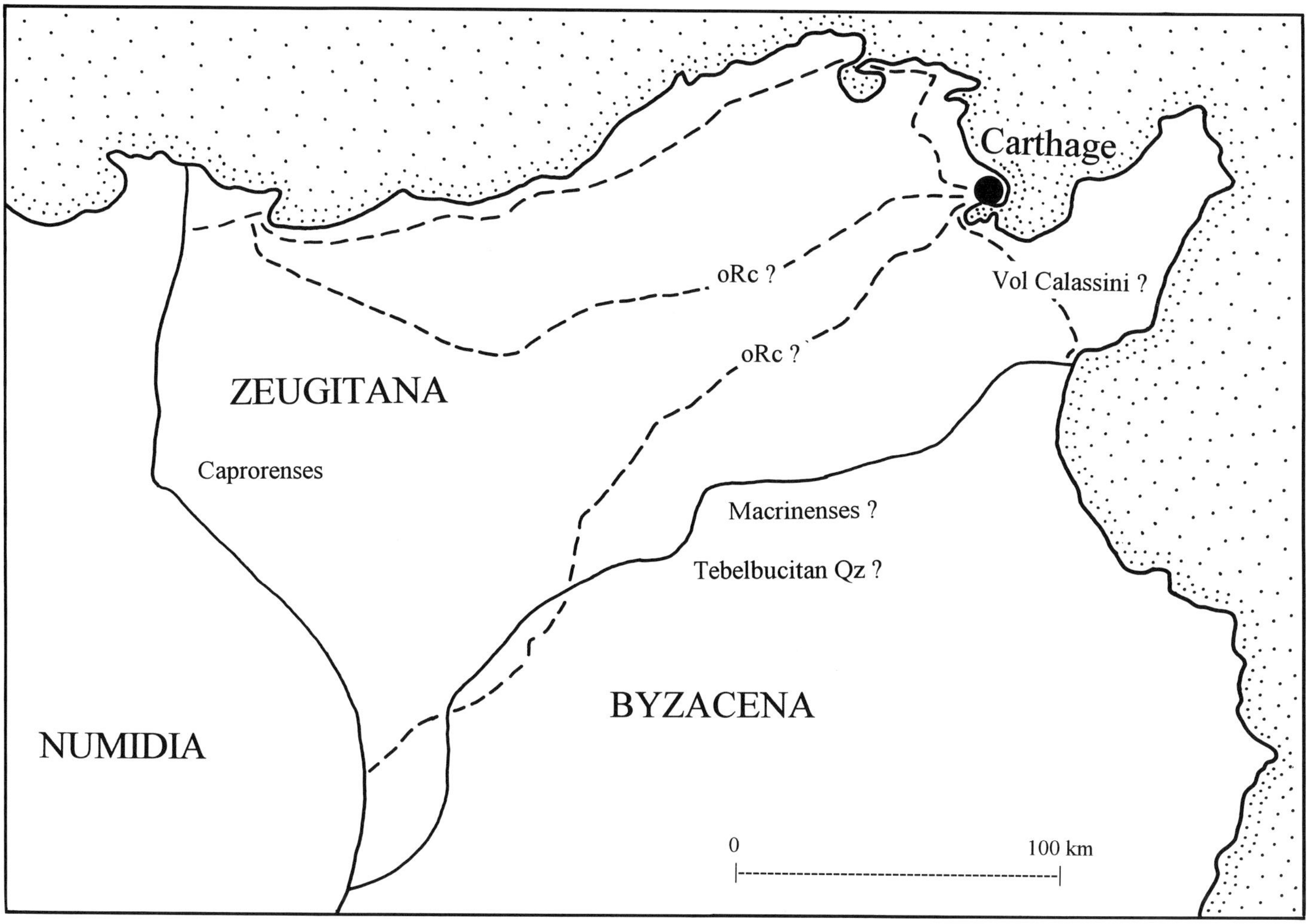

Fig. 12. Map showing major road routes leading to Carthage and conjectural locations of oil collection districts recorded in the *ostraca.*

an ethnic, is presumably a district corresponding to one of the three different bishoprics of a *plebs Macrianensis* referred to in these works.[177] One of these was located in Byzacena and another in Mauretania Sitifensis, while the province in which the third was situated remains uncertain. If either of these first two districts was located in Byzacena, a possibility that is supported by the possible expansion of the *as a ꝑ* container type as *ascopa a byzacena*, the fact that oil from this area was brought to Carthage over land rather than being trans-shipped through one of the ports on the eastern seaboard of Tunisia suggests that the district in question lay in the north-central part of the province, perhaps in the vicinity of Mactaris (Maktar), from which it might have proven more economical to move produce northward to Carthage rather than eastward to Hadrumetum for export (fig. 2). The third designation, Vol Calassini, presumably represents a district corresponding to the bishopric of the *plebs Volitana* that is mentioned in both works, the latter locating it in Zeugitana.[178] The name of this bishopric is presumably derived from the settlement of Vol, which Ptolemy places between Maxula and Thimida, roughly 30 km SSW of Carthage.[179] The last of the 4 toponymic designations, Capro-

---

Provinciarum et Civitatum Africae is Quiza/Quizensis; see Lancel 1991, 1450. This settlement lay in the province of Mauretania Caesariensis, however, and thus cannot be relevant if the identification of Tebelbucitan with the *plebs Tubulbacensis* is correct.

177 Lancel 1991, 1412-13.

178 Lancel 1991, 1525.

179 4.3.9. For this identification, see Cagnat and Merlin 1911, 522.

renses, which, like Macrinenses, appears in the form of an ethnic, presumably refers to the territory of the *Caprarienses*, a tribal group that inhabited the *Caprarienses Montes*, an area of uplands to the south of Calama (Guelma) in westernmost Zeugitana, *c.*260 km WSW of Carthage.[180] Oil brought to Carthage from this region would probably have been moved down to the coast on the route that ran from Zattara (Kef Bezioun) to Hippo Regius along the valley of the Ubus (wadi Seybousse), and there trans-shipped to coasting vessels for the completion of the journey. The identification of Caprorenses with this region is thus compatible with the fact that the *caproreses centenaria levia* referred to in Nos. 2-4 were brought to Carthage by *navicula*.

Worth noting is the fact that three of these 4 provenience/ownership designations may correspond to toponyms that appear in the table annexed to the *Règlement*. Perhaps the most convin-cing of these associations is that of Caprorenses with the toponym listed as *pars territori Cap....*[181] Less compelling, though still worthy of mention, are the possible associations of Macrinenses with *Macr...* apparently listed as a *civitas*,[182] and Tebelbucitan qz with *Teb...*, also apparently a *civitas*.[183]

That the oil associated with these 4 provenience/ownership designations pertains to a single mobilization initiative is suggested by the following points:

1) the common toponymic character of the designations;
2) the possible association of as many as three of the four designations (Tebelbucitan qz, Macrinenses, Caprorenses) with tax circumscriptions named in the table annexed to the *Règlement;*
3) the association of three of the four designations (Tebelbucitan qz, Macrinenses, Vol) with the *as a þ*container type;
4) the modest amount of oil associated with each of the designations (under 190,000 lbs. of identified oil);
5) the conveyance of the oil associated with the designations to Carthage in shipments of small size (under 1,500/1,600 lbs., or the equivalent of one *angaria* load) or medium to large size (4,500 to 75,000 lbs., or the equivalent of 3 to 50 *angaria* loads);
6) the conveyance of the oil associated with all four of the designations to Carthage in multiple shipments (three or more).

---

180 For the *Caprarienses*, see *Amm.* 29.5.37. For the Caprarienses Montes, see *Amm.* 29.5.34. The *Tabula Peutingeriana* locates a settlement named Capraria in this area, roughly two-thirds of the way from Tipasa to Thibilis on the Carthage-Constantine route. The precise identification of this settlement remains uncertain. Miller 1916 [1966] col. 936 identifies the site as that of modern Henchir Bu Atfân, for which see *CIL* XII 4836-4844. Gsell 1911, Feuille 18 p. 15 notes previous identifications of two sites in this area (nos. 193 and 194) as Capraria, rejecting both.

181 Saumagne 1950, fig. III, fragment 63, line 5. Note, however, that Lancel 1991, 1342-43 contains two entries that begin with the letters Cap, namely Capsa in Byzacena, and Capsensis Plebs on the Mauretania Sitifensis/Numidia border.

182 Saumagne 1950, fig. II, fragment 55, line 4. The line-drawing suggests that this toponym should perhaps be transcribed *MAM[...]*, in which case fragment 55, line 2, which begins *MA[...]*, can be restored as Macrinenses. Lancel 1991, 1410-15 contains 7 entries that begin with the letters Mac: Macomades (perhaps the same as Macomadia Rusticana and Macomazensis Plebs), in Numidia; Macri/Macrensis Plebs, in Mauretania Sitifensis; Macrianensis Plebs (apparently three different places, as discussed above); and Mactaritana Plebs, in Byzacena. In addition, this work lists one entry that begins with the letters Mam: Mammillensis Plebs, in Mauretania Caesariensis.

183 Saumagne 1950, fig. II, fragment 54, line 4. The line-drawing suggests that the third letter in this toponym may well be a D rather than a B, and Saumagne 1950, 130 transcribes this as *TED[?...]*. While Lancel 1991, 1470-1504 contains no entries that begin with either Teb or Ted, it does list 3 that begin Tab, three that begin Thab, 3 that begin Thib, 6 that begin Thub, 1 that begins Tib, and 3 that begin Tub, some of which may have had alternate spellings that began with Teb.

The fact that the initiative in question involved oil originating in what would appear to have been just four obscure and perhaps widely separated districts would seem to preclude the possibility that it was either the general land tax or the general collection of rent in kind from the tenants of imperially-owned lands. The only remaining possibilities would appear to be either a program of purchase or the collection of one or more surcharges to the land tax, such as those listed under the *Règlement*. However, the modest quantities of oil involved, particularly as regards the Tebelbucitan qz and Macrinenses districts, coupled with the remote location of Caprorenses and also possibly both Tebelbucitan qz and Macrinenses, makes it appear unlikely that this was a program of purchase, since the state could presumably have obtained this amount of oil far more economically by concentrating its efforts on areas lying closer to Carthage. Even if one of the aims of such a program had been that of supporting oleoculture in marginal areas by providing an outlet for otherwise unmarketable produce, it seems unlikely that purchases on this limited scale (perhaps the equivalent of no more than the entire crop of a 5-6 score ha of olive orchard in the cases of both Tebelbucitan qz and Macrinenses) could have made much of an impact in a district of any appreciable size. The only remaining possibility, namely that the initiative in question involved the collection of one or more surcharges to the land tax, is supported by the possible association of at least one and perhaps as many as three of the four provenience/ownership designations with tax circumscriptions listed in the table annexed to the *Règlement*. Also perhaps worth noting in this regard is the fact that the oil associated with each of the four districts reached Carthage in relatively small shipments spread out over periods of several weeks, as this may be indicative of a flexible calendar of payments similar to those attested for some of the surcharges listed in the *Règlement*. Thus, while the evidence is hardly compelling, it would seem to support the inference that the initiative in question represented one or more surcharges to the land tax.

The stocks of oil associated with each of these 4 provenience/ownership designations display characteristics that warrant some comment. In the case of Vol, most notable is the fact that this district provided more oil than the other three districts combined, nearly one-seventh of the total, with this arriving in a large number of shipments of widely varying sizes spread over the entire period for which we possess documentation. Nearly all of this oil (95%) was conveyed to Carthage in oilskins. While this might simply reflect the fact that amphoras were not generally produced in this district, the preponderance of oilskins may relate to Vol's proximity to Carthage. If, as suggested above, empty oilskins were returned to the oil mobilization entity from which they originated for re-use, there may have been comparatively strong incentive for the functionaries responsible for a district such as Vol that lay close to Carthage to employ containers of this kind, since it might have proven possible to re-use the same containers one or more times during the course of a single year.[184] The use of amphoras rather than oilskins for the transport of a small portion of the Vol oil may bear some relation to the time of the year during which the shipment in question was conveyed to Carthage. The containers in question, recorded in Nos. 7 *recto* and *verso*, represent the earliest reference to Vol oil in the documents. The only other containers recorded in the *ostraca* produced on or up through the date of these two documents appear to be shipments of *c.*200 *caprorenses centenaria levia* brought to Carthage by sea on February 3, February 15, and February 16. This raises the possibility that these containers were also delivered by sea, a conjecture that receives some support from the number of amphoras in the consignment, as this may perhaps correspond to two such shipments.[185] If so, this would support the assumption that oil transported by sea was pack-

184 We may gain some insight into how these containers were obtained from *Dig.* 13.7.43.1 (Scaevola), for which see n. 52.

185 If we assume that the 350 cwt. of weighed oil recorded in No. 7 *verso* represent oil brought to Carthage in Vol KN^T and that these containers, the 76 KN^T of unweighed Vol oil reported in this same document, and the 10 KN^T of unweighed Vol oil reported in No. 7 *recto* constituted a single consignment, then the

aged exclusively in amphoras, while also suggesting that the Vol district enjoyed access to the coast, such that it sometimes made sense to transport oil originating there to Carthage by ship.

Caprorenses, the other district that appears to have been located within Zeugitana, supplies the next largest amount of oil — nearly 1.4 times as much as the remaining two districts and just under one-thirteenth of the total. In the case of this district, 100% of the oil was conveyed to Carthage in amphoras. As noted above, this was presumably due to the fact that Caprorenses oil was brought down to the coast at Hippo Regius, where it was transferred to coasting vessels for the trip to Carthage. It is striking that while Caprorenses accounts for the lion's share of the oil attested in the early part of the period for which we possess documentation, oil from this district disappears from the *ostraca* after March 15, and perhaps as early as March 5. As will be discussed below (this section), this may well reflect political events in western Zeugitana during the period in question.

The relatively small amounts of oil associated with the Tebelbucitan qz and Macrinenses districts, respectively just 3.0% and 2.5% of the total, again seem compatible with the conjectural placement of these districts at a greater distance from Carthage. The data regarding the relative proportions of oilskins versus amphoras for these two districts show divergent patterns, with 84% of the Tebelbucitan qz oil in oilskins and just 14% of that from Macrinenses in containers of this kind. Given the small quantities of oil involved, however, the addition of another shipment of even modest size might alter these proportions to a considerable degree, and it is probably wise to forego any interpretation on this point. Unlike either Vol or Caprorenses, yet in common with *oRc*, it appears that consignments from both of these districts sometimes consisted of a mix of both oilskins and amphoras. While this may simply reflect the fact that these two districts embraced an area of complex geology, part of which supported amphora production and part of which did not, it may indicate the presence of a less uniform set of oil collection procedures than those in force in the Vol district.

The possibility that there are differences between, on the one hand, the stocks of oil raised in Tebelbucitan qz and Macrinenses and, on the other, those raised in Vol and Caprorenses suggests that Initiative 1 may have subsumed two distinct surcharges, one that involved circumscriptions in Byzacena and the other circumscriptions in Zeugitana. Interesting in this regard is the fact that a substantial amount of the oil from Caprorenses was conveyed to Carthage under adverse sailing conditions during February, then processed and transferred to some third location by early March, since this may be evidence that the supplement under which it was raised was akin to those listed under the *Règlement* that apparently sought to guarantee through the application of differential rates that substantial amounts of grain would be delivered to the ports of embarcation in time for the re-opening of navigation following the winter hiatus. If so, it follows that the oil mobilized under this initiative was intended for the support of an overseas supply initiative of some kind rather than one such as the *limitis nomine* or *naviculariorum nomine* of the *Règlement*.

We may now turn to Initiative 2, that associated with the *oRc* provenience/ownership designation. The large amount of oil collected under this initiative (the equivalent of the entire crop of *c.*1,500 ha of olive orchard) suggests that it should probably be identified either with the collection of rent in kind payments from tenants on imperial lands or the collection of tax in kind payments under the land tax. If we are correct in inferring that Initiative 1 involved the collection of oil raised under one or more surcharges to the land tax, and that Initiative 1 and Initiative 2 were related to one another in some way, then we should probably identify Initiative 2 with the second of these alternatives.

---

total number of containers comes to *c.*436, equal more or less to two of the shipments of *caproreses centenaria levia* recorded in the Subgroup 1A documents.

This inference receives support from both the timing of the shipments of *oRc* oil and the association of the *as* container type with this initiative. With regard to the first of these points, the documents at our disposal suggest that *oRc* oil reached Carthage in two extremely large shipments, one that arrived after March 15 and prior to April 7, probably on or shortly before the latter date, and the other at some point between April 8 and April 25. As previously noted, the legal sources indicate that one-third of the annual obligation under the land tax fell due on or about the first day of March. Since it would no doubt have taken several weeks to transport *species annonariae* to Carthage from the more distant parts of Zeugitana, the timing of these two shipments is compatible with the assumption that they represent large consignments of oil raised under the land tax that either immediately upon collection or within a short time of being collected were sent on their way to the port of embarcation. The practice of conveying oil raised under the land tax to the port of embarcation immediately upon collection may perhaps explain why the legal sources make no provision for its storage at the state storehouses located at the local collection centers. With regard to the *as*, as already noted, these containers would have permitted the efficient transport of large quantities of oil by means of the heavy wagons operated by the *cursus publicus*, and it seems likely that they were selected as a module for the packaging of oil with this purpose in mind.

If the identification of Initiative 2 with the land tax is correct, then we may speculate that the three letters in the *oRc* provenience/ownership designation stood for some form of the words *oleum*, *Roma/Romanum*, and *canon/canonicus*. Possibilities include *oleum Romae canonicum*, *olei (urbis) Romae canon*, and *olei Romanus canon*, with the second of these perhaps to be preferred. We might, alternatively, propose that the final letter stood for *conditum*, and venture the expansion *oleum Romae conditum*.[186] If any of these expansions is correct, then it would appear that this initiative was, in fact, the *canon olei*, with all of the oil registered under the *oRc* designation thus destined for export to Italy for free distribution and/or sale to the populace of Rome.

It is possible to venture two additional observations regarding this second oil mobilization initiative. First, if, as indicated by the previously cited law of 412, one-third of the annual obligation under the land tax was payable at the conclusion of the first trimester of the tax year, then the amount of *oRc* oil attested in the *ostraca* should represent approximately one-third of that received at Carthage under this initiative during the administrative year 373. Second, the fact that *oRc* oil arrived in what would appear to have been two very large shipments suggests that the tax circumscriptions embraced by the Carthage tax region, which presumably corresponded to part or all of Zeugitana, were organized into two sub-regions. If, as Reed has argued, the bulk of the itineraries listed in the late 3rd/early 4th c. *Itinerarium Antonini* (henceforth *Itinerary*) represent routes employed for the collection of foodstuffs raised under the *annona militaris*,[187] there may be some justification for interpreting this bipartite division in light of the routes that this document reports leading to Carthage. There are 4 such routes listed (fig. 12): the Tingi–Carthage route, which approached from the W along the coast via Hippo Regius, Thabraca, Hippo Diarrhytus, and Utica; the Hippo Regius–Carthage route, which approached from the WSW along the Bagradas Valley via Simittu, Bulla Regia, and Thuburbo Minus; the Cirta–Carthage route, which approached from the SW via Theveste, Altiburos, Musti, and Sicilibba; and the Alexandria–Carthage route, which approached from the E, passing through Vina and Maxula. The *Itinerary* lists various feeder routes connecting to them, making for convenient over-land access between Carthage and most parts of the province.

186 Another possible expansion is *oleum Romae Carthaginiense*. While this has the virtue of mirroring the *frumentum Carthaginiense* referred to in the heading to *CTh* 14.25, the presence of a c rather than a k in the final position weighs against this interpretation.

187 Reed 1978, 244-47. For use of the road system in Zeugitana and Byzacena by the state, see Salama 1987, 72-80.

The first of the four routes is unlikely to have been a major conduit for the shipment of oil, as it would probably have proven more economical to move any produce collected in the associated region by means of coasting vessels. One solution for how to distribute two collection districts over the remaining three routes is to assume that the routes from the SW and WSW served to connect Carthage with a district that embraced the area of prime olive cultivation centered on the valleys of the Bagradas river and the wadi Siliana, while that from the E connected it to a second district that comprised the Cap Bon peninsula and perhaps also the valley of the Wadi Miliana. A second, and perhaps more plausible, solution is to assume that the tax represented by Initiative 2, presumably the *canon olei*, was levied exclusively in the area of prime olive cultivation centered on the Bagradas river and the wadi Siliana, the two *oRc* shipments representing oil conveyed to Carthage over the WSW and the SW routes.

If we accept this second solution, then it becomes possible to interpret Initiative 1 as an effort aimed at extending the collection of tax oil to areas not covered under the *canon olei*. These would include a tax circumscription (or perhaps a group of circumscriptions?) situated either on the Cap Bon peninsula or in the valley of the wadi Miliana, for which the town of Vol served as the collection point, a tax circumscription in the extreme western reaches of the province (Caprorenses), and two tax circumscriptions perhaps located in north-central Byzacena, for which Carthage was more readily accessible than the ports of the eastern seaboard (Tebelbucitan qz and Macrinenses). The arrangement of collection areas as posited in this scheme is illustrated in fig. 2. We can only speculate as to why these four areas would have been chosen for this initiative. Caprorenses, and, perhaps also, Tebelbucitan qz and Macrinenses were remote areas from which it may have been more convenient to extract taxes in kind in the form of oil rather than grain, the former being less prone to spoilage and having a significantly higher value to weight ratio. Alternatively, rugged terrain, poor soils, and/or low rainfall may have meant that these districts were capable of producing only modest amounts of surplus grain, leaving the state little choice but to extract a larger than usual portion of surcharge taxes in the form of oil. That Vol constitutes something of a different case is suggested by its proximity to Carthage and the large size of its contribution. Here the most plausible inference is that it represented a grouping of tax circumscriptions which by virtue of their proximity to Carthage were capable of producing a sizeable oil surplus that could be conveyed to a port of embarcation at a relatively modest cost.

Before leaving the topic of the initiatives under which the oil referred to in the documents was mobilized, we may briefly consider the handling of the oil associated with the *fisci* provenience/ownership designation. As argued above, this is probably weighed oil, the possession of which had passed to the *fiscus*. While most of the oil processed at the weighing facility was apparently consigned to *navicularii* for export, it would appear that a significant portion was transferred to the *conditorium Zeugitanum* for storage. When this stored oil first appears in the documents on March 9 it consists of 167 *ag*, some or all of which were set aside during a period of intense processing activity that occurred during late February and/or early March. This quantity of containers is the equivalent of 501 *amphorae* or *c*.35,905 lbs. of oil, a fact which suggests that the intent of the functionaries charged with the disposition of *fisci* oil was to set aside an amount of oil equal either to 500 *amphorae* or 36,000 lbs. Groups of amphoras were added to this stock on at least three occasions. In the first two instances these consisted of KN^T, the first a group of 50 containers, and the second a group of 12 containers. These figures suggest that after the consignment of the initial group of containers the stock of *fisci* oil was built up by the addition of groups of amphoras corresponding to round numbers. In the third instance, a group of 184 *ψ* was added to the stock. Given the amount of oil held in this number of containers, *c*.73,600 lbs., this probably represented much or all of the oil weighed over a period of at least two days. While the size of this stock — which, by the end of the period for which we possess documentation, reached roughly 118,000 lbs., enough for the annual requirements of *c*.2,100 people — seems appropriate for a supply that served for the provision of oil rations to the various state workers stationed at Carthage, the fact that none of this oil was removed from the storage facility for a period of nearly two months suggests that it was more probably an emergency reserve intended for disbursal in the event of a local or regional food crisis.

The administrative context of oil-handling operations

We may draw on three categories of information in order to identify the specific administrative contexts within which the oil-handling operations reflected in the *ostraca* took place:

1) the identities of the various participants in the activities to which the documents refer;
2) the identities of the administrative departments which operated the facilities to which the documents refer;
3) the functions of the *ostraca*.

With regard to the identities of the participants in the activities to which the *ostraca* pertain, as discussed in Section 4, the inspection/reception operations to which the Group 1 *ostraca* pertain appear to have involved the participation of private shippers, inspectors who may have been *mensores olei*, and an official known as the *mensor olei Fori Karthaginiensis*. As discussed in Section 4, the weighing activities to which the Group 2 *ostraca* refer appear to have involved men termed *centenarii*, who were also probably *mensores olei*. Nothing is known about the authors of the Group 2 documents, save that there would seem to have been several men involved in the production of these *ostraca*, and that they had access to information pertaining to oil being housed at both the storage facility and the weighing facility.

So far as the other participants in these operations are concerned, it is evident that some understanding of the title *mensor olei* is essential if we are to more fully appreciate their rôles. As it turns out, the certain and possible references to *mensores olei* contained in the Group 1 and Group 2 *ostraca* constitute our only evidence for a class of functionaries bearing this title from anywhere in the Roman world. The *mensores olei* presumably carried out a set of functions similar to those undertaken by the *diffusores olearii* in 2nd-c. Baetica. They probably enjoyed an administrative status analogous to that of the *mensores frumenti/frumentarii* (grain measurers), a class of functionaries responsible for the inspection and measuring of state grain.[188] Inscriptions and legal sources document the presence of *corpora* of *mensores frumenti* at both Ostia/Portus and Rome during the middle and late empire, where they were responsible for the inspection and measuring of the state grain brought to Italy for the *annona urbis*. A legal source of the late 2nd/early 3rd c. distinguishes between the *corpus mensorum frumenti iuxta annonam urbis* (guild of grain-measurers attached to the office of the urban *annona*) and *mensores frumenti in provinciis* (grain-measurers in the provinces).[189] The former group presumably included the *mensores frumenti* at Ostia/Portus and Rome, who were closely affiliated with the *praefectura annonae*,[190] while the latter presumably included the functionaries who measured and certified the quality of the grain collected for the *annona* at the ports of embarcation in the main provinces which provided this *species annonaria*, such as Egypt, Africa Proconsularis, and Sardinia.

The *mensores olei* at Carthage and the *diffusores olearii ex Baetica* presumably served a function analogous to that of the *mensores frumenti in provinciis*, measuring and certifying the quality of state oil being exported from Zeugitana and Baetica, respectively. The presence at Carthage of the *praefectura annonae Africae*, however, raises the possibility that the former group may have had a status similar to that of *mensores frumenti iuxta annonam*, enjoying some

---

188 For the *mensores frumenti*, see Pavis d'Escurac 1976, 231-39; Hermansen 1981, 56-57, 65-66; Cébeillac-Gervasoni 1994, 50-52, 54-55; France and Hesnard 1995, 92-93.

189 *Dig.* 50.5.10.1 (Paulus).

190 For the affiliation between the *corpus* of *mensores frumenti* at Ostia and the *praefectura annonae*, see Pavis d'Escurac 1976, 238-39; Cébeillac-Gervasoni 1994, 54-55.

sort of formal association with this branch of the state bureaucracy. They may also have enjoyed recognition as a *corpus*, although there is no evidence on this score.[191] *Centenarius* may simply have been a job title held by those members of the group who were directly involved in weighing operations.[192] The apparent prominence of the Felix named in the Subgroup 1A *verso* documents in the oil weighing operations documented in the Group 2 *ostraca* raises the possibility that the title *mensor olei Fori Karthaginiensis* was reserved for the chief officer or leading member of the group.

With regard to the identities of the entities that operated the facilities referred to in the documents, the fact that the *conditorium Zeugitanum* served for the storage of unweighed oil raised under the land tax that had yet to be consigned to the *fiscus* suggests that it was under the control of the provincial administration of Zeugitana rather than under the control of either the provincial branch of the *fiscus* or the *praefectura annonae Africae*. This inference is compatible with the evidence of the textual sources, which, as discussed in Section 3, indicate that provincial governors in Africa retained control of tax grain after its arrival at the ports of embarcation. That the weighing facility was operated by the same entity as that which controlled the storage facility may be indicated by the fact that newly arrived consignments of oil containers were sometimes placed in temporary storage there before being transferred to the *conditorium Zeugitanum* for long-term storage.

If we turn now to the functions of the *ostraca*, it is evident that while the Subgroup 1A *recto* documents and the single document of Subgroup 1B were working notes, the Subgroup 1A *verso* documents were formal records of a transaction between the shippers and the organization to which the inspectors and receivers belonged, presumably the organization of the *mensores olei*. The fact that these were dated to the year may indicate that they retained their significance beyond the end of the administrative year to which they pertained. Functionaries with access to the set of Group 1 *ostraca* would have been able to keep track of the number of oil containers delivered to Carthage by ship and the numbers of these accepted and rejected by date, provenience/ownership designation, container type, shipper, and functionary responsible for their reception. If similar documents were produced for consignments of oil conveyed to Carthage over land, functionaries with access to both series of records, by comparing these with the registers of tax payments entered into the municipal records by *tabularii* and the annual accounts produced by the *susceptores* and *praepositi horreorum*,[193] would have been able to track the mobilization of the oil raised under the two initiatives to which the documents refer through to the port of embarcation, detecting any excessive waste and/or misappropriation.[194]

With regard to the Group 2 *ostraca*, the extensive use of abbreviations and the absence of any indication of either the name or title of the functionary responsible for their compilation suggests that these were records intended for use within a single administrative department. That the dates on these documents include no reference to the year suggests that they ceased to be of significance at the close of the administrative year in which they were produced, if not earlier. While the frequency with which they were drawn up remains unclear, it seems likely they were composed less frequently than on a daily basis, perhaps on each day on which oil weighing operations took place.

---

191 On the prominence of *corpora* at Carthage, in contrast with the remainder of Africa, see Hurst 1994, 66.

192 For the distinct job titles within the *corpus* of *mensores frumenti* at Ostia, see Meiggs 1960, 282; Pavis d'Escurac 1976, 235-36; Hermansen 1981, 56-57.

193 See *CTh* 12.6.24 (397), addressed to the Senate and people, for the obligation of *susceptores* and *praepositi horreorum* to submit annual accounts of their activities.

194 See *CTh* 12.6.26 (400), addressed to the *vicarius urbis Romae*, for the investigation of irregularities in the amount of wine consigned by *susceptores vini* (wine collectors).

The Subgroup 2A and 2B *ostraca* contain three different items of information that may have been of administrative significance: the estimate for the total weight of oil, the figure for the sum of weighed oil, and the weight of oil figures for individual oil weighers. That the first of these figures was of interest is self-evident, as the compilers of these documents went through a set of complex calculations in order to derive it. This figure must have served to enable administrators to know the approximate amount of oil present at the two facilities on a given day. That the figure for the sum of weighed oil was significant in and of itself (and was not calculated solely for the purpose of deriving the figure reported in the Type 4 entry under the *inpletu* heading) is indicated by the fact that, as discussed in Appendix 4, the latter figure more often than not was based not on the figure for the sum of weighed oil, but rather on the number of oil containers processed on that day, the figure for the sum of weighed oil then sometimes being adjusted to bring it into line with this value. The figure for the sum of weighed oil was thus calculated even in instances in which it did not serve as the basis for the Type 4 entry figure, and was viewed as significant enough to warrant adjustment. The purpose of this figure must have been to allow administrators to determine how much oil had been processed either on a given day or over some longer period of time.

With regard to the weight of oil figures for individual oil weighers, that these represented significant information in and of themselves and did not serve merely to permit the derivation of the figure for the sum of weighed oil is indicated by the fact that in the two cases in which men with the same *cognomen* appear in the same document (No. 10: Victor a Serve, Victor a Nobis; No. 13: Felix ab Ucubi, Felix ab ....c) care was taken to distinguish them from one another by indicating their place of origin. The clear implication of this practice is that these figures were administratively relevant, credit for the amount of oil in question being attributed to each weigher. The practice of adjusting the figures for the sum of weighed oil to bring them into line with the figure in the Type 4 entry noted above also underscores the significance of these figures, since, had they served solely for the purpose of deriving the figures for the sum of weighed oil, overriding them in this fashion would have rendered them meaningless. Whether the information contained in these figures was important on a document by document basis or over some longer interval remains unclear. The fact that men with the same two *cognomina* as those noted above are also identified by their place of origin in other documents in which they are the only weigher with this name (No. 7: Victor Mercur(ialis); No. 11: Victor Utumm(ensis)) suggests that it was important to distinguish men with the same name over a period of time embracing two or more such documents. By the same token, however, the fact that in yet other instances men with these same two *cognomina* receive no such designation (Victor: No. 14; Felix: No. 7 *recto*, No. 9, No. 18), would seem to suggest that the information contained in these entries was relevant on a document by document basis.

Also worth noting with respect to the function of the Group 2 documents is the fact that the provenience/ownership designations are omitted for the entries under the *fieri in conditZ* heading in Nos. 9 and 11, since this would seem to indicate that the documents in this group were not used to determine the amount of unprocessed oil on hand from each of the various provenience/ownership designations. It is unclear, in any case, what usefulness such information would have had, as it would not have enabled administrators to calculate the total contribution made by any of these. While this observation suggests that the principal reason for compiling the list of weighed oil and oil container entries in Element 3 was to permit the derivation of the estimate for the total weight of oil, we should not overlook the possibility that the functionaries in charge of processing operations made use of the entries reporting the numbers of containers of unweighed oil for planning purposes.

On the basis of these considerations we may now attempt to identify the specific administrative contexts within which the operations recorded in the *ostraca* took place. The Group 1 *ostraca* appear to have been produced by the *mensores olei*, a group (perhaps a *corpus*) of functionaries perhaps with some more or less formal connection to the *praefectura annonae*

Africae. The *mensores olei* were responsible for inspecting shipments of state oil raised under one or more supplements to the land tax and perhaps also the *canon olei* that were brought to Carthage by shippers, perhaps *navicularii*, working either under contract or within the context of a *munus*. They then supervised the consigning of this oil at a storehouse known as the *conditorium Zeugitanum* probably operated by the provincial administration. The Group 1 *recto* documents would have permitted the *mensores olei* and/or functionaries attached to the provincial administration to provide a full accounting of the tax oil that had been delivered to Carthage by sea, or, if similar documents were produced for over land shipments, a full accounting of the oil conveyed to Carthage under both initiatives.

The specific administrative context within which the Group 2 documents were produced is somewhat less clear. Oil raised under the *canon olei* and one or more supplements to the land tax was brought to Carthage both over land and by sea, with some consigned to the *conditorium Zeugitanum* and some to a special weighing facility. Men termed *centenarii*, who were presumably *mensores olei*, weighed the oil consigned to the latter facility, transferring some or all of it to amphoras in the process, with the possession of the oil passing to the fisc upon completion of the operation. The bulk of the weighed oil was probably handed over directly to *navicularii* for export to Italy, while a minor portion was consigned to the *conditorium Zeugitanum* for long-term storage as an emergency food reserve.

The weight of oil figures for individual oil weighers in the Group 2 documents probably served to determine the amount of reimbursement due to the *centenarii* for their labor, with payments perhaps being tendered on a day by day basis rather than over some longer interval of time. The sum of weighed oil figures was probably employed to determine the amount of oil weighed and/or consigned to the fisc by the province over the course of the administrative year. These figures presumably represented the principal means whereby it could be established whether or not the province had met the oil obligation specified in its *delegatio* for the two or more taxes in question. That these figures were used for this purpose appears problematic, however, if we assume that Macrinenses and/or Tebelbucitan qz lay within Byzacena. There would seem to be two solutions: either all 4 of the toponymic provenience/ownership designations lay, in fact, in Zeugitana, or certain of the surcharges to the land tax, even though they included circumscriptions located in Byzacena, were subsumed under the *delegatio* prepared for Zeugitana. The fact that a surcharge directed at Byzacena was included in the *Règlement* can perhaps be taken as evidence in support of the latter alternative. The use to which the estimate for the total amount of oil was put remains somewhat uncertain. As it includes both unweighed oil still apparently in the possession of the province that was due for transfer to the fisc and weighed oil that had already been transferred to the fisc, it would appear to represent an estimate for the total amount of oil on hand at the two facilities that was potentially at the disposal of the fisc. This might perhaps have proved useful information for planning the allocation of state shipping. Further, by taking into account the sum of figures of weighed oil from previous dates (and subtracting the amount of *fisci* oil from the estimate) it would have been possible to judge the extent to which the province was positioned to fulfill its obligations under its *delegatio*, providing advance warning of any impending shortfall.

Some or all of this information might have been of interest either to provincial authorities and/or to the fisc, and it may well be that these records were produced by the group of the *mensores olei*, with the relevant information summarized and supplied to the appropriate administrative department. The span of dates on the Group 2 documents, which runs from February 16 to June 6, raises the possibility that these may have been discarded following an accounting procedure undertaken half-way through an 8 month administrative year that ran from early February to early October. If the assumption that both the Group 1 and Group 2 *ostraca* were produced by the group of the *mensores olei* is correct, then it seems likely that both series were housed in a *tabularium* (archive) located within a set of administrative offices that this group maintained. As discussed below, this may well have been located on the Ilôt de l'Amirauté.

As previously noted, a law of 365 required the *praefectura annonae Africae* and the *officium urbanum* to account for the amounts of *species annonariae transmissum* (passed on?) and *pervectum* (delivered?). The *praefectura annonae Africae* may well have employed the sum of weighed oil figures in the Group 2 documents to prepare its accounting for the oil collected under the two or more taxes represented. Interesting in this regard is the practice of increasing the cwt. values in some of these figures to bring them into line with the number of KN^T processed. This would seem to suggest that for some higher accounting purpose (quite possibly the derivation of the *oleum transmissum* statistic by the *praefectura annonae Africae*), the practice was to multiply the number of containers of processed oil by a standard weight value. The *praefectura annonae* would presumably have employed this method at Ostia/Portus to derive its accounting for the amount of *oleum pervectum*, thereby obviating the need to engage any *mensores olei* at this terminus of the transport route.[195] This technique was presumably regarded as permissible due to the high degree of standardization in the capacities of the amphoras employed for the bottling African oil. In the case of the KN^T, data derived in Appendix 4 suggest that values for effective capacity may have fallen in the 95-100% range for individual containers and in the 98-99% range for groups of these containers. Dressel 20 amphoras, to judge from the *corpus* of gamma *titulus* components, displayed a far greater range of values, and it may be for this reason that the weighing/bottling of Baetican oil came to involve the production of the complex *titulus pictus* that appears on this class of amphora.[196] Indeed, it may be due to the relatively low level of standardization associated with the Dressel 20 amphora that the state adopted the practice of weighing oil rather than measuring it by volume as part of the bottling process.[197]

---

195 Perhaps worth noting in this regard, however, is the fact that the *Not.Dig.Occ.* 4.16 lists under the administrative jurisdiction of the *praefectus urbi* a post termed *centenarius Portus* (*centenarius* for Portus). While it cannot be excluded that in this instance the term *centenarius* refers to the salary grade of this official, it would be the only case of this kind in the *Notitia Dignitatum*, and it may be that the duties of this official were somehow concerned with the handling of state oil. Jones 1964, 691 suggested that the *centenarius Portus* was the assistant to the *comes Portus*. The fact that this post is listed immediately after that of *curator horreorum Galbanorum* (overseer of the Horrea Galbana), the official in charge of the warehouse complex in the Emporium district where fiscal goods were stored, may be seen as adding weight to the conjecture that it was in some way concerned with the handling of state oil. Compare in this regard the pairing in *Not.Dig.Occ.* 4.9-10 of the *rationalis vinorum* and the *tribunus fori suarii*, the officials who presumably supervised the disposition of the wine and pork brought to Rome under the *canon vinarius* and *canon suarius*. If so, he may have stood in a relationship to the *praefectus annonae* analogous to that which prevailed between the *praefectus annonae Africae* and the *mensor olei Fori Karthaginiensis*.

196 African oil amphoras very rarely bear *tituli*, and when they do they do not resemble the *titulus* on the Dressel 20 amphora. See Blázquez Martínez *et al.* 1994, 126 no. 220, for a *titulus* on what may be an *Africano* 1/Keay 3 amphora from a 2nd-c. context at Monte Testaccio, and Peña (forthcoming) no. 48 (inv. #5089) for a *titulus* on an *Africano* 2/Keay 7 amphora manufactured in a fabric from the Leptiminus area (and quite possibly a container for fish products) that was recovered in a context of early 4th-c. date on the Palatine Hill.

197 The oil rations issued to recipients at Rome during this period may, however, have been measured in terms of volume. Evidence for this are the theta *titulus* components on a small number of Dressel 20 amphoras from Monte Testaccio. Rodríguez-Almeida 1989a, 30 argues that these record the amount of oil left in the container as this was measured out by functionaries attached to the *praefectura annonae*. Since the unit referred to in these is the *hemina*, an amount equal to one half of a *sextarius*, it appears that the state measured the oil that it distributed to the inhabitants of Rome during at least parts of the 2nd/3rd c. in terms of volume. In later periods the oil rations provided to soldiers were measured sometimes by weight and sometimes by volume. For weight, see *P.Beatty Panop.* 2.245-249, of

The calendar of operations

The fact that both the Subgroup 2A and 2B *ostraca* are titled *ad Octobrem* suggests that the operations referred to in these documents were probably tied to the calendar for state shipping which, as noted in Section 3, a law of 380 established to run from April 13 to October 15, with April 1 and October 1 as the beginning and ending dates for the loading of cargoes. It cannot be excluded, however, that this heading refers to the tax year, which, as discussed in Section 3, appears to have concluded on November 1 in Africa. While it is impossible to reconstruct the rhythm of oil processing operations due to the fragmentary nature of the series of Group 2 *ostraca* at our disposal, the sum of weighed oil figures in these documents suggest that there were periods of intensive weighing activity at the beginning of the series (late February/early March) and again at its end (late May/early June), corresponding to the Subgroup 2A and 2C documents, respectively, with a slack period in the middle, corresponding to the Subgroup 2B documents. While it might be argued that the beginning of operations was tied to the calendar for oil production, in which the months of December and January are devoted to pressing, there need have been no connection of this kind. There were presumably storage facilities both at the local collection centers and at the agricultural establishments where oil was produced, and, since oil can be stored for up to three years without spoiling, there would have been no necessity to collect newly pressed oil at the earliest possible opportunity. More convincing is the assumption that the patterning apparent in the calendar of operations reflects variation in the availability of state shipping. The period of intensive oil weighing activity at the beginning of the series can best be explained as reflecting an effort to process and hand over to the *praefectura annonae Africae* as large a quantity of oil as could be mustered so that this could be consigned to *navicularii* for export at the earliest moment that sailing conditions permitted.[198] That the transfer of this oil occurred at least three weeks prior to the April 1 opening date for the loading of fiscal cargoes is a point of interest, although not necessarily a problem for this interpretation, since, as noted in Section 3, there is reason to suspect that in the years prior to 380 the state compelled *navicularii* to undertake sailings earlier in the year.

The dropoff in the rate at which oil was processed over the next two and a half months may well reflect a shortage of state shipping in the period following this early season sailing. Of particular interest in this regard is the handling of the two shipments of *oRc* oil upon their arrival at Carthage. As reconstructed in Section 4, all but *c.*21,000 lbs. of this oil was placed in storage at the *conditorium Zeugitanum*, where it remained through to the end of the period for which we possess documentation. Thus, while the calendar for the collection of the land tax/*canon olei* would have made it possible to move large quantities of tax oil down to the ports of embarcation by the middle of April, in the instance for which we possess documentation there appears to have been little effort on the part of the provincial authorities and the *praefectura annonae Africae* to see that this oil was readied for export in the weeks subsequent to its arrival. This practice, if typical of oil mobilization operations, may explain why in 397 the state required that one-third of the *urbanus canon* be shipped at the opening of the sailing season, and also perhaps why there was a shortage of state oil in Rome during 384. The fact that these functionaries did not elect to build up a large backlog of processed oil during this slack period may be taken as evidence either that there was no convenient means for storing substantial amounts of weighed oil, or for a lack of amphoras suitable for use as secondary

---

Diocletianic date; *CTh* 8.4.17 (389) issued to the *praefectus praetorio* of Oriens; also Marichal 1992, 103-4, where deliveries of unnamed foodstuffs reckoned in terms of pounds rather than volumetric measurements in two of the 3rd-c. Golas *ostraca* (nos. 75 and 88) are interpreted as relating to consignments of oil. For volume, see *P.Oxy.* 1920 and 2046, both dating to the 6th c.

198 Interesting in this regard is the fact that No. 4 *verso*, compiled on March 4, bears a postconsular date. This suggests that knowledge of the consuls for that year had yet to reach administrators at Carthage, hence that no ship sailing from Portus since early January had made port there by early March.

containers.[199] The apparent return to more intensive levels of oil processing by late May/early June may reflect an increase in the availability of amphoras or an increase in the amount of available shipping. While in the latter case this might be thought to be connected with the return to Carthage of the ships involved in the late February/early March sailing, this seems unlikely, as African *navicularii* were apparently expected to undertake only one voyage on the behalf of the state every two years.[200]

While it is unclear whether the effort to process and export a large amount of oil during late February/early March reflects the pressure to replenish the stock of oil in the state storehouses at Rome or some peculiar set of circumstances, a case can be built in favor of the latter alternative. This is grounded in the observation that there may have been some connection between this activity and the revolt of Firmus, an uprising in the western part of the Diocese of Africa that probably lasted from 372 to 374 or 375.[201] According to Zosimus, an important contributing factor to the spread of the revolt was the adoption of more vigorous procedures for the collection of taxes.[202] It seems possible, on the one hand, that one or both of the oil collection initiatives referred to in the documents constituted part of the offending fiscal policy. On the other, preoccupation on the part of functionaries in the office of the *proconsul Africae* and/or the *praefectura annonae Africae* with regard to the security of the urban food supply as the revolt spread eastward from Mauretania during the winter of 372/373 may have resulted in an effort to collect, process, and dispatch to Italy as much oil and grain as possible from the threatened districts as soon as weather conditions permitted. The fact that coasting vessels, quite possibly sailing from Hippo Regius, were engaged in the transport of oil to Carthage in early to mid February, well outside the period for safe navigation, is compatible with such a suggestion. That such concerns were not ungrounded may be reflected by the fact that Caprorenses oil disappears from the documents no later than March 15. An inscription from Calama, located immediately to the north of the Montes Caprarienses, indicates that the *ordo* of that town recognized Firmus as emperor at some point during 373.[203] According to Ammianus Marcellinus, the Montes Caprarienses were the scene of skirmishing between forces allied to the cause of Firmus and troops sent out under the command of Theodosius for the purpose of crushing the rebellion either during or shortly after February of 374.[204] It thus appears all but certain that tax collection operations were interrupted in western Zeugitana at some point during 373, recommencing no earlier than the spring of 374, and the lack of any reference to Caprorenses oil in the Ilôt de l'Amirauté *ostraca* after the middle of March may well be a reflection of this development.

The location and physical nature of the oil-handling facilities

We can say little of substance regarding either the location or the physical nature of either

199 In recent years pottery production has been carried out year-round at both Nabeul and Moknine on the eastern seaboard of Tunisia. This probably reflects a recent intensification of operations, however, and at the latter town operations were traditionally concentrated during the summer months in order to coincide with the slack period in the agricultural cycle; see Peacock 1982, 38-39. Two leases for the rental of pottery workshops from Oxyrhynchus dating to the 3rd c. indicate that in this instance the firing of amphoras was deferred until the period extending from May to August; see Cockle 1981, 92-94. Perhaps worth noting in this connection is the fact that the largest of the container types identified as an amphora, the ψ, appears in the documents beginning only at the end of April.

200 *CTh* 13.5.26 (396), issued to the *praefectus praetorio Italiae et Africae*.

201 On the chronology and geography of the revolt of Firmus, see *RE* 6.2 col. 2383-84 s.v. Firmus 8; *PLRE* 340 Firmus 3. I have been unable to consult Gsell 1902.

202 *Zos.* 4.16.3.

203 *CIL* VIII 5338.

204 29.5.31, 34, 37.

the *conditorium Zeugitanum* or the weighing facility on the basis of the information contained in the documents. The fact that in at least two instances large numbers of containers of unweighed oil appear to have been placed in temporary storage at the weighing facility, then shifted to the *conditorium Zeugitanum* unprocessed for storage, suggests that the two facilities were probably located close to one another, and may perhaps have inter-communicated. The fact that the *conditorium Zeugitanum* was used for the long-term storage of tax oil suggests that it was both covered and enclosed. It cannot have been a small structure, as it was capable of housing a large number of oil containers, at least 184 *ψ*, 167 *ag*, 2,844 *as a ƀ*, 757 *as*, and 1,644 *KN*^{T}. While the standard order in which entries appear under the *fieri inconditZ* heading in Nos. 9, 14, 16, and 18 may well reflect the disposition of groups of oil containers within the *conditorium Zeugitanum*, suggesting some internal division of the storage space, it is impossible to advance from this observation to any useful inferences regarding this facility's specific configuration. It presumably lay at no great distance from harbor facilities, and it must also have been possible for sizeable trains of wagons and pack animals either to approach or to enter it.

Even less can be said about the weighing facility. The fact that containers of unprocessed oil were transferred from this facility to the *conditorium Zeugitanum* suggests that, perhaps in contrast with the facilities at which oil was weighed in Baetica, it was not a *portus* in the legal sense — that is, an enclosed facility that served for the clearing of goods across a customs boundary. It must have been capable of holding at least 27 *as a ƀ* and 161 *as*, if only on a temporary basis, and may have been large enough to accommodate as many as 13 balances in simultaneous use. It also presumably had space to accommodate large numbers of primary containers that had been emptied of their contents and large numbers of amphoras awaiting use as secondary containers. As with the *conditorium Zeugitanum*, it presumably lay at no great distance from harbor facilities, and it must also have been possible for it either to be approached or to be entered by trains of wagons and pack animals.

The so-called *Aula dei Mensores/Horrea dei Mensores* complex at Ostia may provide us with a good idea of the various structures likely to have been associated with the weighing facility.[205] This complex, situated in the NW quarter of the town (*Regio* I. *Insula* XIX.2-4), was the seat of the *corpus* of the *mensores frumenti*, as is demonstrated by the presence there both of a dedication to the *patronus* of the *corpus* and of a mosaic depicting a *mensor frumenti* at work. It was presumably the location where the state grain that was off-loaded at Ostia was measured in preparation for transfer to river-boats for transport up the Tiber to Rome. The location of the complex would have provided convenient access both to the port facilities along the Tiber and to *horrea* that might have served for the storage of grain. The original phase of its construction appears to date to the early 2nd c., with evidence for restructuring during the 3rd c. The complex consists of a trapezoidal enclosure encompassing a small prostyle temple that presumably served for the organization's religious observances, a sizeable hall that served as the group's *schola* or meeting place, and rows of work rooms ranged around an oblong courtyard. Some of these last measure 12 m across, and presumably served for the measuring of grain. Others may have served for its temporary storage. An unusually large doorway provided access to the complex, while an interior ramp led to a second storey. While the weighing process for oil presumably had requirements that were substantially different from those associated with the measuring of grain (e.g., it may well have required substantially less roofed space, as there was less need to protect oil from exposure to moisture), we may nonetheless imagine that the oil weighing facility at Carthage was similarly located with respect to the city's port facilities and *horrea*, and may have contained both a temple and a *schola* in addition to spaces suitable for the weighing and temporary storage of oil.

---

205 For this complex, see Rickman 1971, 70; Pavolini 1983, 122-23; Cébeillac-Gervasoni 1994, 50.

On the basis of these observations we may now consider whether it is possible to identify the *conditorium Zeugitanum* and the weighing facility with specific known structures. As noted above, logical considerations suggest that both facilities probably lay close to one another in a part of the city that enjoyed ready access to harbor facilities. Further, given the functions of the two facilities, we would expect that the *conditorium Zeugitanum* and perhaps also the weighing facility had a plan resembling that of a storage building, quite possibly that of a set of *horrea*. None of the late imperial structures documented to date in the vicinity of the Rectangular and Circular Harbors has the appearance of a storage building,[206] and, basing our evaluation solely on the two expectations given here, we can point to no set of remains that seems a plausible candidate for either of the two facilities.

The fact that the *ostraca* that refer to the two facilities were recovered on the Ilôt de l'Amirauté should lead us to consider, however, whether either or both were not located there. As a result of Hurst's excavations on the Ilôt de l'Amirauté, we now enjoy a reasonably detailed picture of its development over the course of the middle and late empire. At some point during the second half of the 2nd c., or perhaps a little later, the island was the scene of an ambitious architectural redevelopment.[207] This included the construction around the island's perimeter of an annular portico, with both an inward-facing and an outward-facing colonnade, and with a monumental entrance at the point where the causeway from the mainland provided access to the island, the reconstruction of the small rectangular temple at the center of the island, and the construction of a small circular building, perhaps to be reconstructed as an open-sided *tholos* on a high podium, immediately to the south of the temple. Hurst connects this monumentalization of the island with the organization in 186 of the *Classis Commodiana* (fleet of Commodus), a formally constituted fleet charged with the transport to Italy of African grain.[208] While there is considerable structural evidence for modifications to these buildings during the period *c.*200-450, the remains are hard to date and, due to their fragmentary nature, difficult to interpret.[209] It would appear, however, that at some point during this period the external colonnade was interrupted at several points by cross walls, perhaps for the construction of enclosed rooms, while a wall was constructed around the edge of the interior colonnade immediately inside the line of columns, apparently creating a pair of closed semi-annular spaces, perhaps subdivided by cross walls. In addition, a small set of rooms was constructed, perhaps in mudbrick, in the northeast part of the island, no more than *c.*10 m from the probable find-spot of the *ostraca*.

If we assume that the various constructions belonging to this last period were already in place by 373, it is possible to assign all of the activities associated with the *conditorium Zeugitanum* and the weighing facility to the Ilôt de l'Amirauté in a reasonably satisfactory manner. The *conditorium Zeugitanum* may correspond to the pair of semi-annular rooms created by the construction of the wall inside the inner colonnade of the portico. The weighing facility, in turn, may correspond to the area enclosed by the portico, with the open court serving for weighing operations, the temporary storage of both empty and full oil containers, and the unloading of wagons and draft animals, while the structures in the northeast area would have housed the offices of the organization of the *mensores olei*, within which were stored the records pertaining to its activities.[210] The small temple may have served for the religious

---

206 The vaulted substructures preserved in the area immediately to the north of the Rectangular Harbor, sometimes identified as the remains of late imperial *horrea*, are more likely to belong to the substructures of a temple; see Hurst 1994, 113.

207 Hurst 1977, 242-45; 1979, 33-37.

208 Hurst 1979, 46-7.

209 Hurst 1979, 37-39.

210 See also Hurst 1979, 47 for the possibility that the *mensores olei* had their offices on the Ilôt de l'Amirauté.

observances of the group, and the small round building perhaps for its *schola*.[211] With regard to the accessibility of the Ilôt de l'Amirauté, the causeway connecting it with the mainland, which was supported on piers *c*.12-13 m wide, would have been wide enough to accommodate heavy wagons, while the open court at the center of the island could have held large numbers of draft animals or wagons. At the same time, the fact that there was but one means of access to the Ilôt de l'Amirauté would have rendered any storage facilities located there highly secure. Further, it need hardly be remarked that any facilities on the island would have enjoyed ready access to ships moored in the Circular Harbor. Perhaps the single difficulty with this interpretation is the fact that the distance between the inner faces of the central piers of the portico's monumental entrance is just *c*.2.5 m, more than adequate for draft animals burdened with a pair of oilskins or amphoras, but perhaps insufficient for heavy wagons.

Whether the set of late 4th-c. structures on the Ilôt de l'Amirauté should be identified as the *Forum Karthaginiense* alluded to in the title of the presumed author of the Group 1 *verso* documents, rather than as the main civic forum of the city (probably located between *kardines* XII and XIII East and the *decumanus maximus* and *decumanus* I South), remains unclear. Hurst has argued in favor of this interpretation,[212] which has much in its favor the fact that, according to Procopius, Justinian provided for the rebuilding of colonnades on both sides of a structure that he refers to as ἡ μαρίτιμος ἀγορὰ (the seaside market).[213] Augustine twice refers to a *platea maritima* (seaside court), which may perhaps have been this same facility.[214]

Broader implications of the *ostraca*

While the *ostraca* that are the focus of this study reveal a wealth of information regarding specific aspects of oil handling operations at Carthage, our ability to employ this information to draw broader inferences regarding the mobilization of state oil in Zeugitana and Africa is circumscribed by 4 circumstances:

1) the partial nature of the data (i.e., the fact that both groups of documents represent an undefinable portion of the total amount of oil received and processed at the two facilities during the course of the year 373);
2) the possibility that certain of the operations represented in the documents were extraordinary, undertaken either as part of a possibly short-lived initiative for the more vigorous collection of taxes or (perhaps more likely) as a response to the revolt of Firmus;
3) the possibility that there were other such oil handling facilities at Carthage, the activities of which are not reflected in the *ostraca*;
4) the lack of evidence regarding the specific territory for which Carthage served as the regional collection center/port of embarcation for tax oil, and regarding the number of other such centers that existed both in the province and in the diocese.

Despite the limitations that these factors impose, it is nonetheless possible to draw several inferences regarding more general aspects of oil mobilization operations in Zeugitana.

While the *ostraca* at our disposal do not allow us to formulate an accurate estimate for the total amount of oil that passed through the weighing facility and the storage facility in the course of the year 373, they do provide some basis for inferring the general scale of oil handling operations at these two facilities. The analysis of the *ostraca* presented above suggests that the minimum oil inputs at the two facilities over the period for which we possess documen-

211 For the identification of a large room with a mosaic pavement in a structure excavated on the NE side of the Circular Harbor as the *schola* of a *corpus* of cloth-workers connected with the Carthage *gynaeceum*, see Hurst 1994, 65-6, 69-70.

212 Hurst 1979, 47; 1994, 111. For the debate regarding this identification, see Hurst 1994, 114-15.

213 *De aedif.* 6.5.10.

214 *Retract.* 2.58; *Civ. dei* 16.8.

tation came to just under 1,337,000 lbs. (*c.*437,000 kg/481,000 l). Since the documents represent what may be no more than spotty coverage for a 4-month period within what would appear to have been an 8-month administrative year, there is good reason to assume that the actual amount of inputs in 373 came to substantially more than this. In particular, the interpretation of the *oRc* designation suggests that the quantity of oil indicated in the documents may represent only one-third of the amount taken in under Initiative 2 over the course of the administrative year. Since this designation accounts for nearly 527,000 lbs. of oil, we may be justified in suggesting a figure of *c.*1,580,000 lbs. for the total amount mobilized under this initiative, yielding a minimum of *c.*2,390,000 lbs. (*c.*782,000 kg/860,000 l) of oil as an estimate for minimum amount of inputs for the year 373. We have no similar basis for estimating the likely additional inputs of oil under Initiative 1. Here, the best that can be done is to extrapolate on the basis of the figures at hand, employing a figure for mean daily inputs for the period for which we possess documentation and then extending it over the entire administrative year. If we combine the inputs of oil associated with the 4 toponymic provenience/ownership designations for the 91-day period from February 4 to May 6, and then divide by the number of days, we obtain a figure of 3,937 lbs. of oil per day. While a disproportionate amount of the oil raised under Initiative 1 may have been collected during the first trimester of the tax year, this figure may nonetheless represent a substantial under-estimate. First, a large portion of the inputs for which the provenience/ownership designation is unknown probably consisted of oil mobilized under this initiative. Second, any missing Group 2 documents probably listed groups of containers with one of these designations that were processed, the oil that they contained subsequently being transferred to some third location. If, however, we extend this figure over the remainder of the period from May 6 to October 1, the estimated amount of oil inputs under Initiative 1 comes to slightly more than 940,000 lbs. A conservative estimate for the total amount of oil received at the two facilities between February and October, 373 thus comes to *c.*2,521,000 lbs. (*c.*824,000 kg/907,000 l), or the equivalent of the total produce of *c.*7,500 ha of olive orchard.

It remains difficult to specify the extent of the territories within which this oil was mobilized. If the second of the two interpretations offered above regarding the division of the oil raised under Initiative 2 into two different shipments is correct, however, then it appears likely that the *oRc* oil registered at Carthage represented all of that raised in Zeugitana under the *canon olei*. The oil registered there under Initiative 1 might likewise represent all of that collected in Zeugitana and perhaps some neighboring parts of Byzacena under one or perhaps two supplements to the regular land tax that were also concerned with the mobilization of oil for export.

The total amount of oil that may have passed through the two facilities in the course of the year would have been enough to provide for the annual oil requirements of *c.*45,000 people, or the equivalent of *c.*4.5-5.3% of the population of Rome, assuming a figure of *c.*850,000-1,000,000 individuals.[215] If we assume that the number of people qualified for the oil dole at Rome was the same as that entitled to receive state bread, roughly 100,000-200,000, and that each of these was entitled to an amount of oil equal to a soldier's annual ration in 6th-c. Egypt, that is, 54-68 lbs. (17.7-22.2 kg/19.4-24.5 l), then this amount would have been equal to *c.*18.4-46.3% of the oil distributed under this program. It is clear, however, that not all of the oil received at the two facilities could have been placed at the disposal of the *praefectura annonae* for distribution to the populace of the *urbs*. First, as emerges from the analysis of the weight of oil figures for individual oil weighers, it would appear that *c.*2.5% of the oil processed at the

---

215 The population figure given here is that developed for the early 1st c. in Morley 1996, 33-39. For the population of Rome during the 4th-5th c., see Hodges and Whitehouse 1983, 48-52; Barnish 1987, 160-64. These studies conclude that the city's population underwent substantial contraction from its 1st-c. levels only during the late 4th or 5th c.

weighing facility was set aside as a allowance of some sort, perhaps either for the *navicularii* or for the group of *mensores olei*. The amount of processed oil available for distribution would have been further reduced by wastage. While a law of 414 makes it clear that *navicularii* engaged on the Africa to Portus run were permitted to lose a set percentage of their cargo, the precise amount is not specified.[216] The Group 1 *ostraca* suggest, however, that on coasting voyages to Carthage, perhaps from Hippo Regius, a wastage rate of 4% was allowed, and we might not be far wrong if we assumed a similar or slightly higher figure for the Carthage to Portus run. Finally, it is unclear what was done with the oil associated with the *fisci* designation that was placed in storage at the *conditorium Zeugitanum*. As noted above, this oil, roughly one-tenth of the total for which we possess documentation, may have been intended to serve as an emergency store of some sort in the event of some local or regional food crisis. If so, whether any oil that remained towards the end of the administrative year would have been consigned to *navicularii* for transport to Ostia/Portus or some other destination remains unknown. Taking these factors into account, it would appear that the oil mobilized under these two initiatives in the Carthage collection district might have represented perhaps one-tenth to four-tenths of the total amount disbursed at Rome under the oil dole. It would thus appear that Zeugitana played a significant, if perhaps only secondary, rôle in the provision of this oil. A substantially larger share was presumably obtained by the application of similar initiatives in Byzacena.[217]

Whether there were other such facilities at Carthage is uncertain. As interpreted here, however, the *ostraca* leave entirely out of the equation oil collected as rent in kind from imperial lands in the Carthage area that might have been transferred to the *fiscus* for the support of state supply initiatives. It is hard to imagine what would have been done with much of the oil produced on imperial estates had it not been employed for state supply initiatives of some sort, and it may be that it was oil of this kind that was sold at the *mensae oleariae*, while that raised under the *canon olei* was employed for free distributions. In light of these observations, it seems possible that there were separate facilities at Carthage devoted to the storage and processing of oil originating with the *res privata*. Perhaps worth noting in this connection is the fact that the Group 2 documents refer to the storage facility as the *conditorium Zeugitanum* (rather than simply as the *conditorium*), since this may indicate that the group of *mensores olei* was involved in operations at more than one such facility.

The Ilôt de l'Amirauté *ostraca* raise several points of interest with regard to the use of African oil amphoras. Roughly one-half to as much as three-quarters of the oil referred to in these documents appears to have been transported to Carthage in oilskins, where it was transferred to amphoras in the course of weighing for export. As we have already seen, the location of the production sites for Dressel 20 amphoras suggests that a similar approach was employed for the bottling of oil in Baetica. This also appears to have been the method used for the export of oil produced in central Tunisia. In this instance, a systematic effort by Peacock and colleagues to locate pottery production sites through a program of surface investigation has yielded important evidence regarding the geography of amphora production in this region from the late 2nd to the 5th c.[218] This research identified a number of pottery workshops engaged in amphora production in the coastal zone, with concentrations around the port cities of Sullecthum and Leptiminus,[219] and a third such concentration on the southern shore of the Sebkhet Sidi el Hani, a salt lake lying roughly 60 km inland. In the area from Kairouan to the environs

216 *CTh* 13.5.38 (414), issued to the *praefectus urbi*.

217 For comparative statistics for oil production in northern, central, and southern Tunisia in recent decades, see Mattingly 1994b, 100-3.

218 Peacock *et al.* 1989; Peacock *et al.* 1990.

219 For further evidence for amphora production at Sullecthum, see Lavoie 1989. For Leptiminus, see Dore 1992, 155; Stone, Stirling and Ben Lazreg 1998.

of Sufetela (Sbeitla), the pottery workshops identified appear to have concentrated on the manufacture of tablewares, cookwares, and lamps. Amphora production at these workshops was limited, and the containers may have enjoyed only local distribution. In light of this evidence, it is clear that we should exercise a degree of caution in the use of amphoras as evidence for the geography of the production and distribution of African oil, since much of the oil produced in inland districts is likely to have been exported in amphoras manufactured in the environs of the major ports, including, but by no means limited to, Carthage, Leptiminus, and Sullecthum.

While the amphora evidence from several parts of the western Mediterranean makes it clear that the large-scale export of African olive oil survived the Vandal conquest of the 430s,[220] it seems highly unlikely that the oil mobilization practices reflected in the Ilôt de l'Amirauté *ostraca* can have survived this event without very substantial alterations. Interesting in this regard is the fact that the previously-mentioned survey of pottery production sites undertaken in central Tunisia by Peacock and colleagues has uncovered evidence for a possible shift in the locus of amphora production in the area around Sullecthum that may be related to changes in the packaging of African oil that occurred with the advent of Vandal rule.[221] The workshops for the production of amphoras located either at or in the immediate environs of the town appear to have ceased to operate at some point during the first half of the 5th c., several new workshops being established at roughly the same time at a distance of *c.*8-10 km from the town. These new workshops were very probably (and, in at least one case, demonstrably) associated with villas. This pattern suggests that at this time the bottling of oil for export shifted away from centralized processing facilities located at the town to the estates where the oil was produced.[222] This is precisely the sort of development that one would expect to find in the aftermath of the discontinuation of the state-sponsored system for the mobilization of oil described above.[223]

Finally, the documents provide evidence regarding the relative proportions of the different types of amphoras employed for the operations to which they refer. As here interpreted, the *ostraca* document the use of *c.*99 *ψ*, 144 *ƀ*, and 2,983 *centenaria levia*/KN^T for the transport of tax oil to Carthage.[224] At the same time, they suggest that the bottling of weighed oil involved the use of 184 *ψ*, 167 *ag*, and 1,026 KN^T.[225] Interestingly, the first two of these three container types appear to have been used exclusively for the long-term storage of oil at the *conditorium Zeugitanum*, while the latter was employed largely, if not exclusively, for oil slated for immediate export. This no doubt was a function of the great weight of the *ψ* and the *ag*, which must have made them more suitable for use as storage containers rather than as transport containers. While it would be a mistake to read too much into these data, given the speculative nature of the analyses from which they have been derived, they do suggest that the amphora class or classes which correspond to the *centenarium leve*/KN^T container type should be many times more abundant in the archaeological record than those which correspond to the *ψ* and the *ag* container types, with the latter classes perhaps somewhat less rare in the

---

220 Reynolds 1995, 53-60.

221 Peacock *et al.* 1989, 199-201.

222 While Peacock and colleagues inferred a similar pattern for the Leptiminus region, more recent research has shown that here amphora production in the area of the town continued into the Vandal period; see Dore 1992, 155.

223 Another response might have been a shift away from oleoculture to the cultivation of other crops. Perhaps relevant in this regard is settlement evidence from the territory of Segermes, a *civitas* in the northeast corner of Byzacena, which suggests that there was a transition from oil to grain production at some point during the course of the 5th c.; see Ørsted and Sebaï 1992, 83.

224 These data derive from the last row in Table 6.

225 These data represent a combination of the figures for the *fisci* provenience/ownership designation in No. 18 with the numbers of containers posited for weighing operations in Appendix 4.

Carthage area than they are outside Africa. In general, the identification of the Keay 25 amphora as the class that corresponds to the *centenarium leve*/KN^T, the Keay 35 amphora as the class that corresponds to the *ag*, and the wide-bodied Keay 35 amphora as the class that corresponds to the *ψ*, would appear to receive support from these data, as containers of the former class are extremely abundant in contexts of the later 4th c., while those of the latter two classes are uncommon.

We may close this section by commenting on two areas of study in which a re-orientation of research objectives might serve to improve our understanding of some of the topics touched on in this essay. The first of these concerns the field of amphora studies. Here it appears that we might achieve an enhanced understanding of the function of amphoras if we were to broaden our field of interests to include not just the traditional areas of classification, provenience, and chronology, but also the study of vessel capacity and the identification of vessel contents through residue analysis.[226] This study of the Ilôt de l'Amirauté *ostraca* underscores in particular the need for a comprehensive evaluation of the capacities of the various classes and subclasses of African amphoras, since it is clear from these documents that both the amphoras and oilskins used for the packaging of state oil were regarded as corresponding to (and to some extent did correspond to) standardized volumetric and/or weight modules. Once these amphora classes have been examined from this point of view and the underlying system or systems exposed, it should be possible to translate the somewhat abstract information that typically results from the quantitative analysis of amphora assemblages into data sets that offer more meaningful measures of the ebb and flow of economic interaction between Africa and the other parts of the Roman world.

The second area is that of research on shipwrecks. Wrecks are extraordinarily important resources in that they represent our only source of direct information regarding the specific modalities employed for the distribution of African oil, fish products, and pottery (excluding serendipitous finds such as the *ostraca* that are the subject of this study). We have great need of more comprehensive studies of the amphoras and other items of cargo recovered from merchantmen lost along the routes that served to connect the principal ports of Africa with the regions where these products were consumed.[227] Here again, a more comprehensive investigation of this evidence should permit us to move beyond the abstract models that figure in much recent discussion of trade in the Roman world to develop a more nuanced vision that takes proper account of the specific institutional, geographic, logistical, historic, and other components of exchange.

---

226 For the determination of vessel capacity, see Senior and Birney 1995, 319-25. For a recent overview of techniques of residue analysis, see Heron and Evershed 1993.

227 For some recent studies that begin to redress the situation, see Pontacolone and Incitta 1991; Bost *et al.* 1992; McCann and Freed 1994, 23-37.

6. SUMMARY

The Ilôt de l'Amirauté *ostraca* belong to two distinct sets of records concerned with the mobilization of state oil during the year 373. Those in one group, termed Group 1, record the inspection and receipt of consignments of tax oil brought to Carthage by ship. Those in the other, termed Group 2, record amounts of tax oil weighed in preparation for its export, a summation of these figures, and an estimate for the total amount of oil held at two facilities, one a weighing facility, the other a storage facility termed the *conditorium Zeugitanum*. Both sets of documents were probably produced by a group of functionaries known as *mensores olei*, who assisted with the reception and processing for export of tax oil brought to Carthage. The information in these documents was probably summarized and forwarded to provincial tax officials and/or functionaries attached to the *praefectura annonae Africae* so that it could be employed to monitor oil mobilization operations and determine the amount of reimbursement due to the oil weighers for their efforts. Both sets of documents may have been stored in offices of the organization of the *mensores olei*, probably located on the Ilôt de l'Amirauté.

Through the analysis of these documents it is possible to draw numerous inferences regarding the mobilization of state oil in Zeugitana and the handling of this oil upon its arrival at Carthage. The oil referred to in the documents appears to have been raised under two distinct initiatives. One of these was probably the *canon olei*, a special levy subsumed under the land tax that was earmarked for the supply of the city of Rome. Much or all of the oil raised under this initiative may have originated in the Bagradas valley and the valley of the wadi Siliana to the southwest of Carthage. The other initiative may have been a supplement to the land tax that was also directed towards the mobilization of oil for export, perhaps again for the supply of the city of Rome. The oil raised under this second initiative was apparently levied in just four collection districts: one known as Vol or Vol Calassini that may have consisted of one or more tax circumscriptions in eastern Zeugitana, one known as Caprorenses that probably corresponded to a tax circumscription in the extreme western part of the province, one known as Tebelbucitan qz that may have corresponded to a tax circumscription in NW Byzacena, and one known as Macrinenses that may have corresponded to a tax circumscription in this same general area. Geographical considerations suggest that this initiative may have been intended to extend the collection of tax oil into portions of Zeugitana and also perhaps adjacent parts of Byzacena that were not covered by the *canon olei*.

The oil raised under the first initiative was bottled in containers of two different kinds: oilskins with a capacity equal to 7 *amphorae* (*c.*504 lbs. of oil) that were probably termed *ascopae* or *ascoperae*, and amphoras termed *centenaria* and/or *centenaria levia* that held slightly less than 100 lbs. of oil. Many, perhaps even most, of the containers of the second type were probably examples of the amphora class that archaeologists term Keay 25. The oil raised under the second initiative was also bottled in two different kinds of containers, in this case *centenaria* and oilskins with a capacity equal to 1 *amphora* (*c.*72 lbs. of oil) that were perhaps termed *ascopae/ascoperae a byzacena*. Some of the oil raised under either or both of these initiatives was also bottled in a type of amphora with a 400-lb. capacity, the name of which remains unknown, and also possibly amphoras with a capacity equal to 1 *amphora*, that were perhaps termed *byzacenae*. The containers belonging to the first of these two types were probably examples of the amphora class termed the wide-bodied Keay 35, while those belonging to the second were probably small examples of the Keay 25 amphora. While the bulk of the oil raised under these two initiatives was apparently brought over land to Carthage by means of wagons and also perhaps pack animals operated by the *cursus publicus*, that from the Caprorenses district and perhaps one or more other districts was transported in coasting vessels that were operated by private individuals working either under contract or under the obligations of a *munus*.

The *mensores olei* inspected the shipments of oil containers brought to Carthage by sea, after which the containers that had passed the inspection were consigned to the *conditorium Zeugitanum*. The *mensores olei* documented these operations by means of the Group 1 *ostraca*. Whether or not shipments brought over land to Carthage were subject to a similar inspection procedure is uncertain. Upon arrival at Carthage, the bulk of the oil raised under both initiatives was directed to the *conditorium Zeugitanum* for storage, while a minor portion was sent directly to the weighing facility. These two facilities were probably located close to one another somewhere in the vicinity of the city's two harbors, and a reasonably convincing argument can be made that the *conditorium Zeugitanum* should be identified with the annular portico around the perimeter of the Ilôt de l'Amirauté, and the weighing facility identified with the area enclosed by this structure. The *conditorium Zeugitanum* and perhaps also the weighing facility were probably operated by the provincial administration.

The oil consigned to the weighing facility was weighed and then consigned to the *fiscus*, presumably here represented by functionaries attached to the *praefectura annonae Africae*. The weighing of the oil was no doubt undertaken so that it would be possible to determine the amount of tax oil turned over to the *fiscus* by the provincial administration under the two oil mobilization initiatives to which the *ostraca* pertain. The weighing procedure, which was carried out by men apparently termed *centenarii*, involved weighing allotments of oil by cwt. and lbs. Functionaries probably attached to the organization of the *mensores olei* documented weighing operations by means of the Group 2 *ostraca*.

As part of the weighing process, the oil brought to Carthage in oilskins was apparently transferred to amphoras, presumably because skin containers were unsuitable for long-distance maritime transport and/or long-term storage. The weighing of this oil was probably accomplished using the same technique as that employed during the 1st to 3rd c. for the weighing of oil in Baetica, with an amphora weighed empty, the oil poured into the amphora, the filled amphora weighed, and the second figure then subtracted from the first. The amphoras used for this purpose were of three types, the previously mentioned *centenarium* and 400-lb. capacity amphora, and an amphora with a capacity equal to 3 *amphorae*/2 *metretes* (*c.*216 lbs. of oil) that was probably known as an *amphora gemellaria*. The containers of this last type were probably examples of the amphora class termed Keay 35. Whether the oil conveyed to Carthage in amphoras was also transferred to a new container in the course of weighing operations is uncertain, although it seems likely that this was the practice. While some *centenarii* operated alone, others appear to have belonged to work groups consisting of two or more men. In the latter case credit for the oil weighed by the group was apportioned to its members according to various procedures. The allotments of unweighed oil assigned to individual *centenarii* and/or work groups for weighing appears to have been based on groups of 12 *centenaria*. The amount of oil weighed on any one day often appears to have been governed by the practice of processing enough oil to fill a group of 39 *centenaria*. This suggests that 2.5% of the oil was being set aside, perhaps as payment either for the *navicularii* who exported the oil or for the *mensores olei*.

Weighing operations ran from at least the middle of February through to October, at which point they were probably suspended for a period of some months. Both the calendar of operations and their intensity were probably determined by the availability at Carthage of state shipping. While the bulk of the weighed oil was probably consigned to *navicularii* for export, a minor, though significant, portion appears to have been transferred to the *conditorium Zeugitanum*, where it was held in storage, perhaps as a reserve to be used in the event of a local or regional food crisis. The very large stock of unweighed oil that was built up at the *conditorium Zeugitanum* over the course of the late winter and spring was presumably transferred to the weighing facility for processing during the late spring and summer so that it could be exported before the close of the sailing season in October. The desultory pace of weighing operations from early March to early May suggests why in 397 the state required that one-third of the *species* raised under the *canon urbis Romae* be shipped at the beginning of the sailing season in April, and also perhaps why in 384 there was a shortage of state oil at Rome.

The overall amount of oil received at the two facilities during the period for which documentation exists probably came to at least *c.*1,337,000 lbs. (*c.*437,000 kg/481,000 l). The amount handled in the course of the full administrative year may well have been as much as *c.*2,521,000 lbs. (*c.*824,000 kg/907.000 l), enough for the annual requirements of *c.*45,000 people, or *c.*18.4-46.3% of the amount disbursed each year for the urban oil dole. Since not all of this oil could have been placed at the disposal of the *praefectura annonae* for distribution to the urban populace, it would appear that the Carthage collection district may have provided about one-tenth to four-tenths of the oil disbursed at Rome under this program.

While many aspects of the operations to which the Ilôt de l'Amirauté *ostraca* refer remain obscure, they can be used to construct an unusually detailed view of the specific mechanisms that the state employed to collect and process a foodstuff that was both one of the principal *species annonariae* and one of the most important components of the Roman diet, and to provide this to the inhabitants of the *urbs*. In addition, by furnishing information regarding the way in which oil amphoras functioned during the late empire, these documents provide an enriched context for the study and interpretation of what is one of the most abundant and economically significant classes of material culture available to us from the Roman world.

Department of Classics, The University at Buffalo, S.U.N.Y

Appendix 1
Unassigned ostraca

Among the group of *ostraca* examined by the author were 9 that preserved too little text to permit them to be assigned to either Group 1 or Group 2. These are as follows:

24. Fragment of *ostracon* of unclear form. Traces of 5-7 lines of text on the exterior surface perpendicular to the vertical axis of the parent amphora. Traces of 1-2 lines of text on the interior surface. The length and disposition of the texts suggests that this *ostracon* probably belongs to Subgroup 1A.
25. Fragment of *ostracon* of unclear form. Traces of text on the exterior surface with lines perpendicular to the vertical axis of the parent amphora.
26. Fragment preserving approximately one-half of a shield-shaped *ostracon;* salt scum on the exterior surface. Traces of at least 5 lines of text on the interior surface parallel with vertical axis of the parent amphora.
27. Fragment probably from a shield-shaped *ostracon*. Small portion of the lower right-hand part of the text preserved on the exterior surface. Probably a Group 2 document.
28. Fragment of lower (?) portion of a shield-shaped *ostracon*. Small portion of the text preserved on the exterior surface. Probably a Group 2 document.
29. Fragment of a shield-shaped *ostracon*. Portion of the right-hand part of text on the exterior surface consisting of series of container type designations and numbers. Perhaps a Subgroup 2C document.
30. Two joining fragments preserving part of an *ostracon* of uncertain form. Fragments apparently joined with glue in 1911. There are traces of glue on a different fracture surface, indicating that an additional fragment of this *ostracon* was recovered in 1911, attached with glue, and then subsequently separated and was lost. Traces of 9-10 lines of text on the exterior surface.
31. Fragment of a shield-shaped *ostracon*. Traces of 6 lines of text on the exterior surface.
32. Fragment of a shield-shaped *ostracon*. Traces of 4 lines of text on the exterior surface.

Appendix 2
The method employed in the *ostraca* of Group 2 to derive the estimate for the total weight of oil

Element 3 in the Subgroup 2B documents concludes with an entry consisting of a pair of figures, the first introduced by the sum of cwt. sign and the second by the lbs. sign. These are evidently an estimate for the total weight of the oil represented by the entries that appear under the *inpletu* and *fieri inconditZ* headings in this element. This estimate must have been obtained by multiplying the quantity of container figures listed under these entries by a standard weight value for the associated container type and then adding the resulting products. The figure in the Type 4 entry under the *inpletu* heading was also presumably included in this total. Evidence discussed in Appendices 3 and 4 can be used to build a strong case that a standard weight value of 100 lbs. was assigned to the KN^T container type for this purpose. Taking this as a given, it is possible to treat Element 3 in each of the 4 documents that preserve both their oil container entries and this pair of numbers intact (Nos. 9, 14, 17, and 19) as a polynomial equation and solve for the standard weight values assigned to the other 4 container types to which reference is made (*ag*, *as a ƀ*, *as*, and ψ).

The relevant portions of the 4 documents can be formulated as equations as follows:

No. 9: 3,400 + 167A + 27B = 41,320
No. 14: 15,600 + 167A + 1,847B + 433C + 1,191D = 526,520
No. 17: 3,875 + 167A + 2,679B + 757C + 1,644D = 785,275
No. 19: 11,110 + 167A + 2,844B + 757C + 1,644D + 184E = 880,275

Where A = *ag*, B = *as a ƀ*, C = *as*, D = KN^T, and E = ψ

Substituting a value of 100 for D, and then solving No. 14 for C in terms of A and B, No. 17 for B in terms of A, No. 9 for A, and then No. 19 for E, yields the following results:

A (*ag*) = 215.0 lbs.
B (*as a ƀ*) = 74.9 lbs.
C (*as*) = 505.6 lbs.
E (ψ) = 397.3 lbs.

As is discussed in Appendix 3, these figures are close approximations of the notional weight equivalents in olive oil of regular modules of volumetric measure, and there can be little doubt that the compilers of these documents employed the first three of these numbers in their whole number forms (215, 75, and 505 lbs.), and the fourth increased to the nearest 5 (400 lbs.), as standard weight values for these 4 container types in order to derive the estimate for the total weight of oil.

That figures of 215, 505, 75 and 100 lbs. were the standard weight values employed by the compilers of the Group 2 documents is confirmed by the fact that, with only a minor amount of *ad hoc* adjustment, it is possible to employ these values to reproduce the exact figures indicated for the estimate for the total weight of oil in two of the 4 documents (Nos. 9 and 17) that were used to derive these values. In order to understand the method employed for deriving the estimate for the total weight of oil, we may begin with the formulation of No. 17 as an equation that was earlier employed to derive the standard weight value estimates:

3,875 + 167A + 2,679B + 757C + 1,644D = est. total wt. of oil

Where A = *ag*, B = *as a ꝑ*, C = *as*, and D = KN^T

Substituting the standard weight values either assumed or derived above, we obtain the following:

3,875 + 35,905 + 200,925 + 382,285 + 164,400 = 787,390

The figure obtained for the estimate for the total weight of oil, 787,390, surpasses that actually recorded in the document, 785,275, by 2,115 lbs. This suggests that, if the assumptions made here regarding the standard weight values and the method employed for deriving this estimate are correct, some sort of rounding procedure was employed to obtain some or all of the figures used for the left-hand side of the equation. The fact that the value for the sum of weighed oil appearing in the first term of the equation and the value obtained for the estimate for the total weight of oil on the right-hand side of the equation both end in 75 suggests that the procedure employed to derive the latter figure involved the addition of the former value to some rounded number or set of rounded numbers. If we truncate the figures derived from A, B, and C at the nearest 1,000, we obtain the following:

3,875 + 35,000 + 200,000 + 382,000 + 164,400 = 785,275

This reproduces the exact figure for the estimate for the total weight of oil given in the document. It seems likely that this was the technique employed by this document's compiler, who truncated at the nearest 1,000 the values obtained in the more complex multiplication operations, that is, those involving the standard weight values for the *ag*, *as a ꝑ*, and *as*, and then added to the resulting figures the sum of weighed oil and the figure obtained for the KN^T, which involved the relatively straightforward operation of multiplying the quantity of containers figure by the standard weight value of 100.

A similar procedure may have been employed to derive the estimate for the total weight of oil in No. 9, with the figures for the weight of oil in the *ag* and *as a ꝑ* truncated at the nearest 10 rather than the nearest 1,000. In this case the operation can be represented as follows:

3,400 + 167A + 27B = est. total wt. of oil
3,400 + 35,905 + 2,025 = 41,330
3,400 + 35,900 + 2,020 = 41,320

Since the difference between the value obtained by simply multiplying the standard weight values by the quantity of containers figures and the figure recorded in the document for the estimate for the total weight of oil amounts to only 10 lbs., it cannot be excluded that in this instance we are looking at the result of a computational or transcriptional error rather than a truncation procedure such as that illustrated for No. 17. If, on the other hand, the truncating of these three figures at the 10s level rather than at the 1,000s level, as in No. 17, was the procedure employed, this practice can perhaps be ascribed to the relatively small amount of oil on hand at the two facilities at the time that this *ostracon* was composed, or to the fact that this document was drawn up by a functionary different from the one responsible for No. 17.

While a variety of rounding procedures was evaluated in an effort to reproduce the procedures employed for deriving the estimate for the total weight of oil in Nos. 14 and 19, in neither case did it prove possible to obtain the figure recorded in the document. The inability to reproduce these figures should perhaps be attributed to the presence of a minor computational error on the part of the compiler of these documents. Worth noting, however, is the fact that the substitution of the standard weight values assumed above for the various container types yields a value only 1,245 lbs. larger than the actual estimate for the value of the total weight of oil in the case of No. 14, and a value only 325 lbs. larger than this figure in the case of No. 19.[228]

---

228 No. 14: 527,795-526,550 = 1,245 (= + 0.2%); No. 19: 880,600-880,275 = 325 (= + 0.04%).

The calculations presented above obtained progressively greater departures from the standard weight values that it is here conjectured were employed by the compilers of these documents for the value of the container types in question (i.e., 0.1 lbs. for the *as a ƀ*, 0.6 lbs. for the *as*, and 2.7 lbs. for the *ψ*). This should perhaps be ascribed to cumulative error deriving from the use of rounding procedures of the sort illustrated here for Nos. 9 and 17 and/or from the presence of minor computational errors of the sort conjectured for Nos. 14 and 19.

Appendix 3

Nature and capacity of the container types referred to in the *ostraca*

By combining evidence contained in the *ostraca* with various kinds of external evidence, it is possible to ascertain both the nature and capacity of the 7 different container types to which these documents refer. For the discussion of this topic readers will find it helpful to consult Table 8, which summarizes the results.

Table 8: Container types referred to in the Group 2 documents

Standard weights are those assumed by compilers for estimating total weight of oil. Notional weights and volumes are those for which standard weights are assumed to have served. Gross weights are those inferred for container plus content. CALC = calculated; lg. = large; sm. = small; w-b = wide-bodied.

DESIGNATION	SUGGESTED EXPANSION	CONTAINER TYPE	STANDARD WT. (LBS.)		NOTIONAL WT.		NOTIONAL VOL.		GROSS WT.
			CALC.	TRUE	LBS.	KG	AMPH.	L	KG
as a ƀ	ascopa a byzacena	sm. oilskin	74.9	75	72	23.5	1	26.1	26
ƀ	byzacena	med. amph./ (sm. Keay 25)	-	-	?72	23.5	1	26.1	34
KN^T	kentenarium	med. amph./ (lg. Keay 25)	-	100	100	32.7	-	36.0	45
ag	amphora gemellaria	lg. amph./ (Keay 35)	215.0	215	216	70.6	3	78.3	98
ψ	?	w.-b. amph./ (w.-b. Keay 35)	397.3	400	400	130.8	-	143.9	166
as	ascopa	lg. oilskin	505.6	505	504	164.8	7	182.7	180

We can begin by considering the KN^T and the related *centenarium leve* container types. The discussion of the format of the Subgroup 2A documents in Section 2 yielded two observations regarding these two container types:

1) The *centenarium leve* was either identical to or subsumed under the KN^T container type.
2) The KN^T was probably assigned a standard weight value of 100 lbs. by the compilers of the Group 2 documents for the purpose of calculating estimates for the total weight of oil.

The second of these observations is corroborated by additional evidence, including the fact that assuming a standard weight value of 100 lbs. for the KN^T yields a set of plausible values for the other container types in the analysis presented in Appendix 2, the fact that the compilers of the Group 2 documents eschewed the use of the sign *N* for groups of KN^T in quantity of container entries, apparently because these figures were regarded as the equivalent of a cwt. figure, and the fact that, as discussed in Appendix 4, the set of weight of oil figures for individual oil weighers recorded in No. 7 *verso* is compatible with the assumption that weighing operations involved sets of containers with a capacity that ranged between *c.*95 and 100 lbs. (with perhaps both larger and smaller outliers) and a group mean on the order of 99 lbs. It thus seems fair to infer that the abbreviation KN^T should be expanded *K(e)NT(enarium)*, presumably a variant of the word *centenarium*. As previously noted, it was common practice in the Roman empire to measure olive oil in terms of *centenaria*, and it seems a reasonable inference that this container type was conceived of as having a capacity equal to, or, as the name *centenarium leve* suggests, just slightly less than 100 lbs. of oil.[229]

Turning now to the 4 remaining container types, it is possible to build a strong case that the weight values obtained for these in Appendix 2 (215.0, 74.9, 505.6, and 397.3 lbs.) correspond to standard weight values of 215, 75, 505, and 400 lbs. that the compilers of the Group 2 documents used for the purpose of deriving estimates for the total weight of oil. Of fundamental importance in this regard is the apparent relationship between the figure of 215.0 lbs. obtained for the *ag* and that of 216 lbs. that the corpus of *tituli* on Dressel 20 amphoras indicates was the standard module employed for the bottling of Baetican oil during the 2nd and 3rd c.[230] The basis for this module of 216 lbs. lies in the system of liquid measures. A container that held this weight of oil would thus have had a capacity of 144 *sextarii*, an amount exactly equal to 3 *amphorae* or 2 *metretes*.[231] That this module may in some cases have been regarded as a double *metretes* rather than a triple *amphora* is suggested by a passage in a metrological treatise attributed to Africanus, a writer of the late 2nd or early 3rd c.:[232]

> καὶ τὰ ἐλαιηρὰ παραπλησίως, πλὴν ὅτι ἀπὸ τοῦ καλουμένου κεντηναρίου τὴν αρχὴν ἔχει, ὅ δὴ λίτρας ἔχει ρ̅. ἔστι δὲ καὶ ὁ ἐλαιηρὸς μετρητὴς τοῦδε διπλάσιος.
>
> It is similar for oil measurements, with the exception that they have as their basis the so-called *centenarium*, which contains 100 lbs. The oil *metretes*, however, is the double of this.

Read literally, this passage states that a module called the oil *metretes* was twice the size of the *centenarium*. This makes little sense from a metrological point of view, however, as the various types of *metretes* recognized in the ancient world were all considerably smaller than 134 *sextarii*, the volume equivalent of 200 lbs. of oil. A more plausible interpretation of this passage is that it meant to indicate that the *metretes* was the module that was doubled in order to obtain the module that did service as the double *centenarium*. That the *metretes* may in some cases have served as the base module for the bottling of Baetican oil is suggested by the fact that a set of standard measures corresponding to a *metretes*, a quarter *metretes*, and a *sextarius* has been found at Vélez Málaga,[233] roughly 20 km east of Malaca (Málaga), an important center for the bottling of

---

229 Hilgers 1969 contains no entry under either *kentenarium* or *centenarium*, and the origin of this term as the name for this container type is unclear. *SHA, Elagab.* 19 mentions *vasa centenaria argentea*, though referring to the vessels' weight rather than their capacity, and it seems doubtful that this name was originally a modifier for a word such as *vasum* or *dolium*. The name may perhaps have been taken back into Latin from a Greek term κεράμιον κεντηνάριον. See Oxé 1940, 128 for κεντηνάριον as the Greek term for the Latin *centenarium* in the sense of hundredweight. For the use of the term *kentenarion* in Byzantine metrology, see Schilbach 1970, 109, 174; Dagron and Morrisson 1975.

230 As discussed in Section 3, the evidence for this module consists of the figures that appear in the gamma and sometimes also the delta *titulus* components. The vast bulk of the known examples of these *tituli* come from Monte Testaccio. For a systematic presentation and discussion of the corpus of examples published in *CIL* XV and Rodríguez-Almeida 1984a, see Rodríguez-Almeida 1984b, 133-51; Martin-Kilcher 1987, 152-57. For additional examples recovered in the 1989 excavations at Monte Testaccio, see Blázquez Martínez *et al.* 1984, 39-124. While, as noted above, the numbers in these *tituli* range from a low of 162 to a high in the 230s, 216 is by far the most common figure. In *CIL* XV, for example, the examples with this figure account for over 30.4% of the total, while those with 214 and 215 account for another 5.2%. Rodríguez-Almeida 1989a, 28 puts the figure at over 50% of all examples from Monte Testaccio.

231 The *metretes* in question is the so-called Attic *metretes*, equal to 1.5 *amphorae* (72 *sextarii*), for which see Hultsch 1882, 107-10. Rodríguez-Almeida 1989a, 28 also notes that this number is equal to 1 gross *sextarii*

232 For the text, see Viedebantt 1917, 136. For a discussion of this passage and related passages from three other metrological sources, see Oxé 1940, 136, 145-46. I find unconvincing the reconstruction and interpretation of this passage offered in this work.

233 For this set of measures, see Hultsch 1884, 690. The fact that the *metretes* was subdivided into quarters rather than thirds suggests that it was not in this case regarded as 1.5 *amphorae*, and that the *amphora* was not relevant to the set of operations for which this set of measures served. That those who manufactured the Dressel 20 amphora sometimes conceived of its volume in terms of the *modius*, a measure equal to 16 *sextarii*, or one-third of an *amphora*, is indicated by the presence of a graffito made prior to firing on an example of this class that reads *VIII S*. This almost certainly represents eight and

Baetican oil.[234] Similarly, that the standard containers for Baetican oil were conceived of as the double of some base module may be indicated by the fact that Columella, whose home town was Gades (Cádiz), refers to a receptacle used for the storage of freshly pressed oil as a *gemellar structile* ('built twin'?),[235] perhaps alluding to an amphora that was anchored in some sort of masonry structure to serve a basin. Also perhaps worth noting in this regard is the existence of a *figlina gemelliana* responsible for the manufacture of Dressel 20 amphoras, apparently located in the vicinity of Corduba.[236]

If we accept this interpretation, the passage in question provides an exact description of the approach employed for the bottling of the oil designated *fisci* in the Group 2 documents, which was packaged exclusively in the 100-lb. KN^T and the 215-lb. *ag*, save that beginning at some point after April 25 and before May 6 the 400-lb. capacity *ψ* was also used. The evidence would thus seem to suggest that the *ag* was a container with a capacity equal to 3 *amphorae*/2 *metretes*, with its notional weight rounded from 216 to 215 lbs. for the purpose of deriving the estimate for the total weight of oil. The rounding of the final 6 to a 5 would have greatly simplified the task of multiplying the figure for the quantity of containers by the standard weight value as part of the operation employed for estimating the total weight of oil, since it would have eliminated the need to include any ones in the calculation. That the error introduced by this practice would not have been significant is suggested by the fact that, as shown in Appendix 2, the compilers of these documents sometimes truncated the resulting figure.

The precise nature of the connection between the use of this 216 lb. module for the packaging of oil owned by the *fiscus* in later 4th-c. Zeugitana and its use for the bottling of Baetican oil during the 2nd and 3rd c. remains unclear. As already noted, however, during the 2nd and 3rd c. Baetica appears to have furnished a large portion, perhaps the overwhelming bulk, of the state oil employed both for the provisioning of military units in the western provinces and for the supply of the city of Rome, and it may be that during this period a 216-lb. container came to be generally regarded as a standard unit for the packaging of state oil. That this module eventually came to be adopted in Africa as the equivalent of a double *centenarium* seems plausible. It is particularly interesting to note in this connection that Augustine and Quodvultdeus, both Africans of the later 4th/early 5th c., refer to the receptacle used to receive newly pressed oil as a *gemellarium*.[237]

As previously noted, the figure of 505.6 lbs. obtained for the *as* in Appendix 2 probably corresponds to a standard weight value of 505 lbs. This presumably represented a rounding up to the nearest 5 of 504 lbs., the notional weight of 336 *sextarii*, or 7 *amphorae* of oil. Data in Appendix 4 suggest that this container type may have had a capacity more nearly equal to 507.4 lbs. of oil. As discussed in Section 4, the reason for the adoption of this module, attested exclusively with oil associated with the *oRc* provenience/ownership

---

one-half *modii*, equal to 136 *sextarii*, or 204 lbs. of oil; see Martin-Kilcher 1987, 157, 156 Abb. 88.2. The other graffiti on Dressel 20 amphoras discussed by Martin-Kilcher that indicate vessel capacities in terms of *modii* appear to relate to the secondary use of these containers; see van der Werff 1989.

234 For Malaca as a center for the bottling of olive oil, see Rodríguez-Almeida 1993, 103.

235 12.52.10.

236 See Mayet 1986, 293, 300; Blázquez Martínez *et al.* 1994, 63 no. 64 (A.D. 221), and also perhaps 94 no. 135 (A.D. 161). Certain occurrences of the letter g in the delta *titulus* component on Dressel 20 amphoras may also be interpreted as abbreviations for the term *gemellar*. Several Dressel 20 amphoras from the mid-2nd c. Saint Gervais 3 wreck bear the formula *acc g* or *g acc* in association with a name in the nominative. Rather than expanding these as *acc(epit) g(ustavit)/g(ustavit) acc(epit)* as suggested in Liou and Tchernia 1994, 137, 150, a more plausible solution may be *acc(epit) g(emellar)/g(emallar) acc(epit)*. Similarly, in several *tituli* of A.D. 161 the first line of the delta *titulus* component presents a small number immediately after the barred R that is generally taken to be an abbreviation for *recensitum*, with the values of this number ranging from a low of 11 to a high of 30. See Blázquez Martínez *et al.* 1994, 81 no. 107, 92 no. 132, 93 no. 134, 95 no. 139, 96 no. 140, 97-98 no. 143, and also perhaps 108 no. 170. These are in the same general range as the numbers that appear in the epsilon *titulus* component, and both may perhaps refer to the same thing. What this is, however, remains uncertain. Worth noting is that in one of these *tituli* (Blázquez Martínez *et al.* 1994, 92 no. 132) the number is preceded by a letter g. If expanded as *gemellaria*, this may perhaps be taken as referring to the total number of containers in the group to which the container in question belonged.

237 Augustine: *Psalm* 80.1, 80.11, 136.9, *Serm.* 24.11; (attributed to) Quodvultdeus: *De Tempore Barbarico* 2.6.11. To my knowledge, this term is nowhere else attested in Latin literature of the classical period.

designation, probably lay in the fact that it permitted maximum efficiency in the use of the two classes of heavy wagons operated by the *cursus publicus*, which had load limits of 1,000 and 1,500 lbs.

The interpretation of the 74.9-lb. figure obtained in Appendix 2 for the *as a ƀ* is more problematic. While this presumably represents a standard weight value of 75 lbs., the identification of the module that underlies this figure is somewhat uncertain. That it represents either three-quarters of a *centenarium* or a unit consisting of 50 *sextarii* seems doubtful, as there is no evidence that a module of this size was employed for the measuring of liquids in the Roman world.[238] Data in Appendix 4, however, suggest that this container type may have had a capacity equal to *c.*72.5 lbs. of oil. In light of this fact, a more plausible suggestion is that the standard weight value of 75 lbs. represents the rounding upward of 72 lbs., the notional weight of one *amphora* of oil. This value was presumably rounded up to 75 rather than down to 70 since this practice would have simplified the task of converting a figure for the quantity of vessels to its equivalent in cwt. of oil (i.e., 4 x 75 = 300). Whether the container type designation *ƀ*, which appears only in No. 6, should be regarded simply as a variant of *as a ƀ* or a distinct type of container is uncertain.

The figure of 397.3 lbs. obtained for the *ψ* presumably represents a container having a standard weight value of 400 lbs., or 4 *centenaria*. While there is no evidence that 400 lbs. ever represented a standard module for the packaging of oil, the analysis of the sum of weighed oil figures in the Group 2 *ostraca* suggests that oil was often processed in lots equal to 40 cwt. (see Section 4 and Appendix 4), and the reason for the use of a container with a capacity of 4 cwt. may perhaps have been grounded in this practice.

We may next endeavor to identify the nature of the containers to which these designations refer. Here the task is to establish whether a designation served to indicate either an oilskin or an amphora and, if the latter, the specific class or classes of amphora. The evidence that can be mobilized towards this end includes the capacity of the container type in question, its name, and, since it seems unlikely that oilskins were employed for long-term storage or marine transport, whether or not that container type was used for either of these purposes.

Turning first to container type capacities, it is possible to compare the capacities of the container types referred to in the *ostraca* with capacity values for known container types. The notional capacity of each container type can be determined by converting the standard weight value derived above for that container type to its equivalent volume, as indicated in Table 8.

While nothing is known about the capacities of the oilskin container types employed for the bottling of liquids in late imperial Africa, we can determine the capacities of the various amphora classes produced in Africa during this period. According to Freed,[239] during the later 4th c. African amphoras were manufactured in four general size classes: small, represented by the class termed Keay 26 (or *spatheion*); mid-sized, represented by the classes termed Keay 25, 27, and 50, large-sized, represented by the classes termed Keay 7-8, 30-35, 37-43, 45-46, 59, 77-78, and 90, and wide-bodied, represented by the classes termed Keay 35 (wide-bodied variant) and 89.[240] The two amphora classes in the wide-bodied size class are the largest known from the Roman world.[241] While the evidence is far from conclusive, that available suggests that most of the amphora classes listed here were employed for the packaging of both oil and fish products.[242]

It is evident from the size of the Keay 26 amphora, the single amphora class assigned to the small size class, that examples of this class had capacities well below *c.*26 l (the volume equivalent of *c.*72 lbs. of oil), and this size class need not concern us further. In order to determine the capacities of the amphora classes assigned to the other size classes I made use of a computer program that calculates a vessel's capacity from a profile drawing by means of an electronic digitizing pad. The program in question, produced by Senior and Birney, operates by converting a vessel profile to a series of stacked conic sections, calculating the volume of

---

238 For a βοῦττις (cask?) with a capacity of 50 *sextarii*, however, see *Edictum de Pretiis* 12.37.

239 Freed 1995, 166-68.

240 Note that while Keay 1994, assigned the Keay 35 amphora to the 5th c., more recent evidence indicates that it more probably dates to the late 4th/early 5th c.; see McCann and Freed 1994, 31-32; Freed 1995, 170.

241 McCann and Freed 1994, 31.

242 For the content of African amphoras during the late imperial period, see McCann and Freed 1994, 24; Bonifay and Piéri 1995, 95-106; Mattingly and Hitchner 1995, 200-1.

each, and then summing the results.[243] Trials undertaken by the author demonstrate that this procedure is fairly accurate, yielding values that fall within *c*.92-100% of the true value for African amphoras belonging to classes assigned to Freed's medium and large size classes.[244] The values obtained represent the maximum capacities of the containers in question, and, in practice, amphoras belonging to these classes may not have been filled to the lip.[245] Of the three amphora classes that comprise the mid-sized size class, the Keay 25 amphora is far and away the most abundant in archaeological contexts of the 4th c.[246] Capacity measurements were carried out for 15 examples of this class for which profile drawings were available in the literature, as well as one example of the Keay 27 amphora. The values obtained for the examples of the Keay 25 amphora ranged between 26.8 and 35.1 l, with a single outlier at 40.5 l (mean = 31.3; standard deviation = 3.8 l),[247] while a value of 36.9 l was obtained for the single example of the Keay 27 amphora.[248] These data suggest that examples of the Keay 25 amphora and probably also the Keay 27 amphora normally had maximum capacities of *c*.75-110 lbs. of oil, with some capable of holding up to *c*.115-20 pounds of oil. Similar measurements were carried out for five containers belonging to amphora classes assigned to Freed's large-size size class, including two examples of the Keay 31 amphora, two examples of the Keay 35 amphora, and one example of the Keay 42 amphora.[249] A value of 60.4 l was obtained for the Keay 31 amphora, values of 60.8 and 80.2 l were obtained for the two examples of the Keay 35 amphora, and a value of 60.2 l was obtained for the Keay 42 amphora. These data suggest that, while most containers in these classes were capable of holding up to *c*.165-185 lbs. of oil, some examples of the Keay 35 amphora (and also perhaps examples of some of the other classes assigned to this size class) had maximum capacities of *c*.225 lbs. of oil. Finally, a measurement was carried out for a single container belonging to a class assigned to Freed's wide-bodied size class, in this case an example of the wide-bodied Keay 35 amphora missing the spike and a small portion of the lower body.[250] A value of 143 l was obtained for this container in its fragmentary condition, and it is estimated that, when complete, it had a maximum capacity of *c*.148 l. This suggests that some examples of this class could have held as much as *c*.415 lbs. of oil.

With regard to the names of the container types, the similarity between the *as* and *as a ƀ* designations suggests that these two container types were related in some fashion.

---

243 For a description of this program, see Senior and Birney 1995, 324-30. I would like to thank the two developers of this program for making a copy of it available for this study, as well as J. McCaw for carrying out the vessel capacity measurements reported here

244 For a full exposition of the procedures employed to obtain the capacity measurements reported here, see Peña (forthcoming).

245 How closely amphoras were filled to their maximum capacity presumably varied from class to class as a function of various factors, including the method employed for stoppering. A lease for the rental of a pottery workshop from Oxyrhynchus dating to the 3rd c. indicates that in this instance the capacity of wine amphoras was measured μέχρι χείλου (up to the lip); see Cockle 1981, document A, line 37. Similarly, the theta *titulus* component that occurs on some Dressel 20 amphoras from Rome indicates that the capacity of these was reckoned *ad summum labrum* (to the top of the lip); see Rodríguez-Almeida 1989a, 30. In contrast, van Alfen 1996, 203-7 argues that Late Roman 1 amphoras from the 7th-c. Yassi Ada shipwreck were filled only to the junction of the body and the neck.

246 On the abundance of the Keay 25 amphora relative to other classes of African amphoras during the period running from the beginning of the 4th to the mid 5th c., see Reynolds 1995, 49-50, 51-52; McCann and Freed 1994, 27; Freed 1995, 167 for the Catalan sites studied in Keay 1984; Freed 1995, 172 for the Canadian excavations at the Theodosian Wall at Carthage; Peña (forthcoming) for an early 4th c. deposit from the Palatine Hill at Rome.

247 The amphoras in question and the capacity values obtained are as follows: Carandini and Panella 1977 [=*Ostia* IV] 263 no. 1/116 fig. 1 [30.2 liters]; 263 no. 2/116 fig. 2 [29.1 l]; 263-64 no. 3/116 fig. 3 [34.8 l]; 264 no. 5/116 fig. 5 [31.4 l]; 264 no. 6/116 fig. 6 [40.5 l]; 265-66 no. 7/116 fig. 7 [26.8]; 266 no. 8/116 fig. 8 [33.3 l]; 257 fig. 17 [36.1 l]; 258 fig. 18 [29.7 l]; 258 fig. 19 [32.4 l]; 258 fig. 20 [35.1 l]; 258 fig. 21 [27.2 l]; 258 fig. 23 [34.0 l]; Freed 1995, 189 no. 3/190 fig. 1.2 [29.7 l]; 189 no. 3/190 fig. 1.3 [28.6 l]. For a complete discussion of these data, see Peña (forthcoming).

248 The amphora in question is Carandini and Panella 1977 [= *Ostia* IV] 264 no.4/116 fig. 4 [36.9 l].

249 The amphoras in question are McCann and Freed 1994, 29 no. 4/25 fig. 23.4; 28-29 no. 3/25 fig. 23.3; 32 no.6/25 fig. 23.6; Freed 1995, 190 no. 12/183 fig. 2.2; McCann and Freed 1994, 30 no. 5/25 fig. 23.5.

250 The amphora in question is Freed 1995, 190 no. 11/183 fig. 2.1.

Finally, with regard to the uses to which the various container types were put, the Group 1 documents demonstrate that during February and early March the KN^T was employed for what was probably the short-haul shipping of oil to Carthage, while during July both the *ƀ* and the *ψ* were used for this purpose. Also worth noting is that in the Subgroup 2B documents the KN^T, the *ag*, and the *ψ* are associated with the *fisci* provenience/ownership designation. As argued in Section 4, these were probably containers of weighed oil that were consigned to the *conditorium Zeugitanum* for long-term storage.

On the basis of this evidence we may draw five conclusions regarding the identities of the 7 container types referred to in the *ostraca*:
1) The *as a ƀ* and *ƀ* may correspond to examples of Keay 25 amphora near the lower end of the size range attested for this amphora class (fig. 4.A).
2) The *centenarium leve*/KN^T may correspond to examples of Keay 25 amphora near the upper end of the size range attested for this amphora class (fig. 4.B) and to examples of Keay 27.
3) The *ag* may correspond to examples of Keay 35 amphora near the upper end of the size range attested for this amphora class (fig. 4.C), and possibly other amphora classes belonging to the large-size size class.
4) The *ψ* may correspond to the wide-bodied Keay 35 amphora (fig. 4.D).
5) The *as* is too large to have been an amphora.

In light of this last observation, it seems possible that the *as* designation was, in fact, an abbreviation for the word *ascopa* (or the variant *ascopera*), a Latinization of the Greek ἀσκὸς (skin bag) that is well attested in late Latin.[251] If this inference is correct, then we should probably interpret the first two characters in *as a ƀ* as an abbreviation for this word. This container type thus may have been an oilskin rather than a small example of the Keay 25 amphora, as just suggested. If the assumption that oilskins were not regarded as suitable containers for marine transport is correct, then the container type designation *ƀ*, which No. 6 documents in connection with two groups of containers delivered to Carthage by sea, would appear not to be simply a variant of *as a ƀ*, but rather the designation for a distinct class of container that was an amphora. Its similarity to the *as a ƀ* designation, however, suggests that there was some connection between the two, and we may surmise that it too had a capacity of 1 *amphora*. It may thus correspond to a small example of Keay 25.

The identification of five of the container types mentioned in the *ostraca* with specific amphora classes is a point of considerable interest. A more ambitious program of capacity measurement than the one reported here would no doubt yield important information regarding the existence of different size variants within these classes, the degree of standardization realized in the production of these variants, and so forth.

With regard to the expansions of the names of the container types, we have already seen that KN^T very probably stood for *kentenarium*/*centenarium*, while *as* probably stood for *ascopa*. With regard to the *as a ƀ* designation, the fact that two of the three provenience/ownership designations associated with this container type, Tebelbucitan qz and Macrinenses, correspond to toponyms that may have been located in Byzacena (see Section 5) suggests that the final character may have been an abbreviation for *byzacena*, with the designation to be expanded *as(copae) a by(zacena)* (oilskins from Byzacena). The irregular rendering of this container type designation that appears in No. 9, Entry 4, which can perhaps be read *as a b ce*, may support this conjecture. Since the third provenience/ownership designation associated with this container type, Vol Calassini, probably lay in Zeugitana (see Section 5), it may be that containers of this kind, while associated with Byzacena in some general way, were also employed for the bottling of oil in some parts of Zeugitana. If this expansion is correct, then the *ƀ* designation presumably stood for the adjectival substantive *byzacena*. With regard to the *ag* container type, if the 216-lb. module that it apparently represents was regarded as a double *metretes*, and if it was the practice in late 4th/5th-c. Africa to refer to certain oil containers as *gemellaria*, we may conjecture that this was an abbreviation for *a(mphora) g(emellaria)* or some related term, such as *a(mphora) g(emella)* or *a(mphora) g(emina)*. Alternatively, if this module was regarded as a triple *amphora*, we may conjecture that this abbreviation stood for *a(mphora) g(amma)*. A third possibility is that it simply stood for *a(mphora) g(randis)* (large amphora). The nature of the *ψ* designation remains enigmatic, and no plausible expansion can be suggested.

On the basis of the reconstructed weight figures presented above, we may venture rough estimates for the gross weights of the container types referred to in the Group 2 documents. These figures are of interest in that they allow us to infer how each of these container types was transported to Carthage and how it was handled upon arrival. As there is no evidence available regarding the weight of the oilskins used in the

251 See *TLL s.v.* ascopera; *Glossarium Mediae et Infime Latinitatis s.v.* ascopa.

Roman world, any estimates suggested for the gross weights of the two oilskin container types remain conjectural. The figures presented here are based on the assumption that oilskins were substantially more efficient than amphoras and that their efficiency increased with their capacity. In accord with these assumptions, we can estimate the gross weight of the 5 container types as follows:

as a ℔: *c*.26 kg (23 kg oil + 3 kg oilskin)
℔: *c*.34 kg (23 kg oil + 11 kg amphora)[252]
centenarium leve/KN^T: *c*.45 kg (33 kg oil + 12 kg amphora)[253]
ag: *c*.98 kg (70 kg oil + 28 kg amphora)[254]
ψ: *c*.166 kg (131 kg oil + 35 kg amphora)[255]
as: *c*.180 kg (165 kg oil + 15 kg oilskin).

The *as a ℔*, *℔*, and *centenarium leve*/KN^T would have been light enough that they could have been moved by a single porter.[256] The *ag*, *ψ*, and *as*, on the other hand, were probably carried by teams of two or more men using *phalangae*, wooden poles, as we know was sometimes done for the Dressel 20 amphora and the *cupae* (large casks) employed for the storage of state wine at Rome.[257] How poles of this kind would have been attached to the *as* is unclear, although they may have been inserted through belts that circled its body or rows of loops attached to the upper part of the bag.

As previously noted, it seems unlikely that oilskins were regularly employed for maritime transport. With regard to transport over land, the crucial observation is that the mule, the type of animal most likely to have been employed in Zeugitana,[258] can generally carry up to *c*.30 % of its own weight, or roughly 90-122 kg, provided that the load can be divided into two nearly equal portions so that it can be balanced on the animal's back.[259] Thus, while the *as a ℔*, *℔*, and *centenarium leve*/KN^T could have been loaded onto mules in pairs (or in the case of the first of these container types, perhaps in fours) for transport to Carthage,[260] the *as*, *ψ*, and *ag* must have been transported by wagon.

---

252 Freed 1995, 189 reports weights of 11.0, 11.3, 11.5, and 13.0 kg for 4 examples of the Keay 25 amphora. An example of this class with a capacity of 26 liters/72 lbs. of oil would probably have weighed *c*.11 kg.

253 An example of the Keay 25 amphora with a capacity of 36 1/100 lbs. of oil would probably have weighed *c*.12 kg; see n. 252.

254 Freed 1995, 190 no. 12 reports a weight of 27.0 kg for an example of the Keay 35 amphora missing the spike. When complete, this vessel probably weighed *c*.28 kg.

255 Freed 1995, 190 no. 11 reports a weight of 32.5 kg for an example of the wide-bodied Keay 35 amphora missing the lower wall and spike. When complete, this vessel probably weighed *c*.35 kg.

256 See, for example, the so-called Tabularii Relief of probably 3rd-c. date from Portus, which depicts two stevedores, each carrying what appears to be an example of *Africano* 1/Keay 3 amphora, the mid-imperial predecessor of Keay 25, down a gangway from a ship onto a quay. In both instances the man is supporting the amphora on his left shoulder, the mouth pointing forward and the spike to the rear, with his left hand grasping one of the handles and his right arm extended for balance. For photographs of this relief, see Meiggs 1960, 301 pl. XXVIa; Pavis d'Escurac 1976, 231; France and Hesnard 1995, 91 fig. 5.

257 A fresco on the wall of a warehouse at Augusta Rauricorum depicts a pair of porters carrying a Dressel 20 amphora suspended from a *phalanga* by straps; see Martin-Kilcher 1987, Abb. 94; 1994, 520. For the involvement of men termed *falancarii* in the handling of *cupae* used for the storage of state wine at Rome, see *CIL* VI 1785. A fresco from the Catacombs of Priscilla dated to *c*.325-50 depicts 4 pairs of men equipped with *phalangae* and staffs engaged in the transport of a *cupa*; see Giuliani 1997.

258 For a *collegium mulionum* (association of mule drivers) at Carthage, see *CIL* VIII 24686. Camels may also have been employed for the transport of state oil in Africa.

259 Landels 1978, 172.

260 Worth noting in this regard is the fact that the *Portoria Palmyrenorum* (*OGIS* 629), a regulation of A.D. 137 that specifies the customs duties levied on various categories of goods imported into and exported from the territory of Palmyra, indicates (ll.49-58) that both donkeys and camels were employed for the transport of oil, the latter carrying their load in either 2 or 4 goatskin ἀσκοὶ.

Appendix 4

Analysis of weight of oil figures for individual oil weighers in the *ostraca* of group 2

The figures in the various entries in Nos. 7 and 8 *verso* and in Element 2 of the Subgroup 2B *ostraca* presumably correspond to an amount of oil either weighed by the man recorded in that entry or an amount attributed to him on some other basis. From an analysis of these figures it is possible to shed light on the nature of the entries in question and, by so doing, to arrive at a number of inferences regarding the methods employed for oil weighing operations at Carthage.

Logically, oil weighing operations at Carthage must have involved one of two different approaches: either the oil was weighed in the container in which it had been conveyed to Carthage, with a set number of lbs. then being deducted from this figure in order to compensate for the weight of the container, or the oil was transvased into some other container so that it would be possible to weigh either the oil or its container separately. In the latter case, this might have involved one of three different approaches:

1) the oil might have been weighed in its original container, shifted to a second container where it was held while the original container was weighed, and then returned to the original container;
2) the oil might have been shifted from its original container to a pre-weighed container, weighed, and then allowed to remain in this second container;
3) the oil might have been shifted from the original container to a pre-weighed container employed specifically for weighing, weighed, and then either returned to the original container or shifted to some other container.

Worth noting in this regard is the fact that oil was weighed to the lb., since this would appear to indicate that, whatever the method employed, a high degree of precision was required in this operation. As amphoras belonging to the same class and of roughly similar capacity can display a wide range of efficiency ratios, it seems unlikely that the method employed was that which involved weighing the oil in its original container and then deducting an estimate for the weight of the container, since this probably would not have offered the requisite degree of precision. Of the three different methods that would have required the transvasing of the oil, the second — that is, the one which involved the transfer of the oil to a pre-weighed container — seems most likely to have been the technique employed. First, in comparison with the other two techniques, this approach would have required that the oil be transvased just once rather than twice. This would have been advantageous not only in that it would have involved fewer operations, but also would have presented less risk of wastage through spilling and/or the adhering of oil to the interior of an emptied container. Second, this approach would have permitted the transfer of the oil from the container in which it had been brought to Carthage (here termed the primary container) to a container of a size and type more suitable for storage or further distribution (here termed the secondary container). Specifically, this method would have allowed the shifting of the oil conveyed to Carthage in oilskins from containers of this type, which were presumably favored for transport over land due to their relatively high efficiency ratios, to amphoras, which were presumably viewed as more suitable for maritime transport and long-term storage on account of their greater rigidity and strength. The assumption that this was most likely the approach employed receives support not only from the fact that this appears to have been the method used for the weighing and packaging of Baetican oil, but also from some of the data discussed below.

If we now consider the weight of oil figures for individual oil weighers, these presumably represent either an amount of oil actually weighed by the man listed in the entry, or a quantity of weighed oil that was attributed to him on the basis of some other consideration. In the latter case, this might have been a predetermined amount that represented a share of some larger quantity of weighed oil that had been processed by that weigher together with one or more additional weighers who labored as a group. In cases where figures correspond to amounts of oil actually weighed by an individual weigher, while we might expect these to be roughly equivalent to some multiple of the weight of oil held by a particular container type, an exact correspondence would not be expected, since the capacity of individual containers presumably departed somewhat from that type's notional capacity. In contrast, in instances where these figures were assigned as arbitrarily determined shares, we might expect to find round numbers, particularly even cwt., with sets of figures perhaps embodying some set of regular relationships.

The remainder of this appendix examines the weight of oil figures for individual oil weighers in the Group 2 *ostraca* with these expectations in mind, the aim being to uncover regularities in these numbers that can be used to infer the method or methods employed for the weighing of the oil. In following the discussion readers will find it helpful to consult Tables 9 and 10, which summarize the data employed in this analysis.

Table 9. Individual oil weigher entries in Group 2 documents.

For explanation of methods, see Appendix 4. * = problematic value.

ENTRY	WEIGHT OIL	%	TRIAL 1		MODIFIED DATA		
			N.KNT	MEAN WT	WORK GROUP	N.KNT	MEAN WT
A. No. 7 v.	Date: Feb. 17						
1. Maurus	35	0.1	*1	*35.0	A	84	99.0
2. Ianuarius	55	0.2	*1	*55.0			
3. Felix	8,226	23.8	83	99.1			
4. Vindemialis	300	0.9	3	100.0	B	24	99.9
5. Victor M.	2,097	6.1	21	99.9			
6. Augustalis	1,398	4.0	14	99.9	C	35	99.9
7. Maioricus	2,097	6.1	21	99.9			
8. Marianus	4,677	13.5	47	99.5	D	47	99.5
9. Primus	4,660	13.5	47	99.1	E	47	99.1
10. Murc...	3,425	9.6	35	97.8	F	35	97.8
11. Evasius	1,872	5.4	19	98.5	G	60	98.2
12. Restutus	4,022	11.6	41	98.1			
13. Victorinus	1,798	5.2	18	99.7	H	18	99.7
TOTAL	34,658	100.0			8	350	99.0
B. No. 8 v.	Date: *c.*Feb. 17						
?X-Y.							
1.	?		-	-			
2. Obbalus	?		-	-			
3. Metrianus	8,420		85	99.1	A	117	99.3
4. Lampadius	3,200		32	100.0			
5. Marinus	8,868		89	99.6	B	103	99.7
6. Tutus	1,400		14	100.0			
7.	?		-	-			
8. Livianus	≥1,500		≥15	-			
9. ..n.	≥1,000		≥10	-			
10. B....	?		-	-			
11. N....anus	4,214		43	98.0		43	98.0
12. ...du.us	≥2,010		≥20	-			
13. Ignu....	4,200		42	100.0		42	100.0
TOTAL	≥34,812		≥350	-	?	305	99.4
C. No. 9	Date: March 9						
1. Felix	3,363	100.0	34	98.9	1	34	98.9
D. No. 10	?March 10-April 14						
X-Y.							
1.	1,500 -1,999		≥15	-	A		
2.	390 -399		4	97.5 -99.8	B	4	97.5 -99.8
3. ......us	1,804		19	*94.9	C	32	97.8
4. .....vus	1,325		14	*94.6			
TOTAL	22,207		>52	-	3	36	97.8 -98.0
E. No. 11	Date: March 15						
1. Augrinus	206	5.4	3	*68.7	A	39	98.4
2. Victor U.	225	5.9	3	*75.0			
3. Iomunpris	3,405	88.7	35	*97.3			
TOTAL	3,836	100.0	41	93.6	1	39	98.4

F. No. 13	Date: April 7						
1. Flabianus	1,000	6.5	10	100.0	A	33	97.9
2. Felix ab U.	740	4.8	*8	*92.5			
3. Peregrinus	1,490	9.6	15	99.3			
4. Felix ab ..	1,092	7.1	11	99.1	B	11	99.1
5. Doi..anus	11,135	72.0	112	99.4	C	112	99.4
TOTAL	15,457	100.0	156	99.1	3	156	99.1

G. No. 14	Date: April 8						
1. Donatilus	1,250	5.4	*13	*96.2	A	34	99.4
2. Victorianus	715	3.1	*8	*89.4			
3. Vanosus	1,414	6.1	*15	*94.3			
4. Fi...r	4,765	20.5	48	99.3	B	48	99.3
5. Ka....ius	2,400	10.3	24	100.0	C	48	99.0
6. Ar....us	2,353	10.1	24	98.0			
7. Victor	4,660	20.0	47	99.1	D	47	99.1
8. Romanus	5,710	24.5	58	98.5	E	58	98.5
TOTAL	23,267	100.0	237	98.2	5	235	99.0

H. No. 16	Date: April 25						
1. Quintus	560	14.6	*6	*93.3	A	39	98.6
2. Victorianus	2,067	53.7	21	98.4			
3. Bil. ab O.	200	5.2	2	100.0			
4. Tzelica	1,020	26.5	*11	*92.7			
TOTAL	3,847	100.0	40	96.2	1	39	98.6

I. No. 17	Date: April 26						
1. Con...	2,717		*28	97.0	A	46	99.6
2. Iricar.mu.	1,865		19	98.2			
3. ....us	2,102		*22	95.5	B	43	99.3
4. K..uas	2,170		22	98.6			
5. .....s	≥1,052		≥11	-	C		
TOTAL	≥9,906		≥102	-	?3	89	99.5

F. No. 18	Date: May 6						
1. .....inus	994	9.1	10	99.4	A	47	98.3
2.	1,342	12.3	*14	*95.8			
3.	766	7.0	*8	*95.8			
4. ...nus	487	4.5	*5	*97.4			
5. Victor a S.	518	4.8	*6	*87.3			
6. Felix	514	4.7	*6	*85.7			
7. Inventus	3,562	32.7	36	98.9	B	36	98.9
8. Victor a N.	2,718	24.9	*28	*97.1	C	28	97.1
TOTAL	10,901	100.0			3	111	98.2

Table 10. Weighed oil data in Group 2 documents

EST. N. KN^T. = estimated number of KN^T. This reports figure in MODIFIED DATA columns in Table 9. MODULES column reports figure in EST. N. KN^T column divided by 39.

NUMBER/DATE	HAND	AMOUNT WEIGHED	SUM RECORDED	EST. N. KN^T	MODULES	TYPE 4 ENTRY
No.7/17.2	5	34,658	35,078	350	9X-1?	-
No.8/*c*.17.2	5?	?	44,293	-	-	-
No.9/9.3	6	3,363	3,463	34	-	1/ 34
No.10/10.3-14.4	7	?	22,207	-	-	⁊ 224
No.11/15.3	8	?3,836	3,836	39	1X	?
No.13/7.4	7	15,457	15,457	156	4X	⁊ 156
No.14/8.4	7	23,267	23,267	235	6X+1	1} 235
No.16/25.4	7	3,847	3,847	39	1X	1/ 39 Ⲡ 75
No.18/6.5	7	10,901	11,111	111	-	1/ 111 Ⲡ 10

Beginning with No. 7 *verso*, the fact that 4 of the 13 entries are only two or three pounds short of an even hundredweight (Entries 5-7, 13), suggests that the figures reported in this document may represent quantities of oil held in groups of containers having a capacity of or slightly less than 100 lbs. of oil, presumably *centenaria levia*/KN^T. In order to evaluate this conjecture, the figures in these 13 entries were divided by the largest whole number that yielded a product of 100.0 or less. In this operation the divisor represents the number of amphoras in the putative group of containers and the dividend the mean weight of the oil that they held. The results of this operation are reported in Table 9.A in the columns labelled TRIAL 1.

With the exception of the results obtained for Entries 1 and 2, the mean container weight figures, which range from a low of 97.8 to a high of 100.0, appear to be compatible with the conjecture that the weight of oil figures for individual oil weighers in this document represent amounts of oil held in sets of containers termed *centenaria levia*. The figures obtained for Entries 1 and 2, 35 and 55 lbs., respectively, are, of course, incompatible with this conjecture, in that both are considerably smaller than 100 lbs. Worth noting, however, is the fact that these two figures are equal to the weight equivalents of one-half and two-thirds of an *amphora* of oil, 36 and 54 lbs., respectively, rounded to the nearest 5, and it may well be that these represent arbitrarily determined shares that were apportioned to these two weighers out of some larger amount of weighed oil. If we accept this conjecture, we may infer that these two weighers worked in collaboration with the man named in Entry 3, and that they were each attributed a small portion of the extremely large quantity of oil weighed by this three-man work group. The highly unequal division of this oil suggests that the group consisted of something like a master oil weigher and his two assistants, with the latter two men being credited with only a token amount of the oil processed by the group. Entries 4 and 5 may well represent another case of this kind. In this instance, the figure in Entry 4, 300 lbs., is substantially smaller than any of the other figures in Entries 3-13, and it alone of the weight of oil figures for individual oil weighers in this document corresponds to an even hundredweight. Here again this figure may represent an arbitrarily determined share, with the weigher in this entry working as an assistant to the man named in Entry 5.

If we add the 90 lbs. of oil represented by Entries 1 and 2 to the figure for Entry 3 and then divide the sum by the largest whole number that yields a result of 100.0 or less, the figure for the resulting number of containers for this work group comes to 84. Of note is the fact that this number and the number of containers projected for the hypothetical work group represented by Entries 4-5 (24) are both multiples of 12. Following this lead, it will be noted that for Entries 6-12 the figure for the number of containers is either one less than a multiple of 12 (Entries 8-10) or a figure that, when combined with the figure for the entry adjacent to it in the list, produces a sum either equal to a multiple of 12 (Entry 11 plus Entry 12) or equal to one less than a multiple of 12 (Entry 6 plus Entry 7). The figure for the number of containers for the final entry, Entry 13, departs from this pattern, being equal to one and one-half dozens. This pattern suggests both that the men listed in Entries 6-7 and 11-12 represent two 2-man work groups, and that for the weighing operations documented in this *ostracon* KN^T were allotted to individual weighers and to 2- or 3-man work groups either by the dozen or by the near dozen, with the final weigher in the list receiving an irregular number of residual containers. While the fact that all of the containers referred to in the documents dating to this date and earlier are *centenaria levia*/KN^T may be taken as an indication that the containers distributed according to these procedures were filled primary containers, considerations discussed in Section 4 suggest that they were most likely empty secondary containers meant to be filled in the course of weighing operations.

The pairs of men in the work groups represented by Entries 6-7 and 11-12 appear to have divided up their allotment of empty KN^T at the outset of operations, with the amount of oil attributed to each man corresponding to the amount then transvased into the containers in his allotment. For the work group of Entries 6-7 this division was made in accordance with a ratio of 2:3, while in the case of the work group of Entries 11-12 the division was within one container of a ratio of 1:2. This approach to the division of oil is distinctly different from that employed for the work groups of Entries 1-3 and 4-5, suggesting a more equal arrangement between the men in these groups.

The columns in Table 9.A labelled MODIFIED DATA represent a reworking of the Trial 1 data in light of these observations, the entries being grouped by work group and the figures for Entries 1-3 and 4-5 (Work Groups A and B) being averaged to reflect the method apparently employed for the apportioning of weighed oil. Unassociated weighers are also assigned work group designations as these men may have been helped by assistants whose names do not appear in the list (see Section 5), and these men are henceforth referred to simply as work groups for ease of discussion. The results remain virtually unchanged from Trial 1 with regard to the range of mean container weight values, which now span the interval 97.8-99.9 rather than 97.8-100.0. The fact that the figure for the number of containers for 4 work groups is one less than a multiple of 12 raises the possibility that in these cases the true figure may have been one larger than the number assumed for the purposes of this analysis. In order to test this conjecture, another trial was undertaken for the two unassociated weigher work groups (Entries 8 and 9), increasing the figure of the number of containers by one. In both instances, however, the resulting mean container weight figure (Entry 8 = 97.4, Entry 9 = 97.1) was well below the lowest mean container weight figure obtained for any of the other work groups, suggesting that the original set of values is probably the correct one. This suggests that, while an effort was made to distribute containers to work groups by the dozen, the size of an allotment was in some cases shaved by one container, perhaps with a view towards bringing the number of containers available for the final work group on the list up to the even figure of one and one-half dozens. If this last observation is correct, then we may infer that the total number of containers involved in weighing operations on this day was determined on the basis of some consideration other than the desire to assign regularly-sized groups of containers to the several work groups on duty.

Also worth noting with regard to these data is the general downward trend in the mean container weight values registered from Work Group C through Work Group G, with this trend then being reversed with Work Group H. This suggests that the procedure employed for the distribution of KN^T to work groups may have been organized in such a way as to place the groups progressively further down the list at an increasing disadvantage with respect to the size of the containers in their allotment. One possibility is that the assignment of containers to work groups took place in the order in which the groups appear in the list, with each group free to select the KN^T in its allotment from among the group of containers set aside for operations on that day. If work groups had sought to maximize the amount of oil in their allotment, they would presumably have selected those containers which appeared to be the largest, producing a trend similar to that apparent in the data. The reversal of the trend for Work Group H may perhaps be explained by assuming that this work group was allowed to round out the number of containers in its allotment by selecting one amphora from the sets of containers already chosen by the 4 work groups with allotments of one less than an even dozen, i.e., Work Groups C, D, E, and F. If this group had selected what appeared to be the largest among the sets of containers chosen by these 4 groups, this would have had the effect of depressing ever so slightly the mean container weight values for these other groups while inflating more substantially this value in its own case.

The mean container weight values obtained for the various work groups indicate that the average weight of oil that could be held by small groups of KN^T ranged from a maximum of 99.9 lbs. to a minimum of 97.8 lbs. While maximum and minimum capacity values for individual containers cannot be determined on the basis of these figures, if we assume, as seems reasonable, that the largest containers in the group had capacities of no more than *c.*100.0 lbs. of oil, then the smallest may well have held no more than *c.*95-96 lbs. of oil (*c.*34-34.5 l).

The weight of oil figures for individual oil weighers for the other Group 2 documents can be analyzed applying variations on the methods employed for No. 7. While this involves a substantial amount of *ad hoc* adjustment on a document-by-document basis, the results suggest that generally similar approaches were employed for the allocation of credit for weighed oil on the other days on which weighing activity took place. It should be noted at this juncture that while trials were also undertaken dividing the figures in these documents by values equal to the notional capacities of the other container types attested in the Group 2 *ostraca*, these failed to yield any promising results.

The figures for No. 8 *verso* are fragmentary and little can be done with them. Of note, however, is the fact that three of the six intact figures are equal to an even cwt. (Entries 4, 6, and 13). The fact that two of these entries (Entries 4 and 6) immediately follow entries with figures that yield significantly lower mean container weight values, when divided according to the Trial 1 procedures described above, suggests that this series of 4 entries may represent two work groups of two weighers each, as indicated in the MODIFIED DATA column. The final two entries (12-13) might also represent a work group of this kind. The significantly lower mean container weight value for Entry 11 is compatible with the general downward trend for these figures noted for No. 7 *verso*.

If we turn to No. 9, the figure of 3,363 lbs. of oil attributed to the single weigher listed, presumably the same Felix recorded in No. 7 *verso*, Entry 3, is compatible with the weighing of a group of 34 KN^T having a mean capacity of 98.9 lbs. This last figure is very close to that obtained for the work group headed by Felix in No. 7 *verso* (99.0), raising the possibility that the variation in mean container weight values obtained for the several work groups posited for this other document may to some extent reflect differences in weighing technique and/or in the method employed for the filling of secondary containers rather than differences in container capacity.

The figures for No. 10 are again fragmentary and difficult to interpret. When these figures are divided according to the Trial 1 procedures, those for Entries 3 and 4 yield problematic values, in the sense that they are well below the range of mean container weight values obtained for the work groups in No. 7 *verso*. It seems possible, however, that the weighers in these two entries constituted a single work group, as suggested in the MODIFIED DATA columns. If so, it would appear that the first man was assigned a base share of 18 cwt. and the second a base share of 13 cwt., quite possibly prior to the actual weighing of the oil, with credit for the remaining 29 lbs. then divided between them after the completion of weighing operations, the second man receiving a round amount of 25 lbs. and the first man the residual 4 lbs.

All three values in No. 11 are problematic when divided according to the Trial 1 procedures, and here it appears likely that the men in these three entries constituted a single work group, with the first two weighers each assigned a base share of 2 cwt., and the third a base share of 34 cwt. Credit for the remaining 41 lbs. was then divided among the three, with the second man receiving the round amount of 25 lbs., and the first and third men round amounts of 5 lbs., with the 1 residual lb. then allotted to the first man.

In No. 13, dividing the figures in accordance with the Trial 1 procedures yields a problematic result for Entry 2. The most plausible explanation is that the men in the first three entries constituted a single work group, with the first man assigned a base share of 1,000 lbs., the second a base share of 700 lbs., and the third a base share of 1,400 lbs., with credit for the remaining 130 lbs. being divided among the last two men in accordance with the size of their original allotments, 40 lbs. going to the second man and 90 lbs. to the third. This assumption is supported by the fact that a nearly identical pattern occurs in the first three entries in No. 14, a document composed on the following day by the same functionary. The fourth and fifth entries in this document appear to represent unassociated weighers. The figures for the number of containers in the MODIFIED DATA columns are of some interest, in that they suggest container distribution procedures somewhat analogous to those posited for No. 7 *verso*. In this instance, the first work group may have been assigned three dozen containers, the second work group one dozen containers, and the third work group 9 dozen containers, with the last group then allotted one container from each of the dozens assigned to the first two work groups, decreasing the allotments of these groups by 3 and 1 containers, respectively, while increasing its own allotment by 4.

No. 14 may be analyzed much along the same lines as No. 13. In this instance, Trial 1 yields problematic figures for Entries 1-3. As just noted, the figures in these entries exhibit striking similarities to those in Entries 1-3 in No. 13, and here too it seems likely that these represent a single work group. The three men in the group appear to have been assigned base shares of 12, 7, and 14 cwt., with credit for the remaining 79 lbs. being distributed among them, the first man receiving the round amount of 50 lbs., and the residual 29 lbs. being divided evenly between the other two. The remaining entries in this document appear to represent an unassociated weigher assigned 48 KN^T, a two-man work group assigned this same number of containers, and two unassociated weighers assigned 47 and 58 KN^T, respectively. The fact that the men in the two-man work group were attributed with 2,400 and 2,353 lbs. of oil suggests that the former was credited with a base share equal to 24 cwt., while the latter was credited with the balance of the weighed oil. The figures for the number of containers for this document appear to reflect the same distribution practices as those inferred for No. 7 *verso* and No. 13, with containers allotted to work groups by the dozen, and the final work group permitted to increase its allotment by selecting containers from the sets already assigned to some of the other work groups. As with No. 7 *verso*, the mean container weight figures show a pattern of progressive decrease, suggesting that a similar approach was employed for distributing amphoras to the several work groups.

The weight of oil figures for individual oil weighers in No. 14 are of particular importance because, as discussed in Section 4, there is good reason to assume that the 23,267 lbs. of weighed oil registered in this document correspond to the oil held in the 27 *as a ƀ* and 42 of the 161 *as* recorded under the *inpletu* heading in No. 13. This marks the only instance in which we have reasonably clear evidence regarding the identity of the primary containers that served to hold the oil recorded in a set of weight of oil figures for individual oil weighers. As just discussed, the various weight of oil figures for individual oil weighers in No. 14 are compatible with the assumption that they represent amounts of oil held in KN^T, and trials undertaken with a view to identifying likely groups of *as a ƀ* or *as* that might also account for these figures failed to yield any workable result. It would thus appear that for oil brought to Carthage in oilskins the weight figures associated with work groups and unassociated oil weighers correspond to amounts of oil transferred to groups of secondary containers, specifically KN^T, in the course of the weighing process, rather than to amounts of oil held in groups of primary containers. In light of this observation it would appear that groups of empty KN^T were distributed to work groups and unassociated weighers as secondary containers, with the men in these groups then opening as many primary container oilskins as were required to fill the group of amphoras that had been allotted to them. If this was, in fact, the approach employed, it seems likely that there would have been some effort to consign *as a ƀ* and *as* to the weighing facility in groups that held an amount of oil corresponding more or less to a round cwt., as this would have simplified the task of transvasing oil from primary to secondary containers. It thus seems possible that the recurrence at this facility of groups of 21 *as a ƀ*, which would have held *c.*1,512 lbs. of oil, more or less the amount required to fill 15 KN^T, may reflect this consideration rather than the fact that this number of *as a ƀ* represented the maximum load for an *angaria*, as suggested in Section 4.

As discussed in Section 4, it seems likely that this was also the procedure employed for the weighing of oil conveyed to Carthage in KN^T and ψ. If so, it may be that groups of primary container amphoras were employed as the secondary containers for the oil that they held, the contents of the first amphora being shifted to some supplementary container on a temporary basis, the contents of the second amphora transvased into the first, that of the third transvased into the second, and so forth, with the contents of the first amphora then transvased from the supplementary container into the last amphora in the group.

The assumption that the 23,267 lbs. of weighed oil recorded in No. 14 was brought to Carthage in 27 *as a ƀ* and 42 *as* also permits us to calculate the true capacity of these two container types. As discussed in Appendices 2 and 3, these two container types appear to have had notional capacities equal to 1 and 7 *amphorae*, respectively. The total capacity of the containers processed on this day would thus have been equal to 321 of these notional *amphorae* (27 + [42 x 7] = 321). Each such notional unit would thus have been equal to *c.*72.5 lbs. of oil (23,267/321 = 72.48), yielding a capacity equal to this value for the *as a ƀ* and one of 507.4 lbs. for the *as*. The validity of the assumptions and inferences on which these calculations are based receives confirmation from the fact that the resulting figure for the notional *amphora* is virtually identical to that for 1 *amphora* of olive oil, which, assuming values of 26.2 l for the capacity of the *amphora*, 327 g for the pound, and 0.91 for the density of oil, comes to 72.9 lbs. Also worth noting in light of this calculation is the fact that, by rounding up the notional weight of the *as* from 504 to 505 lbs., and by rounding up the notional weight of the *as a ƀ* from 72 to 75 lbs. rather than rounding it down to 70 lbs., the compilers of the Subgroup 2B *ostraca* may not only have been simplifying the task of deriving an estimate for the total weight of oil at the two facilities, but also improving the accuracy of this estimate.

In No. 16, Trial 1 results in problematic figures in the meant container weight column for two of the 4 entries (Entries 1 and 4). The figures in three of the four entries, however, have the appearance of arbitrarily determined shares (Entries 1, 3, and 4), and it may be that all four entries are of this type, with the men listed in this document all belonging to a single work group. They would have been assigned base shares equal to 5, 20, 2, and 10 cwt. Credit for the remaining 147 lbs. of oil would then have been apportioned among 3 of the 4 men, with the weighers in Entries 1 and 2 receiving allotments of 60 lbs. each and the weigher in Entry 4 an allotment of 20 lbs., with the residual 7 lbs. added to the tally of the man in Entry 2.

For No. 17, Trial 1 yields problematic values for two of the four entries for which figures are available (Entries 1 and 3). In this instance, as with No. 9 *verso*, it appears possible that the first four entries represent two 2-man work groups. The two men in the first pairing would have been attributed base shares of 27 and 18 cwt., with credit for the remaining 82 lbs. of oil then divided between them, one-fifth of this amount going to the first man and four-fifths to the second. The two weighers in the second group would each have received base shares of 21 cwt., again dividing credit for the remaining oil between themselves, with the round amount of 70 lbs. going to the second weigher and the residual 2 lbs. going to the first.

In No. 18, Trial 1 results in problematic figures for 6 of the 8 entries (Entries 2-6 and 8). As none of the weight of oil figures for individual oil weighers in this document has the appearance of an arbitrarily determined share, the interpretation of this document remains problematic. The problematic nature of the figure in Entry 8 may perhaps be more apparent than real, as it seems possible that a group of KN^T might have had a mean capacity as low as 97.1 lbs., particularly if the group were one allotted towards the end of the amphora distribution procedure, as imagined above. In every other list of entries for which we possess unambiguous evidence, with the possible exception of No. 17, the list is headed by a work group consisting of three or more weighers. By assuming that this is also the case with this document, and that the group in question extends down to the last of the problematic entries, No. 6, it is possible to produce a workable set of MODIFIED DATA figures, consisting of a group of 47 KN^T with a mean container capacity of 98.3 lbs. The number of containers figure for the resulting work group appears plausible in that it is one short of an even dozen, with the figure for the next work group in the list equal to an even dozen, and that for the third and final work group an irregular number that might include an amphora removed from the set of containers originally allotted to the work group at the head of the list. The mean container weight value is plausible in that it is consistent with the relatively low values attested for the other groups in this document.[261] The lack of any apparent logic to the apportioning of weight values among the 6 weighers assigned to the first work group remains, however, a substantial difficulty with regard to this interpretation.

Given the inelegant nature of the several analyses presented above it will be understandable if readers entertain considerable scepticism with regard to the validity of the approach employed. The validity of both the approach and the results, however, receives corroboration from three different bodies of independent evidence. It should be stressed that in all three cases the connections between the bodies of evidence in question and the results of these analyses were not noted until after the completion of the analyses. The first of these three bodies of evidence consists of the values reported in the Type 4 entries in the Subgroup 2B documents. As noted in Section 2, the values reported in these entries, while clearly related to the sum of weighed oil figures reported at the bottom of Element 1, differ from these in a seemingly inconsistent fashion, most often appearing as a value in cwt. that ranges from the same figure in cwt. reported in the sum of weighed oil figure to a figure as much as 3 cwt. greater than this. As Table 10 illustrates, in every case in which such a comparison can be made (Nos. 9, 13, 14, 16, and 18), the figure in cwt. reported in the Type 4 entry is equal to the number of KN^T projected in the analysis of that document presented above. This suggests that the figure reported in the Type 4 entry was based on the number of KN^T of processed oil on hand at the weighing facility on the day in question, being either equal to this figure or equal to this figure plus a second figure for lbs. of oil that was derived by rounding the figure for lbs. of oil appearing in the sum of weighed oil figure. While the rounding of the lbs. of oil figure from 11 to 10 in No. 18 presents no difficulty, the rounding of the lbs. of oil figure from 47 to 75 in No. 16 is somewhat puzzling. One possibility is that this reflects the fact that among the primary containers emptied on that day were a number of *as a ꝑ*. Since this container type was assigned a standard weight value of 75 lbs., the compiler might have thought it appropriate to terminate the Type 4 entry with this number. Interesting is the fact that the Type 4 entries in these documents are varyingly introduced by three different signs - the cwt. sign, the sum of cwt. sign, and a barred *centenarius* sign. All three, in fact, were employed by a single compiler, Hand 7.

The second set of corroborative evidence consists of the apparent mistakes embodied in the figures for the sum of weighed oil in Nos. 7 *verso*, 9, and 18. In all three cases, the 'mistake' — the recording of 346 cwt. as 350 cwt. in No. 7 *verso*, the recording of 33 cwt. as 34 cwt. in No. 9, and the recording of 109 cwt. as 111 cwt. in No. 18 — brings the cwt. of oil figure into line with the figure posited above for the number of KN^T processed on that day. This suggests that these were not, in fact, errors, but rather efforts to simplify record-

261 Treating Entry 1 as a separate work group, for example, yields a value for the mean container weight of 99.4 for the weigher in this entry, while lowering that for a putative work group consisting of Entries 2-6 to 98.0.

keeping or to avoid being charged with a shortfall by bringing the number of cwt. in the figure for the sum of weighed oil into agreement with the number of KN^T of oil that had been processed on that day.

The third and final set of corroborative evidence consists of the recurrence of values equal to multiples or near multiples of 39 among the figures for the total numbers of KN^T of processed oil projected in this analysis (see Table 10). As discussed in Section 4, this probably represents the processing of groups of containers equal to 97.5 % of 40.

BIBLIOGRAPHY

Albertini, M., "Table de mesures de Djemila," *CRAI* 1920, 315-19.

Aubert, J.-J., *Business managers in ancient Rome: a social and economic study of "institores", 200 B.C. - A.D. 250* (Leiden 1994).

Bagnall, R., A. Cameron, S. Schwartz, and K. Worp, *Consuls of the later Roman Empire* (Atlanta 1987).

Barnish, S. J. B., "Pigs, plebeians and *potentes*," *PBSR* 55 (1987) 157-85.

Barrow, R. H. (ed.), *Prefect and emperor. The* relationes *of Symmachus A.D. 384* (Oxford 1973).

Belli Pasqua, R., "Il rifornimento alimentare di carne a Roma nel I-V secolo d.C.," *Agricoltura e commerci nell'Italia antica (Atlante tematico della topografia antica, Suppl.* 1, 1995) 257-72.

Blázquez (Martínez), J. M., "The latest work on the export of Baetican olive oil to Rome and the army," *G&R* 39.2 (1992) 173-88.

Blázquez Martínez, J. M., J. Remesal Rodríguez, and E. Rodríguez-Almeida, *Excavaciones arqueológicas en el Monte Testaccio (Roma). Memoria campaña 1989* (Madrid 1994).

Bonifay, M., and D. Piéri, "Amphores du Ve au VIIe s. à Marseille: nouvelles données sur la typologie et le contenu," *JRA* 8 (1995) 94-120.

Bost, J.-P., M. Campo, D. Colls, V. Guerrero, and F. Mayet, *L'épave Cabrera III (Majorque): échanges commerciaux et circuits monétaires au milieu du IIIe siècle après Jésus-Christ* (Paris 1992).

Cagnat, R., "Table de mesures-étalons trouvées en Afrique," *CRAI* 1905, 490-97.

Cagnat, R., "14 Décembre 1911. Séance de la Commission de l'Afrique du Nord," *BAC* 1911, ccxxv-ccxliv.

Cagnat, R., "L'annone d'Afrique," *Mém.Acad.Insc.* 40 (1916) 247-77.

Cagnat, R., *L'armée romaine d'Afrique et l'occupation militaire de l'Afrique sous les empereurs* (1913; repr. New York 1975).

Cagnat, R. and A. Merlin, "Ostraka latins de Carthage," *JSav* 9 (1911) 514-23.

Carandini, A. and C. Panella (edd.), *Ostia* IV: *Le Terme del Nuotatore* (*StMisc* 23, 1977).

Carignani, A., "La distribuzione delle anfore africane tra III e VII secolo," in Giardina (ed.) (1986) 273-77.

Carignani, A., A. Ciotola, F. Pacetti, and C. Panella, "Roma. Il contesto del Tempio della Magna Mater sul Palatino," in Giardina (ed.) (1986) 27-43.

Carignani, A., and F. Pacetti, "Anfore tardoantiche degli scavi del Palatino," in Lenoir *et al.* (edd.) (1989) 610-15.

Carignani, A. and F. Pacetti, "Le importazioni di anfore bizantine a Roma fra IV e V secolo: le evidenze di alcuni contesti urbani," in V. Deriche and J. M. Speiser (edd.), *Recherches sur la céramique byzantine* (*BCH* Suppl. 18, 1989) 5-16.

Carrié, J.-M., "Les distributions alimentaires dans les cités de l'empire romain tardif," *MEFRA* 87.2 (1975) 995-1101.

Casson, L., *Ships and seamanship in the ancient world* (Princeton 1971).

Cébeillac-Gervasoni, M., "Ostie et le blé au IIe siècle ap. J.-C.," in *Le ravitaillement en blé de Rome* (Collection de Centre Jean Bérard 11/CollEFR 196, 1994).

Chastagnol, A., *La préfecture urbaine à Rome sous le Bas-Empire* (Paris 1960).

Cockle, H., "Pottery manufacture in Roman Egypt: a new papyrus," *JRS* 71 (1981) 87-97.

Dagron, G., and C. Morrisson, "Le *Kentènarion* dans les sources byzantines," *RN* 17 (1975) 145-62.

Déléage, A., *La capitation du Bas-Empire* (1944; repr. New York 1975).

di Vita-Evrard, G., "'*Regio Tripolitana*' – a reappraisal," in D. Buck and D. Mattingly (edd.), *Town and country in Roman Tripolitania* (BAR S 274, Oxford 1985) 143-63.

Dore, J., "First report on the pottery," in N. Ben Lazreg and D. Mattingly (edd.), *Leptiminus (Lamta): a Roman port city in Tunisia. Report no. 1* (*JRA* Suppl. 4, 1992) 115-56.

Duncan-Jones, R., *Structure and scale in the Roman economy* (Cambridge 1990).

Durliat, J., *De la ville antique à la ville byzantine: le problème des subsistances* (CollEFR 136, 1990).

Formenti, F., "Analyse de traces organiques dans les amphores," in Lenoir *et al.* (edd.) (1989) 562-63.

France, J. and A. Hesnard, "Une *statio* du quarantième des Gaules et les opérations commerciales dans le port romain de Marseille (place Jules-Verne)," *JRA* 8 (1995) 78-93.

Freed, J., "The late series of Tunisian cylindrical amphoras at Carthage," *JRA* 8 (1995) 155-91.

Frier, B., "Roman law and the wine trade: the problem of vinegar sold as wine," *ZRG* 17 (1983) 257-95.

Fulford, M., and D. P. S. Peacock, *Excavations at Carthage. The British mission* II,2. *The Circular Harbour, North side. The pottery* (Oxford 1994).

Funari, P. P., "Baetica and the Dressel 20 production. An outline of the province's history," *DHA* 20.1 (1994) 87-105.

Giardina, A. (ed.), *Società romana e impero tardoantico* III: *le merci, gli insediamenti* (Bari 1986).

Giacchero, M. (ed.), *Edictum Diocletiani et collegarum de pretiis rerum venalium* 1 (Genova 1974).

Giuliani, R., "Mercatores vinarii nelle catacombe," *Forma Urbis* 2.7-8 (1997) 5-9.

Gsell, S., "Observations géographiques sur la révolte de Firmius," *RecConstantine* 36 (1902) 21-46.

Gsell, S., *Atlas archéologique de l'Algérie* (Paris-Algiers 1911).

Hermansen, G., *Ostia: aspects of Roman city life* (Edmonton 1981).

Heron, C. and R. Evershed, "The analysis of organic residues and the study of pottery use," *Archaeological method and theory* 5 (1993) 247-73.

Herz, P., *Studien zur römischen Wirtschaftsgesetzgebung: Die Lebensmittelversorgung* (Historia Einzelheft Bd. 55, 1988).

Hilgers, W., *Lateinische Gefässnamen* (Beihefte BonnJb 31, 1969).
Hodges, R., and D. Whitehouse, *Mohammed, Charlemagne & the origins of Europe* (Ithaca 1983).
Holmberg, E., *Zur Geschichte des cursus publicus* (Lund 1933).
Hostetter, E. *et al.*, "A late Roman domus with apsidal hall on the NE slope of the Palatine Hill," *Rome papers* (*JRA* Suppl. 11, 1994) 135-85.
Hultsch, F., *Griechische und römische Metrologie* (Berlin 1882).
Hultsch, F. (ed.), *Metrologicorum scriptorum reliquiae* (1864-66 Stuttgart; repr. 1971).
Hurst, H., "Excavations at Carthage 1976. Third interim report," *AntJ* 57 (1977) 232-61.
Hurst, H., "Excavations at Carthage 1977-8. Fourth interim report," *AntJ* 59 (1979) 19-49.
Hurst, H., *Excavations at Carthage The British mission* II,1. *The Circular Harbour, North side. The site finds other than pottery* (Oxford 1994).
Jones, A. H. M., *The later Roman Empire 284-602* (Norman 1964).
Keay, S., *Late Roman amphorae in the western Mediterranean: a typology and economic study of the Catalan evidence* (BAR S 196, Oxford 1984).
Keay, S., *Roman Spain* (London 1988).
Kehoe, D., *The economics of agriculture on Roman imperial estates in North Africa* (Hypomnemata 89, 1988).
Lafaurie, J., "L'empire gaulois. Apport de la numismatique," *ANRW* 2.2 (1975) 853-1012.
Lancel, S. (ed.), *Gesta Conlationis Carthaginiensis anno 411* (CCSL vol. CXLIX A, 1974).
Lancel, S., *Actes de la Conférence de Carthage en 411*, tome IV (Sources chrétiennes 373, 1991).
Landels, J. G. *Engineering in the ancient world* (Berkeley 1978).
Lavoie, C., "Les traces d'ateliers du poterie à Sullecthum," *CEA* 22 (1989) 93-109.
Le Bohec, Y., N. Duval, and S. Lancel, "Le garnison de Carthage," *BCTH* ns 15-16B (1980) 33-89.
Lenoir, M., D. Manacorda and C. Panella (edd.), *Amphores romaines et histoire économique* (CollEFR 118, 1989).
Lequément. R., "Etiquettes de plomb sur des amphores d'Afrique," *MEFRA* 87.2 (1975) 667-80.
Le Roux, P., "L'huile de Bétique et le prince sur un itinéraire annonaire," *REA* 88 (1986) 247-71.
Lewis, N., *Life in Egypt under Roman rule* (Oxford 1983).
Liou, B., "Les amphores à huile de l'épave St. Gervais 3 à Fos-sur-Mer: premières observations sur les inscriptions peintes," in Blázquez Martinez, J. M. (ed.), *Producción y comercio del aceite en la antigüedad. Primero congreso internacional* (Madrid 1980) 161-75.
Liou, B. and A. Tchernia, "L'interprétation des inscriptions sur les amphores Dressel 20," in *Epigrafia della produzione e della distribuzione* (CollEFR 193, 1994) 133-56.
Loyzance, M.-F., "A propos de Marcus Cassius Sempronianus Olisiponensis, *diffusor olearius*," *REA* 88 (1986) 273-84.
Manacorda, D., "Testimonianze sulla produzione e il consumo dell'olio tripolitano nel II secolo," *DialArch* 9-10 (1976-77) 542-601.
Manacorda, D., "Il *Kalendarium Vegetianum* e le anfore della Betica," *MEFRA* 89 (1977) 313-32.
Marichal, R., *Les ostraca de Bu Njem* (LibAnt Suppl. 7, 1992).
Martin, A., "L'importazione di ceramica africana a Roma tra il IV e il V secolo (Santo Stefano Rotondo)," *L'Africa romana* 6 (1989) 475-83.
Martin-Kilcher, S., *Die römischen Amphoren aus Augst und Kaiseraugst* 1: *Die südspanischen Ölamphoren (Gruppe 1)* (Forschungen in Augst 7, 1987).
Martin-Kilcher, S., *Die römischen Amphoren aus Augst und Kaiseraugst* 2: *Die Amphoren für Wein, Fischsauce, Südfrüchte (Gruppen 2-24)* (Forschungen in Augst 7, 1994).
Mattingly, D., "Oil for export? A comparison of Libyan, Spanish, and Tunisian olive oil production in the Roman Empire," *JRA* 1 (1988) 33-56.
Mattingly, D., "Olive cultivation and the Albertini Tablets," *L'Africa romana* 6 (1989) 403-15.
Mattingly, D. *Tripolitania* (Ann Arbor =1994a).
Mattingly, D. "Regional variation in Roman oleoculture: some problems of comparability," in *Landuse in the Roman Empire* (AnalRom Suppl. 22 =1994b) 91-106.
Mattingly, D., and R. B. Hitchner, "Roman Africa: an archaeological review," *JRS* 85 (1995) 165-213.
Mayet, F., "Les *figlinae* dans les marques d'amphores Dressel 20 de Bétique," *REA* 88 (1986) 285-305.
McCann, A. M. and J. Freed, *Deep water archaeology* (*JRA* Supp. 13, 1994).
Meiggs, R., *Roman Ostia* (Oxford 1960).
Millar, F., *The emperor in the Roman world* (London 1977).
Miller, K., *Itineraria romana. Römische Reisewege an der Hand der Tabula Peutingeriana* (1916; repr. Wien 1966).
Morley, N., *Metropolis and hinterland: the city of Rome and the Italian economy 200 B.C. - A.D. 200* (Cambridge 1996).
Neri, V., "*Cod. Theod.* XI.1.6 ed il vino di Cesena," *Atti e Memorie Deputazione di Storia Patria per le province di Romagna* 26 (1977) 107-20.
Nordh, A., *Libellus de Regionibus Urbis Romae* (Lund 1949).
Ørsted, P.,"*Quattuor publica Africae*: custom duties or landtax," *L'Africa romana* 9 (1992) 813-29.
Ørsted, P. and L. L. Sebaï, "Town and countryside in Roman Tunisia: a preliminary report on the Tuniso-Danish survey project in the Oued R'mel basin in and around ancient Segermes," *JRA* 5 (1992) 69-96.
Oxé, A., "Das *centenarium* und seine metrologische Umwelt," *RhMus* 89 (1940) 127-51.
Panella, C., "Le anfore africane della prima, media e tarda età imperiale: tipologia e problemi," *Actes du colloque sur la céramique antique de Carthage, 23-24 juin 1980* (CEDAC Dossier I, 1982) 171-96.
Parker, A., *Ancient shipwrecks of the Mediterranean and the Roman provinces* (BAR S 580, Oxford 1992).

Pavis d'Escurac, H., *La préfecture de l'annone, service administratif impérial d'Auguste à Constantin* (BEFAR 226, 1976).
Pavolini, C., *Ostia* (Guide archeologiche Laterza 8, 1983).
Peacock, D. P. S., *Pottery in the Roman world: an ethnoarchaeological approach* (London 1982).
Peacock, D. P. S. and D. Williams, *Amphorae and the Roman economy* (London 1986).
Peacock, D. P. S., F. Bejaoui and N. Belazreg, "Roman amphora production in the Sahel region of Tunisia," in Lenoir *et al.* (edd.) (1989) 179-222.
Peacock, D. P. S., F. Bejaoui, and N. Ben Lazreg, "Roman pottery production in central Tunisia," *JRA* 3 (1990) 59-84.
Peña, J. T., *The urban economy during the early dominate: ceramic evidence from the Palatine hill* (forthcoming BAR Int. Ser.)
Petschenig, M. (ed.), *Victoris Episcopi Vitensis historia persecutionis Africanae provinciae* (1881; repr. New York-London 1967).
Pflaum, H.-G., *Les carrières procuratoriennes équestres sous le Haut-Empire romain* (Paris 1960-61).
Pontacolone, L. and M. Incitti, "Un relitto con carico di merci africane di età imperiale alle Trincere (Tarquinia)," *L'Africa romana* 8 (1991) 543-70.
Reed, N., "Pattern and purpose in the Antonine Itinerary," *AJP* 99 (1978) 228-54.
Remesal Rodríguez, J., "Die Ölwirtschaft in der Baetica: Neue Formen der Analyse," *SaalJb* 38 (1982) 30-71.
Remesal Rodríguez, J., "Transformaciones en la exportación del aceite bético a mediados del siglos III d.C.," in Blázquez Martínez, J. M. and J. Remesal Rodríguez (edd.), *Producción y comercio del aceite en la antigüedad. Segundo congreso internacional* (Madrid 1983) 115-31.
Remesal Rodríguez, J., *La annona militaris y la exportación de aceite bético a Germania* (Madrid 1986).
Remesal Rodríguez, J., "Mummius Secundinus. El *Kalendarium Vegetianum* y las confiscaciones de Severo en la Bética (*HA Severus* 12-13)," *Gerión* 14 (1996) 195-221.
Reynolds, P., *Trade in the western Mediterranean, A.D. 400-700: the ceramic evidence* (BAR S 604, Oxford 1995).
Rickman, G., *Roman granaries and store buildings* (Cambridge 1971).
Rickman, G., *The corn supply of ancient Rome* (Oxford 1980).
Robinson, O. E., *Ancient Rome: city planning and administration* (London 1992).
Rodríguez-Almeida, E., "Monte Testaccio: I *mercatores* dell'olio della Betica," *MEFRA* 91 (1979) 873-975.
Rodríguez-Almeida, E., "Vicissitudini nella gestione del commercio dell'olio betico da Vespasiano a Severo Alessandro," in J. D'Arms and E. C. Kopff (edd.), *The seaborne commerce of ancient Rome* (MAAR 36, 1980) 277-90.
Rodríguez-Almeida, E., *Il Monte Testaccio* (Rome =1984a).
Rodríguez-Almeida, E., "Varia de Monte Testaceo," *Cuadernos de la Escuela Española de Historia y Arqueología* 15 (=1984b) 105-64.
Rodríguez-Almeida, E., *Los tituli picti de las ánforas olearias de la Bética* I: *tituli picti de los Severos y la ratio fisci* (Madrid =1989a).
Rodríguez-Almeida, E., "Diffusores, mercatores, negotiatores olearii," *BullCom* 92.2 (=1989b) 299-306.
Rodríguez-Almeida, E., "Graffiti e produzione anforaria della Betica," in Harris, W. (ed.), *The inscribed economy* (JRA Suppl. 6, 1993) 95-106.
Rougé, J., "La navigation hivernale sous l'empire romain," *REA* 54 (1952) 316-25.
Rougé, J., "*Periculum maris* et transports d'etat: la lettre 49 de Paulin de Nole," *Studi tardoantichi* 2 (1986) 119-36.
Rowland, R., "The case of the missing Sardinian grain," *AncW* 10 (1984) 45-48.
Rowland, R., "The production of Sardinian grain during the Roman period," *Mediterranean Historical Review* 5.1 (1990) 14-20.
Salama, P. *Bornes milliares d'Afrique proconsulaire. Un panorama historique du Bas-Empire romain* (CollEFR 101, 1987).
Saumagne, C., "Un tarif fiscal au quatrième siècle de notre ère," *Karthago* 1 (1950) 105-206.
Schilbach, E., *Byzantinische Metrologie* (Handbuch der Altertumswissenschaft 12.4, 1970).
Senior, L. and D. Birney III, "Accurately estimating vessel volume from profile illustrations," *American Antiquity* 60.2 (1995) 319-34.
Sirks, B., *Food for Rome* (Amsterdam 1991).
Stone, D. S., L. M. Stirling and N. Ben Lazreg, "Suburban land-use and ceramic production around Leptiminus: interim report," *JRA* 11 (1998) 305-17.
Tengstrom, E., *Bread for the people: studies of the corn supply of Rome during the late Empire* (ActInstRomSuec ser. 8.12, 1974).
van Alfen, P., "New light on the 7th-c. Yassi Ada shipwreck: capacities and standard sizes of LRA1 amphoras," *JRA* 9 (1996) 189-213.
van der Werff, J., "Sekundäre Graffiti auf römischen Amphoren," *ArchKorr* 19 (1989) 361-76.
Viedebantt, O., "Metrologische Beiträge I," *Hermes* 47 (1912) 422-65.
Viedebantt, O., *Forschungen zur Metrologie des Altertums* (Abh., phil.-hist. Kl., Kgl. Sächs. Gesell. d. Wiss. 34.3, 1917).
Whitehouse, D., G. Barker, R. Reece, and D. Reese, "The Schola Praeconum I: the coins, pottery, lamps, and fauna," *PBSR* 50 (1982) 53-101.
Wilcken, U., *Griechische Ostraka aus Aegypten und Nubien: Ein Beitrage zur antiken Wirtschaftsgeschichte* 1-2 (1899; repr. Amsterdam 1970).
Zevi, F. and A. Tchernia, "Amphores de Byzacène du Bas Empire," *AntAfr* 3 (1969) 173-214.